# A WRITTEN CONSTITUTION FOR QUEBEC?

DEMOCRACY, DIVERSITY, AND CITIZEN ENGAGEMENT SERIES
Series editor: Alain-G. Gagnon

With the twenty-first-century world struggling to address various forms of conflict and new types of political and cultural claims, the Democracy, Diversity, and Citizen Engagement Series revitalizes research in the fields of nationalism, federalism, and cosmopolitanism, and examines the interactions between ethnicity, identity, and politics. Works published in this series are concerned with the theme of representation – of citizens and of interests – and how these ideas are defended at local and global levels that are increasingly converging. Further, the series advances and advocates new public policies and social projects with a view to creating change and accommodating diversity in its many expressions. In doing so, the series instills democratic practices in meaningful new ways by studying key subjects such as the mobilization of citizens, groups, communities, and nations, and the advancement of social justice and political stability.

Under the leadership of the Interdisciplinary Research Centre on Diversity and Democracy, this series creates a forum where current research on democracy, diversity, and citizen engagement can be examined within the context of the study of nations as well as of nations divided by state frontiers.

1 The Parliaments of Autonomous Nations
*Edited by Guy Laforest and André Lecours*

2 A Liberal Theory of Collective Rights
*Michel Seymour*

3 The National Question and Electoral Politics in Quebec and Scotland
*Éric Bélanger, Richard Nadeau, Ailsa Henderson, and Eve Hepburn*

4 Trust, Distrust, and Mistrust in Multinational Democracies
Comparative Perspectives
*Edited by Dimitrios Karmis and François Rocher*

5 Constitutional Politics in Multinational Democracies
*Edited by André Lecours, Nikola Brassard-Dion, and Guy Laforest*

6 Fiscal Federalism in Multinational States
Autonomy, Equality, and Diversity
*Edited by François Boucher and Alain Noël*

7 The Symbolic State
Minority Recognition, Majority Backlash, and Secession in Multinational Countries
*Karlo Basta*

8 Taking Pluralism Seriously
Complex Societies under Scrutiny
*Félix Mathieu*

9 A Written Constitution for Quebec?
*Edited by Richard Albert and Léonid Sirota*

# A Written Constitution for Quebec?

*Edited by Richard Albert*
*and Léonid Sirota*

McGill-Queen's University Press
Montreal & Kingston • London • Chicago

ISBN 978-0-2280-1385-3 (cloth)
ISBN 978-0-2280-1477-5 (ePDF)
ISBN 978-0-2280-1478-2 (ePUB)

Legal deposit first quarter 2023
Bibliothèque nationale du Québec

Printed in Canada on acid-free paper that is 100% ancient forest free (100% post-consumer recycled), processed chlorine free

Funded by the Government of Canada | Financé par le gouvernement du Canada | Canada

Canada Council for the Arts | Conseil des arts du Canada

We acknowledge the support of the Canada Council for the Arts.
Nous remercions le Conseil des arts du Canada de son soutien.

---

Library and Archives Canada Cataloguing in Publication

Title: A written constitution for Quebec? / edited by Richard Albert and Léonid Sirota.
Names: Albert, Richard (Law professor), editor. | Sirota, Léonid, editor.
Series: Democracy, diversity, and citizen engagement series ; 9.
Description: Series statement: Democracy, diversity, and citizen engagement series ; 9 | Includes bibliographical references and index.
Identifiers: Canadiana (print) 20220437203 | Canadiana (ebook) 20220437254 | ISBN 9780228013853 (cloth) | ISBN 9780228014775 (ePDF) | ISBN 9780228014782 (ePUB)
Subjects: LCSH: Constitutional history—Québec (Province)
Classification: LCC KEQ740.W75 2023 | LCC KF4483.Q4 W75 2023 kfmod | DDC 342.71402/9—dc23

---

This book was typeset in 10.5/13 Sabon.

# Contents

# Tables and Figures

## TABLES



## FIGURES

# Acknowledgments

A project like this is possible only with the help of many persons. We thank Patrick Baud, Josée Bergeron, Marianne Bonnard, Lisa Brennan, Rahima Chaudhury, Laura Coughlan Woodring, Jay Gitlin, Lourdes Haynes, Sameer Jaywant, Ryan Manucha, Chaghig Torikian, and Marilyn Wilkes for their generous help and support at various stages of this years-long undertaking. We also thank the MacMillan Center for International and Area Studies at Yale University, the Howard R. Lamar Center for the Study of Frontiers and Borders also at Yale University, the Research Support Program on Intergovernmental Affairs and Québec Identity, the Québec – United States University Grant Program, and the William Stamps Farish Professorship Fund at the University of Texas at Austin for their generous financial support.

We are also extraordinarily grateful to the team at McGill-Queen's University Press for their enthusiasm for this project. In particular we thank Neil Erickson, Filomena Falocco, Kathleen Fraser, Jacqueline Mason, Louise Piper, Joanne Pisano, and Richard Ratzlaff.

We reserve our biggest thanks of all to the contributors to this volume. Their chapters are informative and important, and they have joined together to create a valuable resource for Quebec to consult as it considers whether to formalize a written constitution for itself and its peoples.

Richard Albert
*Ottawa, Canada*

Léonid Sirota
*Reading, United Kingdom*

# A WRITTEN CONSTITUTION FOR QUEBEC?

INTRODUCTION

# Constitution and Codification

*Léonid Sirota and Richard Albert*

The contemporary world is a world of written – that is to say, (more or less) codified and (more or less vigorously) entrenched – constitutions. These instruments "aspire not only to establish the forms of governmental authority ... but also to reconstitute the people in a particular way."[1] They define and delimit public power, yet also serve as symbols for the highest commitments of the polity and indeed of the polity's very existence. Very few countries lack one, and these holdouts now face questions about whether they ought to conform to the global trend.[2]

Yet as Michael Burgess and Alan Tarr point out, in "most" federal polities "the federal constitution is an 'incomplete' framework document ... It leaves 'space' to be filled by the constitutions of its sub-national units."[3] Just how much space is left to subnational constitutionalism – and how much of what is left is actually used by framers of subnational federations – varies among, and sometimes within, federations. But, as with national constitutions, their subnational counterparts provide "an opportunity for constituent units [of federations] to define their own goals and establish their own governmental institutions and processes."[4]

In many federations, including the United States and Germany, subnational constitutions take a form that closely resembles their associated national constitutions, at least at first blush. They are codified and entrenched texts. Australian state constitutions are also codified, although not necessarily entrenched. By contrast, as we explain more fully below, the constitutions of Canadian provinces are neither codified (with one limited exception) nor entrenched; they are unwritten.

## AN UNDEREXPLORED QUESTION

In a world of written constitutions, it is worth asking whether Canada's provincial constitutions should remain unwritten. This question may seem theoretical to most Canadians, but in Quebec it is a live one. The issue of constitutional codification and entrenchment has arisen in Quebec a number of times over the last several decades, including in a bill introduced in the National Assembly by Daniel Turp,[5] one of the contributors to this book. Recent political developments – notably the enactment of the secularism legislation colloquially known as Bill 21[6] and the introduction of Bill 96,[7] dealing primarily with linguistic matters – have put constitutional issues and the self-definition of the province at or at least near the top of the political agenda in Quebec, and this has provoked serious discussion across the country.[8] Quebec's unique history and circumstances help explain why the question whether its constitution should be "written down" has attracted more attention there than elsewhere.[9] But the considerations that bear on it are relevant to other Canadian provinces, and indeed to subnational polities beyond Canada's borders, just as the experiences of federations abroad are in turn relevant to how Quebeckers think about their own constitutional arrangements.

This question – does Quebec need a written constitution? – is the one we set out to explore in this book, with insights from both legal scholars and political scientists, and from Quebec, the rest of Canada, and beyond. To be clear, to ask the question is not to prejudge that the answer ought to be in the affirmative. The different contributions in this volume each have their own perspective on the question. Some are enthusiastic about the prospect of a Quebec constitution; others are skeptical. In bringing them together, our aim is not to produce a manifesto, but to encourage reflection.

Our invitation to reflect on subnational constitutions in Quebec and Canada may be especially valuable because subnational constitutions everywhere attract comparatively little attention.[10] It is sometimes suggested that this is due to their legally inferior status.[11] But even in those polities where subnational constitutions are written in the same sense as the national ones, they are something of a niche interest. To be sure, there is, in fact, a not-insubstantial body of literature on subnational constitutions, whether considering them generally,[12] or focusing on particular issues in relation to the phenomenon of subnational constitutionalism,[13] on the subnational constitutions in a particular polity[14] or, indeed, on the constitutions of particular subnational polities.[15] Nonetheless, it seems fair to say that this literature pales in comparison with the vast body of scholarship on national constitutions.

Yet this is not because subnational constitutions do not deserve interest on the part of scholars, policymakers, and citizens. As we have already noted, subnational constitutions are the means through which, within the limits allowed by national constitutions, (subnational) political communities define and give legal form to their values and aspirations, establish their governing institutions and empower them, and protect the rights of citizens and communities. It is true that the authors of subnational constitutions often follow the model provided by the national constitutional framework within which they work, even when they are not legally required to do so. But this is far from always the case. As John Dinan notes, "sub-national constitution-makers have made significant use of the constitutional space allotted to them, but in certain areas more than others."[16] In particular, they have often streamlined their legislative and constitutional amendment processes, and tended to "provide more opportunities for direct democracy" than the framers of national constitutions.[17] Some have also provided more expansive protections for a variety of rights. In all this, subnational constitutions can serve as experiments and models for other subnational polities within, and even outside, their home federation.[18]

## PROVINCIAL CONSTITUTIONS IN CANADA

The lack of interest in subnational constitutions has been especially marked in Canada, both among political actors and among constitutional scholars. In Gerald Baier's words, "[t]o all but the closest observers, the 'action' in Canadian constitutionalism takes place exclusively at the state rather than at the sub-state level"[19] – that is to say, it concerns the federal constitution rather than the constitutions of the provinces. More generally still, Canadian legal and political scholars pay remarkably little attention to provincial institutions, let alone constitutions.[20] Yet as Baier notes this is not because the provinces "lack the ability or opportunity to define and assert themselves constitutionally. Against the measure of other subnational constitutional traditions, the Canadian provinces have multiple options for defining and expressing themselves constitutionally. But these opportunities have simply not been seized."[21] As several of the contributions to this volume explain (especially chapter 2 by Maxime St-Hilaire and Patrick Baud), the Canadian constitutional framework does impose significant constraints on the provinces' freedom of action in the constitutional sphere, including arguably on the provinces' ability to entrench their constitutions. Yet the provinces have not sought to exercise their constitutional powers to anything approaching their limits.

Notably, with one exception, the provinces have not sought to codify their constitutions, and even British Columbia's *Constitution Act* is only a very incomplete codification.[22] Nor is it entrenched. Provincial constitutions are to be found in part in the various documents that make up the "Constitution of Canada," as that term is defined in the *Constitution Act, 1982*.[23] This includes notably (but not only) Part V of the *Constitution Act, 1867*,[24] entitled "Provincial Constitutions"; the *Canadian Charter of Rights and Freedoms*;[25] and section 45 of the *Constitution Act, 1982*, which provides that, with certain (narrow but significant) limitations "the legislature of each province may exclusively make laws amending the constitution of the province." Other parts of provincial constitutions are set out in provincial legislation dealing with specific subjects (such as elections) or institutions (such as legislatures). Others still belong to the realm of constitutional convention, which may or may not partly entrenched.[26] The situation of Canada's three territories is similar, although fewer provisions of the Constitution of Canada apply to them directly.

With the limited exception of British Columbia, there has been little effort to change this state of affairs, reflecting perhaps what Emmett Macfarlane has described as "the Canadian political class's avoidance of major constitutional change since the early 1990s,"[27] not to mention the difficulty of bringing about any such change within the confines of Canada's demanding amending procedures.[28] Whatever its causes, this situation stands in contrast with what prevails in ordinary politics. There, as Baier notes, the provinces not only claim "that they are culturally and linguistically diverse and that provincial communities have differing ideas of the role of government and the nature of the welfare state that have to be acknowledged in the federal constitution" but they translate these claims into a diversity of policy-making initiatives.[29]

When it comes to provincial constitutions, however, provincial diversity "is not expressed in constitutional practice, or even, seemingly, in a pent-up desire for constitutional self-expression."[30] As Baier notes, "[t]hat is especially surprising in light of the fact that some of the more radical political traditions in Canadian history," at least some of which might have been expected to have constitutional as well as policy agendas, "have asserted themselves primarily at the provincial level."[31] Of course, provinces have sometimes engaged in substantive constitutional innovation. Perhaps the most salient recent example is the introduction of fixed election dates in British Columbia and then Ontario.[32] The Canadian Parliament then followed suit by enacting fixed-election legislation of its own.[33] Other provinces did the same. Yet such innovation is not presented or understood in explicitly constitutional terms,[34] nor is it connected to a broader constitutional reform agenda. It is not "constitutional self-definition,"[35] but piecemeal improvement (or at least hoped-for improvement) of particular institutions; not grand design, but tinkering.

To simply take note of this reality is not to criticize the provinces. For one thing, as Burgess and Tarr note, subnational polities may consciously choose to forgo constitutional innovation. They "may seriously consider alternatives to what is found in the constitutions of other constituent units or in the federal constitution" – or, we would add, to their own past approach – "but conclude that there is no reason to diverge from those models."[36] For another, as Baier points out, "provincial constitutions are demonstrative of the kinds of compromises and self-restraint that make the stability and relative peace of Canadian federalism possible."[37] It may well be that a system that is tolerably well understood by its key actors if not also by the general public is good enough.

## THE POLITICS OF PROVINCIAL CONSTITUTIONS IN QUEBEC

That said, Quebec has been something of an exception to the general trend of a lack of interest in provincial constitutions. If any society among those comprising Canada is interested in self-definition, it is Quebec, and its institutions and fundamental laws have long been part of its efforts at self-definition. Recent and proposed legislation, to which we have already referred, is part of this trend. Thus, the preamble of Bill 21 refers to the "constitutional foundations" of the "Québec state," "enriched over the years by the passage of a number of fundamental laws" and proclaims that "in accordance with the principle of parliamentary sovereignty, it is incumbent on the Parliament of Québec to determine the principles according to which and manner in which relations between the State and religions are to be governed in Québec."[38] The reference to parliamentary sovereignty, with its obvious constitutional undertones, would also be added to the preamble of the *Charter of the French Language* by Bill 96.[39]

It is perhaps unsurprising that Quebec's internal constitutional arrangements – in addition to, of course, its place inside or outside the Canadian federation – have attracted the attention of scholars and, to a more limited but still noteworthy degree, the interest of some political actors. Canada's leading French language constitutional and administrative law treatises dissect the functioning of the Quebec government in as much detail as they do for the Canadian government.[40] To our knowledge, Quebec is the only province whose legislative assembly publishes a comprehensive procedural manual, which is rich with constitutional scholarship.[41] And, as we have noted above, the framing of a written constitution for Quebec is a matter of recurring discussion on the political agenda.

But the question whether Quebec needs a written constitution is not a simple one, even taking Quebec's relative interest in constitutional self-definition as a starting point, and even in abstraction from the competition for the attention of both political actors and the broader public which it would inevitably face from other issues. This question is connected to several others. Some of these have to do with constitutionalism, constitutional entrenchment, and codification both generally and more specifically in the context of subnational polities. Others concern the Canadian constitutional context: the history of Canadian constitutionalism, its rules, and its future. And yet another set of questions concern specifically Quebec: its future in Canada, its aspirations, its values, its governance, and its relationship with its people(s). The process of making a "written" constitution for Quebec, and indeed of deciding whether one would be useful, would need to address all these multifaceted issues.

## AIMS AND LIMITS OF CONSTITUTIONAL CODIFICATION

The obvious question for any polity considering whether it needs a new written constitution is why undertake the effort of drafting and enacting one. Mark Tushnet argues that, for new states, the need for such a constitution is clear and pressing: "a constitution is probably regarded by the international community as a prerequisite to statehood" in practice if not in law.[42] Moreover, the constitution will serve as a symbol of the polity's very existence and unity, and it will fulfil the more prosaic task of creating, regulating, or legitimating governance institutions, or all three.[43] If Quebec were to become an independent state, these reasons would of course apply to it. Together with the need to "patriate" those aspects of its constitution that are now part of the "Constitution of Canada" – and the likely desire to introduce substantive constitutional change such as a transition to republicanism – they would make constitution-making unavoidable.

Yet the prospect of Quebec's independence seems, at present, remote – to the point where pollsters no longer even assess it with any regularity.[44] For the foreseeable future, then, and perhaps beyond, Quebec will not become a new polity, but remain an already-existing one. Why might such a polity wish to acquire a new constitution, despite already having one and not facing the pressures that impel new polities to engage in constitution-making? Tushnet suggests two hypotheses.[45] First, a new constitution may be a more efficient way of introducing some desirable constitutional change than a process of piecemeal amendment. Second, a new constitution may be thought necessary to break with a "discredited" constitutional or political past.[46] It seems fair to say that the latter reason is unlikely apply to Quebec so long as it remains within the Canadian federation. By contrast, the idea that a new, written constitution is necessary to achieve needed constitutional reform even within the Canadian framework is more plausible, although, to be sure, legislative enactments like Bills 21 and 96 are more in the vein of piecemeal amendment than wholesale reform.

The most fundamental reform that could be achieved by the making of a written constitution for Quebec is a change in the very nature of the province's constitution. Alexander Hamilton famously contrasted constitutions born out of "reflection and choice" with those that are the products of "accident and force."[47] He was arguably wrong to neglect a third category: constitutions that have evolved over time, as a result of judicial and political developments that cannot be fairly described as implementing choices in the way written constitutions do. The English constitution and its progeny throughout the Commonwealth (insofar as even the partly written constitutions of Commonwealth nations such as Canada and Australia incorporate important common law and conventional rules), are of this character.[48] Be that as it may, the making of a written constitution for Quebec could radically increase the proportion of the province's constitutional rules that are derived from "reflection and choice," which might be thought to be a worthwhile objective in itself.

There may be other reasons for making a written constitution even in the absence of pressing necessity. Perhaps most obviously, the framing of such a constitution could be part of a polity's process of self-definition, to which we have already referred above. It would, in other words, be a significant symbolic and historical event. For Quebec, the creation of a written constitution would highlight its distinctiveness, even within, let alone outside, the Canadian constitutional order. As a milestone, it could be comparable to, or indeed more salient than, the codification of Quebec's civil law, or the enactment of the *Charter of Human Rights and Freedoms* and *Charter of the French Language*.[49] As Turp's proposal in this volume illustrates, the contents of a written constitution for Quebec might further emphasize Quebec's unique character.

Needless to say, insofar as it attempts and results in the self-definition of Quebec's large and diverse society, constitution-making raises difficult questions about language, culture, and identity. Most obviously: who will be involved in the constitution-making process? Will they speak on behalf of the Quebecois considered as one people, or on behalf of the various groups that together make up Quebec's society? Will the resulting constitution make room for a recognition of aspects of Quebec's society that its current legal symbols may not acknowledge, as Mark Walters suggests in chapter 6, notably Quebec's relationship with Indigenous peoples? More broadly, to which collective aspirations will the constitution seek to give concrete, enduring form?

Sir Geoffrey Palmer and Andrew Butler, two proponents of a constitution-writing endeavour for New Zealand, argue that it would also have the benefit of making constitutional arrangements more transparent, leading to a better public understanding of how political power is exercised.[50] However, there is good reason for skepticism about this. The existence in the United States of a written constitution structured around the three branches of government has not prevented a majority of the American public from being unable to name these branches; a substantial minority cannot name a single one.[51] More generally, as Ilya Somin points out, Americans are and have long been unfamiliar with "the basic structure of government and how it operates"[52] due to a lack of incentives to become informed. Could the same fate befall a Constitution for Quebec?

Beyond the question why even take the trouble to make a written constitution in a polity that already has a set of existing and tolerable constitutional arrangements, the next general question that the would-be framers of such a constitution, in Quebec as anywhere else, need to address is what it would include in its text. Like their counterparts elsewhere, Quebeckers would need to decide how much to depart from the models provided by the existing arrangements, both provincial and federal. Quebec already differs from the federal model in some significant ways, having like all Canadian provinces a unicameral legislature and, unlike the other provinces, an elaborate and original bill of rights, the Quebec *Charter*.[53] The framing of a provincial constitution could serve as the occasion for considering more fundamental changes.

This consideration would interact with the degree of completeness a proposed constitution would have. To what extent should the "written" (and entrenched) constitution spell out detailed rules? Baier argues that one possible reason for the aversion of Canadian provinces to constitutional reform and codification is that "[k]eeping constitutional rules informal serves the purposes of provincial governments, and particularly the political parties in power."[54] This incentive may be outweighed by the considerations in favour of writing down a provincial constitution, but it will not disappear altogether. And of course the desire to preserve a freedom of constitutional action for future legislatures and governments need not be entirely self-serving. The framers of any constitutional system must balance future stability and flexibility.

Any aspiration to produce a complete code of constitutional rules would be unrealistic. Even a fairly detailed constitutional text cannot be exhaustive. It will have to be supplemented by further legislation and by judicial interpretation.[55] It will also, in all likelihood, leave room for the development of constitutional conventions.[56] The real question that the framers of a written constitution face is not whether they will be able to make it a complete code of constitutional law, but what parts of the "complete constitution"[57] to leave in and out. The modern tendency, as identified by Mila Versteeg and Emily Zackin, is towards lengthy and detailed constitutional texts.[58] Even so, which issues such a text will cover, which it will explicitly or implicitly leave to be decided by subsequent legislation, and which it will address in vague terms requiring subsequent elaboration in the course of adjudication is of considerable importance.[59]

## PROVINCIAL CONSTITUTIONS IN THE CANADIAN CONSTITUTIONAL ORDER

Finally, at the risk of preempting the considerably more detailed discussion in the chapters to come, notably chapter 2 by St-Hilaire and Baud as well chapter 3 by Patrick Taillon and Hubert Cauchon, the freedom of action of the framers of a hypothetical Quebec constitution would be constrained in very significant ways by the Canadian constitutional framework.[60] These constraints would involve both the contents of any proposed provincial constitution and its entrenchment against future amendment, and therefore any effort to make their constitution truly "written" as that term is commonly understood.

In the words of the Supreme Court of Canada, "Part V of the *Constitution Act, 1982* provides the blueprint for how to amend the Constitution of Canada."[61] The blueprint, however, only provides partial guidance. For example, Quebec would not be able to make any changes to the "office of … the Lieutenant Governor" without the unanimous consent of the Senate and House of Commons and all other provincial legislative assemblies, although it is not clear just what the "office of … the Lieutenant Governor" is, or how far its entrenchment extends.[62] Notably, it is important to recall Justice Jean Beetz's warning "that the principle of responsible government could, to the extent that it depends on … important royal powers, be entrenched to a substantial extent,"[63] as a consequence of the entrenchment of the "office of … the Lieutenant Governor."

Justice Beetz's caution seems all the more prescient if one generalizes the Supreme Court's conclusion that its own composition and fundamental features have been entrenched by implication through references to them in Part V of the *Constitution Act, 1982*.[64] Along these lines, one might wonder, as Guy Tremblay has, whether it would be possible for the Quebec legislature to provide for the direct election of Quebec's premier.[65] Any efforts to constrain the lieutenant governor's power to dissolve and prorogue the legislature or to limit the premier's power (and duty?) to provide advice on the exercise of those powers would raise similar questions.[66]

Likewise, a province is not authorized to make changes to the *Canadian Charter of Rights and Freedoms* without the consent of the Senate, the House of Commons, and seven of the ten provincial legislative assemblies representing at least 50 per cent of the population of the provinces.[67] Without this depth of cross-national agreement, Quebec remains bound by the *Charter*'s guarantees of individual rights (subject of course to its ability to suspend some of them for limited but renewable periods under section 33 of the *Charter*, a power that is now front and centre in relation to Bills 21 and 96[68]). For example, any attempts to constitutionalize Quebec's peculiar understanding of the principle of secularism,[69] so as to avoid the need to renew Bill 21's resort to the *Charter*'s section 33 every five years, would risk conflicting with the *Charter*'s protection of religious liberty. It is notably for this reason that Emmanuelle Richez has claimed that the Canadian constitutional framework "restricts the provinces' capacity to adopt provisions that would enhance their cultural identity,"[70] although there is room to wonder just how rigid those restrictions really are. Attempts to reform the *Charter*'s democratic rights, which cannot be suspended by the invocation of section 33, would also bear on any attempt to frame a provincial constitution, although their constraints may not be as keenly felt.

Furthermore, a hypothetical constitution for Quebec would also be constrained by two other provisions of the *Constitution Act, 1867*, which cannot be repealed for Quebec without the agreement of Parliament.[71] One is section 96, which protects the jurisdiction of the federally-appointed superior courts, and prevents provinces from insulating the administrative tribunals they create from these courts' supervision.[72] Section 96 also limits the ability of the provinces to transfer exclusive jurisdiction from the superior courts to the provincial courts.[73] The other is section 133, which protects the use of English and French in Quebec's institutions, as well as the federal ones. Acting on its own, Quebec could not do away with the right to use English and French in the debates of the National Assembly and the courts, or the requirement that its laws be enacted in French and English.[74]

On other issues, however, much must be inferred from Part V's sometimes unhelpful words, and its pregnant silences. Most significantly for any project of making a "written" constitution for a province, it is not clear by what means a provincial constitution may be entrenched. Part V also makes no explicit reference to unwritten constitutional principles, such as judicial independence,[75] nor to the concept of "constitutional architecture" that it was held, in the Senate Reform Reference, to protect. To what extent principles other than judicial independence might constrain provincial constitutional reform is not especially clear.

The opportunity to frame a written constitution for Quebec must therefore be assessed in light of the potential benefits of such an endeavour, its possible downsides, as well as the constraints – some known and some uncertain – to which it would be subject. We cannot stress strongly enough that, in this introduction and in this book taken as a whole, we take no position on this ultimate question whether Quebec or any other province should adopt a codified constitution, although some of the individual chapters do so, while others are content to ask questions or to shed light on the relevant issues. Overall, this volume explores answers to the questions that bear on the desirability of a written constitution for Quebec, putting them in their legal, social, and comparative contexts.

## IN THIS VOLUME

The book is divided in three main parts. In part I entitled "Framing the Debate," contributors debate the question directly: should Quebec codify its constitution? In chapter 1, "Oui, Quebec Needs a Written Constitution," Daniel Turp answers the question in the affirmative. He makes two principal arguments: first, that adopting a Quebec constitution would give Quebec its own constitutional identity; and second, that it could also help end the constitutional impasse which resulted from the patriation of the Constitution of Canada without Quebec's consent. This chapter sets the parameters for the rest of the volume, with various authors either supporting or opposing the idea, drawing from the Quebec experience in particular or from theoretical approaches or comparative reflections from outside the province and the country.

Maxime St-Hilaire and Patrick Baud respond to Turp in chapter 2 on "Legal Roadblocks to Proposals for a Quebec Constitution." Their point of departure is the site where the written and the material constitution of Quebec merge in Canadian constitutional law. St-Hilaire and Baud argue that provinces have only limited constitution-making powers within the context of the federal distribution of legislative powers. They then define the concept of a provincial constitution, concluding that provinces do not have free rein to codify the political component, which is to say the conventional component, of the province's constitution.

In chapter 3, Patrick Taillon and Hubert Cauchon offer their own response to Turp and to the larger idea of writing down a constitution for Quebec. They make two important distinctions in their chapter. First, they distinguish the constitutional norms of the Canadian federation from those of the provinces, along the way explaining their interrelations and the consequences of constitutionalizing the norms of the federated entities. Second, they distinguish between codifying and formalizing a provincial constitution, the former referring to the process of bringing together in a single written package the various disaggregated parts of the constitution, and the latter referring to an act of constitutional lawmaking that creates a formal hierarchy between ordinary and higher law. These two distinctions illuminate key challenges and prospects for a Quebec constitution.

In part II, contributors advance perspectives on the purposes and prospects of a Quebec constitution. In chapter 4 on "A Codified Quebec Constitution: A Vain Pursuit or the Making of a Sovereign People?," Nelson Wiseman probes the genesis, contents, and conundrums of a Quebec constitution potentially codified in a single document. The chapter touches on some competing constitutional conceptions, and concludes by addressing some challenges and possibilities that may follow the adoption of a new Quebec constitution. Wiseman argues that, emblematically, such a constitution would serve as a concrete symbol of an abstract idea, a way of representing and communicating the collective life and values of the Quebecois to themselves and their children. Such a constitution may also contribute to moving Quebec in the direction of independence and changing its relationship to the rest of Canada. Or not, he concedes. There are many open questions about the effect of writing down a constitution for Quebec, and Wiseman's chapter helps us identify and understand them.

In chapter 5, Alain-G. Gagnon and Arjun Tremblay explore "Interculturalism and the Plea for an Informal Constitution: Responding to the Challenge of Polyethnicity in Quebec." Suggesting that Quebec might be better off with its informal constitution – as opposed to a formalized one – Gagnon and Tremblay suggest that formalizing Quebec's constitution could actually do more harm than good, if the aspiration of the peoples of Quebec is to fulfill their promise of interculturalism.

Mark D. Walters suggests in chapter 6, entitled "Constitutive Power and the Nation(s) of Quebec," that the question whether Quebec needs a written constitution helps shed light on the general concept of constituent power for two reasons. First, given that Quebec is already a component part of a constitutional system, it is unclear whether the constitution that it could make for itself today would be an exercise of constituent power in the standard sense of that term. Considering this point may shed light upon what constituent power really means. Second, given the constitutional and national pluralism that defines Quebec's legal character today, it is unclear whether there is a "nation" that could be the holder of a constituent power. In particular, Walters' chapter explores how the "nation-to-nation" relationship that Quebec has developed with Indigenous peoples bears on this point. He suggests that this too may assist the inquiry into whether the standard view about constituent power is valid.

The last chapter in part II features an Albertan perspective on the need for a provincial constitution, suggesting that written constitutions could be a point around which provinces could become allies in the federation. In "Why Alberta Needs a Constitution," F.L. Morton offers a distinctly economic justification for a provincial constitution. He explains how the failure to entrench fiscal responsibility led to Alberta's recent $50 billion deficit-debt spiral and how constitutionalized spending rules could be used to ensure greater fiscal responsibility and to protect the Heritage Savings Trust Fund from political raids. Morton also explores some of the problems associated with a provincial constitution and how those problems might be resolved. He argues that this is not just an Alberta problem, but a problem faced by all democratically elected governments in Canada and the world.

The third and final part of this volume is titled "Insights from Abroad." Its chapters explore how other countries have tackled subnational constitutions and what we in Canada might learn from them. They enrich our analysis of constitutional codification in general, and specifically reveal some of the challenges Quebec could face with a subnational constitution of its own. We have chosen to highlight three jurisdictions in particular because they each offer something new and important to consider in evaluating whether Quebec should codify its constitution. Brazil, for its part, raises an important contrast with Canada. While both are federal states, the Brazilian Constitution requires states to codify subnational constitutions, unlike the Canadian Constitution which only authorizes provinces to do so. Does this constitutional mandate make a difference? The United States shines a different light on subnational constitutions insofar as the original thirteen states predated the United States Constitution, and each of those states had a codified constitution of its own before joining the Union. In addition, some states have a distinguishable identity of their own, separate from their larger identity as part of the country, a phenomenon that brings to mind how Quebec has long both defined itself and been defined by others. And the case of Scotland is fascinating not only because its position within the United Kingdom raises some useful analogies to the position of Quebec within Canada but, moreover, because Scotland's recent constitution-making activities suggest possibilities and pitfalls for similar plans in Quebec. These three case studies bring the richness of experiences abroad to the domestic context in Canada.

In chapter 8, Jonathan Marshfield offers an American perspective in his study of the "Political Functions and Limitations of Contemporary State Constitutions in the United States." Marshfield argues that state constitutions in the United States serve various important political functions that may be relevant and helpful to constitutional designers in other political systems. His contribution explores two striking features of contemporary state constitutionalism with an eye towards their value for those considering a written Quebec constitution. First, state constitutionalism is characterized by frequent formal amendment through popular political processes. This has resulted in a form of constitutionalism that often prioritizes swift democratic responsiveness over entrenched prior commitments. Because recent empirical scholarship suggests that this is a broader phenomenon often occurring in federal countries with written subnational constitutions, Quebec reformers should be mindful of how formal amendment under a written constitution can energize popular constitutional politics. Second, state constitutions have not been particularly effective in protecting state political identities or community. In fact, because of frequent amendment and the strong pull of national political parties, the dominant trend in state constitutionalism is convergence on national issues and identities. This, he concludes, should raise questions for Quebec nationalists regarding the real, long-term value of a written provincial constitution.

Chapter 9, by Débora Costa Ferreira and Juliano Zaiden Benvindo, is called "The Brazilian Experience with Subnational Constitutions: What Went Wrong?" Their chapter draws from the Brazilian experience to offer general insights about the role subnational constitutions may play in a federal state. They examine six factors that can explain the failure of the Brazilian subnational constitutional project, which has been characterized by an increasing mimicry of the federal constitution: (1) the short drafting period for state constitutions; (2) the centralized federal model that left only narrow space for constitutional innovation; (3) the uncertainty of the current status of state constitutional autonomy, as defined by the courts; (4) the Supreme Court's centralizing behaviour and the difficulty in defining the norms with which states have to comply; (5) the overlapping structure of judicial review in constitutional states; and (6) the challenge of subnational amendment procedures. Their contribution complicates the debate over whether Quebec should have its own constitution.

Part III closes with chapter 10 by Erin F. Delaney's on "Constitutionalization à L'Écosse: Subnational Constitutionalism as Constitutional Reconciliation." Delaney dives into subnational constitutionalism from the perspective of its ability both to extract concessions from and to exert influence on national, or federal, constitutionalism. After first reviewing the current efforts to promote Quebecois provincial constitutionalism, the chapter turns to the experiences of the Scottish Constitutional Convention, 1989–95. In comparing the two, Delaney highlights the differing substantive and procedural approaches to constitutionalization and the ways in which subnational constitutionalism functioned as a mechanism of subnational influence in the Scottish context. The chapter closes by outlining the most effective aspects of the Scottish experience and evaluating their relevance to Quebec.

The volume concludes with a final chapter by Hoi Kong. In "Should Quebec Adopt a Written Constitution? A (But not the) Conclusion,"

Kong first addresses two preliminary questions: "What is the value of a written constitution to a polity?" and "What is the value of writing a constitution to a polity?" In answering these questions, Kong advances a qualified answer to the question whether Quebec should adopt a written constitution. Kong offers a compelling conclusion that presses us to look beyond the question whether a codified or formalized constitution would serve Quebec's purposes. He invites us to ask the deeper question why Quebec might want to write down its constitution. If it is for the purpose of codification alone, or even to express the distinct identity or identifies of the peoples of the province, that might not be sufficient. But the challenge of codifying a written constitution for Quebec would be worth the risk and effort, argues Kong, if this historic collective action would give effect to the democratic values of deliberative constitutionalism. Kong elaborates his thesis with reference to the previous chapters, offering a contextual conclusion to a volume that asks many questions but by design leaves many of them open for readers to answer for themselves.

* * *

Unlike many other federal countries, Canada does not have a history of codifying provincial constitutions. Part of the reason why reflects our inherited British traditions of constitutional conventions and unwritten constitutionalism. Nonetheless, there is no legal barrier to provincial constitutions. Canada's federal system allows it, though of course no provincial constitution could ever trump the Constitution of Canada as a matter of federal law. The Canadian Constitution would remain paramount and supreme. But if Quebec can do it, why not other provinces and the territories, too?

Neither the provinces nor territories need to wait for Quebec to act if they wish to consider the option for themselves. They can begin today, if they and their peoples wish. And if they choose to give serious consideration to adopting a codified constitution, we hope the critical insights in this volume – drawing from legal, political, historical, theoretical, and comparative perspectives – will prove useful to the task. Our objective here is to illuminate the risks and benefits of provincial constitutions, and to give attention to this understudied subject in Canada. Whatever provinces and territories choose in consultation with their peoples is less important to us than that they consider the question and decide for themselves whether they should adopt a written constitution.

NOTES

The authors are grateful to Patrick F. Baud and to anonymous reviewers for comments on previous versions of this text.

1 Martin Loughlin and Neil Walker, "Introduction," in *The Paradox of Constitutionalism: Constituent Power and Constitutional Form*, eds. Martin Loughlin and Neil Walker (Oxford: Oxford University Press, 2007), 1–8, at 1.

2 See House of Commons Political and Constitutional Reform Committee, *A New Magna Carta* HC 463, 10 July 2014, http://www.publications.parliament.uk/pa/cm201415/cmselect/cmpolcon/463/463.pdf (for the United Kingdom) and Constitutional Advisory Panel, *New Zealand's Constitution: A Report on a Conversation*, November 2013, http://www.ourconstitution.org.nz/store/doc/FR_Full_Report.pdf (for New Zealand).

3 Michael Burgess and G. Alan Tarr, "Introduction: Sub-national Constitutionalism and Constitutional Development," in *Constitutional Dynamics in Federal Systems: Sub-national Perspectives*, eds. Michael Burgess and G. Alan Tarr (Montreal and Kingston: McGill-Queen's University Press, 2012) 3–39, at 3.

4 Ibid.

5 Quebec, Bill 191, *Constitution of Québec*, 1st Sess., 38th Leg., 2007 (introduction 22 May 2007).

6 *An Act respecting the laicity of the State*, CQLR c. L-0.3 ["Bill 21"].

7 Bill 96, *An Act respecting French, the official and common language of Québec*, 1st Sess., 42nd Leg., Quebec, 2021.

8 See e.g., Erin Crandall, "What Is a Provincial Constitution and How Do We Amend It?" *Policy Options*, 28 May 2021, https://policyoptions.irpp.org/magazines/may-2021/what-is-a-provincial-constitution-and-how-do-we-amend-it/ (arguing that the questions surrounding provincial constitutions, especially that of Quebec, and their relationship with the federal constitution require urgent parliamentary study).

9 See Emmanuelle Richez, "The Possibilities and Limits of Provincial Constitution-Making Power: The Case of Quebec," in *Constitutional Amendment in Canada*, ed. Emmett Macfarlane (Toronto: University of Toronto Press, 2016) 164–84, at 170 ("the desire to [adopt a comprehensive written constitution] in Quebec has been present for a long time, part of a wider nation-building strategy").

10 Burgess and Tarr, "Introduction," 7; Stephen Tierney, "'We the Peoples': Constituent Power and Constitutionalism in Plurinational States," in Loughlin and Walker, *Paradox of Constitutionalism*, 229–45, at 233.

11 See Gerald Baier, "Canada: Federal and Sub-National Constitutional Practices," in Burgess and Tarr, *Constitutional Dynamics*, 174–92, at 176.

12 See e.g., Burgess and Tarr, "Introduction"; John Dinan, "Patterns of Subnational Constitutionalism in Federal Countries," *Rutgers Law Journal* 39, no. 4 (2008): 837–61.

13 See e.g., Tierney, "We the Peoples"; Tom Ginsburg and Eric A. Posner, "Subconstitutionalism," *Stanford Law Review* 62, no. 6 (2010): 1583–628; Cheryl Saunders, "The Constitutional Credentials of State Constitutions," *Rutgers Law Journal* 42, no. 4 (2011): 853–80.

14 See e.g., Gerard Carney, "State Constitutions," in *The Oxford Handbook of the Australian Constitution*, eds. Cheryl Saunders and Adrienne Stone (Oxford: Oxford University Press, 2018), 277–312; Arthur B. Gunlicks, "State (Land) Constitutions in Germany," *Rutgers Law Journal* 31, no. 4 (2000): 971–98; Sanford Levinson, *Framed: America's 51 Constitutions and the Crisis of Governance* (New York: Oxford University Press, 2018); Jeffrey S. Sutton, *51 Imperfect Solutions: States and the Making of American Constitutional Law* (New York: Oxford University Press, 2018); and the various chapters in Burgess and Tarr, *Constitutional Dynamics*.

15 For Australian examples, see Bradley Selway, *The Constitution of South Australia* (Annandale, NSW: Federation Press, 1997); Greg Taylor, *The Constitution of Victoria* (Annandale, NSW: Federation Press, 2006); Anne Twomey, *The Constitution of New South Wales* (Annandale, NSW: Federation Press, 2004).

16 Dinan, "Patterns," 841.

17 Ibid.

18 Burgess and Tarr, "Introduction," 18–19.

19 Baier, "Canada," 174.

20 Canadians, even those citizens of Canada's three largest anglophone provinces – Ontario, British Columbia, and Alberta – would search in vain for studies of their constitutions comparable to the Australian ones referred in note 15, above. The last monograph on the Ontario government, for instance, was published well over thirty years ago: Graham White, *The Ontario Legislature: A Political Study* (Toronto: University of Toronto Press, 1987).

21 Baier, "Canada," 174.

22 *Constitution Act*, RSBC 1996, c. 66.

23 *Constitution Act, 1982*, being Schedule B to the *Canada Act, 1982* (UK), 1982, c. 11, s. 52(2), Schedule [*Constitution Act, 1982*].

24 30 & 31 Vict., c. 3 (UK) [*Constitution Act, 1867*].

25 *Constitution Act, 1982*, Part I.

26 See *Ontario (Attorney General) v. OPSEU*, [1987] 2 SCR 2 at 108 ("[i]t may very well be that the principle of responsible government could, to the extent that it depends on ... important royal powers, be entrenched to a substantial extent") (Beetz J.). See also Léonid Sirota, "Immuring Dicey's Ghost: The Senate Reform Reference and Constitutional Conventions," *Ottawa Law Review* 51, no. 2 (2020): 313–60.

27 Emmett Macfarlane, "Introduction" in Macfarlane, *Constitutional Amendment in Canada* (Toronto: University of Toronto Press, 2016), 3–15, at 7.

28 See e.g., Richard Albert, "Constructive Unamendability in Canada and the United States," Supreme Court Law Review (2nd) 67 (2014): 181–219; Richard Albert, "The Difficulty of Constitutional Amendment in Canada," *Alberta Law Review* 53, no. 1 (2015): 85–113; Richard Albert, "The Conventions of Constitutional Amendment in Canada," *Osgoode Hall Law Journal* 53, no. 2 (2016): 399–441.

29 Baier, "Canada," 175.

30 Ibid.

31 Ibid., 179.

32 *Constitution (Fixed Election Dates) Amendment Act*, 2001, SBC 2001 c. 26; *Election Statute Law Amendment Act*, 2005, SO 2005, c. 35.

33 *An Act to amend the Canada Elections Act*, SC 2007 c. 10.

34 See Crandall, "Provincial Constitution," (suggesting that the amendment of provincial constitutions, taking the form of an ordinary statute, "is ... designed to go unnoticed" and thus amounts to "amendment by stealth").

35 Baier, "Canada," 179.

36 Burgess and Tarr, "Introduction," 15.

37 Baier, "Canada," 176.

38 Bill 21, Preamble.

39 Bill 96, cl. 1.

40 See Henri Brun, Guy Tremblay, and Eugénie Brouillet, *Droit constitutionnel*, 6th ed. (Cowansville, QC: Éditions Yvon Blais, 2014); Patrice Garant, *Droit administratif*, 5th ed. (Cowansville, QC: Éditions Yvon Blais, 2010).

41 National Assembly of Quebec, *Parliamentary Procedure in Quebec* (Quebec, QC: National Assembly of Quebec, 2013). The Legislative Assembly of British Columbia publishes annotated standing orders: E George MacMinn, *Parliamentary Procedure in British Columbia*, 4th ed. (Victoria: Queen's Printer for British Columbia, 2008); the House of Assembly of Newfoundland and Labrador publishes a *Members' Parliamentary Guide* (St John's: House of Assembly, 2016).

42 Mark Tushnet, "Constitution-Making: An Introduction," *Texas Law Review* 91, no. 7 (2013): 1,983–2,013, at 1,983 (footnote omitted).

43 Ibid., 1984.

44 Philippe Teisceira-Lessard, "Appui à la souveraineté: une Saint-Jean dans le noir," *La Presse,* 24 June 2020. https://www.lapresse.ca/actualites/2020-06-24/appui-a-la-souverainete-une-saint-jean-dans-le-noir.

45 Tushnet, "Constitution-Making," 1985.

46 Ibid.

47 Alexander Hamilton, "The Federalist No. 1," in John Jay, James Madison, and Alexander Hamilton, *The Federalist Papers*, ed. Ian Shapiro (New Haven, CT: Yale University Press, 2009), 7–10, at 7.

48 See e.g., A.V. Dicey, *Introduction to the Study of the Law of the Constitution*, 8th ed. (London: Macmillan, 1915), 192 ("some polities, and among them the English constitution, have not been created at one stroke, and, far from being the result of legislation, in the ordinary sense of that term, are the fruit of contests carried on in the courts on behalf of the rights of individuals"); Dicey, of course, also emphasized the importance to the constitution of conventions originating in political practice rather than judicial decisions.

49 See e.g., *Civil Code of Quebec*, CQLR c. CCQ-1991; *Charter of the French Language*, CQLR c. C-11; *Charter of Human Rights and Freedoms*, CQLR c. C-12 [Quebec *Charter*].

50 Sir Geoffrey Palmer and Andrew Butler, *Constitution Aotearoa* (Wellington: Victoria University Press, 2016), 25–7.

51 Ilya Somin, *Democracy and Political Ignorance: Why Smaller Government Is Smarter*, 2nd ed. (Stanford: Stanford University Press, 2016), 20 (more precisely, 36 per cent of the respondents to a 2014 survey were able to name the three branches, and 35 per cent failed to name one).

52 Ibid.

53 Alberta and Saskatchewan have bills of rights of their own, but rather more minimalist than the Quebec *Charter*: *Alberta Bill of Rights*, RSA 2000, c. A-14 and *The Saskatchewan Human Rights Code, 2018*, SS 2018, c. S-24.2, Part 2.

54 Baier, "Canada," 181.

55 Even the paradigmatic model of a written constitution consists of rules that exist "outside" the codified constitutional text. See Ernest A. Young, "The Constitution Outside the Constitution," *Yale Law Journal* 117, no. 3 (2007): 408–73.

56 W.S. Holdsworth, "The Conventions of the Eighteenth-Century Constitution," *Iowa Law Review* 17, no. 2 (1932): 161–80, at 162

("conventions must grow up at all times and in all places where the powers of government are vested in different persons or bodies – where in other words there is a mixed constitution").

57 See Matthew S.R. Palmer, "Using Constitutional Realism to Identify the Complete Constitution: Lessons from an Unwritten Constitution," *American Journal of Comparative Law* 54, no. 3 (2006): 587–636.

58 Mila Versteeg and Emily Zackin, "Constitutions Unentrenched: Toward an Alternative Theory of Constitutional Design," *American Political Science Review* 110, no. 4 (2016): 657–74.

59 Stephen A Scott, "Pussycat, Pussycat or Patriation and the New Constitutional Amendment Processes," *University of Western Ontario Law Review* 20, no. 2 (1982): 247–306, at 254 (warning that "every word, – indeed every punctuation mark, – in the *Proposed Resolution* will undergo repeated and lengthy analysis in the courts of this country and this for a time extending indefinitely into the future … Profound consequences may turn on the meaning of any single word.").

60 For another study of these constraints and their application to Daniel Turp's 2007 proposal, see Richez, "Possibilities and Limits."

61 *Reference re Senate Reform*, 2014 SCC 32 at para. 28, [2014] 1 SCR 704; *Constitution Act, 1982*, Part V.

62 *Constitution Act, 1982*, ss 41(a), 47 (note that the Senate has a suspensive veto). See *Motard v. Canada (Attorney General)*, 2019 QCCA 1826 at para. 92; Philippe Lagassé and Patrick F. Baud, "The Crown and Constitutional Amendment after the Senate Reform and Supreme Court References," in Macfarlane, *Constitutional Amendment in Canada*, 247–70; 253–8.

63 *Ontario (Attorney General) v. OPSEU*, [1987] 2 SCR 2 at 46 [*OPSEU*].

64 Adam M Dodek, "Uncovering the Wall Surrounding the Castle of the Constitution: Judicial Interpretation of Part V of the *Constitution Act, 1982*," in Macfarlane, *Constitutional Amendment in Canada*, 42–64, at 49.

65 Guy Tremblay, "La réforme des institutions démocratiques au Québec: commentaires en marge du rapport du Comité directeur," *Les Cahiers de droit* 44, no. 2 (2003): 207–35.

66 Warren Newman, "Of Dissolution, Prorogation, and Constitutional Law, Principle and Convention: Maintaining Fundamental Distinctions during a Parliamentary Crisis," *National Journal of Constitutional Law* 29 (2010): 217–29; 224–5. But see Fabien Gélinas and Léonid Sirota, "Constitutional Conventions and Senate Reform," *Revue québécoise de droit constitutionnel* 5 (2013): 107–23; 114–5 (distinguishing the governor general's powers from the prime minister's advice).

67 *Constitution Act, 1982*, s. 38(1); *Reference re Senate Reform* at paras 34, 36 (the general amending procedure set out in s. 38(1) is the residual procedure for amendment).
68 Bill 21, s. 34; Bill 96, cls. 118 and 200.
69 Bill 21, ibid.
70 Richez, "Possibilities and Limits," 176.
71 *Constitution Act, 1982*, s. 43.
72 *Reference re Residential Tenancies Act*, [1981] 1 SCR 714; *Crevier v. Quebec (Attorney-General)*, [1981] 2 SCR 220.
73 *MacMillan Bloedel Ltd v. Simpson* [1995] 4 SCR 725; *Reference re Code of Civil Procedure (Que.)*, art. 35, 2021 SCC 27.
74 *Quebec (Attorney-General) v. Blaikie*, [1979] 2 SCR 1016.
75 *Reference re Remuneration of Judges of the Provincial Court (PEI)*, [1997] 3 SCR 3.

PART ONE

# Framing the Debate

# 1

# Oui, Quebec Needs a Written Constitution

*Daniel Turp*

The idea of giving Quebec its own constitution is part of its national history.[1] This idea received the support at the Estates General on the reform of democratic institutions, where 82 per cent of the participants said they were in favour of "the reforms that could be proposed by the Estates General eventually leading to a Québec constitution."[2] Its steering committee was of the view that "the adoption of a Québec constitution is an essential action that will promote democratic development by broadening the field of awareness and knowledge of democratic practices [and that] [a]ny measure relating to the form of government, the relationship between those who govern and those who are governed, and the organization of democratic institutions should be included in a fundamental law, voted by the National Assembly and confirming the popular decision expressed by referendum."[3]

The proposal to adopt a Quebec constitution has had its advocates among federalists who believe that Quebec should have a constitution as a member of the Canadian federation,[4] as well as among the supporters of Quebec independence.[5] Several pro-independence advocates have also called for the adoption of a Quebec constitution before it becomes independent.[6] I am among those who favour the adoption of such a Quebec constitution regardless of Quebec's political status and have intervened on several occasions to this end,[7] notably by introducing two draft constitutions of Quebec during my tenure as a member of Quebec's National Assembly.[8]

Obviously, this issue continues to be debated as is evidenced by the theme of the Yale Symposium: "Does Quebec need a written constitution?" To this question, then, and now – my answer is an unequivocal "Oui." Such an answer is based on a strong belief that there is a need for a written constitution in order for Quebec to affirm its distinct constitutional identity (I) and to end Canada's continuing constitutional impasse (II).

## I. THE NEED FOR A WRITTEN CONSTITUTION TO AFFIRM QUEBEC'S DISTINCT CONSTITUTIONAL IDENTITY

The distinguished academic and former deputy premier of Quebec, Professor Jacques-Yvan Morin, referred to the issue of identity in his 21 May 1985 covering letter to the Avant-projet de Constitution du Québec which he drafted at the request of Prime Minister René Lévesque. The introductory words of this letter read as follows: "You kindly asked me to undertake the drafting of a document intended to prepare the discussion on the advisability of giving Québec a formal constitution. The Committee [...] drafted the texts that we will present in the form of a draft Constitution. We have drawn on a number of sources (international instruments, foreign constitutions, political programs), taking care to adapt them as closely as possible to Québec realities. In its current form, which we wanted to be as concise as possible, it gives an overview of the kind of society that the government could propose to Quebeckers. In our view, such a socio-economic and cultural project can not only be an instrument of progress for our society, but also a *factor of identity.*"[9] (Italics mine.)

Furthermore, in a seminal article published the same year promoting the adoption of a constitution for Quebec, Professor Morin appears to focus on the identify factor in referring to a constitution as a "mirror" and a "portrait." His plea is as follows: "Undoubtedly, the mere fact of adopting a formal constitution does not provide a guarantee of good government and equal rights for all. Any hope for pure constitutional rationality constitutes magical thinking, to the extent that the norms are not securely attached to the realities, needs and aspirations. But if they can be and the conditions exist to allow a basic law to become a compendium of societal values, a pedagogical instrument for socio-political education, then one is entitled to give Québec a "living" Constitution, its mirror, and at the same time its ideal portrait."[10]

Akin to this notion of an identity factor is the concept of "constitutional identity." This concept has emerged in Europe and the United States of America and has been the subject of significant debates in the legal literature[11]. It has recently been referred to with relation to the Indigenous peoples of Canada[12] and has also been explored in the Quebec context.[13]

It has been suggested that the concept of "constitutional identity" is defined by its content, and more specifically by the rules and principles that are inherent to a society and enshrined in its constitution.[14] It has also been affirmed that a "constitutional identity" is to be defined as the identity of the legal order of which the constitution is the guarantor."[15]

In light of these definitions, Quebec might be seen as having a constitutional identity. The rules and principles that are inherent to the Quebec society have been enshrined in laws such as the *Charter of Human Rights and Freedoms*[16] which has been labelled by courts as quasi-constitutional[17] and the recent *An Act respecting the laicity of the State*[18] which also possesses a similar quasi-constitutional status. Other statutes, such as the *Civil Code of Quebec*,[19] the *Charter of the French Language*,[20] and the *Act respecting the exercise of the fundamental rights and prerogatives of the Québec people and Québec State*[21] also convey such rules and principles. These statutes and others[22] are considered to be part of Quebec's material constitution and reveal, albeit in a patchy and desultory fashion, Quebec's constitutional identity. Qualifying such material constitution as a "constitution in the substantive sense" and reminding us rightly so that such a constitution is also comprised of conventions and principles, Professor Benoît Pelletier seems to be of the same opinion:

> Québec already has a constitution in the substantive sense. It consists of measures contained in the constitutional laws, conventions and principles established by the courts. But something is missing in Québec: a constitution in due form, a fundamental text which citizens can identify as having an indisputable authority from the legal or moral standpoint. [...]
>
> Concerned that Québec must preserve its identity, I firmly believe that one of the avenues to maintain such identity is to enshrine it in a basic law, that is to say, a constitution having

> precedence over any ordinary legislation enacted by the National Assembly.
>
> The drafting of a document of such importance would allow Québecers to take stock of their common values. Those values that bring us together are also those which distinguish us from any other society in North America. It seems imperative that we determine all together what we are and where we want to go in a collective way.[23]

The values on which Quebec's constitutional identity is based – and which should be enshrined in a basic law are, inter alia, laicity, interculturalism, French as Quebec's distinctive language, and Quebec's national character. They do however come into collision with values that are enshrined in the Constitution of Canada, and especially in its *Constitution Act, 1982* and *Canadian Charter of Rights and Freedoms*.

The affirmation of the supremacy of God in the preamble of the *Canadian Charter of Rights and Freedoms* is hardly compatible with the principle of laicity now affirmed Quebec. The will of Quebec to abide by the principle of interculturalism also runs afoul with the maintenance and enhancement of the multicultural heritage of Canadians promoted by article 27 of the *Canadian Charter of Rights and Freedoms*.[24] Moreover, the imposition by the Supreme Court of Canada of official bilingualism in relation to the language of the legislature and of the courts in Quebec and the adoption in 1982 without Quebec's consent of linguistic rights had the effect of overriding the provisions of Quebec's *Charter of the French Language*. It thus thwarted Quebec's attempt to define its own constitutional identity. And the repeated refusal to recognize Quebec's status as a distinct society within Canada or to identify Quebec as a people or nation in the Constitution of Canada have been interpreted as a clear opposition to what Quebec considers at its own constitutional identity.

Thus, many have argued that Quebec must consolidate or, even better, strengthen its constitutional identity by initiating a process to adopt a written constitution of Quebec.[25] Such an initiative could involve two steps, one being the adoption of a constitution of Quebec and the other, amendments to the Constitution of Canada.[26] Embarking on such an avenue could, in my opinion, lead to the end of Canada's continuing constitutional impasse.

## II. THE NEED FOR A WRITTEN CONSTITUTION TO END CANADA'S CONTINUING CONSTITUTIONAL IMPASSE

If the adoption of a written constitution could provide Quebec with its own constitutional identity, its drafting could be useful, and indeed might be needed, to bring an end to the constitutional impasse resulting from the 1982 patriation of the Constitution of Canada without Quebec's consent. In my opinion, the end of the impasse could come about through the adoption of a Quebec constitution and a resolution to amend the Constitution of Canada in order to accommodate Quebec's distinct constitutional identity or by the adoption of a *Constitution of a sovereign and independent Quebec* rendered necessary by the refusal by Canada to negotiate or to agree to changes that would allow Quebec to develop its own basic law and constitutional identity.

Almost forty years have now elapsed since the 1982 "constitutional coup."[27] It is not acceptable to trivialize this event and agree to continue to be subject to a constitutional order against the will of Quebec. The constitutional question is not a matter of "old quarrels" and should cease to be made subject to repeated "moratoriums."[28] The adoption of a Quebec constitution could help end the constitutional impasse in two ways.

On the one hand, the drafting of a Quebec constitution could help define both the standards of a new Quebec constitutional order and identify the amendments to the Constitution of Canada needed to allow such a new order to be consistent with the Constitution of Canada. A draft Quebec constitution could therefore be accompanied by a draft resolution containing the various amendments which may be necessary to ensure the coexistence of the constitutional orders of both Canada and Quebec. Preceded by the approval of the Quebec people in a referendum, the adoption by Quebec's National Assembly of a draft Quebec constitution and a draft resolution to amend the Constitution of Canada would qualify as a legitimate attempt to change the Canadian constitution. It would therefore, as stated by the Supreme Court of Canada in its *Reference re secession of Québec*,[29] trigger "the corollary obligation of all parties to come to the negotiating table."[30] If negotiations succeeded and amendments to the Constitution of Canada proposed by Quebec were accepted, Quebec could bring its own constitution into force and accept the Canadian constitutional order as amended. Such actions would end the constitutional impasse.

If, on the other hand, the negotiations were not successful due to the fact that all parties did not agree to come to the negotiating table and the constitutional amendments sought by Quebec be refused, the drafting process of a Quebec constitution would end the constitutional impasse and allow Quebec to adopt the constitution of a sovereign and independent country.

In fact, the obligation of Canada to negotiate with Quebec on the constitutional amendments required to a allow the coexistence of the Constitution of Canada and a new constitution of Quebec would put Canada before a real choice: respect Quebec's demand for more constitutional autonomy reflected in a draft Quebec constitution and also effect the changes in the Constitution of Canada desired by Quebec, or face the possibility of Quebec adopting the constitution of a sovereign and independent Quebec.

Without doubt, it is on the content and scope of the constitutional amendments required by Quebec that the outcome of the negotiations would depend. They could lead to the end of the constitutional impasse. Constitutional lawyers and scholars who promoted the idea of drafting a Quebec constitution have not always identified explicitly the constitutional changes that should be required to allow the coexistence of a new Quebec constitution and the Constitution of Canada. Others who promote the idea of a domestic constitution for Quebec have been vague on the constitutional amendments needed for coexistence. Benoît Pelletier speaks of "the exercise that needs to be undertaken in order that a *Québec Constitution* is adapted to the federal context, in other words can co-exist seamlessly with the Constitution of Canada," while adding that "[obviously] the scope of each of the Constitutions would become difficult to delineate with precision."[31]

In the same fashion, Alain-G. Gagnon and Raffaele Iacovino do not define the constitutional changes that would allow Quebec to adopt a basic law in line with its aspirations.[32] As for Jocelyn Caron, he presents three options in order to "clearly define Québec demands in constitutional matters [… :] a Québec Constitution […], a sketch of Canadian Constitution amended or a list of constitutional demands."[33] He does not further define the advantages and disadvantage of his three options.

Two promoters of a Quebec constitution are slightly more explicit on the content of the constitutional amendments needed in order to allow the coexistence of a new Constitution of Quebec and the Constitution of Canada. Indeed, André Binette suggests introducing "provisions abolishing the Canada-British monarchy in Québec," and the "transformation of the Province of Québec into an associated republic of Québec."[34] These changes would be necessary to replace the lieutenant governor and appoint a governor or a president or to allow their election by universal suffrage or by the members of the National Assembly. In a later text in which he presents a model of the constitution of a more autonomous Quebec, Binette suggests the transfer of some powers to Quebec over such matters as unemployment insurance and expresses the opinion that the adoption of a significantly more autonomous Quebec "would require profound changes to the Canadian Constitution."[35]

For his part, in introducing his sketch of a republican constitution, Professor Marc Chevrier believes that for Quebec "it is not forbidden to want to go beyond the limits of Canadian constitutional law."[36] He adds that, "if Québec wants to officially become a republic [and] extend its powers, it must clearly indicate the changes it wants, have them approved by a referendum and thus engage the rest of Canada in the negotiation of a constitutional reform it will have initiated with the support of the population."[37] And before presenting the elements of such a republican constitution, he adds: "Among the proposals, two types of constitutional provisions should be distinguished: the first may come into force without using the amending procedure. These provisions would have immediate effects. The second would require amendments to the Canadian Constitution that the National Assembly could incorporate in the draft Constitution without putting them into force. The effect of these declaratory provisions would be delayed. The National Assembly has already resorted to this method to adopt legislation [...]. Following a successful referendum on a draft Québec Constitution, the declaratory provisions would automatically become the basis of a constitutional amendment proposal to the rest of the country over which the talks should engage in good faith."[38]

For many, the solution to the constitutional impasse therefore requires the adoption of a Constitution of Quebec. To inspire those who would take part in the constituent process and give an idea of what could be on the "menu of public discussion"[39] and building on previous texts I have drafted over the years,[40] I present hereinafter a new version of a draft Constitution of Quebec (appendix 1) as well as a draft Amendment to the Constitution of Canada (Quebec) presenting amendments to be made the *Constitution Act, 1867* and the *Constitution Act, 1982*. The adoption of such amendments would be needed to ensure a harmonious coexistence of a new Constitution of Quebec and the Constitution of Canada (appendix 2).

The text of a preamble draft Constitution of Quebec reveals elements of Quebec's constitutional identity. Part I covers such topics as common values and principles, nationality, the national capital and territory, official language and linguistic diversity of Quebec, and its natural and cultural heritage. It also describes Quebec national symbols, such as its flag, emblems, national day, and anthem. In Part II, the draft enumerates the powers, both exclusive and concurrent, that the Parliament of Quebec would be granted in order to make laws in relation to matters coming within several additional classes of subjects. It also refers to intergovernmental agreements and deals with the issue of federal financial initiatives in relation to matters coming within the classes of subjects. The exercise of Quebec's jurisdiction in the area on international relations is dealt with in the Part III of the draft constitution. Part IV confers a constitutional status to fundamental rights by way of incorporation of articles of Quebec's *Charter of Human Rights and Freedoms*, of the *Charter of the French Language*, and of *An Act respecting the laicity of the State*. Part VI describes the institutions of Quebec, including a novel head of state as well as designing the Parliament, the government, the judiciary, and municipal institutions. Part VII proposes the pathways relative to the amendment and supremacy of the Constitution of Quebec.

In its final provisions, the draft Constitution of Quebec contains an article relating to the date of its coming into force. It also includes of provision relating to the articles whose consistency with the Constitution of Canada require the adoption of the Amendment of the Constitution of Canada (Quebec) and indicates that these articles come in force at a date to be fixed by proclamation of the government. This provision would have the effect of suspending the coming into force, inter alia, of articles 8 and 9 relating to the powers of Quebec, articles 12 to 14 on the head of state and article 23 relating to the judiciary of Quebec. An additional article describes the consequences of the rejection of the

Amendment of the Constitution of Canada (Quebec) within the three-year period provided for in the *Constitution Act, 1982*. Were this rejection to occur, the National Assembly would be authorized to declare Quebec's independence. This proclamation could also be made as soon as the National Assembly determined that the amendment could not or would not be adopted. The last article of the draft Constitution of Quebec would govern constitutional transition and provides that, if a proclamation of independence were to be made, the Constitution would remain in force after such proclamation.

With regards to the draft Amendment of the Constitution of Canada (Quebec) in appendix 2, it contains the text of six amendments to be made the *Constitution Act, 1867*. They would allow Quebec to appoint a head of state, to obtain more exclusive and concurrent powers, confirm its powers in the area of international relations, allow it to make all appointments of the members of its judiciary and provide Quebec courts with exclusive jurisdiction on matters relating the *Civil Code of Quebec* on civil law and apply its language legislation to federal companies in Quebec. Five amendments would be required to ensure a harmonious coexistence of a new Constitution of Quebec with the *Constitution Act, 1982*. They would relate to the linguistic rights of the English-speaking minority in matters of education, laicity, interculturalism, the rights of Quebec and the amendment procedure as it applies to the office of the Lieutenant-Governor so as allow Quebec to appoint its own head of state.

* * *

I am more convinced than ever before that Quebec needs to adopt its own written basic law to foster its own constitutional identity. A written constitution would also allow Quebec to define the path it prefers to end the constitutional impasse it has been experiencing within Canada since the entry into force and imposition on Quebec of the *Constitution Act, 1982*. As I have had the opportunity to write and say for the last twenty-five years, a constitution is first and foremost a document aimed at establishing the foundations of the life of a nation. It can also empower a people and enhance the participation of its citizens in the democratic life of the nation. To achieve these goals for its people and citizens, "Oui," Quebec needs a written constitution.[41]

ADDENDUM: Since the Yale Symposium, the most significant development concerning matters that relate a "Québec constitution" has been the adoption by the National Assembly of Quebec on 24 May 2022 of *An Act respecting French, the official and common language of Québec* (Bill 96).[42] This act confers a quasi-constitutional status to the *Charter of the French Language*. In conformity with section 45 of the *Constitution Act, 1982* which states that "the legislature of each province may exclusively make laws amending the constitution of the province," this act inserts in chapter 5 of the *Constitution Act, 1867* relating to "Provincial Constitutions" a new section 90Q.1, which affirms that "Quebecers form a nation" and a new section 90Q.2 which adds that "French shall be the only official language of Québec" and that "[i]t is also the common language of the Quebec nation." I have commented on these provisions and their constitutional validity elsewhere[43] and suggested that they would "successfully pass the stages of its challenge that its opponents are already preparing." I also added: "If this were not the case, it should come as no surprise that the Quebec nation, in exercising its right to self-determination, would wish to adopt its own constitution and, presumably, to reflect its national aspirations, that of a sovereign and independent State."[44]

## APPENDIX 1: CONSTITUTION OF QUEBEC

### *Preamble*

WHEREAS Quebec is free to choose its own destiny, to determine its political status, and pursue its economic, social, and cultural development:
WHEREAS the French language, the distinctive language of a people that is in the majority French-speaking, is the instrument by which that people has articulated its identity;
WHEREAS the First Nations and the Inuit nation, the first inhabitants of this land, form distinct nations and have specific characteristics and a historical continuity rooted in their territory;
WHEREAS the English-speaking community in Quebec constitutes a national and linguistic minority and possesses its own institutions;
WHEREAS ethnic minorities contribute fully to the development of Québec;

WHEREAS Quebec must be guided by the principle of human and sustainable development in order to ensure the ability of future generations to meet their own needs;
WHEREAS it is important for Quebec to contribute to fair globalization, to the respect of the rules of international law, ensuring the peaceful settlement of international disputes and cooperating with international institutions and the enhancement of the common heritage of humankind;
WHEREAS it is committed to apply the principle of interculturalism and to protect and promote cultural and linguistic diversity;
WHEREAS the importance of affirming and guaranteeing fundamental rights, including the fundamental language rights of the individual;
WHEREAS the laicity of the State of Quebec is based on the principles of the separation of State and religions, the religious neutrality of the State, the equality of all citizens and freedom of conscience and freedom of religion.
WHEREAS Quebec has exercised its rights through parliamentary, governmental, and judicial institutions, which have adopted several basic laws and have laid the foundations to the further expression by Quebec of its constitutional identity;
Therefore, WE, THE PEOPLE OF QUEBEC, through the voice of our Parliament, ordain and enact this Constitution of Quebec as follows:

## *Part I: Quebec*

### CHAPTER I: THE COMMON VALUES AND PRINCIPLES IN QUEBEC

1. Quebec is a democratic and peaceful society.
   Quebec is a lay State.
   Quebec is governed by the rule of law.
   Quebec is a land where human beings are free and equal in dignity and rights and where the importance of ensuring equality between women and men is paramount.
   Quebec is a society that cares for the vulnerable, especially children and the elderly.
   Quebec ensures the promotion and protection of French language and culture, as well as the diversity of linguistic and cultural expressions.
   Quebec is committed to ensuring human and sustainable development.

CHAPTER II: THE NATIONALITY OF QUEBEC

2. A Quebec nationality is established.
Quebec's nationality may be combined with any other nationality or citizenship.
Other matters concerning Quebec nationality are prescribed by law.

CHAPTER III: THE NATIONAL CAPITAL OF QUEBEC

3. The national capital of Quebec is Quebec City.

CHAPTER IV: THE TERRITORY OF QUEBEC

4. Quebec exercises full powers on its territory.
Quebec's territory cannot be changed without the consent of the Parliament of Quebec.
Other matters concerning the protection and the integrity of Quebec's territory are prescribed by law.

CHAPTER V: THE OFFICIAL LANGUAGE AND LINGUISTIC DIVERSITY OF QUEBEC

5. French is the official language of Quebec.
The languages of the First Nations and the Inuit; and the English language contribute with the French language to Quebec's linguistic diversity.
Other matters concerning the protection and promotion of Quebec's official language and of its linguistic diversity are prescribed by law.

CHAPTER VI: THE NATURAL AND CULTURAL HERITAGE OF QUEBEC

6. Quebec preserves, protects, and promotes all its natural and cultural heritage of an archaeological, architectural, archival, artistic, ethnological, historical, and religious nature. Other matters concerning the preservation, protection, and promotion of natural and cultural heritage of Quebec are prescribed by law.

CHAPTER VI: THE FLAG, THE EMBLEMS, THE NATIONAL DAY, AND ANTHEM OF QUEBEC

7. The national flag of Quebec is a white cross on a blue field, with a white fleur-de-lis in each canton or, in heraldic terms, azure, a cross between four fleurs-de-lis argent.

The emblematic tree of Quebec is the yellow birch, its emblematic flower is the blue flag, and its emblematic bird is the snowy owl.
Quebec's motto is: "Je me souviens."
The blazon of Quebec's coat of arms is tierced (divided into three parts) in fess, first azure, two fleurs-de-lis Or; second gules, a lion *passant guardant* of the second, armed and langued of the first; third, of the second, a sprig of three sugar maple leaves vert, nerved of the field. Ensigned with the royal crown. Under the shield, a scroll argent bordered azure bearing the motto "Je me souviens" of the same.
The national anthem of Quebec is: "Gens du pays."
Other matters concerning the national flag and emblems, the National Day, and the national anthem are prescribed by law.

## *Part II: The Powers of Quebec*

### CHAPTER 1: EXCLUSIVE POWERS OF QUEBEC

8. Quebec may exclusively make laws in relation to matters coming within the classes of subjects hereinafter enumerated:
   1 language and culture, including communications, radio and television broadcasting, and new information technologies;
   2 education, higher education, and research in colleges and universities;
   3 health and social services;
   4 the environment, including energy and natural resources;
   5 the economy, including agriculture, regional development, industry, trade, research, and development and tourism;
   6 support for individuals and families, the youth and elderly, including leisure and sports, social affairs, family policy, marriage and divorce, employment insurance, and income security;
   7 social affairs, including policies related to labour, employment insurance, and income security;
   8 municipal affairs, including housing policies;
   9 the administration of justice and public security;
   10 collection of all taxes levied in Quebec, including federal income and goods and services taxes.

No form of federal financial initiative in relation to matters coming within the classes of subjects referred to above is authorized.

CHAPTER II: CONCURRENT POWERS OF QUEBEC

9. Quebec may concurrently make laws in relation to matters coming within the classes of subjects hereinafter enumerated:
   1 Indigenous affairs;
   2 immigration;
   3 financial institutions;
   4 justice, including the appointment of judges;
   5 fisheries;
   6 transportation;
   7 taxation and income.

Intergovernmental agreements define the exercise of such concurrent jurisdiction between Canada and Quebec.
In the absence of an intergovernmental agreement, no form of federal financial initiative in relation to matters coming within the classes of subjects is authorized.

## *Part III: The International Relations of Quebec*

10. Quebec conducts its international relations on matters coming within its jurisdiction.
    In its international relations, it abides by the rules of international law, including the norms relating to the peaceful settlement of international disputes, and through cooperation with international institutions.
    The government establishes and maintains relationships with other States and international institutions. It ensures its representation those States and institutions.
    It may enter into international agreements. The Government of Quebec ratifies or gives assent to international agreements.
    An international agreement which is an important international agreement must be approved by the Quebec National Assembly before it is ratified or given assent to by the Head of State.
    The expression "important international agreement" means an international agreement which:
    1 requires, for its implementation by Quebec, the passing of an act or the making of regulation, the imposition of a tax, or the acceptance of an important financial obligation;

2 concerns human rights and freedoms;
3 concerns international trade; or
4 should be approved in other cases prescribed by law.
International agreements in force, decisions of international institutions to which Quebec must comply, rules of customary international law and general principles of law which confer rights and impose obligations are part of domestic legal order and take precedence over rules of domestic law.

### *Part IV: The Fundamental Rights in Quebec*

11. Articles 1 to 56 of the *Charter of Human Rights and Freedoms* (chapter C-12) are an integral part of this Constitution.
Articles 1 (right to life, and to personal security, inviolability and freedom, and to a juridical personality), 3 (freedom of conscience and freedom of religion), and 37 of this *Charter* are not subject to the power of derogation conferred by article 52 of the *Charter*. Such power does not authorize the suspension of legal rights essential for the protection of such rights.
Articles 2 to 6 of the *Charter of the French Language* (chapter C-11) are part of this Constitution.
Articles 2 to 10 *of An Act respecting the laicity of the State* (chapter L-0.3) are also part of this Constitution.
The interpretation and application of the abovementioned articles must be consistent with the common values and principles set out in article 1 of this Constitution.

### *Part V: The Institutions of Quebec*

CHAPTER I: THE HEAD OF STATE OF QUEBEC

12. The National Assembly appoints the Head of State.
13. In exercising its powers, the Head of State:
  a) appoints the Prime Minister and, at his request, the members of Quebec's Executive Council;
  b) appoints, after confirmation by the National Assembly, the members of the Supreme Court of Quebec;
  c) after their adoption by the National Assembly, promulgates laws;
  d) accredits persons occupying key positions in general

delegations, delegations, and other Quebec international offices and antennas abroad;

e) ratifies or gives assent to important international agreements approved by the National Assembly.

14. Other matters concerning the Head of State are prescribed by law.

CHAPTER II: THE PARLIAMENT OF QUEBEC

15. The National Assembly and the Head of State form the Parliament of Quebec. The Parliament of Quebec exercises all the powers attributed to the Quebec Legislature.
Parliament exercises legislative power.
The National Assembly has a supervisory jurisdiction over any act of the government, its departments, and agencies.
The Head of State shall convene, prorogue ,and dissolve the National Assembly.
A legislature lasts at most five years. The Head of State can dissolve the National Assembly before the end of those five years.

16. The National Assembly consists of 125 members. This number can be changed by law to take account of demographic trends in Quebec.
An elected member may sit in the National Assembly after having taken the following oath: "I swear that I will be loyal to Quebec and that I will perform my duties with honesty and justice with respect for the Constitution of Quebec."

17. The legislative initiative belongs to members of the National Assembly. However, only a member of the Executive Council may introduce a bill for which public funds can be committed, imposing a burden on taxpayers, levying a debt to the state, or disposing of property owned by the State.
A bill adopted by the National Assembly shall be submitted to a referendum if, at the time of its presentation, it contains a provision to this effect and the text of the question submitted to referendum. Such a bill may be promulgated after being submitted to voters in a referendum.

18. The Prime Minister or fifty members of the National Assembly can submit to the Supreme Court of Quebec the question of the consistency of a draft bill or an important international agreement with this Constitution. A draft bill or an

international agreement declared inconsistent with this Constitution may not be adopted or approved by the National Assembly.

19. Other matters concerning the Parliament of Quebec are prescribed by law.

CHAPTER III: THE GOVERNMENT OF QUEBEC

20. The government conducts the domestic and foreign policy of Quebec. It ensures the effective implementation of legislation and the use of the regulatory power.
The government is led by an Executive Council composed of the Prime Minister, ministers, and secretaries of State acting under the authority of the Prime Minister.
The appointment of the Prime Minister is made by the Head of State in accordance with election results.
The appointment of members of the Executive Council is made by the Head of State at the request of the Prime Minister.
The Prime Minister chairs the Executive Council and is responsible for the general policy of Quebec.
Only an elected member of the National Assembly can be appointed at the Executive Council. However, a person may be appointed and remain a member of the Executive Council if elected in the year following the appointment.

21. The government must retain the confidence of the National Assembly and can engage its responsibility on a bill or on its overall program. Government accountability can also be challenged by the vote on a motion of confidence.

22. Other matters concerning the Government of Quebec are prescribed by law.

CHAPTER IV: THE JUDICIARY OF QUEBEC

23. The courts are independent and impartial. Judges shall cease to hold office upon attaining the age of seventy-five years and can be suspended or dismissed only by virtue of a resolution of the National Assembly.
The Court of Quebec and the Superior Court of Quebec are the trial courts having jurisdiction in civil and criminal matters as well as in matters concerning minors.
The Court of Appeal of Quebec is the appellate court with jurisdiction over causes, matters, and things appealable.

The Supreme Court of Quebec is the highest court in Quebec. The appointment of judges of the Court of Quebec and the Superior Court of Quebec is made by the Minister of Justice; the judges of the Court of Appeal of Quebec are appointed by the Prime Minister on the recommendation of the Minister of Justice; the judges of the Supreme Court of Quebec are appointed by the Head of State after the confirmation by National Assembly.

24. If in the course of litigation, there are issues relating to the consistency a draft bill or an important international agreement with this constitution, a judge must suspend the proceedings and submit the draft bill or important international agreement to the Supreme Court of Quebec. In case of a declaration of inconsistency of a draft bill or an important international agreement with this Constitution, its application is suspended until the amendment of this Constitution.
25. Other matters concerning the judiciary of Quebec are prescribed by law.

CHAPTER V: THE MUNICIPAL INSTITUTIONS OF QUEBEC

26. The municipal institutions in Quebec are territorial divisions with their own legal personality. The number of municipal institutions cannot be altered except by law.
    Municipal institutions are guaranteed the right to independent management in their areas of jurisdiction and the right to adequate funding.
    Other matters concerning municipal institutions are prescribed by law.

## *Part VI: The Supremacy and Amendment of the Constitution of Quebec*

27. The Quebec Constitution is the supreme law of Quebec.
    Any rule of law that is inconsistent with the provisions of this Constitution is, to the extent of the inconsistency, of no force or effect.
28. The provisions of this Constitution are subject to amendment.
    The initiative of the amendment belongs to the Prime Minister. Such an initiative can also be taken with the support of fifty members of the National Assembly.

An amendment of this Constitution may also be initiated by 15 per cent of registered voters.
An amendment must be introduced by a bill in the National Assembly.
The amendment bill is submitted to a vote in a referendum. If the bill receives a majority of valid votes cast, namely 50 per cent of the votes plus one vote, it is presented to the National Assembly for its adoption.
An amendment bill can be put to a vote of the National Assembly before it is submitted to a vote in a referendum. If it obtains the support of seventy-five members of the National Assembly, it is adopted without the obligation to hold a referendum.
Other matters concerning the amendment of the Constitution of Quebec are prescribed by law.

### *Part VII: The Publication and Distribution of the Constitution of Quebec*

29. The text of this constitution is published in the official language which is authoritative.
The text of the Constitution is also published in the languages of First Nations and the Inuit as well as in the English language.
The Head of State of Quebec must send to very citizen reaching the voting age or upon a written request a copy of this Constitution and a copy of the articles of the *Charter of Human Rights and Freedoms* (chapter C-12), the *Charter of the French Language* (chapter C-11), *and An Act respecting the laicity of the State* (chapter L-0.3) which are referred to in this Constitution.Educational institutions must include in their program of studies teachings on this constitution and its content.

### *Transitional and Final Provisions*

30. This constitution comes into force on [insert date here].
31. However, articles of this constitution whose consistency with the Constitution of Canada require the adoption of the Amendment of the Constitution of Canada (Quebec) approved by the Quebec National Assembly on [insert date here] will

come in force at a date to be fixed by proclamation of the government.

32. If the Amendment of the Constitution of Canada (Quebec) is not adopted within three years, the National Assembly is authorized to adopt a proclamation of the independence of Quebec. This declaration can also be made as soon as the National Assembly has established that this modification could not or would not be adopted.
33. In the event that a proclamation of independence is made pursuant to article 32, the present Constitution shall remain in force after this proclamation and will be subject to the amendment procedure provided for in article 29 of this Constitution. Articles 31 to 33 will cease to have effect on the date of this proclamation.

## APPENDIX 2: AMENDMENT TO THE CONSTITUTION OF CANADA (QUEBEC)

### *Part I*

DRAFT RESOLUTION

WHEREAS the National Assembly adopted and the people of Quebec approved the *Constitution of Quebec* during the referendum held on [insert date here];

WHEREAS the entry into force of certain provisions of the Constitution of Quebec would be facilitated by the adoption of amendments to the Constitution of Canada;

WHEREAS the Constitution of Quebec provides that if the Amendment of the Constitution of Canada (Quebec) is not adopted within three years, the National Assembly is authorized, under the Constitution, to declare the independence of Quebec and that this proclamation can also be made as soon as the National Assembly has established that this amendment will not be adopted.

*Therefore Be It Resolved,*

THAT the National Assembly authorizes the Amendment of the Constitution of Canada by proclamation of His Excellency the Governor General under the Great Seal of Canada in accordance with the following:

*Amendment to the Constitution of Canada (Quebec)*
*Constitution Act, 1867*

1. The *Constitution Act, 1867* is amended by inserting after section 90, the following:
   "90A. As of [insert date here], sections 58 to 90 of this Part shall not apply in Quebec."[45]
2. The act is amended by inserting after section 93A the following:

*Powers of Quebec93B. Quebec may exclusively make laws in relation to matters coming within the classes of subjects hereinafter enumerated:*

1 language and culture, including communications, radio and television broadcasting, and new information technologies;
2 education, higher education, and research in colleges and universities;
3 health and social services;
4 the environment, including energy and natural resources;
5 the economy, including agriculture, regional development, industry, trade, research and development, and tourism;
6 support for individuals and families, the youth and elderly, including leisure and sports, social affairs, family policy, marriage and divorce, employment insurance, and income security;
7 social affairs, including politics of labour, employment insurance, and income security;
8 municipal affairs, including housing policies;
9 the administration of justice and public security;
10 collection of all taxes levied in Quebec, including federal income and goods and services taxes.

No form of federal financial initiative in relation to matters coming within the classes of subjects mentioned above is authorized.
93C. Quebec may concurrently make laws in relation to matters coming within the classes of subjects hereinafter enumerated:

1 Indigenous affairs;
2 immigration;
3 financial institutions;
4 justice, including the appointment of judges;
5 fisheries;

6 transportation;
7 taxation and income.

Intergovernmental agreements define the exercise of such concurrent jurisdiction between Canada and Quebec.

In the absence of an intergovernmental agreement, no form of federal financial initiative in relation to matters coming within the classes of subjects is authorized.

93D. Quebec exercises jurisdiction over international relations concerning matters coming within the classes of subjects enumerated in this sections 93B and 93C. In exercising such jurisdiction, it may enter into international agreements and ensure its representation in other states and international institutions.

3. The act is amended by inserting after section 96 of the following:
96A. "The judges of the courts created by the laws of the Parliament of Quebec are appointed by ways and means prescribed by such laws."[46]
4. Section 98 of the act is repealed.[47]
5. Section 101 of the act is amended by inserting the following:
101A. "The Appeals Court General for Canada does not have jurisdiction to rule on questions relating to the interpretation and application of the Civil Code of Quebec and civil law."[48]
6. The act is amended by inserting after section 133 the following:
"133A. Interpretation of the Constitution of Canada should be consistent with the duty of Parliament and the Government of Quebec to protect and promote the French language and its use in Quebec."
"133B. The Parliament of Quebec can make laws regarding the use of the French language by any company established by an act of Parliament of Canada."[49]

*Constitution Act, 1982*

7. The *Constitution Act, 1982* is amended by inserting after section 23, the following:
"23A. Subsections (1) to (3) of Article 23 shall not apply in Quebec."[50]
8. Section 27 of the act is amended by inserting the following:
"27A. In Quebec, this *Charter* shall be interpreted in a manner consistent with the principle of laicity."[51]
9. The act is amended by inserting after section 35.1 the following:

*Part II*

RIGHTS OF QUEBEC

"35.2 (1) The right of Quebec to choose its own destiny, to determine its political status, and pursue its economic, social, and cultural development is hereby recognized and affirmed.

(2) The Parliament and Government of Quebec have a role to protect and promote the abovementioned right."

10. Section 45 of the act is amended by inserting after the first paragraph, the following:

"45A. Notwithstanding section 41 or any other provision of the *Constitution of Canada*, the Parliament of Quebec may amend its constitution to replace the office of the Lieutenant Governor by the office of the Head of State of Québec."[52]

11. Section 59 of the act is repealed.[53]

12. Title of this amendment, "Amendment of the *Constitution of Canada* (Quebec) (*insert here the year of proclamation*)."

NOTES

1 For a detailed account of such historical underpinnings, see Daniel Turp, "La constitution québécoise: une perspective historique," *Revue québécoise de droit constitutionnel* 2 (2008):16–71.

2 See Secrétariat à la réforme des institutions démocratiques, *Prenez votre place – Cahier de participation* (Gouvernement du Québec: 2003), 19–20.

3 See Comité directeur de la réforme des institutions démocratiques, *Prenez votre place – La participation citoyenne au cœur des institutions démocratiques québécoises – Rapport* (Quebec: March 2003), 37. The broad consensus on this issue was also reflected in a survey conducted in 2007 which showed that 63 per cent of people were in favour the adoption of a Quebec constitution: see Léger Marketing, *L'opinion des Québécois à l'égard d'une constitution du Québec*, dossier 10943-001 (November 2007), http://danielturpqc.org/upload/2020/Constitution_Québecoise_Sondage_Leger_Marketing_14-18_novembre_2007.pdf.

4 See Benoît Pelletier, *Une certaine idée du Québec: Parcours d'un fédéraliste de la réflexion à l'action* (Quebec: Presses de l'Université Laval, 2010), 165–72.

5 See Jacques Dufresne, *Le courage et la lucidité: essai sur la Constitution d'un Québec souverain*, (Sillery: Septentrion, 1990); Marc Chevrier, "Une Constitution pour le peuple québécois," *L'Agora* 2, no. 10 (1995): 13–14;

Marc Brière, "L'acte fondateur de la nation – L'établissement d'un nouveau contrat social s'impose," *Le Devoir*, 25 April 2000, A-7; François Rocher, "Une nouvelle constitution pour le Québec?," in *L'annuaire du Québec 2003*, ed. Fides (Montreal: Fides, 2002), 485–8; Denis Monière, "Le besoin d'une Constitution québécoise," *L'Action nationale* 95, no. 2 (2005): 30–5; Danic Parenteau, *L'indépendance par la République – De la souveraineté du peuple à celle de l'État*, (Montréal: Fides, 2015): 169–95.

6 See David Payne, *Pour une constitution du Québec*, March 1984 and David Payne, *Pour une constitution du Québec*, November 1984; Jacques-Yvan Morin, "Pour une nouvelle Constitution du Québec," *McGill Law Journal* 30, no. 2 (1985): 171–220; André Binette, "Pour une constitution du Québec," *Le Devoir*, 11 December 1992, B-8; Guy Laforest, *Pour la liberté d'une société distincte – Parcours d'un intellectuel engagé* (Quebec: Presses de l'Université Laval, 2004); Michel Seymour, "Pour une Constitution québécoise," *Spirale: Arts, Lettres, Sciences humaines* 222 (2008): 16–17; André Larocque, "Constitution et citoyenneté québécoise. Pourquoi pas?," *Le Soleil*, 2 April 2007, 17; Marc Chevrier, *La République québécoise: Hommages à une idée suspecte* (Montréal: Boréal, 2012).

7 For the collected essays that I have written on the issue of a Quebec constitution, see Daniel Turp, *La Constitution québécoise – Essais sur le droit du Québec se doter de sa propre loi fondamentale* (Montreal: Éditions JFD, 2013) [hereinafter Daniel Turp, *Essais sur la Constitution québécoise*].

8 See Bill 191, *Constitution of Québec*, (Introduction), 1st Sess., 38th Leg., Quebec, 22 May 2007, http://assnat.qc.ca/en/travaux-parlementaires/projets-loi/projet-loi-191-38-1.html; and Bill 196, *Québec Constitution*, (Introduction), 1st Sess., 38th Leg., Quebec, 18 October 2007, http://m.assnat.qc.ca/en/travaux-parlementaires/projets-loi/projet-loi-196-38-1.html.

9 This letter is reprinted in Daniel Turp, *Essais sur la Constitution québécoise*, 416–17.

10 Morin, "Pour une nouvelle Constitution," 220 (translation mine). The reference to a "living" constitution appears to be an allusion to the "living tree" metaphor first used by the Judicial Committee of the Pricy Council in relation the *British North America Act* (now the *Constitution Act, 1867*) in the "Persons case," *Edwards v. Canada (Attorney General)*, [1930] AC 24 and referred to by the Supreme Court of Canada in *Re BC Motor Vehicle Act*, [1985] 2 SCR 486 and *Reference Re Same-Sex marriage*, 2004 SCC 79, [2004] 3 SCR 698. The meaning of the metaphor is very well captured by the Court in this latter case: "The 'frozen concepts' reasoning runs contrary to one of the most fundamental principles of Canadian constitutional interpretation: that our Constitution is a living

tree which, by way of progressive interpretation, accommodates and addresses the realities of modern life" (at para. 22). For an in-depth study of the application of this metaphor, see, Eugénie Brouillet and Alain-G. Gagnon, "La constitution canadienne et la métaphore de l'arbre vivant: quelques réflexions politologiques et juridiques," in *Constitutionalisme, droits et diversité: Mélanges en l'honneur de José Woehrling*, eds. Alain-G. Gagnon and Pierre Noreau (Montréal: Thémis, 2017), 79–107.

11 In Europe, the concept of constitutional identity has been anlaysed by Anne Levade, "Quelle identité constitutionnelle nationale présenter face à l'Union européenne," in *Annuaire de droit européen*, vol. II: *L'État membre de l'Union européenne*, ed. Hélène Gaudin (Bruxelles: Bruylant, 2004), 173–88; Michel Troper, "L'identité constitutionnelle," in *1958–2008: Cinquantième anniversaire de la Consittution française*, ed. Bertrand Mathieu (Paris: Dalloz, 2008), 123–9; Laurence Burgorgue-Larsen, *L'identité constitutionnelle saisie par les juges en Europe* (Paris: A. Pedone, 2011); and François Xavier Millet, *L'Union européenne et l'identité constitutionnelle des États membres* (Paris: LGDJ, 2013). In the United States of America, the notion has also been studied by Gary Jeffrey Jacobsohn, *Constitutional Identity* (Cambridge: Cambridge University Press, 2010); Heinz Klug, "Constitutional Identity and Change," *Tulsa Law Review* 47, no. 1 (2011): 41–50; Peter Kruzlicz, "Le sens et les limites du terme de l'identité en droit constitutionnel: à la recherche d'une définition juridique," *Synergies Roumanie* 13 (2018): 111–29.

12 See Patrick Macklem, "L'identité constitutionnelle des peuples autochtones au Canada: groupes à statut particulier ou acteurs fédéraux?," *Revue juridique Thémis de l'Université de Montréal* 51, no. 2 (2017): 389–432.

13 See Stéphane Bernatchez, "L'identité constitutionnelle du Québec: l'émergence d'un nouveau concept juridique," in *Un regard québécois sur le droit constitutionnel: Mélanges en l'honneur d'Henri Brun et Guy Tremblay*, eds. Patrick Taillon, Eugénie Brouillet, and Amélie Binette (Montreal: Yvon Blais, 2016), 101–30.

14 See Dominique Rousseau, "Identité constitutionnelle, bouclier de l'identité nationale ou branche de l'étoile européenne," in Burgorgue-Larsen, *L'Identité constitutionnelle*, 89–100.

15 See Bernatchez, "Identité constitutionnelle du Québec," 117.

16 CLRQ, c. C-12.

17 The Supreme Court of Canada has affirmed in at least twelve of its judgments the quasi-constitutional nature of Quebec's *Charter of Human Rights and Freedoms*: see inter alia *Mouvement laïque québécois v. Saguenay (City)*, 2015 SCC 16, [2015] 2 SCR 3, at para. 45.

18 CLRQ, c. L-0.3.

19 CLRQ, c. C-1991.

20 CLRQ, c. C-11.

21 CLRQ, c. E-20.2

22 For a compendium of statutes which can be considered as part of Quebec's "material" constitution, see Daniel Turp, "Le pouvoir constituant et la constitution du Québec," in Taillon, Brouillet, and Binette, *Un regard québécois*, 694–701.

23 See Pelletier, *Une certaine idée du Québec*, 165 (translation mine).

24 A definition of the concept of interculturalism was put forward by the Quebec Government in its "Policy on Québec affirmation and Canadian Relations" which refers to the "emergence of a unique pluralistic model of integration and coexistence: interculturalism" and adds: "The model of interculturalism in Québec, based on the principle of reciprocity, aims to strike a balance between openness to diversity and the continuity and vitality of Québec's distinct French-speaking identity": see Government of Quebec, *Quebecers: Our Way of Being Canadian* (Québec: Secrétariat aux affaires intergouvernementales canadiennes, 2017), https://www.sqrc.gouv.qc.ca/documents/relations-canadiennes/politique-affirmation-en.pdf, 69. For in an in-depth discussion on interculturalism, see Alain-G. Gagnon and Arjun Tremblay, "Interculturalism and the Plea for an Informal Constitution: Responding to the Challenge of Polyethnicity in Québec," in this volume.

25 Such is the case of Jacques-Yvan Morin, Benoît Pelletier, and myself, but also Marc Chevrier: see Chevrier, *La république québécoise*, 239; see also André Binette, "La succession royale, la Constitution canadienne et la Constitution du Québec," *L'Action nationale* 98, no. 4 (2008): 84–133 and Jocelyn Caron, *Choisir le progrès national* (Montreal: Druide, 2013), 400.

26 From an historical perspective, it is interesting to note that such a constitutional roadmap was proposed as far back as 1967 by Paul Gérin-Lajoie in his capacity as chairman of the Constitutional Affairs Committee of the Political Committee of the Québec Liberal Federation. That committee proposed "two new constitutions, two deadlines" and the conclusion of the report included the following passage in this regard: "It is clear from the foregoing that Québec requires a new Constitution of Canada and a new Constitution of Québec. There was a time when a patch or a few specific amendments, could meet its needs. But the requirements of the present, both from the standpoint of the national symbol and he perspective of the effective functioning of government, require entirely new

documents – documents designed at home, prepared at home, adopted at home, with the approval of the sovereign people": see See Paul Gérin-Lajoie, *Rapport du comité des affaires constitutionnelles de la commission politique de la Fédération libérale du Québec* (Montreal, October 1967). For a comment on this report, see Marc Chevrier, "La République associée du Québec et sa constitution," *Encyclopédie de l'Agora,* 1 April 2012, http://agora.qc.ca/documents/Constitution_quebecoise--La_Republique_associee_du_Quebec_et_sa_constitution_par_Paul-Gerin_Lajoie.

27 See Frédéric Bastien, *The Battle of London: Trudeau, Thatcher, and the Fight for Canada's Constitution* (Toronto: Dundurn, 2014), 313.

28 See Jocelyn Caron, "Question constitutionnelle – La voie du progrès national – En niant le problème et en l'associant bassement à des 'vieilles chicanes', les libéraux ont fini par faire oublier l'importance de la loi fondamentale," *Le Devoir*, 28 March 2013, A-9.

29 [1998] 2 SCR 217.

30 Ibid., at para. 88. The full text of this paragraph reads as follows: "In Canada, the initiative for constitutional amendment is the responsibility of democratically elected representatives of the participants in Confederation. Those representatives may, of course, take their cue from a referendum, but in legal terms, constitution-making in Canada, as in many countries, is undertaken by the democratically elected representatives of the people. The corollary of a legitimate attempt by one participant in Confederation to seek an amendment to the Constitution is an obligation on all parties to come to the negotiating table."

31 See Pelletier, *Une certaine idée du Québec*, 171.

32 See Alain-G. Gagnon and Raffaele Iacovino, *De la nation à la multination* (Montreal: Boréal, 2007), 222–30.

33 See Caron, *Choisir le progrès national*, 400.

34 See Binette, "Pour une constitution du Québec." See also Gilbert Paquette and André Binette, "L'accession du Québec à l'indépendance," in *L'indépendance maintenant!*, eds. Gilbert Paquette, André Binette, and Ercilia Palacio-Quintin (Montreal: Michel Brûlé, 2012), 282–303.

35 See André Binette, "Le peuple québécois doit se donner sa propre constitution," notes for a speech delivered at the États généraux sur la souveraineté, 6 April 2013, 2 (on file with author).

36 See Chevrier, *La République québécoise*, 305.

37 Ibid.

38 Ibid., 309–10.

39 See ibid., 309.

40 Apart from Bill 191 and 196 that were introduced in Quebec's National Assembly referred to above, my other draft constitutions for Quebec can be found in Daniel Turp, *Essais sur la Constitution québécoise*, 14–39, 69–88, 165–88, 185–7, 247–68, 319–22, 339–44, 526–38, and 591–600.

41 My strongly held conviction that Quebec needs a written constitution has been reinforced by my experience as co-chair of the Citizen Constituent Assembly set up during the course of the CONSTITUONS!; https://inm.qc.ca/constituons/. Coordinated by the Institut du Nouveau-Monde, this project brought together forty-two citizens of Quebec chosen by a draw and led to the adoption of a *Constitution citoyenne du Québec*, https://inm.qc.ca/sites/inm.qc.ca/wp-content/uploads/docs/CONSTITUONS/constitution_citoyenne_quebec_INM.pdf

42 *An Act respecting French, the official and common language of Québec* (Bill 96), Statutes of Québec 2022, chapter 14, http://www2.publicationsduquebec.gouv.qc.ca/dynamicSearch/telecharge.php?type=5&file=2022C14A.pdf.

43 Daniel Turp, "La validité de la proposition du Québec de modifier sa constitution provinciale," *Options politiques/Policy Options*, 30 June 2021, https://policyoptions.irpp.org/fr/magazines/june-2021/la-validite-de-la-proposition-du-quebec-de-modifier-sa-constitution-provinciale.

44 Ibid. (translation mine). See also my article published after the adoption of *An Act respecting French, the official and common language of Québec:* Daniel Turp, "De la primauté de la Charte québécoise dans la future Constitution du Québec," *Le Devoir*, 30 June 2022, A-7, https://www.ledevoir.com/opinion/idees/728511/droits-de-la-primaute-de-la-charte-quebecoise-dans-la-future-constitution-du-quebec.

45 Part V of the *Constitution Act, 1867* relates to "Provincial Constitutions" and comprises sections on Executive Power (58–68) and Legislative Power (69–90).

46 Section 96 reads as follows: "The Governor General shall appoint the Judges of the Superior, District, and County Courts in each Province, except those of the Courts of Probate in Nova Scotia and New Brunswick."

47 Section 98 reads as follows: "The Judges of the Courts in Québec shall be selected from the Bar of that Province."

48 Section 101 reads as follows: "The Parliament of Canada may, notwithstanding anything in this Act, from Time to Time provide for the Constitution, Maintenance, and Organization of a General Court of Appeal for Canada, and for the Establishment of any additional Courts for the better Administration of the Laws of Canada."

49 Section 133 reads as follows: "Either the English or the French Language may be used by any Person in the Debates of the Houses of the Parliament of Canada and of the Houses of the Legislature of Québec; and both those Languages shall be used in the respective Records and Journals of those Houses; and either of those Languages may be used by any Person or in any Pleading or Process in or issuing from any Court of Canada established under this Act, and in or from all or any of the Courts of Québec. The Acts of the Parliament of Canada and of the Legislature of Québec shall be printed and published in both those Languages."

50 Subsections 1 to 3 of section read as follows:

(1) Citizens of Canada

(*a*) whose first language learned and still understood is that of the English or French linguistic minority population of the province in which they reside, or

(*b*) who have received their primary school instruction in Canada in English or French and reside in a province where the language in which they received that instruction is the language of the English or French linguistic minority population of the province, have the right to have their children receive primary and secondary school instruction in that language in that province.

(2) Citizens of Canada of whom any child has received or is receiving primary or secondary school instruction in English or French in Canada, have the right to have all their children receive primary and secondary school instruction in the same language.

(3) The right of citizens of Canada under subsections (1) and (2) to have their children receive primary and secondary school instruction in the language of the English or French linguistic minority population of a province

(*a*) applies wherever in the province the number of children of citizens who have such a right is sufficient to warrant the provision to them out of public funds of minority language instruction; and

(*b*) includes, where the number of those children so warrants, the right to have them receive that instruction in minority language educational facilities provided out of public funds.

51 Section 27 reads as follows: "This Charter shall be interpreted in a manner consistent with the preservation and enhancement of the multicultural heritage of Canadians."

52 Section 41 now in force read as follows in the relevant part: "An amendment to the Constitution of Canada in relation to the following matters may be made by proclamation issued by the Governor General under the

Great Seal of Canada only where authorized by resolutions of the Senate and House of Commons and of the legislative assembly of each province: the office of the Queen, the Governor General and the Lieutenant Governor of a province"; section 45 reads as follows: "Subject to section 41, the legislature of each province may exclusively make laws amending the constitution of the province."

53 Section 59 reads as follows: "(1) Paragraph 23(1) (*a*) shall come into force in respect of Québec on a day to be fixed by proclamation issued by the Queen or the Governor General under the Great Seal of Canada. (2) A proclamation under subsection (1) shall be issued only where authorized by the legislative assembly or government of Québec."

# 2

# Legal Roadblocks to Proposals for a Quebec Constitution

*Maxime St-Hilaire and Patrick F. Baud*

There have been several proposals over the years for the adoption of a Quebec constitution. But Quebec, like all Canadian provinces, already has a constitution, which is made up of both political and legal norms. The legal norms include formally constitutional provisions and jurisprudentially-derived principles supreme over ordinary law; formally ordinary provisions scattered across the provincial statute book and their judicial interpretation; and common law rules.

So the proposal that Quebec adopt a constitution is not so much about adopting a constitution as such. The aim is rather to adopt a constitution with different characteristics than the existing one. From our brief review of proposals for a Quebec constitution, which we describe in part I, two characteristics (aside from substantive changes) differentiate the proposed constitution from the existing one: (1) a greater degree of codification;[1] and (2) subjecting the constitution to an amending procedure more onerous than that for amending ordinary laws with the aim of making a Quebec constitution supreme over other provincial laws.

Though we take no view here on the merits of codification, we see no legal impediment to it as such. To cite an oft-quoted example, British Columbia, for instance, has codified a portion of its constitution in a *Constitution Act*.[2] There is no reason Quebec could not do the same. Indeed, Quebec too has already codified portions of its constitution. The *Act respecting the National Assembly*, for instance, codifies some aspects of the relationship between the National Assembly and the executive Government of Quebec. To that end, section 4 provides that "[t]he Assembly has the power of supervision over all the acts of the Government and of its departments and agencies."[3] Likewise, the *Executive Power Act* provides for the appointment of members of the Executive Council as ministers by the lieutenant governor and empowers the government (defined as the lieutenant governor and the Executive Council) to specify ministerial duties.[4] Care must of course be taken to ensure that codification does not stray beyond the legislature's jurisdiction.

However, given the fundamental distinction between supreme law and ordinary law, which we describe in part II, the other main characteristic of proposals for a Quebec constitution – subjecting that constitution to an amending procedure more onerous than that for amending ordinary laws, thus making a Quebec constitution supreme over other provincial laws – gives us greater pause. As desirable as these things might be as a matter of policy, in our view, as we detail in part III there are reasons to doubt bringing these changes about is possible in law.

The Quebec legislature's adoption of a constitution that would have these characteristics – and, in effect, the same legal authority in Quebec as the supreme law of Canada has throughout this country – transcends the bounds of Canada's existing legal order, which leaves no room for a third category of laws that stands above ordinary provincial law and below the supreme law of Canada. A Quebec constitution with the status of supreme law in that province could be adopted only through significant changes to the Canadian legal order effected by amending the Constitution of Canada.

Our focus in this chapter is not on the "addition" of two provisions to the *Constitution Act, 1867* proposed in Bill 96.[5] Although aspects of the analysis in this chapter may be relevant to the debate about the proposals in Bill 96, that debate raises considerations well beyond the scope of this chapter, as one of us has explored elsewhere.[6] As a result, we will not venture any definitive views on the proposals in Bill 96 here.

## I. PROPOSALS FOR A QUEBEC CONSTITUTION

As Daniel Turp and Nelson Wiseman have chronicled,[7] concrete proposals for a Quebec constitution date at least as far back as the Union Nationale's 1966 election platform, which called for a "constituent assembly ... to revise and complete the internal constitution of Quebec" and to make Quebec's constitution subject to "an amendment procedure, which would consecrate the Quebec people's sovereignty and right to be consulted through a referendum on any subject that concerns its own mastery of its fate" (our translation).[8]

In 1985, Jacques-Yvan Morin, a former minister of intergovernmental affairs, proposed a draft constitution.[9] Section 2 provides that the "Constitution being Quebec's fundamental law, courts shall invalidate any act that is inconsistent with it" (our translation).[10] Section 95 adds that the Constitution "shall be amended in accordance with the rules it prescribes" (our translation). Sections 98 and 99 provide that a constitutional amendment must be passed by a two-thirds majority in the National Assembly and approved in a referendum.

In 2007, Daniel Turp, a contributor to this volume, then a member of the National Assembly, introduced a bill to establish a Quebec constitution.[11] Subsection 14(2) provides that a bill to amend the Constitution "must be supported by a two-thirds majority of Members of the National Assembly." Subsection 15(1) continues the "laws and constitutional conventions applicable in Québec when th[e] Constitution comes into force," "provided they are consistent with the Constitution." Subsection 15(2) adds that the "Constitution prevails over any rule of Québec law that is inconsistent with its provisions."

The parallels with the Constitution of Canada are striking.[12] Both Morin and Turp's proposed constitutions would be supreme over other law, with Morin's constitution expressly recognizing the power of courts to declare invalid law inconsistent with the constitution. Like the Constitution of Canada, Morin and Turp's proposals also create a procedure for constitutional amendment different from that for adopting ordinary laws, as does the Union Nationale's more inchoate proposal.[13] The Quebec constitution proposed by Morin and Turp would, in effect, have the same status in Quebec as has the Constitution of Canada throughout this country.

Our concern is not whether these characteristics are desirable as a matter of policy, but whether they are legally viable.

## II. THE DISTINCTION BETWEEN SUPREME AND ORDINARY LAW

Our analysis in the rest of this chapter relies heavily on the hierarchical relationship between supreme law and ordinary law and the distinctions that can be drawn among ordinary laws, which we briefly describe here.

### *A. Conflict between Supreme Law and Ordinary Law*

Our understanding of the distinction between supreme and ordinary law is grounded in the rules governing constitutional amendment. As Richard Albert has persuasively argued the rules concerning constitutional amendment are the most important part of any constitution.[14] Those rules are the source of the distinction between supreme law and ordinary law, central to a legal system like Canada's, founded on the principles of constitutionalism and the rule of law.[15] If law must conform to some higher law, as constitutionalism presupposes, there must be some way to distinguish ordinary law from the higher law on which its validity depends.

Section 52 of the *Constitution Act, 1982* draws a fundamental distinction between "supreme law" and ordinary "law." The Constitution of Canada, it tells us, "is the ***supreme law*** of Canada, and any ***law*** that is inconsistent with the provisions of the Constitution is, to the extent of the inconsistency, of no force or effect."[16] Supreme law thus has primacy over ordinary law. Subsection 52(1) supplies a rule for resolving inconsistency between supreme law and ordinary law: the ordinary law is invalid.[17]

What is the content of that supreme law? Subsection 52(2) defines the Constitution of Canada as including "(*a*) the *Canada Act 1982*, including the [*Constitution Act, 1982*]; (*b*) the Acts and orders referred to in the schedule; and (*c*) any amendment to any Act or order referred to in paragraph (*a*) or (*b*)." This definition has long been recognized as underinclusive, as the Constitution encompasses fundamental principles, as well as certain provisions of the *Supreme Court Act*, despite their not being expressly enumerated in section 52(2).[18]

But the definition in section 52(2) is also overinclusive because it includes provisions that can be amended or repealed by Parliament or the provincial legislatures.[19] A law amending or repealing a provision is, by definition, inconsistent with that provision, so if Parliament or the legislature can validly amend or repeal a provision, it must not be part of the supreme law. Were it otherwise, the law effecting the amendment or repeal would be invalid under section 52(1).

The true definition of the Constitution is as those provisions that cannot be amended (or repealed) by ordinary law and can only be amended (or repealed) through a constitutional amendment.[20]

Subsection 52(3) provides that "[a]mendments to the Constitution of Canada shall be made only in accordance with the authority contained in the Constitution of Canada." This provision directs those looking to amend the Constitution to seek out the "authority" it "contain[s]." In our view, that authority is largely contained in Part V of the *Constitution Act, 1982*.[21]

The default rule found in Part V is that the Constitution of Canada is amended by proclamation authorized by the Senate, the House of Commons, and seven of ten provincial legislative assemblies representing at least 50 per cent of the total population of the provinces.[22] (The Senate has only a suspensive veto.)[23] This is known as the "general procedure" and applies to all constitutional amendments, subject to limited exceptions.[24]

There are two such exceptions, which vary the number of provincial legislative assemblies which must agree to the amendment in addition to the Senate and the House of Commons. (Here too, the Senate has only a suspensive veto.) Some subjects fall under the "unanimity" procedure, which requires that all provincial legislative assemblies agree to the amendment.[25] Unanimity is required to amend Part V, which is to say the authority for amending the Constitution.[26] An amendment to the Constitution "in relation to [a] [...]provision that applies to one or more, but not all provinces" falls under the "special arrangements procedure," which only requires the agreement of the Legislative Assembly of any province to which the amendment applies.[27]

Both the general procedure and the exceptions to it – the unanimity and special arrangements procedure – are different and more demanding than the procedure for making ordinary law, which requires passage by the Senate and House of Commons or the Legislative Assembly and assent in the Queen's name by the governor general or lieutenant governor, as the case may be.[28]

The conventional account of Part V of the *Constitution Act, 1982* holds that there is a third exception to the general amending procedure.[29] Section 44 of the *Constitution Act, 1982* provides that "Parliament may exclusively make laws amending the Constitution of Canada in relation to the executive government of Canada or the Senate and House of Commons."[30] Section 45 provides that "the legislature of each province may exclusively make laws amending the constitution of the province."[31] On the conventional view, ss 44 and 45 empower Parliament and the provincial legislatures to amend (or at least legislate inconsistently with) certain provisions of the Constitution that concern "the executive government of Canada," "the Senate," or the "House of Commons," or, in the case of the provincial legislatures, "the constitution of the province."

In our view, these provisions do not in fact allow for the enactment (or repeal) of supreme law; they are no exception to the general amending procedure. Rather, like their predecessor provisions sections 91(1) and 92(1) of the *British North America Act, 1867*,[32] they confer on Parliament and the provincial legislatures the exclusive authority to make laws concerning certain subject matters: "the executive government of Canada" and the Senate and the House of Commons and "the constitution of the province," respectively.[33] Just as other grants of jurisdiction to Parliament and the provincial legislatures, sections 44 and 45 of the *Constitution Act, 1982* allow, in other words, for the making of ordinary law. Since ordinary law inconsistent with supreme law is invalid,[34] supreme law cannot be altered by ordinary law. It follows that any provision that can be altered by ordinary law must itself be ordinary, rather than supreme, in nature.

Like any other legislative power, Parliament and the provincial legislature's powers under sections 44 and 45, respectively, are subject to constitutional limits. Those limits consist not only of the familiar ones established by the guarantee of rights by the *Canadian Charter of Rights and Freedoms* and the recognition and affirmation of the rights of aboriginal peoples in section 35 of the *Constitution Act, 1982*, but also by the procedures for amending the supreme law.[35] Despite its jurisdiction in relation to the Senate, for instance, Parliament cannot change the method of selecting senators, as that requires a constitutional amendment under the general amending procedure.[36]

The legislature's power under section 45 is similarly limited by the rest of the Constitution. To our mind, section 45 consists of the power to make laws in relation to the provincial executive and legislature. But it does not extend to the offices of the Queen, the Governor General, and the lieutenant governor of the province, whose continued existence and role is guaranteed, absent constitutional amendment.[37] Nor does it extend to the judiciary, which, to the extent its existence, independence and jurisdiction is not constitutionally protected, is the subject of a distinct head of power. Nor does section 45 concern municipal institutions, which are covered by a distinct head of power.[38] Nor, finally, does it encompass the creation of "quasi-constitutional" rights, which are best understood as incidental to each of the legislature's substantive heads of power.

In the remainder of this chapter, when we refer to the "supreme law," we refer solely to the provisions of the Constitution that can only be amended or repealed by constitutional amendment, rather than by an act of Parliament or the provincial legislature.

### *B. Conflict between Ordinary Laws Enacted by Parliament or Legislature*

A statute enacted by Parliament or a legislature does not take precedence over one enacted by the same body. As a result, inconsistency among statutes does not make either invalid. Instead, the common law supplies rules for resolving conflicts. For instance, the special prevails over the general.[39] More rarely, a later statute might be found to have impliedly repealed an earlier one.[40]

As there exist common law rules for the resolution of conflicts between statutes, Parliament and the legislatures are free to depart from them, provided they do so clearly.[41]

This is how human rights laws and other laws described as "quasi-constitutional" produce their effects.[42] Both Quebec's *Charter of Human Rights and Freedoms*[43] and, at the federal level, the *Canadian Bill of Rights* provide that they prevail over all other laws with which they conflict, unless the law specifically provides otherwise.[44] The effect is similar to that of the paramountcy doctrine:[45] the law over which another has prevailed continues to exist, albeit deprived of legal effect. Should the prevailing law be amended or repealed, the other law can become operative once more.[46]

## III. SUBJECTING AMENDMENT OF A QUEBEC CONSTITUTION TO "MANNER AND FORM" REQUIREMENTS

We doubt that any ordinary law, including a codified Quebec constitution, may subject a provision of ordinary law to an amending procedure more onerous than the procedure for amending other ordinary laws. In Quebec, that means passage in English and French by the National Assembly and assent by the lieutenant governor.[47]

No Canadian case has definitively settled the issue whether Parliament or a provincial legislature may impose an effective manner and form requirement on itself. An effective manner and form requirement is a requirement about the procedure by which a law is adopted, which, if not followed, would result in the law's invalidity.[48] For instance, rather than the usual majority, a law might require a two-thirds majority to pass a bill repealing it.

We distinguish such an effective requirement from one, which while not legally effective, would be considered politically unavoidable and could, perhaps, give rise to a constitutional convention requiring that it be followed. We also would have no quarrel with a proposal for a Quebec constitution enacted as an ordinary law and given precedence over all other law in the event of an unavoidable conflict and then only to that extent, as has been partly done for the Quebec *Charter*.[49] But, as we have explained, we do not understand that to be what most proponents of a Quebec constitution have in mind. As we read their proposals, their objective is for a Quebec constitution to have the same status in that province as the supreme law of Canada has throughout Canada.

Although statements made in *Mercure*, *Reference re Canada Assistance Plan*, *Mikisew Cree First Nation*, and the *Reference re Pan-Canadian Securities Regulation* suggest that the Supreme Court is prepared to accept that certain self-imposed manner and form requirements are effective,[50] the issue should be resolved, with the benefit of full submissions, in a case in which it squarely arises.[51]

The Supreme Court's statements concerning manner and form requirements rely on case law from other countries which, like Canada, share in the British constitutional tradition, and scholarship emerging from that tradition. There is, in our view, reason to doubt that all the arguments canvassed in those cases and that scholarship can be directly transplanted into the Canadian context.

Although we are aware of the rich theoretical debates about the nature of parliamentary sovereignty,[52] our view does not depend on any particular theory of parliamentary sovereignty. Instead, what makes Canada different, to our minds, is that our Constitution expressly provides that it is "supreme law" and provides a distinct procedure for amending the supreme law, more onerous than that for enacting ordinary law. Together, these features leave little room (if any) for legislative power to be limited by ordinary law and mean that most self-imposed manner and form requirements are ineffective. There can be no third category of law that stands above the ordinary law of a province and below the supreme law of Canada.

### *Supreme Court's Case Law on Self-Imposed Manner and Form Requirements*

The Supreme Court has referred to the notion of self-imposed manner and form requirements on several occasions, most recently in *Mikisew Cree First Nation* and *Reference re Pan-Canadian Securities Regulation*. With varying degrees of clarity, these statements suggest that the Supreme Court is prepared to accept that some self-imposed manner and form requirements may be effective. But a close reading of the statements and, crucially, the examples on which they rely indicates that this acceptance is at times equivocal and its conceptual foundations remain shaky.

The first in this line of cases is the Saskatchewan case of *Mercure*[53] and its Alberta companion case, *Paquette*,[54] which concerned section 110 of the *Northwest Territories Act*, a provision in federal law which required that the territory's legislature enact its ordinances in English and French.[55] When Parliament established Alberta and Saskatchewan from part of the Northwest Territories, it continued all laws existing in the new provinces at the time of their creation.[56] And Parliament expressly continued "all provisions of the law with regard to the constitution of the Legislative Assembly,"[57] a category of provisions which, according to Justice La Forest, includes section 110.[58]

The Alberta and Saskatchewan legislatures could repeal any laws that fell within their jurisdiction even if, as was the case with section 110, they had originally been enacted by Parliament.[59] Justice La Forest held that the legislatures could repeal section 110, but that they would have to comply with section 110's "manner and form" requirement to do so.[60] Thus, an act repealing section 110 as it applied to either Alberta or Saskatchewan would itself need to be enacted in English and French. Failure to enact a French version would make the repeal of section 110 invalid.

We have doubts about the Supreme Court's reasoning in *Mercure* and *Paquette*. For one, Justice La Forest seems to have premised his conclusion in part on the fact that, since section 110 was binding on the Northwest Territories legislature, that did not change when Parliament created Alberta and Saskatchewan.[61] But we are not sure that follows. Parliament's relationship with the territories is fundamentally different from its relationship with the provinces. Parliament's plenary power over the territories means it can impose manner and form requirements on their legislatures that they would have no power to change.[62] By contrast, when Parliament exercises its one-time authority to establish a new province and provide for its constitution, it cannot prevent the new legislatures from later exercising their authority to amend the "constitution of the province."[63]

In *Mercure,* Justice La Forest cites the Australian case of *Trethowan*, the South African case of *Harris*, and the Ceylonese case of *Ranasinghe*.[64] Justice La Forest in *Mercure* places particular emphasis on *Ranasinghe*, describing it as "clearly stat[ing]" the law on manner and form requirements and concluding that he "cannot accept that in a nation founded on the rule of law, a legislature is free to ignore the law in its constituent instrument prescribing the manner and form in which legislation must be enacted."[65]

*Trethowan*, as Justice La Forest acknowledges, was premised on a requirement in section 5 of the *Colonial Laws Validity Act 1865* that amendments to the constitution of the legislature be made in accordance with the applicable manner and form requirements.[66] As an imperial law applicable to the Australian states, the *Colonial Laws Validity Act 1865* had, by its own terms, the status of supreme law in those states.[67] The *Colonial Laws Validity Act 1865* largely ceased to apply to Canada in 1931 and no longer applies since 1982.[68] There is no equivalent to section 5 of the *Colonial Laws Validity Act 1865* in the supreme law of Canada. *Harris* and *Ranasinghe* presented closer analogies to the case before Justice La Forest, as they both involved manner and form requirements that were externally imposed, but that did not enjoy the status of supreme law. But those authorities do not deal directly with self-imposed manner and form requirements.

Justice La Forest also refers to Sir Ivor Jennings' *The Law and the Constitution* in which Jennings explains that, since the "powers of [the] Parliament [of the United Kingdom] are not expressed in an Act of Parliament," they must come from common law, according to which "Parliament may make any law in the manner and form provided by the law."[69] The *Parliament Act, 1911*,[70] in Jennings' view, provided an alternative manner and form to that supplied by the common law and implies that Parliament is free to provide other alternatives, including for specific purposes.[71] But Justice La Forest stops short of endorsing Jennings' broad view of manner and form requirements.[72] *Mercure* (and thus, *Paquette*) should be read narrowly as concerning a manner and form requirement not self-imposed, but externally imposed through Alberta and Saskatchewan's "constituent instrument[s]," the *Alberta* and *Saskatchewan Acts*.

The Supreme Court's next comments on manner and form requirements came in *Reference re Canada Assistance Plan*, in which Justice Sopinka, writing for a unanimous court, concluded that "parliamentary sovereignty prevents a legislative body from binding itself as to the substance of future legislation,"[73] a point the court reiterated in *Reference re Securities Act*.[74] Justice Sopinka described a requirement that a person or group outside the legislature consent to the enactment of legislation is a requirement as to its substance, rather than the manner and form of its enactment.[75] This significantly narrows the possible scope for recognizing self-imposed manner and form requirements.

However, Justice Sopinka left open the possibility that self-imposed manner and form requirements might be effective, writing that "[i]t may be that where a statute is of a constitutional nature and governs legislation generally, rather than dealing with a specific statute, it can impose requirements as to manner and form."[76] Such a statute would also need to demonstrate the legislature's "intent[ion] ... to bind itself or restrict the powers of its members who are also members of the executive."[77] The need to manifest such intention flows, at least in an immediate sense, from the *Interpretation Act*, which "applies, unless a contrary intention appears, to every [Act]" and provides that "[e]very Act shall be so construed as to reserve to Parliament the power of repealing or amending it."[78]

Justice Sopinka cited *R v. Drybones* and *Mercure* as examples of cases in which manner and form requirements were held to be effective.[79] As we have explained, we harbour doubts about the holding in *Mercure* and, in any event, *Mercure* was not concerned with a self-imposed manner and form requirement. In *Drybones*, the court held that a provision of the *Indian Act* making it an offence to be an "Indian who is ... intoxicated ... off a reserve" is inoperative because it is inconsistent with the equality rights recognized by the *Canadian Bill of Rights*.[80] As we read it, the *Canadian Bill of Rights* does not create a manner and form requirement. Instead, the *Canadian Bill of Rights* communicates Parliament's intention to depart from the ordinary rules governing conflicting statutes by dictating the result where another federal statute conflicts with the *Canadian Bill of Rights*.[81]

The next reference in the Supreme Court's case law to manner and form requirements was in keeping with the ambiguity with which it dealt with the issue in *Reference re Canada Assistance Plan*. In *British Columbia v. Imperial Tobacco*, Justice Major, writing for a unanimous court, explained that "[a]ctions of the legislative branch are constrained [by the rule of law] … but only in the sense that they must comply with legislated requirements as to manner and form (i.e., the procedures by which legislation is to be enacted, amended and repealed)."[82] Though providing a helpful definition of the term "manner and form," Justice Major cited no specific examples of "legislated requirements as to manner and form," leaving open to discussion where he meant solely to refer to requirements imposed by the supreme law or also to those imposed by Parliament or a legislature on itself.

The Supreme Court revisited the effectiveness of manner and form requirements in two recent cases: *Mikisew Cree First Nation* and the *Reference re Pan-Canadian Securities Regulation*. In *Mikisew Cree First Nation*, three sets of reasons concurred in by eight judges of the Court suggested that self-imposed "manner and form" requirements enacted were enforceable. We begin with the views expressed by Justices Karakatsanis and Rowe who each wrote for themselves and two others.

Justice Karakatsanis wrote that her conclusion that the duty to consult does not apply to the law-making process "does not affect the enforceability of … provisions [of treaties between the Crown and Indigenous peoples], implemented through legislation, that explicitly require pre-legislative consultation … Manner and form requirements (i.e., procedural restrains on enactments) imposed by legislation are binding."[83] Justice Karakatsanis cited Peter W Hogg's *Constitutional Law of Canada* and *Mercure*. She also referred to the Nisga'a Final Agreement and its implementation by federal and British Columbia statutes as an example of an effective manner and form requirement. As we have explained, we harbour doubts about *Mercure*. And, in any event, the law at issue in *Mercure* is not an example of self-imposed manner and form requirement, since the requirement was imposed by Parliament on the Northwest Territories and continued for the new provinces of Alberta and Saskatchewan on their creation.

It is also far from clear that Nisga'a Final Agreement supplies an example of a self-imposed manner and form requirement, at least in the usual sense. The provisions of the Nisga'a Final Agreement that Justice Karakatsanis refers to require that British Columbia (i.e., the provincial Crown) consult the Nisga'a Lisims Government before amending a provincial law if the amendment would have certain effects on Nisga'a law.[84] The "Nisga'a Final Agreement is a modern treaty, so, assuming these provisions are sufficiently clear to be binding, British Columbia's commitment to consult the Nisga'a Lisims Government is constitutional in nature.[85] The binding effect flows from section 35 of the *Constitution Act, 1982*, rather than from the British Columbia law concerning the Nisga'a Final Agreement (and still less so the federal law).[86] And it is not clear that Justice Karakatsanis meant to say anything different. It is more likely that her aim was to ensure that manner and form requirements imposed by treaty would remain effective.[87]

As for Hogg's *Constitutional Law of Canada*, which Justices Abella and Rowe also cite, he takes the view that Parliament or a legislature can redefine itself by changing the nature of the legislative process. Since the legislatures of several provinces could validly abolish their upper houses, a legislature could thus "re-define" itself "either generally or for particular purposes."[88] Hogg gives as examples of such redefinition the requirement that a law can be amended only with a two-thirds majority or only after approval in a referendum.[89] As we will explain, the notion of redefinition is not without limits, which constrain its potential as a basis on which to construct self-imposed manner and form requirements. As for referenda, we accept that holding a referendum can be made mandatory, but the rejection of a proposal put to referendum does not legally preclude Parliament or the legislature from enacting that proposal.[90]

In *Mikisew Cree First Nation*, Justice Rowe wrote that "[i]f Parliament or a provincial legislature wishes to bind itself to a manner and form requirement incorporating the duty to consult Indigenous peoples before the passing of legislation, it is free to do so."[91] This passage suggests that Justice Rowe would be prepared to accept the effectiveness of such a requirement.

In explaining that the duty to consult is no mere rule of procedure, but rather a constitutional obligation to be satisfied, Justice Abella noted that "constitutional (*and self-imposed*) manner and form requirements ... [are] another accepted instance of court review of legislative processes ... Failure to comply to comply with a manner and form requirement will result in the legislation being invalid, as there is 'no doubt as to the binding character of the rules of the Constitution,'" quoting Hogg's *Constitutional Law of Canada*.[92]

Justice Abella cited the *Reference re Manitoba Language Rights* and *Gallant v. The King* as examples of a courts reviewing the legislative process for compliance with manner and form requirements. The famous *Reference re Manitoba Language Rights* concerned Manitoba's failure to comply with section 23 of the *Manitoba Act, 1870*, a constitutional provision requires that Manitoba statutes be enacted in English and French.[93] The somewhat less exalted case of *Gallant* concerned an amendment to Prince Edward Island's *Prohibition Act*.[94] The amending bill was passed by the Legislative Assembly, but the lieutenant governor withheld assent in April 1945. After the lieutenant governor left office, his successor purported to assent to the bill in September 1945. The Supreme Court of Prince Edward Island held since the bill in question had not been passed anew, there was nothing for the lieutenant governor to assent to in September 1945.

Although Justice Abella's quotation from Hogg and examples (which are drawn from Hogg) refer to manner and form requirements imposed by the Constitution, her reference to "self-imposed" requirements suggests that, like Justices Karakatsanis and Rowe, she is prepared to accept self-imposed manner and form requirements.

By contrast, Justice Brown referred only to manner and form requirements imposed by the supreme law, citing as examples section 23 of the *Manitoba Act, 1870*, as interpreted by the *Reference re Manitoba Language Rights*; ss 48 and 49 of the *Constitution Act, 1867*, which impose a quorum on the House of Commons and require majority voting, respectively; and section 52(1) of the *Constitution Act, 1982*.[95]

The reference to section 52(1) may seem somewhat puzzling since the provision does not, on its face, create a manner and form requirement, but it was likely included by Justice Brown because section 52(1) is what makes constitutionally-imposed manner and form requirements effective. The failure to follow such a requirement in enacting a law makes it inconsistent with the supreme law and, to the extent of the inconsistency, without force or effect.[96] Justice Brown made no comment concerning "self-imposed" manner and form requirements.

Finally, in *Reference re Pan-Canadian Securities Regulation*, a unanimous Supreme Court wrote that "a legislature intending to bind itself to rules respecting the manner and form by which the statute is to be amended *must* do so in clear terms."[97] The Court cited *Reference re Canada Assistance Plan* and its application in *Canadian Taxpayers Federation* by the Ontario Superior Court of Justice.[98] Though giving its opinion weeks after giving judgment in *Mikisew Cree First Nation*, the Court did not cite any of the statements on manner and form requirements made in *Mikisew Cree First Nation*.

Nonetheless, the tentative terms in which Justice Sopinka couched his discussion of manner and form requirements in *Reference re Canada Assistance Plan* are absent in *Reference re Pan-Canadian Securities Regulation*. And Justice Brown, who avoided making any statement about manner and form requirements in *Mikisew Cree First Nation*, was prepared to sign on to an opinion in the *Reference re Pan-Canadian Securities Regulation* recognizing the possibility that at least some self-imposed manner and form requirements could be effective.

The relatively narrow statement made in the *Reference re Pan-Canadian Securities Regulation* and the more expansive ones made in three sets of reasons in *Mikisew Cree First Nation* have yet to receive further judicial consideration. The lower courts have, however, considered the statements made in *Mercure* and, particularly those made in *Reference re Canada Assistance Plan*.[99]

Beginning with the *Canadian Taxpayers Federation* case, the lower courts generally treat *Reference re Canada Assistance Plan* as having established three conditions for finding an effective manner and form requirement: "(a) a clear statement of intent by the legislature that, despite the clear words of ... the *Interpretation Act* [reserving the power to amend or repeal an act], the legislature intended to bind itself or restrict the legislative powers of its members; (b) [the statement of intent] would normally be contained in a statute that is constitutional or quasi-constitutional; and (c) the statute would specify the manner and form to be followed by the legislature itself to effect the amendments ... [and] would not remit the decision to an entity not forming part of the legislative structure."[100] This passage in *Canadian Taxpayers Federation* was in turn cited with approval by the Supreme Court in *Reference re Pan-Canadian Securities Regulation*,[101] but this was in reference to the clear intention condition, rather than the test as a whole, so should not be taken as endorsing the latter.

Moreover, the test derived from *Reference re Canada Assistance Plan* is probably best understood as expressing a common law rule for resolving conflicts among ordinary laws, like the rule that the special prevails over the general, rather than a rule for determining whether an ordinary law is valid. In this sense, a manner and form requirement would be effective in the same way that a statute guaranteeing "quasi-constitutional" rights, such as the *Canadian Bill of Rights* or the Quebec *Charter*, would be.

Even on its own terms, the test leaves something to be desired. For one, as Justice Sopinka acknowledges in *Reference re Canada Assistance Plan* itself, the *Interpretation Act* is nothing more than the statutory recitation of the underlying constitutional principle that, within constitutional limits, Parliament and the provincial legislatures can make or unmake any law.[102] Further, it is not plain what is meant by a "constitutional" or "quasi-constitutional" statute. Justice Sopinka suggests that the distinguishing feature may be that manner and form requirement be established by a statute that (at least presumptively) applies to all legislation,[103] such as the *Canadian Bill of Rights*, the Quebec *Charter* and perhaps Ontario's *French Language Services Act*'s legislative bilingualism requirement.[104]

To our knowledge, there are no Canadian cases in which a self-imposed manner and form requirement has been enforced. This may of course be because the self-imposed requirements (of which there exists no comprehensive survey) are generally respected. Aside from *Mercure* itself, (which, in our view, did not concern a self-imposed manner and form requirement) we know of only one instance of a court finding an effective, self-imposed manner and form requirement and then only in *obiter*.[105]

Although *Mikisew Cree First Nation* and *Reference re Pan-Canadian Securities Regulation* suggest the Supreme Court is prepared to recognize at least some self-imposed manner and form requirements, the statements in its case law are not definitive and in many cases rely on examples that are not self-imposed manner and form requirements. We maintain that the Supreme Court should decide the issue of self-imposed manner and form requirements in a case where the issue squarely arises. If the issue arises, the Supreme Court must take in account the distinctive features of Canada's constitutional order.

### *Putting Manner and Form Requirements in Canada's Constitutional Context*

Despite the Supreme Court's statements on manner and form requirements, particularly in *Mikisew Cree First Nation* and *Reference re Pan-Canadian Securities Regulation*, we remain skeptical that there is a place for such requirements in the Canadian legal order. Our skepticism is threefold.

First, the Constitution of Canada, which is the only source of supreme law in Canada, contains no provision giving effect to manner and form requirements. By contrast, the *Australia Act, 1986* expressly recognizes such requirements in Australian states as concerns laws respecting "the constitution, powers or procedure of the Parliament of [a] State."[106] Such laws are "of no force or effect unless ... made in such a manner and form as may ... be required by a law made by [the State's] Parliament."[107] This makes authorities concerning Australian state constitutions, including *Trethowan*, largely irrelevant to the Canadian situation. The Supreme Court acknowledged this point of distinction in *Mercure.*[108]

Second, the structure of the supreme law of Canada leaves us wondering where self-imposed manner and form requirements would fit into Canada's constitutional order. As the Supreme Court recently noted in *Reference re Pan-Canadian Securities Regulation*, Parliament and the provincial legislatures are, within constitutional limits, on the same footing as the legislatures of countries without supreme laws, such as New Zealand and the United Kingdom.[109] But what of those limits?

The supreme law of Canada guarantees rights and freedoms set out in the *Charter* and recognizes and affirms aboriginal and treaty rights in section 35 of the *Constitution Act, 1982.*[110] With a few exceptions, both *Charter* and section 35 rights are equally applicable to Parliament and the provincial legislatures, effectively limiting their legislative powers.[111] The supreme law further specifies the subject matters in relation to which Parliament and the provincial legislatures may legislate, further limiting their powers.[112] The supreme law also sets out the procedure for changing the limits on Parliament and the provincial legislature's powers.[113] As we explained, most such changes require the use of the general amending procedure.[114]

It is difficult to see why a supreme law like Canada's that states limits on the powers of Parliament and the provincial legislatures and specifies a detailed procedure for changing those limits leaves room for those powers to be further constrained by ordinary law. Allowing their legislative powers to be limited by ordinary law risks blurring the line between supreme law and ordinary law, a distinction that is implied by the unwritten principles of the rule of law and constitutionalism, and, in our view, flows form the express words of section 52(1).[115]

To our ken, this is what explains why Parliament and the provincial legislatures cannot impose substantive limits on their legislative powers.[116] Neither Parliament nor a provincial legislature can enact a statute that prevents it from legislating on a particular subject or imposes a substantive limit on legislation the way that does the division of powers between Parliament and the provincial legislatures or the guarantee of rights and freedoms by the *Charter*. Even if a statute purported to do so, it would not be effective: a future statute concerning that subject matter would not be invalid.[117]

Were it otherwise, Parliament and the provincial legislatures could effectively circumvent the amending procedures. We do not see why it should be any different for procedural limits. Accordingly, a Quebec constitution enacted by ordinary law cannot place substantive limits on the province's legislative powers nor can it subject itself to a special amending procedure.

One might be tempted to draw an analogy between Canada and other federations, such as South Africa and the United States, to suggest that a federating unit's constitution should be supreme at the subnational level just as the federal constitution is at the national level.[118] Though that may be as a matter of federal theory, the argument faces an insurmountable obstacle in Canadian constitutional law.

In Canada, there are undoubtedly a federal constitution and ten "provincial constitutions," which is to say a set of legal and political norms belonging to the federal order of government and to each province. But there is only a single supreme law in Canada. As Justice Karakatsanis put in *Windsor*, commenting on the phrase "supreme law of Canada," the Constitution is "neither federal nor provincial."[119] Instead, the Constitution "logically precedes that distinction" because it is its legal source.[120] It is in this sense that section 133 of the *Constitution Act, 1867* was said to be "'a part of the Constitution of Canada and of Quebec in an indivisible sense' and not a part of the constitution of Quebec" subject to unilateral amendment.[121] Absent amendment, the supreme law of Canada leaves no room for the creation of a supreme law of a province.

There is a stark contrast with the Constitution of South Africa, which provides that a "provincial legislature may pass a constitution for the province or, where applicable, amend its constitution, if at least two thirds of its members vote in favour of the Bill" to pass or amend it.[122] The provincial constitution (or the amendment) must be submitted for certification by the Constitutional Court.[123] Once certified, the provincial constitution is binding on the province on the same terms as the Constitution of South Africa: the provincial legislature "must act in accordance with, and within the limits of, the Constitution and th[e] provincial constitution," as must the executive.[124]

Although the Constitution of the United States does not contain such explicit language, state constitutions are understood as supreme within each state (except where the state constitution is inconsistent with the Constitution of the United States).[125] Though the point merits closer attention, the supremacy of state constitutions seems to reflect the limited sovereignty retained by American states on the formation of the United States or their entry into the Union.[126] But Canadian provinces are not sovereign even in the limited sense that American states remain. Canada is the result of a union of colonies over which the United Kingdom was sovereign.[127] In a legal sense, Canada and its provinces remained colonies after 1867. Largely in 1931, but ultimately in 1982, Canada won independence from the United Kingdom.[128] Though the provincial order of government exercise sovereign authority, it cannot claim to retain sovereignty that it never possessed.

Finally, moving beyond these conceptual points, the Parliament of Canada's power to redefine itself is far more limited than the Parliament of the United Kingdom's. The definition of the Parliament of Canada as the Queen, represented by the governor general; the Senate; and the House of Commons is a matter of constitutional law, not common law.[129] The essential features of the Senate and the House of Commons cannot the changed absent an amendment under the general procedure.[130] The existence of the office of the Queen, her representative the governor general, the Senate, and the House of Commons is specifically protected,[131] as are the powers of the Senate.[132] These limits on Parliament's power narrow the range of possible self-imposed manner and form requirements at the federal level (and possibly preclude them).[133] Absent a constitutional amendment, Parliament cannot reduce the Senate to a suspensive veto nor can it add another body to the legislative process.

Each provincial legislature consists of the Queen, represented by the lieutenant governor and the Legislative Assembly of the province. Just as at the federal level, removing the Queen's representative, the lieutenant governor, from the legislative process would require a constitutional amendment under the unanimity procedure.[134] Unthinkable though it may be, abolition of the Legislative Assembly would likewise require a constitutional amendment, in all likelihood under the unanimity procedure, given the assembly's role in constitutional amendment.[135]

But five provincial legislatures originally consisted of three components: the Queen; the Legislative Council; and the Legislative Assembly. Each of these legislatures, including Quebec's, subsequently abolished their legislative councils, removing one of the components of the legislative process.[136] The legislatures did so under their exclusive authority to make laws in relation to the "amendment of the constitution of the province" under section 92(1) of what was the *British North America Act, 1867*.[137]

Since these provincial legislatures were able to abolish their legislative councils under section 92(1), it seems to follow that any province can establish a legislative council (or another chamber) as a component of the legislature under section 92(1)'s successor provision, section 45 of the *Constitution Act, 1982*.[138] But it does not follow that the legislature's power to redefine itself is unlimited.

As the Judicial Committee of the Privy Council warned in the *Reference re Initiative and Referendum Act* that a legislature does not necessarily have the power to "create and endow with its own capacity a new legislative power not created by the Act to which it owes its existence" or, in modern terms, the supreme law of Canada.[139] Reference was made to this dictum in *OPSEU* in which the Supreme Court commented that "it may stand for the wider proposition that the power of constitutional amendment given to the provinces … does not necessarily comprise the power to bring about a profound constitutional upheaval by the introduction of political institutions foreign to and incompatible with the Canadian system."[140]

Although the restrictions flowing from this dictum are undoubtedly less explicit than those applicable to Parliament under the amending procedures, they may nevertheless render ineffective certain types of self-imposed manner and form requirements.[141] If the *Reference re Initiative and Referendum Act* teaches us that legislatures cannot create a new legislative power, then a fortiori, the legislatures cannot create a new constitution-amending authority.

There is a difference in kind between a legislature redefining itself for all purposes by abolishing an upper house and a legislature giving a law of its making supremacy over other provincial law by making it subject to a more onerous amending procedure. The latter is an attempt to use a power to make ordinary law to make supreme law, a possibility not available in Canadian law and, indeed, inconsistent with the very notion of supreme law.

Both as a conceptual matter and as a matter of positive law, then, there is reason to doubt that the reasoning in comparative authorities relied on in the Supreme Court's case law and Canadian scholarship manner and form requirements can be imported into the Canadian context wholesale as the basis for recognizing self-imposed manner and form requirements.

## CONCLUSION

As we have explained, we doubt that a Quebec constitution can be made subject to an effective manner and form requirement by the provincial legislature. Accordingly, we doubt that a Quebec constitution may be made supreme over other provincial laws. Suggestions to the contrary in the Supreme Court case law should be treated with skepticism because of the extent to which the reasons in which they can be found mistake rules for resolving conflicts among ordinary laws for rules for determining whether an ordinary law is valid. Proponents of a Quebec constitution which would have the same status in Quebec as has the supreme law of Canada are bound for disappointment. The constitution they seek for Quebec requires significant changes to the Canadian legal order and can be effected only through amendments to the supreme law of Canada.

## NOTES

1 See Benoît Pelletier, "La nature quasi constitutionnelle de la *Charte des droits et libertés de la personne du Québec* et l'idée d'une constitution québécoise," *Bulletin québécois de droit constitutionnel* 2 (2007), https://aqdc.quebec/archives/infolettres/bqdc_no2_hiver2007.html.

2 *Constitution Act*, RSBC 1996, c. 66.

3 *Act respecting the National Assembly*, CQLR, c. A-23.1, s. 4.

4 *Executive Power Act*, CQLR, c. E-18, ss 3–4, 6, 9, 11. For the definition of "Government" in Quebec law, see *Interpretation Act*, CQLR, c. I-16, s. 61(12).

5 *An Act respecting French, the official and common language of Québec*, SQ 2022, c 14, s 166.

6 See e.g., Ian Peach "Quebec Bill 96 – Time for a Primer on Amending the Constitution," *Constitutional Forum* 30, no 3 (2021); Maxime St-Hilaire, "Quebec's Bill 96 Is an Unconstitutional Attempt to Amend the Constitution of Canada," Advocates for the Rule of Law, 8 June 2021, http://www.ruleoflaw.ca/quebecs-bill-96-is-an-unconstitutional-attempt-to-amend-the-constitution-of-canada/.

7 Daniel Turp, "La constitution québécoise," *Revue québécoise de droit constitutionnel* 2 (2008): 15–56; Nelson Wiseman, "In Search of a Quebec Constitution," *Revue québécoise de droit constitutionnel* 2 (2008): 130–49; Nelson Wiseman, "The Quest for a Quebec Constitution," *American Review of Canadian Studies* 40 (2010): 56–70.

8 Turp, "La constitution québécoise," 15–56.

9 Turp, "La constitution québécoise," 24–5.

10 Quoted in Turp, "La constitution québécoise."

11 Bill 196, *Québec Constitution*, 1st Sess., 38th Leg., Quebec, 2007, 18 October 2007.

12 See Wiseman, "In Search of a Quebec Constitution," 145–6.

13 Daniel Turp, "Pour une pleine constitutionnalisation et un enrichissement normatif de la *Charte des droits et libertés de la personne*," *Revue québécoise de droit international* (2015): 221–41.

14 Richard Albert, *Constitutional Amendments: Making, Breaking and Changing Constitutions* (Oxford: Oxford University Press, 2019), 1–3.

15 *Reference re Secession of Quebec*, [1998] 2 SCR 217 at para. 72, 161 DLR (4th) 385.

16 *Constitution Act, 1982*, s. 52(1), being Schedule B to the *Canada Act, 1982* (UK), c. 11 (emphasis added).

17 *Reference re Manitoba Language Rights*, [1985] 1 SCR 721 at 746, 19 DLR (4th) 1.

18 *Reference re Remuneration of Judges of the Provincial Court (PEI)*, [1997] 3 SCR 3, 150 DLR (4th) 577 (*Provincial Judges Reference*); *Reference re Secession of Quebec*, [1998] 2 SCR 217, 161 DLR (4th) 385; *Reference re Supreme Court Act, ss 5 and 6*, 2014 SCC 21, [2014] 1 SCR 433.

19 Maxime St-Hilaire, Patrick F. Baud, and Éléna S. Drouin, "The Constitution of Canada as Supreme Law: A New Definition," *Constitutional Forum* 28, no. 1 (2019): 7–17, at 8–10.

20 St-Hilaire, Baud, and Drouin, "The Constitution of Canada," 11.

21 There are authorities for constitutional amendment elsewhere in the Constitution: see *Constitution Act, 1871* (UK), 34 & 35 Vict., c. 28,

ss 2–3; *Constitution Act, 1930* (UK), 20 & 21 Geo. V, c. 26. But there is good reason to think that those authorities have been impliedly repealed by the enactment of Part V of the *Constitution Act, 1982*: see Richard Albert, "The Difficulty of Constitutional Amendment in Canada," *Alberta Law Review* 53, no. 1 (2015): 85–113, at 108; St-Hilaire, Baud, and Drouin, "The Constitution of Canada," 11. See also *Reference re Objection by Quebec to a Resolution to amend the Constitution*, [1982] 2 SCR 793 at 806, 140 DLR (3d) 385.

22 *Constitution Act, 1982*, s. 38.

23 Ibid., s. 47(1).

24 *Reference re Senate Reform* at paras 34, 36.

25 *Constitution Act, 1982*, s. 41.

26 Ibid., s. 41(*e*); *Reference re Senate Reform*.

27 *Constitution Act, 1982*, s. 43. See *Potter c. Québec (Procureur géneral)*, [2001] RJQ 2823, EYB 2001-27194 (CA).

28 St-Hilaire, Baud, and Drouin, "The Constitution of Canada," 11–12.

29 See e.g., Patrick J. Monahan, Byron Shaw, and Padraic Ryan, *Constitutional Law*, 5th ed. (Toronto: Irwin Law, 2017), 213–16.

30 *Constitution Act, 1982*, s. 44. This power is made subject to ss 41–2.

31 Ibid., s. 45. This power is made subject to s. 41.

32 *Reference re Senate Reform* at paras 46–8.

33 St-Hilaire, Baud, and Drouin, "The Constitution of Canada."

34 *Constitution Act, 1982*, s. 52(1).

35 *Reference re Senate Reform* at paras 47–8.

36 *Constitution Act, 1982*, s. 42(1)(*b*).

37 Ibid., s. 41(*a*).

38 *Constitution Act, 1867* (UK), 30 & 31 Vict., c. 3, Preamble and ss 92(8), (14), 96–100.

39 Ruth Sullivan, *Sullivan on the Construction of Statutes*, 6th ed. (Toronto: LexisNexis, 2014), 363–7.

40 *R. v. Mercure*, [1988] 1 SCR 234 at 265, 48 DLR (4th) 1; *Conseil scolaire francophone de la Colombie-Britannique v. British Columbia*, 2013 SCC 42, [2013] 2 SCR 774 at para. 44.

41 *R. v. DLW*, 2016 SCC 22, [2016] 1 SCR 402 at para. 21.

42 Maxime St-Hilaire, "'Quasi-Constitutional' Status as Not Implying a Form Requirement," Blog of the International Journal of Constitutional Law, 8 August 2017, http://www.iconnectblog.com/2017/08/quasi-constitutional-status-as-not-implying-a-form-requirement/; John Lovell, "Legislating Against the Grain: Parliamentary Sovereignty and Extra-Parliamentary Vetoes," *National Journal of Constitutional Law* 24, no. 1

(2008): 1–26, at 15; John Lovell, "Parliamentary Sovereignty in Canada," in *The Oxford Handbook of the Canadian Constitution*, ed. Peter C. Oliver, Patrick Macklem, and Nathalie Des Rosiers (Oxford: Oxford University Press, 2017), 189–210, at 200–1; M.H. Tse, "The Canadian Bill of Rights as an Effective Manner and Form Device: An Analysis of the Supreme Court of Canada Decision in *Authorson v. Canada (Attorney General)*," *National Journal of Constitutional Law* 18, no. 2 (2005–6): 71–104.

43 *Charter of Human Rights and Freedoms*, CQLR, c. C-12, s. 52 (Quebec *Charter*).

44 *Canadian Bill of Rights*, SC 1960, c. 44, s. 2.

45 *Alberta (Attorney General) v. Moloney*, 2015 SCC 51, [2015] 3 SCR 327 at para. 29.

46 *Tranchemontagne v. Ontario (Director, Disability Support Program)*, 2006 SCC 14, [2006] 1 SCR 513 at para. 35.

47 *Constitution Act, 1867*, ss 49, 55, 87, 90, 133; *An Act respecting the Legislative Council*, SQ 1968, c. 9; *Act respecting the National Assembly*, s. 2.

48 Even if a manner and form requirement is effective, its enforcement is not a foregone conclusion owing to parliamentary privilege: see William E. Conklin, "*Pickin* and its Applicability to Canada," *University of Toronto Law Journal* 25, no. 3 (1975): 193–214; Katherine Swinton, "Challenging the Validity of an Act of Parliament: The Effect of Enrolment and Parliamentary Privilege," *Osgoode Hall Law Journal* 14 (1976): 345–405; Henri Brun, Guy Tremblay, and Eugénie Brouillet, *Droit constitutionnel*, 6th ed. (Cowansville, QC: Éditions Yvon Blais, 2014), para. VIII.167.

49 Quebec *Charter*, s. 52.

50 See Noura Karazivan, "Cooperative Federalism v. Parliamentary Sovereignty: Revisiting the Role of Courts, Parliaments and Governments," in *Canadian Federalism and its Future: Actors and Institutions*, ed. Alain-G. Gagnon and Johanne Poirier (Kingston and Montreal: McGill-Queen's University Press, 2020), 291–335; Craig M. Scott, "Consultation, Cooperation and Consent in the Commons' Court: 'Manner and Form' After *Mikisew Cree II*," *Supreme Court Law Review* (2d) 94 (2020): 155–86, at 178.

51 See *Ngaronoa v. Attorney-General*, [2018] NZSC 123, [2019] 1 NZLR 289, at para. 70 (making a similar point in the New Zealand context). See also Timothy Shiels and Andrew Geddis, "Tracking the Pendulum Swing on Legislative Entrenchment in New Zealand," *Statute Law Review* 41, no. 2 (2020): 207–25.

52 See John Lovell, "Legislating Against the Grain"; Vanessa MacDonnell, "The New Parliamentary Sovereignty," *Review of Constitutional Studies* 21, no. 1 (2016): 13–36; Han-Ru Zhou, "Revisiting the 'Manner and Form' Theory," *Law Quarterly Review* 129 (2013): 610–38.

53 *Mercure.*

54 *R. v. Paquette*, [1990] 2 SCR 1103, 137 NR 232.

55 See *Northwest Territories Act*, RSC 1886, c. 50, s. 110.

56 *Alberta Act*, SC 1905, c. 3; *Saskatchewan Act*, SC 1905, c. 42.

57 *Alberta Act*, s. 14(1); *Saskatchewan Act*, s. 14(1).

58 *Mercure* at 262.

59 Ibid., at 270–1. See also *Caron v. Alberta*, 2015 SCC 56, [2015] 3 SCR 511 at para. 79.

60 *Mercure* at 277, 280–1.

61 Ibid., at 277.

62 *Constitution Act, 1871*, s. 4. In contrast to the provincial legislatures, which owe their powers to the Constitution, the territorial legislatures' powers are delegated to them by Parliament under their constitutive statutes: see *Conseil scolaire francophone de la Colombie-Britannique v. British Columbia*, 2020 SCC 13 at para. 65, note 1.

63 *Constitution Act, 1871*, ss 2, 6.

64 *New South Wales (Attorney-General) v. Trethowan*, [1932] AC 526 (PC); *Harris v. Minister of the Interior*, [1952] 2 SALR (NS) 428; *Bribery Commissioner v. Ranasinghe*, [1965] AC 172 (PC).

65 *Mercure* at 277–9.

66 *Colonial Laws Validity Act 1865*, 28 & 29 Vict., c. 63, s. 5.

67 Ibid., ss 1–2.

68 *Statute of Westminster, 1931*, 22 Geo. V, c. 4, ss 2(1), 7(2); *Constitution Act, 1982*, s. 53(1) and schedule (providing for repeal of s. 7(2)).

69 *Mercure* at 278, quoting William Ivor Jennings, *The Law and the Constitution*, 3rd ed. (London: University of London Press, 1943).

70 *Parliament Act, 1911* (UK), 1 & 2 Geo. V, c. 13.

71 *Mercure* at 278.

72 Ibid., at 278–9.

73 *Reference re Canada Assistance Plan (BC)*, [1991] 2 SCR 525 at 563, 83 DLR (4th) 297.

74 *Reference re Securities Act*, 2011 SCC 66, [2011] 3 SCR 837 at para. 118.

75 *Reference re Canada Assistance Plan* at 563.

76 Ibid., at 563–4.

77 Ibid., at 563.

78 *Interpretation Act*, RSC 1985, c. I-21, ss 3(1), 42(1).

79 *Reference re Canada Assistance Plan* at 563.
80 *R. v. Drybones*, [1970] SCR 282, 9 DLR (3d) 473.
81 Maxime St-Hilaire, "'Quasi-Constitutional' Status as Not Implying a Form Requirement."
82 *British Columbia v. Imperial Tobacco Canada Ltd*, 2005 SCC 49, [2005] 2 SCR 473 at para. 60.
83 *Mikisew Cree First Nation v. Canada (Governor General in Council)*, 2018 SCC 40, [2018] 2 SCR 765 at para. 51.
84 "Nisga'a Final Agreement" (1999).
85 *Quebec (Attorney General) v. Moses*, 2010 SCC 17, [2010] 1 SCR 557; *Beckman v. Little Salmon/Carmacks First Nation*, 2010 SCC 53, [2010] 3 SCR 103; *First Nation of Nacho Nyak Dun v. Yukon*, 2017 SCC 58, [2017] 2 SCR 576 at para. 34.
86 See *Nisga'a Final Agreement Act*, SBC 1999, c. 2, ss 3, 5.
87 See Scott, "Consultation, Cooperation and Consent," 170–1.
88 Peter W. Hogg, *Constitutional Law of Canada*, 5th ed. (Toronto: Carswell, 2006), 12-8–19.
89 Hogg, *Constitutional Law of Canada*, 12-8–19.
90 *Alliance Québec c. Québec (Directeur général des élections)*, 2006 QCCA 651 at para. 28, citing *In re the Initiative and Referendum Act*, [1919] AC 935 (PC); *R. v. Nat Bell Liquors Ltd*, [1922] 2 AC 128 and *Haig v. Canada; Haig v. Canada (Chief Electoral Officer)*, [1993] 2 SCR 995, 105 DLR (4th) 577.
91 *Mikisew Cree First Nation* at para. 167.
92 Ibid., at para. 96 (emphasis added).
93 *Manitoba Act, 1870*, SC 1870, c. 3, s. 23; *Reference re Manitoba Language Rights*.
94 *Gallant v. The King*, 1948 CanLII 316, [1949] 2 DLR 425 (PEISC).
95 *Mikisew Cree First Nation* at paras 123–4.
96 *Reference re Manitoba Language Rights* at 745–7.
97 *Reference re Pan-Canadian Securities Regulation*, 2018 SCC 48, [2018] 3 SCR 189 at para. 51.
98 *Canadian Taxpayers Federation v. Ontario (Minister of Finance)* (2004), 73 OR (3d) 621 (SC) (*Canadian Taxpayers Federation*).
99 *Canadian Taxpayers Federation*; *Ordre des comptables généraux licenciés du Québec c. Québec (Procureur général)*, [2004] RJQ 1164, EYB 2004-61113 (CA); *Greater Vancouver Regional District v. British Columbia (Attorney General)*, 2011 BCCA 345, 339 DLR (4th) 251; *Canada (Attorney General) v. Friends of the Canadian Wheat Board*, 2012 FCA 183, [2014] 1 FCR 518, rev'g 2011 FC 1432, [2013] 3 FCR 440; *Oberg v.*

*Canada (Attorney General)*, 2012 MBQB 64, 276 Man R (2d) 189; *Progressive Conservative Party of Manitoba v. Government of Manitoba*, 2014 MBQB 155; *Amalgamated Transit Union Local 1374 v. Saskatchewan (Finance)*, 2017 SKQB 152 (*Amalgamated Transit Union Local 1374*).

100 *Canadian Taxpayers Federation* at para. 49.

101 *Reference re Pan-Canadian Securities Regulation* at para. 51. See also Johanne Poirier, "The 2018 Pan-Canadian Securities Regulation Reference: Dualist Federalism," *Supreme Court Law Review* (2d) 94 (2020), 85–123, at 96–7.

102 *Reference re Canada Assistance Plan* at 548.

103 Ibid., at 563–4.

104 *Canadian Bill of Rights*; Quebec *Charter*; *French Language Services Act*, RSO 1990, c. F32, s. 3(2).

105 *Amalgamated Transit Union Local 1374*.

106 *Australia Act, 1986* (UK), c. 2, s. 6. Before 1986, the governing provision was s. 5 of the *Colonial Laws Validity Act 1865*.

107 *Australia Act, 1986*, s. 6.

108 *Mercure* at 279, citing *New South Wales (Attorney General) v. Trethowan*, [1932] AC 526 (PC). See also *Ranasinghe* at 199.

109 *Reference re Pan-Canadian Securities Regulation* at paras 56–7.

110 *Canadian Charter of Rights and Freedoms*, s. 1; *Constitution Act, 1982*, s. 35(1).

111 *Charter*, s. 32(1); *Tsilhqot'in Nation v. British Columbia*, 2014 SCC 44, [2014] 2 SCR 256 at para. 142. See also Maxime St-Hilaire, "Du non-droit de l'application de la *Charte canadienne des droits et libertés*," *Revue de droit de l'Université de Sherbrooke* 45 (2015): 157–234.

112 Maxime St-Hilaire, "150 Years On: Why Don't We Get Clear on Where the Canadian Federal Distribution of Legislative Powers (Legally) Comes From?" Blogue À qui de droit, 24 August 2017, https://blogueaquidedroit.ca/2017/08/24/150-years-on-why-not-get-clear-on-where-the-canadian-federal-distribution-of-legislative-powers-comes-from/.

113 *Constitution Act, 1982*, s. 38.

114 Ibid.; *Reference re Senate Reform* at para. 27.

115 *Reference re Secession of Quebec* at paras 70–2.

116 *Reference re Canada Assistance Plan* at 563; *Reference re Securities Act* at para. 118.

117 See *Reference re Pan-Canadian Securities Regulation* at para. 67.

118 See Jacques-Yvan Morin, "Pour une nouvelle Constitution du Québec," *McGill Law Journal* 30, no. 2 (1985): 171–220, at 181–3; Benoît Pelletier,

"La nature quasi constitutionnelle." For more on state constitutions in the United States, see Jonathan Marshfield's contribution to this volume.

119 *Windsor (City) v. Canadian Transit Co.*, 2016 SCC 54, [2016] 2 SCR 617 at para. 64.

120 Ibid.

121 *Ontario (Attorney General) v. OPSEU*, [1987] 2 SCR 2 at 40, 41 DLR (4th) 1, quoting *Quebec (Attorney General) v. Blaikie*, [1979] 2 SCR 1016 at 1024, 101 DLR (3d) 394.

122 Constitution of South Africa, ss 104(1)(*a*), 142–3.

123 Ibid., s. 144.

124 Ibid., ss 104(3), 125(6), 133(3)(*a*).

125 United States Constitution, article VI, clause 2.

126 See United States Constitution, Tenth Amendment. See also *Pollard v. Hagan*, 44 US 212 (1845) (all states admitted on an equal footing, which presumably includes their limited sovereignty).

127 *Constitution Act, 1867*, s. 3.

128 *Statute of Westminster, 1931*; *Canada Act, 1982* (UK), c. 11.

129 *Constitution Act, 1867*, ss 17, 91.

130 *Constitution Act, 1982*, s. 38; *Reference re Senate Reform*; *Reference re Supreme Court Act*, ss 5 and 6 at paras 74, 94–5.

131 *Constitution Act, 1982*, s. 41(*a*), (*e*).

132 Ibid., s. 42(1)(*b*).

133 Lovell, "Legislating Against the Grain," 21. For a similar point in the Australian context, see George Winterton, "Can the Commonwealth Parliament Enact 'Manner and Form' Legislation?," *Federal Law Review* 11, no. 2 (1980): 167–202.

134 *Constitution Act, 1982*, s. 41(*a*). The power to give royal assent forms part of the "office" of lieutenant governor, as does the power to reserve a bill: *Reference re Manitoba Language Rights* at 777.

135 Ibid., s. 41(*e*); *Reference re Senate Reform* at para. 110.

136 See *An Act to diminish the expenses of the Legislature of the Province of Manitoba in certain respects*, SM 1876, c. 28; *An Act relating to the Legislative Council*, SNB 1891, c. 9; *An Act respecting the Legislature*, SPEI 1893, c. 1; *An Act Abolishing the Legislative Council and Amending the Constitution of the Province*, SNS 1928, c. 1; *An Act respecting the Legislative Council*, SQ 1968, c. 9.

137 See *R. v. Somers*, 1997 CanLII 22762, 3 WWR 107 (MBQB); *Montplaisir c. Québec (Procureur général)*, JE 97-94 (QCCS); *Larocque c. Beauharnois (Ville)*, 2017 QCCS 6010, leave to appeal denied 2018 QCCA 383, leave to appeal to SCC denied 38190 (29 November 2018). See also *Théodore c.*

*Savard-Déry*, 2019 QCCS 1765 at paras 115, 129–131, leave to appeal denied 2019 QCCA 1450.

138 *Reference re Senate Reform* at para. 48. In Newfoundland and Labrador's case, the possibility is expressly contemplated by its Terms of Union: *Newfoundland Act* (UK), 12 & 13 Geo. VI, c. 22, schedule, Term 14(2).

139 *Reference re Initiative and Referendum Act* at 945.

140 *OPSEU* at 47.

141 For an argument that general recognition of self-imposed manner and form restrictions may be inconsistent with constitutional values, see Robin Elliott, "Rethinking Manner and Form: From Parliamentary Sovereignty to Constitutional Values," *Osgoode Hall Law Journal* 29 (1991): 215–51.

# 3

# Formal Constitutions of the Federating and Federated States of Canada

*Patrick Taillon and Hubert Cauchon*

Can Quebec amend its own constitution? This appears to be at first glance an easy question with an easy answer. Indeed, one can simply read section 45 of the *Constitution Act, 1982*, which provides that a provincial parliament can exclusively make laws amending the constitution of the province, and thus answer the question in the affirmative. But what is the full meaning of the expression "constitution of the province?" In other words, what is the content of a provincial constitution? Why are there rules embedded in the formal texts of the Constitution of Canada that can be modified by section 45? Are the latter rules included in the provincial constitution, in the federation's constitution, or in both?

The history of the Canadian Constitution is unique, as is its content and amending procedures. The Canadian Constitution is a mixture of British constitutional heritage and formalism developed in-house. A prevailing conception, largely influenced by Anglo-American or continental constitutionalism, is that it is compulsory for an amendment to be made through a procedure requiring the consent of more than one legislative assembly in order for it to be part of the "Constitution of Canada" in the sense of the "supreme law." But it is easily forgotten that Canadian constitutional history is widely inherited from the United Kingdom where single parliamentary majority rule is, to date, the cornerstone of British constitutionalism. Let us not forget that it is only in 1982 that the constituent power finally decided to formally include the "consent of more than one legislative assembly" rule into the Constitution of Canada alongside the unilateral amendment procedures that had been in place decades before then. Almost all acts and orders entrenched in the Constitution of Canada and listed in the schedule to the *Constitution Act, 1982* were adopted unilaterally by the parliaments of Westminster or Canada or by Her Majesty in Council.

So how must we understand the amendment procedure enacted in 1982 in relation to Quebec's constitution or any provincial constitution? This study intends to clarify the content and rank of a provincial constitution. In order to do so, we will first distinguish the material constitution from the formal constitution. We take the view that Quebec (a federated state), the federal government (the federating state) and the Canadian federation as a whole (the federal state) have both a material and formal constitution at their disposal. In fact, all these constitutions are deeply interrelated and intertwined. There are no straight boundaries between the constitution of the federation and those of the eleven federating and federated states. Each constitution derives from several sources.

While it is possible to codify, for Quebec or for any other federated state, what already exists in positive law, it is important, however, not to confuse the process of codification with the process of formalization. The latter affords a rule a higher ranking within the normative hierarchy. As such, formalization, far more than codification, raises fundamental questions about the priority that is to be given to one rule over another. Naturally, numerous supralegislative norms already structure the federating and federated states that compose the Canadian federation, and these norms presently comprise the formal constitution of each. How these are outlined, however, is a matter of controversy that we must at present attempt to defuse.

It is possible for the federal and provincial parliaments (the legislative branches of the federating and federated states, respectively) to unilaterally amend certain supralegislative norms. In other words, by express delegation from the Westminster Parliament, the constituent power of 1867, 1949, and 1982 expressly granted unilateral amendment power over certain aspects of the formal constitution of Canada. However, Canadian constitutional law does not offer procedural coherence. Yet, the varying complexity of each type of procedure changes nothing with respect to the supralegislative quality of a norm. This is confirmed by the definition of the Constitution of Canada, which is made partly explicit in subsection 52(2) of the *Constitution Act, 1982* and under Supreme Court of Canada case law.

This means that the Parliament of Quebec may, in certain cases, unilaterally exercise its share of constituent power that the combined reading of sections 45 and 52 of the *Constitution Act, 1982*, provides. In other cases, it must resort to a multilateral process for a constitutional amendment that requires the consent of other federation actors.

Politically, the unilateral use of constituent power has the potential for significant results. The largely positive and consensual support for Quebec's Bill 96 by politicians in Quebec and Canada bears witness to this.[1] Given a federation deeply affected by the failure of its most important attempts at constitutional reform,[2] better use of amendment procedures that do not require the consent of the majority of actors in the federation could allow the introduction of changes to the formal constitution of Canada that would be otherwise politically difficult to carry out.

This comment falls within the scope of work that attempts to qualify the rigidness or inflexibility of Canada's constitutional framework. However, there is very little research on that portion of constituent power entrusted to the federal and provincial parliaments. Yet, sections 44 and 45 of the *Constitution Act, 1982* allow each parliament to not only make laws that amend elements of the material constitution (e.g., *Election Act*),[3] but they also permit amendments to formal constitutional norms, which, consequently, include repealing and adding provisions. This means that Quebec, or another actor in the federation, could turn to its constituent power to modernize several provisions in the *Constitution Act, 1867* without the consent of other federate actors.

It is important to first differentiate between the formal and material constitutions of Quebec, the other federated states, and the federating state, on the one hand, and of the Canadian federation as a whole, on the other.

To date, little work has been done on the sensitive issue of the foreseeable interrelations between a formal Quebec constitution and the Canadian constitutional framework. This issue often amounts to a blind spot in discussions on the matter. Moreover, the issue of these interrelations is even more complex because it reveals several ambiguities, in Canada, within the notion of constitution itself. Unsurprisingly, then, many questions about the nature and legal scope of constitutional rules remain.

To that effect, this chapter sets its sights on a different goal than the one normally pursued by projects involving the codification of a Quebec constitution, undertaken by several authors, including, foremost, Daniel Turp in his contribution to the present publication, as well as Jacques-Yvan Morin, Marc Chevrier, André Binette, and Nelson Wiseman.[4] Our approach is more concerned with the formalization of the constitution than with its codification. At the very least, it seeks to ensure that a significant part of such a codification receives the same rank and force in the normative hierarchy as other rules covered by the definition of the Constitution of Canada set out in subsection 52(2) of the *Constitution Act, 1982*.

We must first show that there already exist, within the vast body that is the material constitution of the entire federation, several subsets (the eleven formal and material constitutions of the federating and federated states) that accumulate, intertwine, and interact according to a dynamic specific to Canadian federalism. The sometime relevant, sometime misleading connection between the issue of amending the formal constitution and the determination of its content must then be examined in order to gauge the extent of the possible reforms to the *Constitution Act, 1867* that sections 44 and 45 of the *Constitution Act, 1982* potentially provide.

## TWELVE MATERIAL CONSTITUTIONS

Every state has at least a material constitution. By definition, a material constitution includes all the rules that define the institutions of a state as well as the rules that determine the relationship between that state and the persons in its territory. Naturally, it embodies not only a broad set of written and unwritten legal norms, but also judicial and administrative decisions, and practises, all corresponding to the various sources of constitutional law.

As a federal state, Canada's exercise of sovereignty is shared between the ten federated states (or provincial units) and the federating state (or federal unit). The "federal state" and "federating state" are therefore not synonymous. On the contrary, the latter term refers only to the federal order of government,[5] the "federating state," which forms only one component of the entire federation, of the "federal state."

In other words, the sovereignty of the Canadian federation belongs neither to the federal government nor to the federal parliament alone. These bodies exercise only a portion of Canada's sovereignty. In truth, the federal state is a collection of eleven states, one federating and ten federated. This description is essential to understanding the net of interweaving formal constitutions in Canada. Indeed, each state is structured by constitutional rules, and while some are specific to each, others are common to several or all.

Following the principle that each federation actor has at least one material constitution, all Canadian federated states must possess one, although it is strewn over several documents and unwritten rules.[6] The scattered nature of these federated states' constitutional provisions has long been recognized by the Supreme Court of Canada: "The constitution of Ontario, like that of the other provinces and that of the United Kingdom, but unlike that of many states, is not to be found in a comprehensive, written instrument called a constitution. It is partly contained in a variety of statutory provisions. Some of these provisions have been enacted by the Parliament at Westminster, such as ss. 58 to 70 and ss. 82 to 87 of the *Constitution Act, 1867*. Other provisions relating to the constitution of Ontario have been enacted by ordinary statutes of the Legislature of Ontario, for instance *The Legislative Assembly Act*, R.S.O. 1970, c. 240; *The Representation Act*, R.S.O. 1970, c. 413, and *The Executive Council Act*, R.S.O. 1970, c. 153."[7]

Similarly, the federating state (or federal unit) has its own material constitution, which is also scattered across various documents. Several provisions of the *Constitution Act, 1867* and the *Constitution Act, 1982*, as well as the *Parliament of Canada Act*, the *Canada Elections Act*, the *Federal Courts Act*, the Letters Patent constituting the office of Governor General of 1947, the *Canadian Bill of Rights*, the *Standing Orders of the House of Commons* and the *Rules of the Senate of Canada* are part of the material constitution of the federating state.

In short, the material constitution of each federated state added to that of the federating state make up the material constitution of the Canadian federal state. The latter thus covers extremely broad content: it includes various documents (laws, regulations, orders in council) and unwritten rules (underlying principles, common law rules, customs, and conventions) of various origins (British, federal, or provincial). The absence of any systematic codification for each of these twelve material constitutions explains its confusing layout: norms are sometimes scattered, sometimes blended together, with no apparent design.

## THE SUBSTANCE OF THE FEDERATING AND FEDERATED STATES' FORMAL CONSTITUTIONS

As a subset of the material constitution, the formal constitution is more limited in its scope, restricted to only those rules that enjoy primacy over other legal norms. It is up to the constituent power to define the perimeter of the formal constitution,[8] which, in fact, can embrace any subject matter. Rules in Switzerland and in several American states regarding tax measures, the liquor trade, the nuclear industry, and other social issues speak for themselves. On the other hand, popular initiatives to amend the constitution blur the boundaries between what normally falls within the legislative or formal constitutional realm.[9]

In any event, the formal nature of a constitution is most often reflected in the presence of a provision that ensures its supremacy. The purpose of this provision is to confer a supralegislative rank on rules that would otherwise be relegated at best to the legislative level. The provision, then, explicitly testifies to the will of the constituent power.

In Canada, subsection 52(1) of the *Constitution Act, 1982* plays this role.[10] It promotes the following texts to the top level of the hierarchy:

> 52. – (1) The Constitution of Canada is the supreme law of Canada, and any law that is inconsistent with the provisions of the Constitution is, to the extent of the inconsistency, of no force or effect.
> (2) The Constitution of Canada includes
> (*a*) the *Canada Act 1982*, including this Act;
> (*b*) the Acts and orders referred to in the schedule; and
> (*c*) any amendment to any Act or order referred to in paragraph (*a*) or (*b*).
> (3) Amendments to the Constitution of Canada shall be made only in accordance with the authority contained in the Constitution of Canada.

Paragraph 52(2)(*a*) provides that the *Canada Act, 1982* and the *Constitution Act, 1982* are part of the formal constitution of Canada. Paragraph 52(2)(*b*) adds that the twenty-four other enactments set out in the schedule to the *Constitution Act, 1982* also form part of the federation formal constitution. Finally, paragraph 52(2)(*c*) specifies that amendments to the *Canada Act, 1982*, the *Constitution Act, 1982* and the twenty-four enactments set out in the schedule are also included in the Constitution of Canada.

Naturally, as specified by subsection 52(3), these amendments must be adopted in accordance with the various amending procedures set out in Part V of the *Constitution Act, 1982*. However, subsection 52(3) does not exclude any of the procedures intended by the Constitution of Canada, no matter what the degree of complexity. In other words, as long as they are conducted in accordance with Part V, any and all amendments to the instruments referred to in subsection 52(2) serve as amendments to the formal constitution of Canada. Indeed, Part V forms a comprehensive code, establishing and delineating the various ways of exercising constituent power within the federation.

The definition included in subsection 52(2) does represent a new trend in Canadian constitutionalism. In many respects, section 7 of the *Statute of Westminster, 1931* and the *Colonial Validity Act, 1865* provided a definition of supralegislative rules in Canadian law.[11]

Ultimately, constituent power is sovereign. It freely determines what texts to include in the formal constitution. In this regard, Canada's constitution is particularly substantial: twenty-six documents, including fifteen British laws, seven federal laws, and four British orders in council.[12] (By way of comparison, the formal constitution of the United States includes only one document, consisting of seven *Articles* and twenty-seven *Amendments*.) Despite this, the definition of Canada's formal constitution is still not exhaustive.[13] The drafters failed to include several fundamental elements in their definition. Consequently, the courts were called upon to identify content that is to be implicitly understood in the explicit definition provided in subsection 52(2).

Even before the *Constitution Act, 1982* was passed, both the account of the committee examining the resolution[14] and the minister's briefing book[15] filed in the archives specified the fragmentary nature of the definition.[16] However, it was not until *New Brunswick Broadcasting Co.* that Justice McLachlin, writing for the majority, resolved the issue of whether or not subsection 52(2) is fully comprehensive.[17] The conclusion, subsequently confirmed by later decisions,[18] was that there is, in fact, implied content in addition to that identified in the definition therein.

The first items to be (judicially) considered as implied by the definition of the formal constitution were unwritten norms. Accordingly, the validation of underlying constitutional principles[19] testifies to the incomplete quality recognized in the definition, despite it being expressly stated. These principles, identified over time by the courts, are: (1) the rule of law;[20] (2) the parliamentary privileges of provincial legislative assemblies;[21] (3) judicial independence;[22] (4) federalism;[23] (5) democracy;[24] (6) constitutionalism;[25] (7) respect for minorities;[26] (8) the honour of the Crown;[27] and, finally, (9) the principle of symmetry between the heads of state of the United Kingdom and Canada as well as the principle of hereditary succession as determined by the United Kingdom.[28]

In addition to these principles, there are other types of unwritten norms that are included in the formal constitution, such as customs[29] or certain rules of common law,[30] insofar as these norms can be connected to various written provisions of the formal constitution. It took a while longer to resolve the fundamental question whether, in addition to these multiple types of unwritten rules,[31] written norms other than those contained in the texts identified in the definition at section 52(2) are included in the formal constitution.

The prevailing opinion, since 2014, is as follows: certain rules contained in written provisions that are not explicitly mentioned in subsection 52(2) are nevertheless entrenched in the Constitution of Canada on the condition that they are connected to a matter set out in one of the amendment procedures provided for in Part V of the *Constitution Act, 1982*. For example, seized with the controversy surrounding the appointment of Mr Justice Marc Nadon, the highest court stated that subsection 4(1) and sections 5 and 6 of the *Supreme Court Act*[32] are part of the formal constitution because of their connection with paragraph 41(*d*) of the *Constitution Act, 1982*, which protects "the composition of and eligibility requirements for appointment to the Supreme Court of Canada as they existed in 1982."[33]

Equally on account of a "connection" to the purposes intended in Part V of the *Constitution Act, 1982*, most norms contained in Letters Patent constituting the office of Governor General of 1947 are obviously enshrined in the Constitution by virtue of paragraph 41(*a*) of the *Constitution Act, 1982*. Similarly, the content of the pre- and postfederative laws defining the boundaries of the federated states must also be given the same rank because of their connection to paragraph 43(*a*) of the *Constitution Act, 1982*.

In short, Canada's formal constitution consists of written rules (i.e., the texts explicitly listed in subsection 52(2) of the *Constitution Act, 1982*), unwritten rules (viz., underlying constitutional principles) and written rules enshrined on account of their connection to subjects mentioned in the various amending procedures.

It is safe to conclude, then, that the expressly stated definition in subsection 52(2) consists only in a starting point. The courts, by interpreting the clear but implicit will of the constituent power, may, on occasion, supplement this definition. However, although the courts have often added implicit content, they have never ventured to subtract from the texts mentioned in the explicit definition in subsection 52(2), and for one very simple reason: removing content would directly contradict the clear intention of the constituent authority.

From the above definition, it is then possible to establish the content of the formal constitution of each state. In the case of Quebec, sections 71 to 80 of the *Constitution Act, 1867*, among other provisions, form part of that state's formal constitution. This is so, first, because Quebec is directly affected by these sections and, second, because these sections have supralegislative status in that they are covered by subsection 52(1) and paragraph 52(2)(*b*) of the *Constitution Act, 1982*.

Aspects of Quebec's material constitution are necessarily included in Quebec's formal constitution and, by extension, in the entire federation's formal constitution. As we have seen, the procedures for amending these supralegislative norms vary according to Part V of the *Constitution Act, 1982*. By way of illustration, whereas unanimous consent of all twelve federal and provincial legislative assemblies of the federation is required to amend the Office of the Lieutenant Governor of Quebec (s 41(*a*)), the unilateral procedure is sufficient to amend inherent parliamentary privileges or to abolish the Legislative Council.[34] In other cases, when it comes, for example, to changing the interprovincial boundaries or the bilingual nature of its institutions, Quebec must act in accordance with the special arrangements procedure provided by section 43 of the *Constitution Act, 1982*.

The same applies to certain aspects of the formal constitution of the federating state.[35] In addition, many sections with supralegislative status are part of the formal constitution of more than one state of the federation.[36]

In short, the degree of complexity of the amending procedures may vary. However, in all cases, the common aim is to modify the norms included (explicitly or implicitly) in the definition of the formal constitution as understood within the meaning of section 52(2).

## THE EQUAL NORMS OF THE FORMAL CONSTITUTION

The content of the formal constitution remains encumbered by a major doctrinal controversy. Some authors, including one of the co-authors of this chapter, cast doubt on the supralegislative nature of certain provisions of the *Constitution Act, 1867* and their subsequent amendments. This interpretative controversy is important and deserves to be addressed here because it affects the way the content of the formal constitution of the federating and federated states is determined.

The controversy lies in an oddity of Canadian constitutional law, where norms that are included in the supreme law of the federation and that are, at first glance, supralegislative, can nevertheless be unilaterally modified by mere provincial or federal legislation. These amendments are made possible by sections 44 and 45 of the *Constitution Act, 1982*, which allow the federal and federated parliaments to exercise constituent power in certain cases.

Several scholars continue to rank the provisions of the Constitution of Canada according to the level of complexity required to amend them.[37] They advocate what we call a procedural approach. They rely, as it were, in a form of hierarchical correlation between the institutions empowered to amend the provisions of the Constitution of Canada and the provisions themselves. In other words, according to these scholars, the amendment procedure set out in Part V of the *Constitution Act, 1982* determines the content of the formal constitution.

As a result, only those provisions that can be amended according to one of the complex procedures would enjoy supralegislative status. Complex procedures refer to amendment formulae that require the consent of at least one provincial legislative assembly and both federal legislative assemblies.[38] Conversely, provisions of the Constitution of Canada that can be amended by one of the two unilateral procedures would enjoy only legislative status, that is, a status equivalent to an ordinary statute passed by any parliament.[39]

According to the procedural approach, then, certain sections of the *Constitution Act, 1867*, despite the fact that it is included in its entirety in the Constitution of Canada, as expressly stated in paragraph 52(2)(*b*), should not be considered part of the supreme law of Canada (subs 52(1)). Herein lies the main flaw of the procedural approach. It ignores numerous provisions, which, as part of the various enactments listed in the schedule to the *Constitution Act, 1982*, are described as supreme norms, but remain subject to unilateral amendment by a provincial or federal parliament.

While most scholars elude this essential and decisive issue, Maxime St-Hilaire, Patrick Baud and Elena S. Drouin have the merit of confronting this difficulty head-on. They straightforwardly identify the definition in subsection 52(2) as "misleading." The clarity of their comments is worth noting. They emphasize not only its incomplete nature (misleadingly underinclusive), but also the specious inclusion, in their view, of norms that, while they are included in the definition, are subject to a unilateral amendment procedure (misleadingly overinclusive).[40]

Yet, as we have seen, not only is the incomplete nature of the definition in subsection 52(2) confirmed by case law, the idea of exempting content from this definition has also never been endorsed by the courts. Although this legal doctrine is highly controversial, the terms of the debate are clear, nevertheless. Either the definition is overinclusive or the consistency of Canadian constitutional law lies elsewhere than in this procedural approach.

Ultimately, the procedural approach's chief oversight resides in its neglect of the written text of Canada's formal constitution. It fails to take into consideration a fundamental provision of the *Constitution Act, 1982*, namely section 52, which states the principle of the supremacy of the Constitution of Canada (subs 52(1)), provides a definition of that Constitution (subs 52(2)) and indicates how it may be amended (subs 52(3)).

Given its position at the crossroads of the British tradition and formal constitutionalism, constituent power exists in many forms in Canada. Indeed, Canadian constitutionalism is the product of the British colonial experience, which in many ways structures the way in which the hierarchy of legal norms has been organized in Canada. Internally, at least initially, the United Kingdom made no distinction between legislative and supralegislative norms. However, with regard to its colonies, Britain observed an imperial logic by giving precedence to the laws of Westminster over those of the colonial parliaments.[41] The hierarchy of norms was designed on this basis in

Canada until the *Constitution Act, 1982*, and its definition of formal constitution in subsection 52(2), was passed. From 1867 to 1982, there was no possible distinction between multilateral and unilateral procedures; legally speaking, the only way to modify imperial and hierarchically superior norms was through legislation.[42]

However, as soon as the *Constitution Act, 1867* – then officially referred to as the *British North America Act, 1867* – was passed, the Parliament of Westminster already expressly stated exceptions to the exercise of its constituent power. Specifically, sections 35, 40, 41, 47, 72, 78, 83, 84, 92(1), 120, and 146 grant the parliaments of federating and federated states the power to amend the British law despite its hierarchical superiority. Their legislative jurisdiction is obviously circumscribed, but the idea that certain aspects of this supreme law can be amended by simple federal or provincial laws is obvious. Consequently, what could retrospectively be described as a constituent power for Canada belonged to the Parliament of Westminster from 1867 to 1982, with some exceptions in favour of the parliaments of the federating and federated states. In those cases, two conditions are necessary. First, the *Constitution Act, 1867* must give the parliament in question jurisdiction to amend the formal constitution. Second, the parliament exercising constituent authority must express a clear intention to change the constitution's content.

The creation of the federated state of Manitoba in 1870 illustrates this phenomenon well. Section 146 of the *Constitution Act, 1867* gives the federal parliament the power to act unilaterally. As a result, the formal constitution of Manitoba was adopted in 1870[43] by a simple act of the federal parliament, without regard for the hierarchical rank of the body that adopted it. Plainly, the constitutions of the new federated states of the Canadian Prairies, passed by the federating state, are granted the same rank in the hierarchy of norms as the supralegislative norms passed by the British Parliament for Canada.[44] An act of the Parliament of Westminster in 1871[45] decisively confirmed and secured the whole in order to discourage any challenge to the creation of the Manitoban state by unilateral federal action. Moreover, the lack of hierarchical discrepancy between the procedures is also reflected in the subsequent authority of Manitoba's parliament to amend certain aspects of the *Manitoba Act, 1870*, initially passed by the federal parliament, by virtue of the partial but very real power of the federated states to amend their own formal constitution.[46]

The capacity of the federating and federated states to amend certain aspects of the formal constitution of the federation was reaffirmed in 1982. The constituent power of 1982 could have abrogated this power; instead, it obviously chose to maintain it. Moreover, to emphasize the importance of this power and its strong relationship with the other procedures contained in Part V of the *Constitution Act, 1982*, it chose to rewrite subsections 91(1) and 92(1) and to move them to Part V. That the supreme law of Canada can be amended unilaterally by a member of the federation without the participation of other federation actors may certainly seem surprising. However, Canada is far from being a typical federation. It is atypical. First, unlike the situation in the United States, the laws of the federated states, that is, the provincial laws, are not subordinate to the laws of the federating state, that is, the federal laws.[47] Second, the Canadian federation is distinguished by its linguistic, bijural and institutional asymmetries. Thus, the unilateral amendment procedure is part of the architecture of the Canadian federation[48] and is one of the essential characteristics that differentiates it from other federations.

## THE CONSTITUENT AUTHORITY OF FEDERATING AND FEDERATED PARLIAMENTS

Norms amended by unilateral parliamentary procedure have been confirmed by case law as forming part of the formal constitution. The courts have repeated that there is no hierarchy between the norms that make up the formal constitution of Canada.[49] In this regard, the constant and recurrent opinion concerning the unilateral amendment of provincial legislative assemblies' parliamentary privilege by provincial parliaments plays a decisive role. While the regularity of the courts' decisions can certainly be criticized,[50] the consequences of this case law cannot be ignored. It includes a complete disavowal of the procedural approach described above and confirms the absence of a connection and hierarchy between the content of the formal constitution and the degree of complexity associated with each amendment procedure.

Just a few years after the Canadian federation was created, the Judicial Committee of the Privy Council ruled that the parliaments of the federated states had the power to legislate with respect to their own constitutions, which included parliamentary privilege.[51] At that time, the legal status of parliamentary privilege had not been established by the Judicial Committee. However, almost a hundred years later, its place in the hierarchy of norms became an issue when it came face to face with the *Canadian Charter of Rights and Freedoms*. The Supreme Court majority concluded that the inherent parliamentary privilege of provincial legislative assemblies enjoyed a supralegislative status following its inclusion within the formal constitution of Canada by virtue of the Preamble to the *Constitution Act, 1867*.[52]

In *Vaid*, the Supreme Court of Canada added that inherent privilege or privilege established by legislation whether provincial or federal in origin,[53] also had supralegislative status. On behalf of the Court, Mr Justice Binnie wrote:

> In *New Brunswick Broadcasting*, Lamer C.J., writing separate concurring reasons, considered that such 'legislated privilege' would lack the constitutional status of 'inherent' privilege, and its exercise would be subject to *Charter* review (p. 364). His reasoning was that s. 32 (1) of the *Charter* itself provides that '[t]his Charter applies ... to the Parliament and government of Canada in respect of all matters within the authority of Parliament.' As s. 18 of the *Constitution Act, 1867* places privilege within the authority of Parliament, therefore legislation affecting privilege, as any other legislation, will be subject to *Charter* review. However, the logic of the separate judgments written by McLachlin J. and La Forest J. points away from such a conclusion, their view was accepted as correct by a majority of the Court, and the point must now be taken as settled.[54]

In short, the inherent privilege of provincial legislative assemblies, by virtue of the Preamble to the *Constitution Act, 1867*, and the privilege established by statutes passed by provincial parliaments, by virtue of their constituent power, all enjoy a supralegislative status. Inherent or legislated privilege can be restricted, extended[55] or repealed under the unilateral provincial amendment procedure set out in section 45 of the *Constitution Act, 1982*. Indeed, until recently, Justice Rowe expressed the view in *obiter* that the unilateral provincial procedure allows for the amendment of parliamentary privilege that has been recognized as having supralegislative status.[56]

In addition to the courts' confirmation of the supralegislative rank of norms that can be amended by the procedure intended in section 45 of the *Constitution Act, 1982*, there are a number of examples of unilateral constitutional amendments that include a clear desire to amend the text of the *Constitution Act, 1867*. A few examples should suffice to illustrate. For each example, it is essential to determine whether the text or provision belonging to the material constitution of the state in question has been promoted to the top rung of the hierarchy of norms by virtue of its inclusion in the definition of what is contained in the formal constitution of Canada.

Paragraph 52(2)(*c*) of the *Constitution Act, 1982* states that amendments to the Constitution of Canada, for instance to any one of the twenty-six enactments referred to in paragraphs 52(2)(*a*) and 52(2)(*b*), also form part of the formal constitution.[57] Its interpretation poses no particular difficulty when the amendment is made under a complex procedure. It does, however, at least for advocates of the procedural approach, when sections 44 and 45 of the *Constitution Act, 1982* are used. Indeed, the problem lies in the fact that these provisions allow amendments of both the formal constitution (at the supralegislative level) and legislative rules of the material constitution of a federating or federated state.[58] Depending on the intention that emerges from the wording, laws passed by the federating or federated parliaments, under the auspice of sections 44 and 45 of the *Constitution Act, 1982*, may be construed as acts amending the formal constitution (e.g., the abolition of the Legislative Council of Quebec)[59] or as ordinary statutes that amend the material constitutional (e.g., the adoption of the *Election Act*).[60]

It was probably to avoid this confusion that the Supreme Court majority, in *Eurig Estate (Re)*, held that it was preferable that a federated parliament, in its capacity as a constituent power, make amendments expressly. Otherwise, if the amendment is interpreted as the result of an ordinary statute, it could be found to be inconsistent with a "sister" provision from the formal constitution of Canada: "By virtue of s. 45 of the *Constitution Act, 1982*, the legislature of each province retains the discretion to exclusively make laws amending the constitution of the province. That power must be read in association with s. 52 (1) of the *Constitution Act, 1982*, which stipulates that any law that is inconsistent with the provisions of the Constitution is, to the extent of the inconsistency, of no force or effect. Subsection 52(1) effectively requires any provincial legislation that seeks to amend the constitution of the province to do so expressly: ... Otherwise, the legislation is liable to being struck down on the basis that it is inconsistent with the Constitution."[61]

The meaning of the word "constitution" here is very clear. It is undoubtedly the constitution in the "formal" and "supralegislative" sense, since the judge clearly writes: "That power must be read in association with s. 52 (1) of the Constitution Act, 1982 […]."

This excerpt from Justice Major's reasons also reveals that an implicit amendment of the formal constitution made under a unilateral procedure is not necessarily invalid. It will not be invalid if it is clear from the intention of the constituent authority that it intended to amend the essence of the provision.[62] For example, the definition of "Parliament of Québec"[63] or the alteration of the maximum duration a legislature can last in order to establish a fixed election date in Quebec,[64] as provided in sections 2 and 6 of the *Act respecting the National Assembly*, respectively, are likely implicit amendments to the *Constitution Act, 1867*. They clearly change the meaning and content of sections 71 and 85 of the *Constitution Act, 1867*. Although this is not done expressly, the terms used are clear and leave no doubt as to the federated parliament's intention. Consequently, pursuant to paragraph 52(2)(*c*) of the *Constitution Act, 1982*, these provisions also contribute to the formal constitution of Quebec. Although the intention would have been more obvious if the constituent power had instead expressly amended section 71 of the *Constitution Act, 1867*, the intention remains clear, nevertheless.

Bill 96 obviously proposes an explicit amendment to the *Constitution Act, 1867*. Although Bill 96 certainly attracts a great deal of attention for political reasons, its proposed amendment is in line with the history of Canadian constitutionalism.

Ultimately, an expressly stated amendment, such as Bill 96, obviously has the advantage of clarity: it eliminates all ambiguity. Consequently, in the context of a codification of the material constitution of Quebec, provisions of this codification could be given supralegislative status in the hierarchy of norms if it were expressly mentioned that they serve as amendments to the *Constitution Act, 1867*. There are two mandatory conditions. First, the change must fall within the limits of the constituent jurisdiction provided in section 45 of the *Constitution Act, 1982*. Second, the federated parliament's intention must be clear.[65]

To summarize, the application of paragraph 52(2)(*c*) of the *Constitution Act, 1982* may sometimes require a careful reading of certain provisions, one norm at a time, to determine whether or not they are part of the formal constitution of the federating state or of a federated state. As a result, each formal constitution of the eleven states, federating and federated, is composed of an assortment of scattered, sometimes interwoven provisions of the formal constitution of the federal state, Canada. Some of these provisions involve only one particular state, while others pertain to more than one formal constitution.[66] Taken individually, these constitutions are intertwined; taken together, they form the Constitution of Canada, the supreme law of the Canadian federation.

## CONCLUSION

As an atypical federation, Canada is made up of several interlocking constitutions. In addition to the classic difference between a constitution in the formal and material sense, there is a distinction to be made between the norms common to the federation as a whole and those specific to one or more of its constituent states. However, it is only through the analysis of these subsets that the outline of each can be established.

This study intended to clarify the rank and content of these material and formal constitutions. Section 52 of the *Constitution Act, 1982*, combined with the Supreme Court of Canada's case law and the architecture of Part V reveal the following: there are supra-legislative norms in the Constitution of Canada that can be amended by ordinary statute. Indeed, the constituent power, by virtue of Part V of the *Constitution Act, 1982*, takes several forms, which vary according to the procedure required to amend the formal constitution of the federation. However, Part V does not propose a hierarchy among the various amending procedures. Each one of the procedures may have its own requirements, with its own varying limits, but there is no gradation among them.

## NOTES

The authors would like to thank Russ Manitt and Amélie Binette for their help in the preparation of this paper. The opinions expressed in this chapter are those of the authors and do not reflect the views of their respective employers.

1 *An Act respecting French, the official and common language of Québec*, Bill 96, 1st Sess., 42nd Leg. (2021); House of Commons, *Journals*, 2nd Sess., 43rd Leg., no. 19 (16 June 2021), 1,115 (*Opposition Motion*

(*Amendment to section 45 of the Constitution and Quebec, a French-speaking nation*)).

2 See "Consensus Report on the Constitution: Final Text, 28 August 1992," *Secrétariat québécois aux relations canadiennes*, accessed 9 October 2021, www.sqrc.gouv.qc.ca/documents/positions-historiques/positions-du-qc/part3/Document27_en.pdf; "Meeting of First Ministers on the Constitution, *1987 Constitutional Accord*, 3 June 1987," *Secrétariat québécois aux relations canadiennes*, accessed 9 October 2021, www.sqrc.gouv.qc.ca/documents/positions-historiques/positions-du-qc/part3/Document22_en.pdf; *Government of Canada*, "*Constitutional Conference – Victoria (1971)*, 14–16 June 1971," https://www.canada.ca/en/intergovernmental-affairs/services/federation/constitutional-conference-victoria-1971.html; "*Act to Provide for the Amendment in Canada of the Constitution of Canada*, 14 October 1964," (better known as the "Fulton-Favreau Formula") reprinted in Canada, Department of Justice, *The Amendment of the Constitution of Canada* (Ottawa: Queen's Printer, 1965), 110. Even the 1982 constitutional amendment is a failure insofar as the National Assembly of the only predominantly French-speaking federated state denounces to this day the content and manner in which the *Constitution Act, 1982* was passed. See *Constitution Act, 1982*, being Schedule B to the *Canada Act, 1982*, 1982, c 11 (UK). On the difficulties associated with amending the formal constitution, see especially Richard Albert, "The Difficulty of Constitutional Amendment in Canada," *Alberta Law Review* 53, no. 1 (2015): 85; Benoît Pelletier, *La modification constitutionnelle au Canada* (Scarborough: Carswell, 1996); Christopher P. Manfredi and Michael Lusztig, "Why Do Formal Amendments Fail? An Institutional Design Analysis," *World Politics* 50, no. 3 (1998): 377.

3 *Election Act*, CQLR c. E-3.3 (QC).

4 Jacques-Yvan Morin, "Pour une nouvelle Constitution du Québec," *McGill Law Journal* 30, no. 2 (1984): 171; Daniel Turp, "L'adoption d'une Constitution nationale du Québec: un test pour la fédération multinationale du Canada ?," in *Le fédéralisme multinational: un modèle viable?*, ed. Michel Seymour and Guy Laforest (Bruxelles: Peter Lang, 2011), 154; Marc Chevrier, "La République du Québec et sa constitution," *Argument* 10, no. 1 (2007–8): 159; Nelson Wiseman, "The Quest for a Quebec Constitution," *American Review of Canadian Studies* 41, no. 1 (2010): 56; André Binette, *L'indépendance, la constitution et la constituante* (Montréal: L'Aut'journal, 2018).

5 See *Re Authority of Parliament in relation to the Upper House*, [1980] 1 SCR 54, 70.

6 For example, many sections from the *Constitution Act, 1867*, 30–31 Vict., c. 3 (UK), and from the *Constitution Act, 1982*, as well as the *Act respecting the National Assembly*, CQLR c. A-23.1 (QC), the *Election Act*, the *Executive Power Act*, CQLR c. E-18 (CQ), the *Courts of Justice Act*, CQLR c. T-16 (CQ), the *Charter of Human Rights and Freedoms*, CQLR c. C-12 (CQ), the *Charter of the French Language*, CQLR c. C-11 (CQ) and the *Standing Orders of the National Assembly*, Provisional ed., 42nd Parl., (Quebec: Secretary General of the National Assembly, Novembre 2018) form part of the material constitution of Quebec in that these various sections or acts indicate how the organs of the state should operate and what the nature of their relationship with the people within their territory should be.

7 *Ontario (AG)* v. *OPSEU*, [1987] 2 SCR 2, 37–8, Justice Beetz for the majority. It should be noted, however, that section 64 of the *Constitution Act, 1867*, should have been removed from the sections enumerated by Justice Beetz. Seeing as the section's purpose is to organize New Brunswick's and Nova Scotia's executive branches, it is certainly not part of the formal constitution of Ontario.

8 This is what many in Europe call the "bloc de constitutionnalité."

9 See Patrick Taillon, *Le référendum expression directe de la souveraineté du peuple? Essai critique sur la rationalisation de l'expression référendaire en droit comparé* (Paris: Dalloz, 2012), 377–411.

10 Section 52 of the *Constitution Act, 1982*, is not the only example of an expressly stated definition that determines the primacy of certain provisions over others. In many respects, section 52 of the *Charter of Human Rights and Freedoms* proceeds in the same way by explicitly identifying the provisions of the charter that must take precedence over other laws and regulations. The main difference rests in the quasi-constitutional nature of these provisions. In other words, although they are supralegislative, they remain infraconstitutional in the sense that they are subordinate to the formal constitution. See *Vriend* v. *Alberta*, [1998] 1 SCR 493.

Other provincial human rights codes do not contain such provisions. The courts, in these cases, have established a supralegislative character based on the implicit intention of the provincial parliaments that enacted them and on the nature of the rights protected. Here, as elsewhere, the legislative procedure followed for the approval of these texts was not considered a decisive factor in establishing whether or not these charters were supralegislative in nature. See *Winnipeg School Division No. 1* v. *Craton*, [1985] 2 SCR 150.

11 See *Colonial Laws Validity Act, 1865*, 28–29 Vict., c. 63 (UK); *Statute of Westminster, 1931*, 22 Geo. V, c. 4 (UK), s. 7(1).

12 Strangely enough, five laws and one federal law, despite being repealed, remain part of the Constitution of Canada. For example, the *British North America Act, 1943*, 6–7 Geo. VI, c. 30 (UK), and the *British North America Act, 1952*, 1 Eliz. II, c. 15 (Can.) are listed in the schedule to the *Constitution Act, 1982*.

13 See e.g., *Reference re Secession of Quebec*, [1998] 2 SCR 217, 239; *Reference re Senate Reform*, 2014 SCC 32, [2014] 1 SCR 704, 723.

14 *Minutes of Proceedings and Evidence of the Special Joint Committee of the Senate and of the House of Commons on the Constitution of Canada*, 1st Sess., 32nd Parl., no. 36 (12 January 1981), concerning the document Canada, *Proposed Resolution for a Joint Address to Her Majesty the Queen respecting the Constitution of Canada*, no. 54 (Ottawa: Parliament of Canada, 1980), 104–8.

15 Jean Chrétien, *Briefing Book for Clause-by-Clause Consideration of the Proposed Resolution*, book II (Ottawa: Government of Canada, 1981), s. 52.

16 When questioned by MP Munro during the hearings of the Joint Committee on the Constitution of Canada, Jean Chrétien, the then-minister responsible for the 1982 constitutional amendment, stated that the list in subsection 52(2) was not complete.

17 In *New Brunswick Broadcasting Co. v. Nova Scotia (Speaker of the House of Assembly)*, [1993] 1 SCR 319, 352–3, Chief Justice Lamer, without ruling definitively on the issue, questioned the exhaustive nature of the documents listed in subsection 52(2) of the *Constitution Act, 1982*, whereas Justice McLachlin, at 378, writing for the majority, was more affirmative.

18 See *Re Secession of Quebec*, at para. 32; *Reference re Remuneration of Judges of the Provincial Court (PEI)*, [1997] 3 SCR 3, 75, Chief Justice Lamer for the majority.

19 It should be noted that underlying constitutional principles do not only include principles sensu stricto, particularly where parliamentary privilege of provincial legislative assemblies is involved. Nevertheless, the term, now enshrined, is used here for convenience to describe all those elements that have been included in the definition of the Constitution of Canada.

20 See *Re Manitoba Language Rights*, [1985] 1 SCR 721.

21 See NB *Broadcasting*.

22 See *Re Remuneration of Judges* at para. 94–109.

23 See *Re Secession of Quebec* at para. 55–60.
24 Ibid., at para. 61–9.
25 Ibid., at para. 70–8.
26 Ibid., at para. 79–82.
27 See *Beckman* v. *Little Salmon/Carmacks First Nation*, 2010 SCC 53, [2010] 3 SCR 103 at paras 41–6.
28 See *Motard et al.* c. *Procureur général du Canada*, 2019 QCCA 1826 (QC); *Motard et al.* v. *Canada (AG)*, leave to appeal to Supreme Court of Canada refused, 38986 (23 April 2020).
29 For instance, customs derived from traditional Aboriginal practices could be analyzed as an implicit extension of the rights protected under section 35 of the *Constitution Act, 1982*.
30 By way of illustration, aspects related to royal assent that are not codified in section 55 of the *Constitution Act, 1867*, and the executive prerogative that flows from the title of head of state, as commander in chief of all armed forces, under section 15 of the *Constitution Act, 1867*, could be characterized as supralegislative common law norms. For further information on royal assent, see Hubert Cauchon, "Sanction royale: un pouvoir discrétionnaire toujours exercé," *National Journal of Constitutional Law* 39, no. 2 (2019): 202. Concerning the prerogative to declare war, see Patrick Taillon and Louis-Philippe Lacombe, "Le rôle des parlements dans le déroulement des opérations extérieures," in *Annuaire international de justice constitutionnelle*, vol. 31 (Paris/Aix-en-Provence: Economica/ Presses universitaires d'Aix-Marseille, 2016), 569.
31 In many respects, the boundary between common law rules (inductive rules drawn from precedent) and principles (deductive rules drawn from the general scheme of the law) is often porous. For example, the unwritten parliamentary privilege of legislative assemblies initially took the form of parliamentary custom, then that of common law rules via the *ratio decidendi* of decisions rendered by the courts of justice in the United Kingdom and, eventually, at least in Canada, the form of underlying constitutional principles through their connection to the Preamble of the *Constitution Act, 1867*.
32 *Supreme Court Act*, RSC 1985, c. S-26.
33 *Reference re Supreme Court Act, ss 5 and 6*, 2014 SCC 21, [2014] 1 SCR 433, 472, McLachlin for the majority.
34 See *Chagnon* v. *Syndicat de la fonction publique et parapublique du Québec*, 2018 SCC 39, [2018] 2 SCR 687, 721, 724, Rowe J. who wrote concurring reasons; *Canada (House of Commons)* v. *Vaid*, 2005 SCC 30, [2005] 1 SCR 667, 692, Binnie J. for the Court. In *Re Upper House*, at 74,

the Supreme Court implicitly recognized that a provincial parliament had the right to unilaterally abolish its legislative council. See also *Montplaisir c. Québec (PG)*, [1997] RJQ 109 (QC) at paras 71–7.

35 For example, sections 50 to 52 of the *Constitution Act, 1867*, serve as part of the formal constitution of the federating state. Because subsection 52(1) and paragraph 52(2)(*b*) of the *Constitution Act, 1982*, apply to those sections, they are located at the top level of the normative hierarchy.

36 This would be the case for most sections of the *Constitution Act, 1867* and *Constitution Act, 1982*. For example, sections 91 to 92A, 94A and 95 of the *Constitution Act, 1867*, which lay down the constitutional division of legislative powers, and sections 1 to 15, subsection 16(3) and sections 23 to 34 of the *Constitution Act, 1982*, which deal with human rights and freedoms, belong to the formal constitution of all federated states, to the formal constitution of the federating state and, by inclusion, to the formal constitution of the federation. Conversely, section 94 of the *Constitution Act, 1867* is excluded from the formal constitution of Quebec, but is included in the formal constitutions of the other federated states and of the federating state. Similarly, subsection 16(2) and sections 16.1 to 22 of the *Constitution Act, 1982* do not contribute to the structure of the formal constitution of Quebec.

37 See e.g., Jacques-Yvan Morin and José Woehrling, *Les constitutions du Canada et du Québec du régime français à nos jours*, book 1 (Montréal: Thémis, 1992), 131, 479; Pelletier, *La modification constitutionnelle*, 42–3, 49; Maxime St-Hilaire, Patrick F. Beau, and Elena S. Drouin, "The Constitution of Canada as Supreme Law: A New Definition," *Constitutional Forum constitutionnel* 28, no. 1 (2019): 7.

38 Three procedures set out in the *Constitution Act, 1982*, satisfy this definition, namely: the unanimity formula (s. 41); the general amendment procedure (subsec. 38(1)) and its variant (subsec. 38(2)); and the special arrangements procedure (s. 43). It should be noted that the lack of Senate authorization may be overridden in accordance with section 47 of the *Constitution Act, 1982*. In other words, the consent of the Senate is not absolutely necessary for complex procedures to succeed.

39 As opposed to complex procedures, which require resolutions to be passed, a unilateral procedure is defined by the isolated involvement of a parliament, whether federal (s. 44) or provincial (s. 45), requiring only that the legislative body pass a statute.

40 St-Hilaire, Baud, and Drouin, "Supreme Law," at 8.

41 See *Colonial Laws Validity Act*, at s. 2; *Statute of Westminster*, at s. 2, 4, 7.

42 Subject, of course, to constitutional conventions. See *Re: Objection by Quebec to a Resolution to amend the Constitution*, [1982] 2 SCR 793.

43 *An Act to amend and continue the Act 32 and 33 Victoria, chapter 3; and to establish and provide for the Government of the Province of Manitoba, 1870*, 33 Vict., c. 3 (Can.).

44 See *Manitoba (AG)* v. *Canadian Pacific Railway Company et al.*, [1958] SCR 744, 750–1.

45 *British North America Act, 1871*, 34–5 Vict., c. 28 (UK).

46 *Constitution Act, 1867*, susbsec. 92(1); *Constitution Act, 1982*, s. 45.

47 In the United States, a federal law passed by Congress can be declared void if it violates the United States Constitution. Similarly, legislation of a federated state may be declared void if it conflicts with the formal constitution of that same state. In addition, a provision included in the formal constitution of a federated state may also be declared void if it violates the formal constitution of the United States, federal laws, or treaties. This last aspect of the hierarchy of formal constitutional norms derives from the *Supremacy Clause*.

48 See *Re Supreme Court Act*; *Re Senate reform*.

49 See especially *Dagenais* v. *Canadian Broadcasting Corp.*, [1994] 3 SCR 835; *Reference re Bill 30, An Act to Amend the Education Act (Ont.)*, [1987] 1 SCR 1148; *NB Broadcasting*; *O'Donohue* v. *Canada*, 109 CRR (2d) 1, [2003] OTC 6 (ON), Rouleau J.; aff'g [2005] OJ no. 965 (ON): the reasons of the Superior Court were upheld by the Ontario Court of Appeal (per curiam).

50 See e.g., Maxime St-Hilaire, "La jurisprudence relative au privilège parlementaire comme modification constitutionnelle inconstitutionnelle," CANLII Connects, accessed 9 October 2021, canliiconnects.org/en/commentaries/67262.

51 See *Fielding* v. *Thomas*, [1896] AC 600 (Privy Council).

52 *NB Broadcasting*, at 368, 377, 378, 384, 394, Justice McLachlin for the majority; Justice La Forest wrote concurring reasons with which Justice McLachlin agreed at 393; Chief Justice Lamer dissented on this point at 354–5.

53 It is important to note that only provincial legislative assemblies enjoy the protection of inherent parliamentary privilege. The two federal legislative assemblies, on the other hand, enjoy only the protection of privilege established by legislation. Indeed, the federal parliament, under section 18 of the *Constitution Act, 1867*, holds the legislative authority to confer parliamentary privileges that do not exceed those held by the British House of Commons.

54 *Vaid*, at 692.

55 Subject to the "test of necessity" established by case law. See NB *Broadcasting*, at 383; *Chagnon*, at 743 at para. 114.

56 See *Chagnon*, at 721, 724, Justice Rowe who wrote concurring reasons.

57 Section 93A of the *Constitution Act, 1867*, which was added following a constitutional amendment, in 1997, exemplifies how paragraph 52(2)(*c*) can apply. The addition constitutes an explicit amendment as intended by paragraph 52(2)(*b*). Seeing as section 93A applies only to Quebec, it would therefore form part of the formal constitution of that state exclusively.

58 It should be noted that several sections of the formal constitution of Canada also allow for the amendment of material constitutions. For example, a federated state can rely on subsections 92(4), 92(13), 92(14) and 92(16) of the *Constitution Act, 1867*, to amend certain aspects of its material constitution. Sections 72, 78, 80, 83, 84, 134, and 135 of the *Constitution Act, 1867*, which confer specific legislative powers, have also made it possible to amend certain aspects of Quebec's material constitution.

See the reasons of the judges of the Supreme Court of Canada with respect to subsections 92(4) and 92(14): *Canada (AG)* v. *Ontario (AG)*, [1898] AC 247 (Privy Council), 254; *OPSEU*, at 15, 16, 49, 58; *R. v. Mercure*, [1988] 1 SCR 234, 271.

59 Quebec abolished its Legislative Council in 1968 by passing the *Act respecting the Legislative Council*, SQ 1968, c. 9 (QC).

60 *Election Act*.

61 *Eurig Estate (Re)*, [1998] 2 SCR 565, 582–3, Justice Major for the majority (emphasis in original).

62 In this sense, the will of a federating or federated parliament to amend aspects of the formal constitution that fall within its purview follows the same logic as the rules governing the expression of the will of parliament to suspend the privileges and immunities of the Crown that are protected by the common law. In both cases, it is in the Parliament's interest to state its will expressly, even if it is always possible for the judge to identify an implicit will. See Pierre Issalys and Denis Lemieux, *L'action gouvernementale. Précis de droit des institutions administratives*, 3rd ed. (Cowansville, QC: Éditions Yvon Blais, 2009), 1323–62.

63 See *Act respecting the National Assembly* at. s. 2: "2. The National Assembly and the Lieutenant-Governor form the Parliament of Québec. The Parliament of Québec assumes all the powers conferred on the Legislature of Québec."

64 Ibid., at. s. 6:

> 6. A Legislature starts upon the receipt by the Secretary General, after a general election, of the list of the candidates …

> A Legislature ends on 29 August of the fourth calendar year following the year that includes the most recent general election polling day.
> […]
> Only the Lieutenant-Governor may dissolve the National Assembly before the expiry of a Legislature.

65 Merely mentioning section 44 or 45 of the *Constitution Act, 1982*, in a preambular provision is not necessarily sufficient to conclude that there has been an amendment to the formal constitutional. To our knowledge, only two federated parliaments have invoked section 45 of the *Constitution Act, 1982* in a preambular provision. However, this was done without any real intention of amending the formal constitution of the state in question. See *Constitution of Alberta Amendment Act*, RSA 1990, c. C-24 (AB); *An Act Respecting Reasonable Limits for Membership in the House of Assembly*, SNS 1986, c. 104 (NS).

In our view, the expressly stated amendment mentioned in *Eurig Estate (Re)*, requires the constituent power to specify the provision of the formal constitution that is being amended. In this regard, section 2 of the *Fair Representation Act*, SC 2011, c. 26 (Can.), is an eloquent example. There is no doubt that the amendment made by this section targets the formal constitution of the federating state.

66 This interconnection was confirmed by a unanimous statement by the Supreme Court of Canada in *Att. Gen. of Quebec* v. *Blaikie et al.*, [1979] 2 SCR 1016, 1025: "section 133 is not part of the Constitution of the Province within section 92(1) but *is rather part of the Constitution of Canada and of Quebec in an indivisible sense*, giving official status to French and English in the Parliament and in the Courts of Canada as well as in the Legislature and Courts of Quebec." (emphasis added).

PART TWO

# Purposes and Prospects

# 4

# A Codified Quebec Constitution: A Vain Pursuit or the Making of a Sovereign People?

*Nelson Wiseman*

This chapter probes the genesis, contents, and conundrums of a potentially codified Quebec constitution, a constitution contained in a single document. The chapter touches on some competing constitutional conceptions and concludes by addressing some challenges and possibilities that may follow the adoption of a new Quebec constitution. Emblematically, such a constitution would serve as a concrete symbol of an abstract idea, a way of representing and communicating the collective life and values of the Quebecois to themselves and their children. Such a constitution may also contribute to moving Quebec in the direction of independence and changing its relationship to the rest of Canada. Or not.

"Technically speaking, there is no Quebec Constitution," states James T. McHugh in the first sentence of his article, "The Quebec Constitution."[1] Au contraire, assert Justice Malcolm Rowe and J. Michael Collins in the first sentence of their chapter on provincial constitutions in the book *Provinces*: "Each province has a constitution."[2] That McHugh is an American ensconced at an American university and that Rowe and Collins are Canadians – Rowe sits on the Supreme Court of Canada – offers a clue to competing assessments; their nationalities influence their conceptions of constitutionalism.

In 2007, Member of the National Assembly (MNA) Daniel Turp for Parti Québécois (PQ), a promoter of a codified constitution for Quebec and whose doctoral dissertation was on the implementation of an international covenant between Quebec and Canada,[3] introduced a bill, "Québec Constitution," in the National Assembly.[4] Turp's bill died the following year with the dissolution of the Assembly for an election. He lost his seat but the MNA who replaced him, Québec Solidaire leader Amir Khadir, also campaigned on a platform in favour of a codified Quebec constitution. Although the bill failed, it represents a reference point for what a future Quebec constitution may contain.

Since the Quiet Revolution, several of Quebec's political parties, civil society groups, and academics have clamoured for a codified Quebec constitution. So-called constitutionitis – the propensity to elevate political issues to constitutional questions – is an elite pleasure industry that has become common in Canadian and Quebec politics. PQ leader Pauline Marois, for example, promised in her party's winning campaign in 2012 to create a distinct Quebec constitution as well as a Quebec citizenship. She had introduced a "Quebec Identity Act"[5] to complement Turp's bill in 2007. It would have created a form of citizenship separate from Canadian citizenship, even though internationally recognized forms of citizenship are the preserve of nation-states. After her party's election, nothing came of her promises. As Marois's government was a minority government, her constitutional enterprise had little prospect of passage and her government did not pursue it.

If such a constitution project succeeds it will pose conundrums and create challenges as well as opportunities. It could set the stage for crises within Quebec and between Quebec and Ottawa: the legal implications of a codified Quebec constitution might lead to challenges in the courts; it might not gain recognition in international law; and it might face fierce opposition from minorities in Quebec and possible pushback in the rest of Canada. On the other hand, the success of such a project may underscore Quebecois identity, reinforce the sense that Quebec and the rest of Canada are increasingly moving apart, and expand Quebec's range of actions as an increasingly sovereign jurisdiction.

## CONSTITUTIONAL CONCEPTIONS

The drive behind a codified Quebec constitution is to create a legal-cultural artifact that would serve as one dimension of an imagined national political community. This idea rests on the well-understood norms of self-determination and independence but it slides over certain uncomfortable aspects of identity in Quebec and Canada: it assumes a "formal universality of nationality as a socio-cultural concept" – that "everyone can, should, will 'have' a nationality, as he or she 'has' a gender."[6] Unlike gender however, which is assigned at birth, nationality in Quebec and Canada is a something of a phantom, an idealist spectre. Both gender and nationality are socially constructed and can vary in content and intensity. Consider native-born Quebecker Mordecai Richler whose novels and essays are set in the province. He was described as "not one of us" and not a "real Quebecker" by federalist Michel Bélanger, the co-chair of the Bélanger-Campeau Commission on the Political and Constitutional Future of Quebec.[7] On a similar note, former PQ premier Lucien Bouchard said "Canada is not a real country" on account of its multicultural complexion.[8]

Prime Minister Stephen Harper said "the *Québécois* are a unique people bonded together by a common language, culture and history – a nation," but when queried further about what Quebecois meant he said "It's up to people to define it."[9] Obviously, Quebecois is an ambiguous term; it may refer to any native or resident of Quebec but it is very often used in reference to Quebec's *pure laine* (dyed in the wool) or *de souche* (old-stock) francophones – those of French ethnic origins whose forbears settled before the Conquest and who share the historical French culture of Quebec. That is how most English Canadians such as native-born Quebecker Conrad Black, who has a law degree from Université Laval and the author of a book on Quebec's longest-serving premier, uses the term.[10] Former PQ premier Jacques Parizeau infamously articulated the distinction between the *Québécois de souche* and the others in Quebec when he declared that "money and the ethnic vote" had determined the outcome of Quebec's 1995 referendum.[11]

The English version of the first sentence of Turp's Quebec constitution bill asserted that the "Quebecers form a nation and Quebec is a French-speaking nation." The French version used the term Quebecois. To be sure, the people of Quebec share the same moral universe, but they do not share a culture: a common language, religion, and literary traditions. As there are different connotations of the terms Quebecois and Quebecker, there are also different definitions of "nation." In the ethnic sense, neither Canada nor Quebec is a nation; both are multinational, polyethnic societies and French Canadians are one of the nations in both. Some have gone further, depicting Canada as a postnational society, a people united by common values and ideas rather than by nationality,[12] something many Quebecois would dispute.

Nation is often conflated with nation-state; a group of people who constitute a political unit in a defined territory personified by a sovereign authority. In international law Canada, unlike Quebec, is a member nation of the United Nations. In the sociological sense, nation refers to a generally large group of people who share a desire to live together and who think of themselves as a distinct nation. In this sense old stock Quebecois, but not most other Quebeckers, think of themselves as a nation. Quebec's francophones have a stronger attachment to Quebec than do Quebec's anglophones and allophones; they have a stronger attachment to Canada.[13]

Propelling the discourse around the development of an entrenched and codified Quebec constitution is what Charles Taylor describes as a political "mode of narration."[14] Such a constitution would articulate how the "Quebec nation" imagines and defines its collective social and political life. It would further Quebeckers understanding of their political practices, of how their political system and its contemporary core values operate, and how they ought to operate in the collective life of their community. Such a Constitution could serve as a venerable interpretive device passed on from generation to generation. Its ratification could represent a national "founding" act, like a referendum favouring independence.

The competing descriptions of Quebec's constitution offered above by McHugh and Rowe and Collins reveal something of the differences between the histories, cultures, and traditions of the United States and Canada. Conceptions of constitutionalism have differed in the two countries. For McHugh, Quebec's existing constitution is not a sovereign constitution because Quebec has not achieved independent statehood. Canada, however, had a constitution long before achieving independence. As with the terms Quebecois and nation, the term constitution has more than one possible interpretation or meaning. Canadian constitutional sensibilities and practices have reflected mixtures and adaptations of British and American usage since Canada's experience has featured the constant interplay of the North American environment and British inheritance. The interaction manifests in spelling, dialects, popular culture, as well as political institutions.

Historically, English and French Canadians have also approached constitutionalism and democracy differently. English Canadians after 1867 thought of constitutionalism as the day-to-day practical resolution of problems and disputes by their parliaments. This utilitarian approach views a constitution as flexible. Quebec's French Canadians have always been more amenable to a grand legal design that spells out abstract social goals and personal rights. Quebec's Cartesian and normative civil code, rooted in the Roman and European heritage, reflects this view of a comprehensive, definitive document that lays down the legal principles that govern property, persons, and relations between persons.

The English Canadian approach of muddling through is how the British, Canadian, and Quebec forms of democratic constitutionalism took shape. In contrast, Pierre Trudeau's *Canadian Charter of Rights and Freedoms* expresses much of the French liberal and American view of constitutionalism, a vision of equal rights-bearing citizens with little room for recognizing the constitutional rights of particular groups of citizens. Influenced by the ideas of Cicero, Aquinas, Locke, and the American Declaration of Independence, the Canadian *Charter* is based on the doctrine of natural right – that the rights of man are universal.[15]

English Canadians have come to embrace this constitutional model and have married it with the principle of classical territorial federalism. In contrast, French Canadians have considered Confederation as animated by cultural dualism; they consider the modern Canadian state as having been fashioned by a solemn pact of two founding nations each with an implicit veto on changing their constitutional relationship. Discussions of a codified Quebec constitution reflect these competing perceptions of Canadian federalism. Simultaneously, Quebec's history as part of a state bound to the English common law tradition has tempered the Quebecois' understanding of a codified constitution. In brief, Quebec's experience with the Westminster model of parliamentary government has witnessed the Quebecois blending their French culture with a British institution.[16]

British Canadians, the once admiring inheritors of the British notion of constitution, thought of a constitution as referring to the powers, procedures, and prerogatives of sovereign parliaments whose edicts were supreme. That is how Britain's *Colonial Laws Validity Act* of 1865 defined "constitution."[17] The British Canadian tradition originally had constitutions coming from above – from the King, his governors and councils, and Britain's Parliament. In contrast, the conception of constitutionalism in the United States has had constitutional change coming from below, directly in the form of a referendum or via the people's elected representatives. Canadians, led by the Quebecois, have moved in an American direction in their growing penchant for referenda. In Canada and Quebec however, so-called referenda are actually plebiscites because unlike in the United States they are not legally binding since they exclude the role of the legislature.[18]

## QUEBEC'S EXTANT CONSTITUTION

British, French, American, and distinct English-Canadian influences have shaped Quebec's constitutional culture. Quebec's original constitution under British rule came in the form of the "Commission and Instructions" issued as *Letters Patent* by the Crown to Governor James Murray in 1763. Supplanting it was the *Quebec Act* of 1774, which is noteworthy as being the first Canadian constitutional document based on British statutory authority rather than royal prerogative.[19] Since 1867, part of Quebec's constitutional infrastructure stems from sections 58–90 of the *Constitution Act, 1867* titled "Provincial Constitutions."

Other parts of Quebec's constitution in the 1867 act include its jurisdictional powers in sections 92 and 93 and section 133, which provides for the use of English and French in Quebec's legislative records and courts. These sections effectively intermingle the Constitutions of Quebec and Canada; the Supreme Court has described them as part of the "Constitution of Canada and of Quebec in an indivisible sense."[20] Quebec's exceptional status is most noteworthy in section 94 because it provides for the possibility of uniform laws for Ontario, New Brunswick, and Nova Scotia – the three other provinces at Confederation – but not for Quebec. In 1875, Quebec secured a special constitutional claim with a guarantee of two of the six seats on the Supreme Court.[21] Although the *Supreme Court Act* is not listed in the schedule to the *Constitution Act, 1982*, the court has read itself into the constitution.[22] Elements of the *Constitution Act, 1982* are also parts of Quebec's constitution, including the *Canadian Charter of Rights and Freedoms* and section 92A dealing with natural resources. Section 59, related to minority language education rights, singles out Quebec for specific attention but is not in force and, as with section 94 of the 1867 act, is a dead letter.

Section 45 of the 1982 act, formerly section 92 (1) of the 1867 act, provides for provinces to change their own constitutions. On that basis in 1968 Quebec abolished its upper house, the Legislative Council, and renamed its Legislative Assembly the National Assembly. Bill 96, *An Act respecting French, the official and common language of Québec*, introduced in 2021 by the Coalition Avenir Québec government and asserting that "Quebecers form a nation" and French is the "only official language" of the province is another example of Quebec changing its provincial constitution.[23] According to Rowe and Collins, Quebec is free to change the operations of its legislature and government so long as the changes do not run afoul of the written constitution's "organizing principles."[24] This presumably refers to the Westminster system of responsible government. Whether Quebec is free to replace its Westminster model, so long as it is a Canadian province, with the American model of checks and balances, as a Quebec government consultation report recommended in 2003,[25] is therefore questionable.

Beyond its written elements, Quebec's constitution includes its unwritten constitution, some judicial decisions, and some quasi-constitutional statutes such as the province's electoral law, its *Charter of Human Rights and Freedoms,* and the *Charter of the French Language.*[26] The *Charter of Human Rights and Freedoms* is notable because it is more extensive than the *Canadian Charter of Rights and Freedoms* and the human rights codes of the other provinces; unlike them, it includes social, economic, and education rights. Quebec's *Charter* enjoys a "preeminent status in Quebec's legal psyche,"[27] just as the Canadian *Charter* does in the rest of the country. The *Charter of the French Language* carries particularly freighted symbolic value because it binds the people of Quebec with its authoritatively definitive statement of an identity related to language.[28] Bill 96 reinforces that identity.

The core of Quebec's constitution is unwritten and rooted in Westminster-style parliamentary government which operates based on custom, usage, and convention. An advocate for a codified constitution, Josée Legault, has described these unwritten elements as Quebec's "informal constitution."[29] Quebec's current constitution is resilient since statutory changes may be de facto constitutional changes. The possibility of litigation makes the Quebec government unwilling to offer an exhaustive list of statutes that constitute the province's written constitution. As Quebec's associate deputy minister of justice wrote in 1992, "[Q]ue pour ne pas préjuger de positions que pourraient ultérieurement prendre le procureur général du Québec devant les tribunaux dans certains litiges constitutionnels, il nous est difficile d'adopter une position précise."[30]

## PROPONENTS OF A CODIFIED QUEBEC CONSTITUTION

Long-held autonomist instincts provide an impetus for a codified Quebec constitution and they mesh well with the compact theory of two equal founding nations popular among French Canadians. Quebec's legislature appointed a commission in the 1870s to codify the province's general statutes, but the project lay dormant.[31] Nevertheless, constitutional preoccupations persisted insofar as Quebec was sensitive to federal intrusions into its jurisdictional fields.

To articulate its constitutional vision of Canada, in the 1950s Quebec created a Royal Commission of Inquiry on Constitutional Problems.[32] In 1963, Premier Jean Lesage created a committee on the constitution – he had the Canadian Constitution in mind[33] – and his successor, Daniel Johnson Sr, won election on a platform that promised to "Établir un mécanisme sauvegardant les droits du people québécois en matières constitutionnelles."[34] Some took this as a commitment to establish a Quebec constitution. In 1966, an États généraux du Canada français met in Montreal but unlike earlier États généraux held in 1912, 1937, and 1952, it took a new turn. Co-ordinated by the Saint Jean Baptiste Society and chaired by Jacques-Yvan Morin, the États généraux proposed a constituent assembly to inquire into the aspirations of the Quebecois and other French Canadians. A rupture between the Quebec representatives and French Canadian organizations from outside the province at the 1967 États généraux, however, resulted in what came to be known as "the day French Canada disappeared."[35] This marked the emergence of Quebec's territorial nationalism with PQ leader René Lévesque reinforcing the break with Canada's other francophone communities in his subsequent description of them as "dead ducks."[36]

An États généraux in 1969, made up of a small group of Quebecois, adopted a resolution calling for a codified Quebec constitution. This constitution would affirm Quebec's right to self-determination, assert Quebec's territorial integrity, guarantee individual rights, provide for universal suffrage, decentralize administration, incorporate the "objectifs fondamentaux du peuple du Québec," and be subject to ratification by the citizenry of Quebec.[37]

The PQ followed this up in its 1970 and 1973 official programs with the latter proposing to "Preparer un projet de constitution" containing among other rights, the right to work, leisure, health, housing, and an adequate standard of living.[38] In its winning campaign of 1976, the PQ platform promised "Doter le Québec d'une constitution assurant l'équilibre entre un gouvernement efficae et une démocratie authentique," but as the government, it did not follow up on the vow.[39] After having served as deputy premier in the PQ government, Morin, the herald most closely associated with the constitution project, chaired a committee in 1985 that drafted a *Constitution du Québec*, a project he pursued later as an academic.[40]

In 1994, the PQ government tabled a bill proposing a Constitution for a sovereign Quebec. It was intended to come into force following a referendum and to serve as a harbinger of Quebec's independence. Its elements included entrenched guarantees for anglophones, recognition of the right to Indigenous self-government, and the devolution of some powers and fiscal resources to municipal governments. It also included a provision making Quebec's Court of Appeal the court of highest jurisdiction until the establishment of a new Quebec Supreme Court.[41] Nothing, however, came of the bill.

When former Premier Parizeau called for the formulation of a Quebec constitution in 1998, his party ignored the call, but in the run-up to the 2003 election both the PQ and L'Action démocratique du Québec (ADQ) endorsed the idea, with the ADQ also proposing dual citizenship. The ADQ described its proposed *Charte du Québec* as "un document de base … la loi des lois de notre communité politiqe," including the right to Quebec's self-determination.[42] That same year, an États généraux convened by the PQ recommended that the province's "fundamental laws be assembled in a Québec constitution" and put to a referendum.[43] A Mouvement Démocratie et Citoyenneté du Québec followed this up in 2006 with what it considered essential elements for such a constitution.[44]

Except for ratification by plebiscite, the principles articulated by the 1969 États généraux appeared in Turp's private member's Bill 196, *Québec Constitution*, in 2007. With Marois's companion Bill 195, *Québec Identity Act*,[45] to create a Quebec citizenship, the related bills were touted as a "gesture of national governance" and garnered the support of the ADQ.[46] With the Liberals in power however, the bills went nowhere, another false start. Nevertheless, Turp's bill serves as a model for a potential codified constitution.

Since Turp's failed bill, former Liberal premier Jean Charest has argued "there are strong and rational arguments that can be made in favour of a good written provincial constitution." In 2016, PQ MNA Martine Ouellet offered a draft of an interim Quebec constitution that includes a question to be posed in a referendum once a PQ government is elected ("Do you accept that Quebec become a sovereign and independent country, according to the initial constitution proposed by the National Assembly. Yes or No"), and the Quebec Liberal Youth wing has more recently called for a Quebec constitution. All the parties in the National Assembly now support the idea of a codified Quebec constitution except for the governing Coalition Avenir Quebec.[47]

## POTENTIAL CONTENT OF A CODIFIED CONSTITUTION

Turp's bill asserted its supremacy – "This Constitution prevails over any rule of Québec law that is inconsistent with its provisions" – and provided for its amendment, which could be initiated by at least 25 per cent of the MNAs or by the premier and required the support of two-thirds of the MNAs. This and the declaration of the Constitution's supremacy were intended to give the bill a superior status to other legislative enactments. To promote a unique Quebec jurisprudence, Turp's bill proposed to establish "independent" Quebec courts, something they could not be so long as Quebec is not an independent state and Ottawa continues to appoint Quebec's superior court judges.

Featuring a tapestry of norms, the bill contained elements that spoke to both ethnic and civic nationalism. The proposed entrenchment of sections of the *Charter of the French Language*[48] and references to Quebec's "cultural heritage" suggested a dominant ethnolinguistic group. ADQ leader Mario Dumont reinforced this by referring to "those who founded Quebec" and their Christian values, "our religious tradition."[49] This sentiment is inconsistent with the recent emphasis on secularism as a foundational principle of the Quebec state and reflected in the 2019 *Act respecting the laicity of the State*.[50] However, CBC's massive Vote Compass survey during the 2015 federal election revealed the Christian religious orientation of old stock Quebecois; those in ridings with their largest concentrations were Canada's most "consistently vehement" opponents of the public presence of non-Christian religious symbols, beliefs, and rituals.

Noting that the "First Nations and the Inuit nation are present in Québec," and that "Québec has an English-speaking community," Turp's bill acknowledged the presence of minority groups but it neither recognized Indigenous self-government rights nor provided any guarantees to anglophones, groups that have historically collided culturally with the Quebecois. In contrast to the bill, the Preamble to the *Charter of the French Language* – the Preamble which the bill did not propose to entrench – states that the "National Assembly of Québec recognizes the right of the Amerinds and the Inuit of Québec, the first inhabitants of this land, to preserve and develop their original language and culture." Earlier, in 1985, a National Assembly motion had acknowledged the autonomy of eleven Aboriginal nations in the province.[51] This raises the questions of how many nations there are in Quebec and whether the rights of one nation, the Quebecois, outrank the rights of the other nations in Quebec. The apparent answer is to see the Quebecois as the ambient nation.

Turp's bill affirmed as a "fundamental value" that "individuals are free and equal in dignity and rights" and proposed entrenching sections of Quebec's *Charter of Human Rights and Freedoms*. Although the Preamble to the *Charter* refers to its enumerated rights and freedoms as "guaranteed by the collective will," the libertarian and egalitarian thrusts of Turp's bill and the *Charter* may be seen as swerving from the communitarian value of solidarity associated with the Quebecois.

A curiously incongruous provision in the bill was its provision for the codification of unwritten conventions. Codifying conventions would reinforce Quebec's current parliamentary practices. In this sense, the bill wanted to follow as well as to guide developments. To be sure, the Quebec legislature is free to put its conventions in statutory form and Turp's bill so provided: "The organization and operation of the Government are provided for by law." One result of such laws federally and provincially has been to increase executive dominance at the expense of legislatures.[52]

Conventions are time-honoured rules that deal with a practical problem. Codifying conventions without spelling out what the conventions are makes them justiciable and problematic. Conventions describe what has occurred in the past and how authority has been exercised in practice. Conventions in the past were not enforceable by courts and the idea of a codified convention once appeared oxymoronic. However, courts have begun to weigh in on conventions, which are at the organizational and operational base of Westminster-style government.[53] Codifying and subjecting conventions to legal review results in the existence of dissimilar constitutional elements. As Peter Hogg has observed, "The existence and definition of a convention has to be ascertained without prior judicial decisions which would support a rule of common law and without the sworn testimony and rules of evidence which would support a finding of fact."[54]

Oddly in this age of increasing democracy, Turp's "Quebec Constitution" bill did not provide for a plebiscite to give it the public's imprimatur. The omission was peculiar because many of the earlier proposals for a Quebec constitution provided for ratification by referendum. Moreover, the Supreme Court had conferred constitutional legitimacy on plebiscites as an embodiment of democracy, one of the "underlying principles" it identified "that animate the whole of our Constitution" in considering whether Quebec could secede unilaterally.[55]

Turp's constitution imparted a sense of eternity to the structures it proposed and the values it espoused. However, the values and structures it identified, like all values and structures of human society, are products of historical accretion and unmistakeably attached to the currently encultured self-perceptions of the Quebecois. His constitution, for example, listed "social progress," "economic development," and "sustainable development," as "fundamental values," values not inherent in Quebec's cultural heritage.

The proposed constitution appeared contradictory, simultaneously referring to the preservation and enhancement of Quebec's "historical and religious heritage" while "guaranteeing equality between women and men, and preserving the secularity of public institutions." As an example of the PQ's clashing norms, the party supported retaining the crucifix above the Speaker's chair in the National Assembly while affirming "the values of State secularism and religious neutrality" in its failed 2013 *Charter of Values* by prohibiting public sector employees from wearing or displaying conspicuous religious symbols.[56]

The proposed constitution referred to Quebec's "deep-rooted historical continuity in a territory over which it exercises its rights through the medium of a state." This was a strange pronouncement because much of the modern territory of Quebec is a product of Ottawa's *Quebec Boundary Extension Acts* of 1898 and 1912 which transferred the far-flung northern District of Ungava, formerly part of the Northwest Territories, to the province.[57] The "deep-rooted historical continuity" of Quebec is largely limited to the north and south shores of the St Lawrence River. The bill also asserted that "Quebec exercises its powers throughout its territory," but military installations, national parks, penitentiaries, seaports, and airports in Quebec are under federal jurisdiction.

## CONUNDRUMS AND CHALLENGES

Like scripture, a codified constitution must be formulated and adapted to the popular mind so that popular values are on its side. This raises the question: what is the popular mind of the Quebec people? To be sure, there is substantial popular consciousness of Quebec's tortured relationship to the Canadian Constitution, but few Quebecois and even fewer of those who may describe themselves as Quebeckers exhibit much interest in a constitution-writing exercise. Quebec's existing constitution barely dwells in their sub-conscious.

If the purpose of a codified and entrenched Constitution is to edify old stock Quebecois and stir their nationalist imagination, it has failed to date. In part this is because no Quebec government, as a foreigner once observed, "has devoted much time or energy to provincial constitution making."[58] The project appears to be embraced by some political parties only when they are not in office. As a government, the PQ's becalmed zeal for a Quebec constitution was notable when its 2014 re-election platform omitted mentioning the project, which it had championed as an opposition party just two years earlier.[59] Nor did the PQ mention it in its 2018 election platform.[60]

If an entrenched Quebec constitution comes to pass, the Canadian regime may adjust with minimal disruption. The response may be muted, with little tumult among other Canadians. Few Canadians in and outside Quebec appear keen in re-engaging the emotional national identity debates that triggered regional tensions in the 1980s and 1990s; compare, for example, the public's rebuff of their elites' exhortations to recognize Quebec as a "distinct society" at that time and the subdued public reaction in 2006 when Parliament recognized the Quebecois as a "nation." It caused barely a stir.

Since provincial constitutions are part of the Canadian Constitution, the Canadian Constitution may be sufficiently elastic to incorporate a codified Quebec constitution. Because the public's trust in judges and courts exceeds the esteem for politicians and political parties, juridical assessments may prove to be vital. As with the attitudes of some Canadian politicians to the Canadian *Charter*, including an attorney general who negotiated it,[61] some Quebec politicians may realize that they underestimated the significance of the transfer of power from their National Assembly and the political arena to the courts. They may come to regret their initiative in that regard.

The courts might approach a Quebec constitution the way they do competing parts of the Canadian Constitution, by treating the two constitutions as complementary rather than opposed. A collision of provisions in the two constitutions would not necessarily imply unconstitutionality. In a clash between them, the courts could rule that there is no hierarchy as between the contents of the two Constitutions and proceed to seek a balance by reconciling the interests at stake. The courts have adopted this method in cases dealing with clashes of the rights in the Canadian *Charter*, approaching them on the contextual facts of actual conflicts.[62]

A new Quebec constitution would continue to be tethered to Quebec's existing constitutional infrastructure of modified parliamentary supremacy – modified by the federal principle and the *Canadian Charter of Rights and Freedoms*. Since a Westminster legislature cannot strictly speaking bind the discretion of a future legislature, could a subsequent assembly override a new Quebec constitution enacted by the National Assembly? McHugh, following Donald Lutz, argues that a codified constitution is not necessarily an entrenched constitution unless the alteration of "fundamental constitutional arrangements" requires rigorous and constrictively defined rules.[63] What those "fundamental constitutional arrangements" or "organizing principles" might be is debatable.

A potential challenge to a new Quebec constitution along the lines of Turp's bill could come from the federal government. Ottawa could challenge the provision for a Quebec citizenship. Judicial decisions and scholarly assessment however might sustain citizenship at the subnational level as they have in the United States.[64] If Ottawa perceives a new Quebec constitution as an irreversible step in the direction of secession, it could resort to its power of disallowance.[65] Although the Supreme Court has referred to this power as spent and disused,[66] Jean Chrétien threatened to use it in the run-up to the Quebec referendum of 1995.[67] Another issue for the federal government is Ottawa's fiduciary obligations to Quebec's First Nations who are likely to oppose severance of those obligations.

In the absence of a codified Quebec constitution, Quebec could still make the case that two of its watershed enactments, the *Charter of Human Rights and Freedoms* and its *Charter of the French Language* are quasi-constitutional statutes that prevail over other laws. To support this line of argument, one could cite Justice Deschamps's opinion in the Chaoulli case.[68] Finding a violation of Quebec's *Charter of Human Rights and Freedoms*, Justice Deschamps said there was no need to rule on whether there was a violation of the *Canadian Charter of Rights and Freedoms*.

The ethnoreligious and linguistic diversity of Quebec may be in tension with the shared identity and cultural solidarity that a new Quebec constitution may be intended to foster. If a codified constitution seeks to preserve and enhance the "historical and religious heritage" of Quebec as the 2007 bill proposed, it will sit uneasily with Quebec's anglophones and Indigenous peoples whose divisions with the Quebecois are deeply rooted. The *Montreal Gazette*, for example, mocked Turp's bill as "absurd" and "surreal," of building a constitutional castle in the sky.[69]

Quebec may be moving on a continuum from ethnic to civic nationalism but xenophobic rants at the hearings of the Consultation Commission on Accommodation Practices Related to Cultural Differences (Bouchard-Taylor Commission) revealed a fair measure of prejudice in the public square.[70] So too did the debate around the PQ's abortive *Charter of Values*. Bill 21, *An Act respecting the laicity of the State*, introduced by the Coalition Avenir Quebec government elected in 2018, has stirred controversy and opposition. The mayor of Hampstead, has described the bill, which prohibits public sector employees including teachers from displaying religious symbols in the workplace, as "ethnic cleansing ... an attempt to remove those who practice minority religions, leaving only non-believers and Christians in Quebec."[71]

To be sure, every society has elements of a dominant ethnic charter group who may resist civic nationalism in its purist form if it excludes recognition of their historic cultural ancestry, and most every ethnic state makes some room for minorities. Quebec is no exception, but that room may diminish with a new Constitution. If a Quebec government introduces a new Constitution and calls for public hearings, it might unleash the type of engagement Ottawa's proposed *Canadian Charter of Rights and Freedoms* generated: a parliamentary committee sat for 357 hours, heard from 267 witnesses, and received close to one thousand written submissions. Supporters of a codified Quebec constitution may see it as complementing their politics, a frame for public policy; skeptics of the endeavour may dismiss it as offering layers of deceptive gauze that substitute for politics. For such critics, the real and deeper issues faced by Quebec are more mundane pressing public policy concerns, not the high politics of constitutional re-engineering.

## CONCLUSION

This chapter has queried the project for a Quebec constitution from various standpoints. Proponents of a codified constitution seek a definitive document that entrenches some egalitarian and libertarian principles together with parts of two landmark enactments – the *Charter of the French Language* and the *Charter of Human Rights and Freedoms* – and gives a nod to Quebec's historical and religious heritage. Supporters of such a constitution wish to crystallize what it means to be Quebecois and they see a precise and permanent document as helping to steer Quebec in the direction of independence by stirring the nationalist imagination of both old stock Quebecois and other Quebeckers.

Although the codified constitution project has had the support of some constitutional entrepreneurs, it has not borne fruit. What is striking is that the PQ has repeatedly promised such a constitution when in opposition but has not acted on it when in power, suggesting the project has served primarily as a rhetorical device in election campaigns. It has not caught the fancy of the Quebecois nor is it currently on the agenda of Quebec public policy.

As a vehicle to further national autonomy, a new Quebec constitution may be inadequate to the task; it may prove less consequential than the promoters of an independent Quebec hope. Josée Legault for example, a one-time political counselor for PQ premier Bernard Landry, described the PQ's proposed constitution in the 2012 election campaign as being of "purely cosmetic value."[72] Nevertheless, however decorative and superficial a codified Quebec constitution may appear at present, it might turn out to give rise to momentous political implications and unpredictable legal consequences.

The rise and fall of the PQ and its constitution project reveal their strengths as well as their vulnerabilities. For critics, a codified Quebec constitution appears as a vanity project of a partisan elite. Critics similarly castigated the PQ's proposed quasi-constitutional *Charter of Values*, the centrepiece of the party's failed 2014 election campaign, as an arrogant and divisive gambit. Intended to stir the issue of Quebecois identity, the *Charter of Values* succeeded in a way that the constitution project has not. If there is a moral to the story of the PQ's electoral defeat, it may be to avoid the pursuit of fundamental, symbolically loaded, constitutional change. Circuitous administrative changes and normal statutory law may accomplish more.

The Quebec constitution project is in abeyance but like a medical condition in temporary remission it may resurface. Proponents of a new Quebec constitution may hope that a calm interval in the project permits *reculer pour mieux sauter*. If a codified Quebec constitution does come about, the PQ as its major agent to date may have its idealistic cake and eat it too. Such a new constitution may come to represent a major leap in Quebec's evolving relationship with the rest of Canada. It may lead to Quebec achieving its sovereignty and independence in the same way that Canada achieved its independence, steadily and purposefully through a series of incremental steps.

That is a definite maybe.

## NOTES

1 James T. McHugh, "The Quebec Constitution," *Quebec Studies* 28 (Fall 1999/Winter 2000): 3.

2 Justice Malcolm Rowe and J. Michael Collins, "What is the Constitution of a Province?" in *Provinces: Canadian Provincial Politics*, ed. Christopher Dunn (Toronto: University of Toronto Press, 2016), 297.

3 Daniel Turp, "*La mise en œuvre du Pacte international relatif aux droits civils et politiques à la lumière de l'expérience du Canada et du Québec*" (Thèse de doctorat d'État, Université de droit, d'économie et de sciences sociales de Paris, 1990).

4 Bill 196, *Québec Constitution*, 1st Sess., 38th Leg., Quebec, 2007, 18 October 2007.

5 Bill 195, *Québec Identity Act*, 1st Sess., 38th Leg., Quebec, 2007. http://www.assnat.qc.ca/en/travaux-parlementaires/projets-loi/projet-loi-195-38-1.html

6 Benedict Anderson, *Imagined Communities: Reflections on the Origin and Spread of Nationalism* (London: Verso, 2006), 5.

7 "Richler, Trudeau, Lasagne et les autres," *Le Devoir*, 22 October 1991, B8; Sarah Scott and Geoff Baker, "Richler Doesn't Know Quebec, Bélanger Says; Writer 'Doesn't Belong,' Chairman of Panel on Quebec's Future Insists," *Gazette* (Montreal), 20 September 1991, 5.

8 Quoted in Bob Rae, "A Canadian Is … ," in *What Is a Canadian? Forty-Three Thought-Provoking Responses*, ed. Irvin Studin (Toronto: McClelland & Stewart, 2006), 259.

9 Tu Thanh Ha, "Of Wool and Old Stocks: When Is a Québécois Not a Québécois?" *Globe and Mail*, 13 March 2015, ProQuest document ID2383783846, accessed 11 September 2021, http://myaccess.library.utoronto.ca/login?qurl=https%3A%2F%2Fwww.proquest.com%2F-blogs-podcasts-websites%2Fwool-old-stocks-when-is-qu%C3%A9b%C3%A9cois-not%2Fdocview%2F2383783846%2Fse-2%3Faccountid%3D14771.

10 Conrad Black, "Conrad Black: 'Vive le Quebec libre!'" *National Post*, 21 November 2014, accessed 11 September 2021, https://nationalpost.com/opinion/conrad-black-vive-le-quebec-libre.

11 "Parizeau Blames 'Money and the Ethnic Vote' for Referendum Loss," CBC Digital Archives, 30 October 1995, accessed 11 September 2021, http://www.cbc.ca/archives/entry/quebec-referendum-reaction.

12 Gunilla Florby, Mark Shackleton, and Katri Suhonen, eds., *Canada: Images of a Post/National Society* (New York: PIE–Peter Lang, 2009).

13 Jack Jedwab, "Quebec Identity in 2011: Attachments, Identity and Diversity," Association for Canadian Studies, 27 December 2010, accessed 11 September 2021, https://acs-aec.ca/old/img/nouvelles/ACS-CIIM-2011EN-R172.pdf.

14 Charles Taylor, *Modern Social Imaginaries* (Durham, NC: Duke University Press, 2004), 176.

15 Pierre Elliott Trudeau, *A Canadian Charter of Human Rights* (Ottawa: Queen's Printer, 1968), accessed 27 July 2022, https://primarydocuments.ca/a-canadian-charter-of-human-rights/. Again, consider quo this earlie

16 Louis Massicotte, "The Successful Combination of French Culture and British Institutions," in *Provincial and Territorial Legislatures in Canada*,

eds. Gary Levy and Graham White (Toronto: University of Toronto Press, 1989), 68.

17 28 & 29 Vict. c. 63.

18 *Reference re the Initiative and Referendum Act* [1919] AC 935.

19 John E. Read, "The Early Provincial Constitutions," *Canadian Bar Review* 26, no. 4 (1948): 621.

20 *Blaikie v. Quebec (Attorney General)*, [1979] 2 SCR 1016.

21 *Supreme and Exchequer Court Act*, SC 1875, c. 11, s. 4.

22 *Reference re Supreme Court Act, ss 5 and 6*, SCC 21, [2014] 1 SCR 433.

23 National Assembly of Quebec, "Projet de loi n° 96," title: *An Act respecting French, the official and common language of Québec*, accessed 11 September 2021, http://m.assnat.qc.ca/en/travaux-parlementaires/projets-loi/projet-loi-96-42-1.html.

24 Rowe and Collins, "What is the Constitution of a Province?" 299.

25 Gouvernement du Québec, "Rapport du Comité directeur des États généraux sur la réforme des institutions démocratiques, " *La participation citoyenne au coeur des institutions démocratiques québécoises* (Québec, 2003), 38–40, accessed 11 September 2021, https://biblio.republiquelibre.org/Rapport_du_Comit%C3%A9_directeur_sur_la_r%C3%A9forme_des_institutions_d%C3%A9mocratiques.

26 *Charter of Human Rights and Freedoms*, CQLR c. C-12, and *Charter of the French Language*, CQLR c. C-11.

27 Jean-François Gaudreault-Desbiens and Charles-Maxime Panaccio, "The Asymmetrical Distinctness of the *Charter of Human Rights and Freedoms* in the Post-*Chaoulli* Era," *Revue du Barreau* 66, no. 5 (2006): 220.

28 *Charter of the French Language*, CQLR c. C-11, accessed 11 September 2021, http://canlii.ca/t/526jl.

29 Josée Legault, "Quebec Needs Its Own Constitution," *Gazette* (Montreal), 8 April 2000, B7.

30 Jean-K. Samson, Le sous-ministre associé, Ministère de la Justice, Québec, to author, 10 December 1992.

31 Government of Quebec, *Judicial Reforms Proposed by the Commission for the Codification of the Statutes: First Report* (Quebec, 1882).

32 Gouvernement du Québec, *Commission royale d'enquête sur les problèmes constitutionnels* (Québec, 1956).

33 La Société du patrimoine politique du Québec, "1960: Le programme politique du parti Libéral du Québec," accessed 11 September 2021, *http://www.archivespolitiquesduquebec.com/programmes/.*

34 *Objectifs 1966 de l'Union Nationale: un programme d'action* (Montreal: Pierre Des Marais Inc., 1966), 5.

35 Christian Rioux, "Les États généraux du Canada français en 1967 – Le jour où le Canada français a disparu," *Le Devoir,* 20 November 2010, accessed 11 September 2021, http://www.ledevoir.com/societe/actualites-en-societe/311368/les-etats-generaux-du-canada-francais-en-1967-le-jour-ou-le-canada-francais-a-disparu .

36 Jane Moss, "The Drama of Identity in Canada's Francophone West," *American Review of Canadian Studies* 34, no. 1 (Spring 2004): 81.

37 Rosaire Morin, "Les États généraux du Canada français," *L'Action nationale* 80, no. 6 (1990): 799–815; and Jacques-Yvan Morin, "Une constitution nouvelle pour le Québec: Le pourquoi, le contenu et le comment," *Revue québécoise de droit constitutionnel* 7, no. 2 (2008): 5–15.

38 *La solution: Le programme du Parti Quebecois présenté par Réné Lévesque* (Éditions du jour: Montréal, 1970), 98; Parti Québécois, *Un gouvernement du Parti Québécois s'engage…* (Québec: Les Editions du Parti Québécois, 1973), 14–15.

39 La Société du patrimoine politique du Québec, "Le programme électorale du Parti Québécois: Programme official Édition 1975," accessed 11 September 2021, http://www.archivespolitiquesduquebec.com/programmes/.

40 Jacques-Yvan Morin, "Pour une nouvelle Constitution du Québec," *McGill Law Journal* 30, no. 2 (1985): 171–220.

41 Text of the draft bill, *Globe and Mail*, 7 December 1994, A4.

42 ADQ, Conseil préélectoral, *Pour un gouvernement responsible: Plan d'action pour un premier mandate de l'Action démocratique du Québec* (Québec, 1 March 2003), 68, accessed 11 September 2021, https://www.bibliotheque.assnat.qc.ca/DepotNumerique_v2/AffichageNotice.aspx?idn=11292; Robert Dutrisac, "Position constitutionnelle: L'ADQ propose une Charte du Québec et la double citoyenneté," *Le Devoir*, 15 May 2001, A2; and "L'ADQ propose une Charte du Québec," *Le Devoir*, 1 June 2001, A9.

43 Report of the Organizing Committee of the Estates General on the Reform of Democratic Institutions, *Citizen Participation at the Heart of Québec's Democratic Institutions* (Québec City: Gouvernement du Québec, 2003), 37.

44 Mouvement Démocratie et Citoyenneté du Québec, Éléments essentiels pour une Constitution pour le Québec d'aujourd'hui (18 June 2006). Reproduced in Association québécois de droit constitutionnel, Troisiéme congrès québécois de droit constitutionnel (23 May 2008), "Fiche Introductive No.2," in *Constitutions!* (Québec: Presses de l' Université Laval), 18–19, https://inm.qc.ca/wp-content/uploads/2018/09/ai_constituons_fichesintroductives.pdf.

45 Bill 195, *Québec Identity Act*, 1st Sess., 38th Leg., Quebec, 2007.

46 Philip Authier and Marianne White, "The Big Stall: PQ 'Under Renovation'," *Gazette* (Montreal), 6 March 2008, 1.

47 La Presse canadienne, "Jean Charest voit de bons arguments en faveur d'une constitution pour le Quebec," Radio-Canada, 4 May 2016, accessed 11 September 2021, https://ici.radio-canada.ca/nouvelle/774027/charest-yale-conference-constitution; Philip Authier, "Ouellet unveils interim constitution for Quebec," *Gazette* (Montreal), 16 August 2016, A7; and Richard Smith and Giuliano D'Andrea, "A Quebec Constitution Could Help Minorities; Proposal Shouldn't Be Dismissed Prematurely," *Gazette* (Montreal), 22 August 2019, A7.

48 RSQ, c. C-11.

49 Quoted in Gerald Owen, "Mario Dumont and Quebec's 'Old Demons'," *National Post*, 2 February 2007, A13.

50 L-0.3 – *An Act respecting the laicity of the State.*

51 Québec (Province), "Motion Recognizing Aboriginal Rights," in *Les fondements de la politique du gouvernement du Québec en matière autochtone*, 20 March 1985, (Québec: Ministère du Conséil exécutive, 1988).

52 Liam Michael O'Flaherty, "Doing Provincial Constitutions Differently: Codifying Responsible Government in the Era of Executive Dominance," (MA thesis, University of British Columbia, 2008), accessed 11 September 2021, https://open.library.ubc.ca/cIRcle/collections/ubctheses/24/items/1.0066683.

53 *Re: Resolution to amend the Constitution*, [1981] 1 SCR 753; *R. (Miller) v. Prime Minister*; *Cherry v. Advocate General for Scotland* [2019] UKSC 41, [2020] AC 373.

54 Peter W. Hogg, "Comments on Legislation and Judicial Decisions: Constitutional Law – Amendment of the British North America Act – Role of the Provinces," *Canadian Bar Review* 60, no. 2 (1982): 320.

55 *Reference re Secession of Quebec*, [1998] 2 SCR 217.

56 Bill 60, *Charter affirming the values of State secularism and religious neutrality and the equality between women and men, and providing a framework for accommodation requests*, 1st Sess., 40th Leg., Quebec, 2013.

57 61 Vict., c. 3; 2 Geo. V, c. 45.

58 Ivo Duchacek, "State Constitutional Law in Comparative Perspective," *Annals of the American Academy of Political and Social Science* 496, no. 1 (1988): 137.

59 La Société du patrimoine politique du Québec, Plateforme du Parti Québécois, *Plus prospère, plus fort, plus indépendant, plus*

*accueilant, 2014–2018*, accessed 11 September 2021, http://www.archivespolitiquesduquebec.com/programmes/.

60 *Un* état fort au service des gens. The text comes from the collection of political texts available at www.poltext.org by The Center for Public Policy Analysis (CAPP) from Laval University, with the financial support of the Fonds de recherche du Québec – Société et culture (FRQSC). (Accessed 11 September 2021.)

61 Roy Romanow, "Courts and the Legislatures in the Age of the Charter," *Canadian Parliamentary Review* 9, no.1 (Spring 1986): 2.

62 For example, *Dagenais v. Canadian Broadcasting Corp.*, [1994] 3 SCR 835 at 877. See also *R. v. Mills*, [1999] 3 SCR 668; *Gosselin (Tutor of) v. Quebec (Attorney General)*, [2005] 1 SCR 238, 2005; *Ross v. New Brunswick School District No. 15*, [1996] 1 SCR 825 at paras 73–4; and *Trinity Western University v. British Columbia College of Teachers*, [2001] 1 SCR 772 at paras 73–4.

63 Quoted in McHugh, "The Quebec Constitution," 3–4; and Donald S. Lutz, *The Origin of American Constitutionalism* (Baton Rouge: Louisiana State University Press, 1988), 13.

64 *Williamson v. Osenton*, 232 US 619 (1914).

65 *Constitution Act 1867*, section 56.

66 *Re: Resolution to amend the Constitution* [1981] 1 SCR 753 at 802.

67 Hugh Winsor and Tu Thanh Ha, "Chretien Signals New Resolve on Quebec," *Globe and Mail*, 12 December 1995, A1.

68 *Chaoulli v. Quebec (Attorney General)*, [2005] 1 SCR 791, 2005 SCC 35.

69 Editorial, "A Surreal Proposal," *Gazette* (Montreal), 20 October 2007.

70 Pierre Anctil, "Introduction," in *Religion, Culture, and the State: Reflections on the Bouchard-Taylor Report*, eds. Howard Adelman and Pierre Anctil (Toronto: University of Toronto Press, 2011), 14.

71 Bill 21, *An Act respecting the laicity of the State*, 1st Sess., 42nd Leg., Quebec, 2019, and quoted in Benjamin Shingler, "Opposition to Quebec's Bill 21 Intensifies as Minister Pleads for Calm," CBC, accessed 11 September 2021, https://www.cbc.ca/news/canada/montreal/quebec-bill-21-opposition-1.5083340.

72 Josée Legault, "Editorial: If Change Is to Come, Let It Be for the Better," *Gazette* (Montreal), 30 August 2012.

# 5

# Interculturalism and the Plea for an Informal Constitution: Responding to the Challenge of Polyethnicity in Quebec

*Alain-G. Gagnon and Arjun Tremblay*

## 1. INTRODUCTION

Does Quebec need a written constitution? In addressing this volume's central question, this chapter explores normative and policy responses to the challenge of polyethnicity in Quebec at the beginning of the twenty-first century. It does so with an eye to identifying the divergence between these responses and to assessing whether or not a formal constitution can help to fulfill the untapped potential of interculturalism.

The challenge of polyethnicity is a distinct and characteristic phenomenon of the "age of migration";[1] it is brought about by immigration and by the resulting cultural, religious, linguistic and customary diversification of national communities. In turn, this diversification engenders four interrelated outcomes: 1. It leads to (an often implicit) reconceptualization of national communities as consisting of a majority and of minority communities; 2. It reveals that institutions tend to reflect the culture, religion, language, and customs of the majority; 3. It exposes the existence of (cultural, linguistic, religious, and customary) barriers preventing members of minority communities from becoming full members of the host society, such as barriers both to the exercise of social, political, and civil rights as well as to belonging to the national community;[2] 4. It compels scholars and public officials to find ways to integrate minorities and, in so doing, to ensure their full membership in the receiving society.

The normative (and also scholarly) response to the challenge of polyethnicity in Quebec has centered on interculturalism. The policy response to the challenge of polyethnicity has, by contrast, resulted in a gradual shift towards the institutionalization of state secularism, culminating in the adoption of a law on state laicity in 2019. Scholars have described this policy response as a form of legislative "degenerative politics"[3] and have argued that it is distinctly anti-intercultural in nature.[4]

Can a written constitution achieve interculturalism's unfulfilled promise? Focusing on three desired yet unattained intercultural outcomes – that is, the development of an ongoing dialogue between majority and minorities, the "indeterminancy" of national identity, and the entrenchment of multinational federalism – this chapter argues, contrary to what Daniel Turp argues in chapter 2, that the formalization of a Quebec constitution may actually do more harm than good at the moment. The chapter concludes that to achieve the goals of interculturalism it might be best for Quebec to revisit and revitalize its informal constitution.

## II. INTERCULTURALISM: THE NORMATIVE RESPONSE TO THE CHALLENGE OF POLYETHNICITY

Interculturalism is rooted in two foundational assumptions. The first foundational assumption is that Quebec is an immigrant-receiving society whose future, both demographically and democratically speaking, depends simultaneously on an openness to immigration as well as to cultural pluralism.[5] The second foundational assumption is that, in light of being a minority nation, Quebec's model of immigrant integration must ensure an openness to ethnocultural diversity and a respect for the cultural communities brought about by immigration and a commitment to ensuring the continuity of the culture and identity of the francophone majority.[6] Beyond sharing these two foundational assumptions there are, however, several variants of interculturalism.

In "Interculturalism or multiculturalism?,"[7] for example, Charles Taylor details one of these variants by focusing on the "'story' that gives the rationale of [multicultural and intercultural] policies."[8] The multicultural "story" in Canada is one that entails a shift away from an integration model of Anglo-conformity to the institutionalization of a multicultural national identity, a change brought about by demographic shifts in immigrant populations, the social and political ascendancy of Canadians of non-British descent, and greater public support for the public recognition of identities.[9] Quebec's intercultural "story," by contrast,[10] requires the emergence of a model of integration that takes into consideration several unique historical factors, such as Quebeckers' desire to see a democratic francophone society persist and "flourish" and the near automatic pull of new immigrants to English language institutions in North America.[11] Taylor sums up the stories and their respective implications as follows: "the 'multi' story decentres the traditional ethnohistorical identity and refuses to put any other in its place. All such identities coexist in the society, but none is officialized. The 'inter' story starts from the reigning historical identity but sees it evolving in a process in which all citizens, of whatever identity, have a voice, *and no-one's input has a privileged status*."[12]

Gérard Bouchard's understanding of interculturalism shares many similarities with Taylor's but it also differs significantly in regards to the privileges of Quebec's constitutive national and cultural communities. In "What is interculturalism?" Bouchard argues that Quebec interculturalism must allow for what he terms the "ad hoc (or contextual) precedence of the majority culture."[13] This is a form of "accommodation that minorities afford to majorities"[14] and it can be used in the service of policies meant to preserve essential features of the national or majority culture, such as religion, language, traditions.[15] To be clear, Bouchard does not argue that all claims to "ad hoc precedence" are legitimate. Rather, as one can see in table 5.1, he distinguishes between "legitimate" and "abusive" applications of "ad hoc precedence."

Bouchard brings forward, in the conclusion to "What is interculturalism?," an important caveat to one of the "abusive" forms of "ad hoc (or contextual) precedence of the majority culture" highlighted above. While he argues that a total ban (or general prohibition) against the wearing of religious signs in public institutions may be wrongly founded "on suppositions and hypotheses that have not been tested enough empirically,"[16] some form of ban can nonetheless be justified under interculturalism. More specifically, he argues that a ban on the wearing of religious signs is permissible under interculturalism for: "officials who embody the neutrality of the state and its autonomy from religion; for officials endowed with coercive power; and in the case of the burka or niqab, which should be banned in state employment locations and even in public spaces if it can be shown to pose a security threat."[17]

Table 5.1 | Legitimate and abusive forms of ad hoc precedence of the majority culture

| *Legitimate criteria for ad hoc precedence* | *Abusive forms of ad hoc precedence* |
|---|---|
| 1. the institution of French as the common public language; | 1. keeping a cross on the wall of the National Assembly and in public courtrooms; |
| 2. allocating a prominent place to the teaching of the francophone past in history courses, or in other words, a national memory that is inclusive but gives predominance to the majority narrative; | 2. the recitation of prayers at municipal council meetings; |
| 3. the current priority position given to the presentation of Christian religions in the new course on ethics and religious culture; | 3. the funding of chaplain or Catholic pastoral care positions in public hospitals with state funds, to the exclusion of other religions; |
| 4. the official burials of heads of state in Catholic churches; | 4. the general prohibition against wearing religious signs for all employees in the public and semi-public sectors; |
| 5. keeping the cross on the Québec flag (which has already been subject to challenges); | 5. the reference to the supremacy of God in the preamble of the *Canadian Charter of Rights and Freedoms*, |
| 6. laying Christmas decorations in public squares or buildings; | 6. including articles or clauses in a charter that establish a formal hierarchy between the cultural majority and minorities; |
| and | and |
| 7. the sounding of bells in Catholic churches at various moments throughout the day. | 7. the prohibition against wearing a burka in streets and public places (except for security or other compelling reasons). |

Source: "What Is Interculturalism?" (2011): 459–60.

Some scholars explore interculturalism within the context of the interaction between the Quebec minority nation and polyethnic minorities and the Canadian state. From this perspective, interculturalism is both a model for immigrant integration as well as an ethos for a harmonious *vivre-ensemble* (i.e., living together). Within this context, Alain-G. Gagnon proposes a variant of interculturalism with three main components: 1. It insists on "continual public debate" over issues of identity and common public culture and it "reveals a deep commitment to political transformation";[18] 2. It is intimately bound to a parliamentary deliberative tradition;[19] and 3. It promotes active citizenship and citizen empowerment.[20]

Gagnon's contributions to the discussion on interculturalism also include his contention[21] that formalizing Quebec's model of *vivre-ensemble* is but one half of a two-part strategy for ensuring Quebec's survival as a democratic polity in an "age of uncertainty" for minority nations. In brief, the point is made that for interculturalism to succeed in providing genuine hospitality for Quebec's minority ethnocultural communities it must be coupled with the institutional development and entrenchment of multinational federalism in Canada.

Multinational federalism is a practical and ethical guideline for the institutional division of powers in a multinational state, which is to say a state comprising a majority nation and at least one territorially-concentrated minority nation. A multinational federation – the institutional realization of multinational federalism – should formally recognize the existence within state boundaries of multiple *demoi* (i.e., peoples) each with their own distinct cultures, identities, and languages and it should also enshrine an asymmetrical division of powers, providing subnational units governed by minority nations with special competencies and jurisdictions. Although there is a growing scholarly consensus that multinational states should adopt multinational federalism, most have not and Canada has only realized the "symbolic recognition ... of the multinational nature of the Canadian state."[22]

Dimitrios Karmis[23] argues that multinationalism – the normative principle that undergirds multinational federalism – and interculturalism constitute different "pluralist" models of national identity that allow for different degrees of inclusion. More specifically, he argues that multinationalism only allows for the "symbolic inclusion" of non-national cultural minorities whereas interculturalism allows for "deep inclusion" and, in turn, for the possibility that "minority communities may participate fairly in the definition and redefinition of national identity."[24] Furthermore, Karmis' version of interculturalism requires that intercultural dialogue include nations and ethnocultural groups as well as other collective identities (e.g., sexual, gender) and nonethnic cultural groups.[25] According to Karmis, interculturalism focuses on processes rather than end-states and therefore "involves a greater measure of indeterminancy than the other models";[26] despite its inclusive potential, he argues that it is an as of yet unimplemented model of national identity.

Scholars such as Marie McAndrew and Daniel Salée show that Quebec interculturalism not only differs from other pluralist models but that it is itself a variable. McAndrew[27] approaches interculturalism diachronically when describing its "Jacobinist" and "pluralist" variants. She associates "Jacobinist" interculturalism with *Cultural Development Policy*, 1978 and *Québecers, Each and Everyone*, 1981, two policy documents produced under the Lévesque governments that embodied a "[promotion] of intercultural rapprochement" but also a "static vision of culture" and the marginalization of nonfrancophone ethnic cultures.[28] She associates "pluralist" interculturalism to *Let's Build Quebec Together*, 1990, the Bourassa government's policy statement on immigration and integration, which "insisted that identities, cultures, and groups were dynamic, rejecting any cultural essentialism that would closely link ethnic origin with community allegiance."[29]

Daniel Salée[30] explores interculturalism synchronically. He identifies and provides a critical assessment of the three variants of interculturalism present in Quebec public and intellectual discourse. He argues that "instrumentalist interculturalism" (*interculturalisme instrumental*) acknowledges that diversity enriches any society yet has little to say about dismantling majority-minority socioeconomic hierarchies.[31] Likewise, "humanist interculturalism" (*interculturalisme humaniste*), a pedagogical approach that combines openness to the "Other" (i.e., *l'Autre*) and education for citizenship, also fails to address power imbalances between the majority and minorities.[32] And "statist interculturalism" (*interculturalisme étatique*), the model articulated by the then Ministère de l'Immigration et des Communautés culturelles (what is now called the Ministère de l'Immigration, de la Francisation et de l'Intégration), espouses the value of diversity and pluralism but also asserts the "majority's normative hegemony"[33] by refusing to discuss or renegotiate specific majority values and principles. As an alternative to these models of interculturalism, Salée proposes[34] a "reimagined interculturalism" (*repenser l'interculturalisme*) based on four principles:

1. The inherent normative value of pluralism; 2. Constant contestation of power relations and hierarchies; 3. Openness to a fundamental re-imagining of new forms of citizenship; and 4. Accepting that dialogue with the "Other" (i.e., ethnocultural minority communities) will also lead to changes in the "Self" (i.e., the majority).

In sum, advocacy for interculturalism both converges and diverges on its main purposes. On the one hand, scholars tend to agree that interculturalism should facilitate, in some way or another, interaction and dialogue between Quebec's historical francophone majority and minority cultural communities borne out of recent immigration to Quebec. On the other hand, scholars differ in regards to their perspectives on whether or not the francophone majority should be given "precedence" over minority cultural communities and the degree to which the majority culture or francophone "Self" should itself be open to re-examination and re-imagining.

## III. LAICITY: THE POLICY RESPONSE TO THE CHALLENGE OF POLYETHNICITY

The policy response to the challenge of polyethnicity has taken place within the context of Quebec's "reasonable accommodation debate" and has led to the gradual institutionalization of laicity rather than interculturalism. The specific origins of the "reasonable accommodation debate" are unclear, however by the middle of the first decade of the twenty-first century Quebec news media had begun to expose "presumed excesses"[35] in the accommodation of minority religious practices and customs by both public and private institutions.[36] Very quickly the number of news reports on "excesses" of accommodation (e.g., a sugar shack's decision to offer a non-pork-based menu to a group of Muslim tourists, the frosting of windows in a YMCA in the Plateau Mont-Royal at the request of a neighboring Hasidic community, and a Quebec major junior hockey team's decision to allow one of its players to miss games that fell on the Sabbath) coalesced together to form a "media tsunami"[37] suggesting the existence of a deep divide between Quebec's francophone majority and the province's immigrant population. This "media tsunami" then caught hold in political discourse and, in turn, set the stage for the articulation of a variant of interculturalism.

On 15 December 2006, Mario Dumont, the then head of the Action démocratique du Québec (ADQ), asked sarcastically that he be permitted a "reasonable accommodation" on behalf of the province's majority to wish his fellow Quebeckers a "Joyeux Noël" rather than be required to employ the nondenominational tidings offered by the leaders of the Parti Québécois (PQ) and the Parti libéral du Québec (PLQ).[38] A month later, Dumont issued a public statement declaring to Quebeckers that the majority should not kowtow ("courber l'échine"[39]) over issues of minority accommodation and that a clear statement should be made about Quebec's core societal values.[40] In and around this time, on 25 January 2007, the town fathers of the small municipality of Hérouxville (population 1,300) issued a "code of conduct" that, among other things, prohibited "killing women by lapidation or burning them alive in public places, burning them with acid, excising them, infibulating them or treating them as slaves"[41] and that was widely seen as an attack on Quebec's Muslim minority community.[42] It was within this increasingly charged atmosphere that Jean Charest, the then Quebec premier and leader of Parti libéral du Québec, interceded in the discussion on "excesses" of accommodation and, on 8 February 2007, launched La Commission de consultation sur les pratiques d'accommodement reliées aux différences culturelles. The commission's two co-chairs, sociologist Gérard Bouchard and philosopher Charles Taylor, were tasked by the government to: "take stock of accommodation [practices] related to cultural differences, analyse the attendant issues bearing in mind the experience of other societies, conduct an extensive consultation on this topic, and formulate recommendations aimed at ensuring that accommodation practices conform to Québec's core values."[43]

In fulfilling its mandate, the Bouchard-Taylor Commission, as it has come to be known, conducted a range of activities including: establishing an advisory committee of fifteen scholarly experts, commissioning thirteen research projects, organizing thirty-one focus groups, holding eighty-two meetings, and holding four public forums as well as fifteen public hearings across the province.[44] In the end, the Bouchard-Taylor Commission arrived at two major conclusions: 1. That any potential worries over "excesses" of accommodation were in fact a "crisis of perception" and, consequently, that the "foundations of collective life in Québec are not in a critical situation";[45] and 2. That, while "sudden media enthusiasm and rumours"[46] contributed to the "crisis of perception," the Commission's investigation revealed that Quebeckers of French-Canadian descent were suffering

Table 5.2 | Bouchard-Taylor report: the objectives of interculturalism

| | |
|---|---|
| Québec interculturalism: | a) institutes French as the common language of intercultural relations;<br>b) cultivates a pluralistic orientation that is concerned with the protection of rights;<br>c) preserves the necessary creative tension between diversity, on the one hand, and the continuity of the French-speaking core and the social link, on the other hand;<br>d) places special emphasis on integration and participation;<br>e) advocates interaction. |

Source: *Building a Future: A Time for Reconciliation* (2008), 121.

from an "anxiety over identity" and that they were "still not at ease with their twofold status as a majority in Québec and a minority in Canada and North America."[47]

Despite dismissing the "crisis" and its ostensible root causes, the Bouchard-Taylor Commission nevertheless issued a series of priority recommendations, chief amongst which was a "call for a definition of new policies or programs pertaining to interculturalism (legislation, a declaration or a policy statement) and secularism (a proposed White paper)."[48] The Bouchard-Taylor report (i.e., *Building a Future: A Time for Reconciliation*) describes interculturalism as a unique "form of integration"[49] that is "characterized by interaction in a spirit of respect for differences."[50] According to the report's authors, Quebec interculturalism "bears a tension between ... ethnocultural diversity and ... the continuity of the French-speaking core and the preservation of the social bond."[51] Therefore, Quebec interculturalism differentiates itself from, on the one hand, Canadian and Australian multiculturalism which "gives priority to diversity"[52] and, on the other hand, from "republican" or "melting pot" forms of

Table 5.3 | The principles of open and rigid secularism

| | |
|---|---|
| Open secularism: | a) The moral equality of persons<br>b) Freedom of conscience and religion<br>c) State neutrality towards religions<br>d) The separation of Church and State |
| Rigid secularism: | a) The moral equality of persons<br>b) Freedom of conscience and religion<br>c) State neutrality towards religions<br>d) The separation of Church and State<br>e) The emancipation of individuals<br>f) Civic integration |

Source: *Building a Future: A Time for Reconciliation* (2008), 135–8.

integration both of which "favour the majority founding culture."[53] As one can see in table 5.2, the Bouchard-Taylor report describes five major objectives of a Quebec policy of interculturalism.

In regard to secularism, the other facet of the Bouchard-Taylor report's central priority recommendation, the commission also recommends that the government "formalize and spell out the conception of secularism that already exists in practice and, in so doing, to confirm and clarify the guidelines that define it."[54] The report defines this model as "open secularism" and, as one can see in table 5.3, it also distinguishes this model from a model of "rigid secularism." Above and beyond their four shared principles, the key difference between the two models is that "rigid secularism" has as a desired end the "erosion of religious belief"[55] (in order to emancipate individuals) and, in pursuing the entrenchment of a common civic identity, it also embraces a "republican position [which] assumes that the removal of difference is a prerequisite to integration"[56] (i.e., thus embracing civic integration).

The commission's endorsement of open secularism comes with two important caveats concerning "the wearing by government employees of religious signs."[57] First, the commission argues that a prohibition on a "full-body veil" would be acceptable for educators and "for the vast majority of duties in our public institutions, where full, open communication between colleagues and with the public is essential."[58] Second, the commission argues that in order to ensure the appearance of state neutrality and impartiality it might be necessary to impose "a duty of circumspection" regarding religious signs[59] on government employees, such as judges, Crown prosecutors, policy officers, prison guards, who "possess a power of punishment and even of coercion."[60] However, the commission also makes it repeatedly clear[61] that they do not endorse a full-scale prohibition on the wearing of religious signs in the Quebec public administration.

Despite these recommendations, the Charest government took no steps to adopt "legislation, a declaration or a policy statement" regarding interculturalism; nor did it draft a White paper on secularism. Immediately following the release of the Bouchard-Taylor Commission's report on 22 May 2008, the Charest government introduced a resolution[62] in the National Assembly declaring that the crucifix prominently displayed in the legislature above the speaker's chair be maintained as a symbol of Quebec's Catholic Heritage[63] thus going against the Bouchard-Taylor Commission's express wishes.[64] And, shortly thereafter, on 1 January 2009, the Charest government implemented a (nonbinding) integration contract that required newcomers to pledge their allegiance to Quebec's six immutable and non-negotiable values,[65] thus indicating to one observer that rather than abiding by the Bouchard-Taylor Commission's conclusions, the Premier "sought to reinforce clear boundaries on practices that would *not* be accommodated."[66]

Over the last decade, the Charest government as well as its successors have also disregarded the Bouchard-Taylor Commission's assessment that "the current situation does not require the adoption of a series of legislative measures aimed at promoting and ensuring secularism."[67] Rather, between 2010 and 2019, the Charest government, the Marois government, the Couillard government, and the

Legault government each set out to legislate secularism in Quebec, albeit in different ways and to different extents.

On 24 March 2010, Kathleen Weil (PLQ), the then minister of justice, introduced Bill 94 – *An Act to establish guidelines governing accommodation requests within the Administration and certain institutions*. Bill 94's stated goal was to "establish guidelines" regarding accommodation requests made by public servants and by individuals interacting with government departments, agencies and budget-funded bodies inter alia. However, Bill 94 also declared that: "the practice whereby a personnel member of the Administration or an institution and a person to whom services are being provided by the Administration or the institution show their face during the delivery of services is a general practice … If an accommodation involves an adaptation of that practice and reasons of security, communication or identification warrant it, the accommodation must be denied."[68] Bill 94 was widely seen by both its proponents and opponents[69] as indirectly targeting Muslim women and implying a ban on the wearing of the niqab and burka in public and semi-public institutions (both by public servants and by consumers).[70] The bill received overwhelming public support[71] however after a year and a half of debate, no consensus on the bill could be achieved and, by mid-2012, Bill 94 became an afterthought in public and legislative discussions in good part due to wide-scale Quebec student mobilization (i.e., the Maple Spring, which lasted from February–September 2012). Bill 94 was effectively abandoned when the Charest government lost the 2012 election and was replaced by the minority Marois government (2012–14).

On 7 November 2013, Bernard Drainville (PQ), the then minister responsible for democratic institutions and active citizenship introduced Bill 60 – *Charter affirming the values of State secularism and religious neutrality and the equality between women and men, and providing a framework for accommodation requests*. By contrast to Bill 94, Bill 60 contained a more extensive ban on the wearing of religious symbols: "In the exercise of their functions, personnel members of public bodies must not wear objects such as headgear, clothing, jewelry or other adornments which, by their conspicuous nature, overtly indicate a religious affiliation."[72] Pauline Marois, the then premier, described the *Charter of Values* (as it is now commonly known) as part of an ongoing process of "deconfessionalization" and situated it as an alternative to other integrationist models such as British multiculturalism under which, she declared, there had been "fistfights and bombings" in Britain.[73] Critics saw the *Charter of Values* as a means for the minority Marois government to rally its rural base, to take votes away from other nationalist political factions[74] and to capitalize on an electoral strategy that had ostensibly helped the Action démocratique du Québec increase its share of seats in the National Assembly.[75] Whatever the precise reasons may have been for the Marois government's decision to introduce a *Charter of Values*, it nevertheless suffered the same fate as Bill 94. After only a few short months in power, the Marois government decided to call a snap election in an attempt to secure a parliamentary majority. The strategy backfired and the PQ lost twenty-four seats and, as a result, the Parti libéral du Québec regained majority control of the National Assembly, this time with Philippe Couillard as premier.

The Couillard government (2014–18) had more success in its attempt to legislate secularism, which came in the form of Bill 62 – *An Act to foster adherence to State religious neutrality and, in particular, to provide a framework for requests for accommodations on religious grounds in certain bodies*.[76] Bill 62 was introduced by Stéphanie Vallée (PLQ), the then minister of justice, on 15 June 2015. Bill 62's main purpose was to "[impose] a duty of religious neutrality, in particular on personnel members of public bodies in the exercise of the functions of office"[77] and, akin to Bill 94, it required that "Personnel members of a body must exercise their functions with their face uncovered"[78] albeit with provisions for "accommodations on religious grounds."[79] Despite these provisions, Bill 62 was panned as a "perversion of secularism,"[80] an "indefensible mess,"[81] and as "what Islamaphobia looks like";[82] a critic who believed that Bill 62 did not go far enough, described it as just plain "sad."[83] Charles Taylor and Gérard Bouchard both criticized Bill 62, the former stating that it was "excessive and badly conceived, in fact, contradictory" and the latter arguing that Bill 62's understanding of secularism was reductive and effectively opposed to "open secularism" in that it "doesn't explore the separation of Church and State, equality of religions and belief, freedom of religion."[84] Although Bill 62 achieved assent on 18 October 2017, it was essentially gelded when its clause on face covering (i.e., clause 10) was struck down by the Cour supérieure du Québec on 30 November 2017 (a decision that was subsequently upheld on 28 June 2018).

The most resounding move towards the institutionalization of secularism has taken place under the Legault Coalition Avenir Québec (CAQ) government (2018–present). On 28 March 2019, Simon Jolin-Barrette (CAQ), the Legault government's minister of immigration, diversity, and inclusiveness, introduced Bill 21 – *An Act respecting the laicity of the State*. In addition to affirming that "The State of Québec is a lay State,"[85] Bill 21 requires that public services be provided and received "with face uncovered."[86] It also comprises the most extensive bans on the wearing of religious symbols; the ban covers[87] inter alia the president and vice-presidents of the National Assembly, justices of the peace, arbitrators, the minister of justice, certain classes of prosecutors and lawyers, peace officers, as well as principals, vice principals and teachers.[88]

Gérard Bouchard and Charles Taylor were invited to testify during deliberations on Bill 21 and both expressed their opposition to the proposed legislation. On the one hand, Bouchard argued that Bill 21 went too far in that it prohibited teachers from wearing religious symbols[89] while Taylor argued that, rather than enshrining religious neutrality as it claimed to do, Bill 21 was effectively discriminatory in that it privileged the rights of some people over others.[90] In justifying Bill 21, François Legault stated that the time had come to put an end to a debate that had "been going on for ten years" and that it "was time to set down the rules because in Québec, that is how we live."[91] In the end, the National Assembly passed Bill 21 into law on 16 June 2019. The government invoked the notwithstanding clause (section 33 of the *Canadian Charter of Rights and Freedoms*) when passing Bill 21, meaning that it is temporarily immunized from judicial review.

The policy response to the challenge of polyethnicity has resulted in the institutionalization of laicity. What does this mean in regards to the design and implementation of interculturalism and, as we will be discussing below, to the need to entrench, or not, a formal Quebec constitution? To be sure, legislators have sometimes argued that the institutionalization of state secularism in Quebec serves the purposes of interculturalism[92] and, during parliamentary deliberations on Bill 21, Simon Jolin-Barrette pointed out to Gérard Bouchard that a ban against the wearing of religious symbols was in fact consistent with his own 2012 treatise on interculturalism that argues in favour of giving "precedence" to the majority culture.[93] However, observers[94] argue that the institutionalization of laicity in Quebec is a distinctly anti-intercultural endeavour and one observer contends that Bill 21, rather than being integrationist, "signifies the actions of an entitled majority that seeks to revoke the 'privilege' of minorities to access public services, as is their right."[95] Furthermore, in June 2019, the Quebec government embraced laicity while Bill 493 – *Interculturalism Act*, introduced by Catherine Fournier (of the opposition Parti Québécois), failed to gain any traction in the National Assembly. Had it been adopted Bill 493 would have declared interculturalism as the official model of integration, enshrined a commitment to interculturalism in the Quebec *Charter of Human Rights and Freedoms*, and asserted French as the common public language and, at the same time, required that the Quebec government "[promote] intercultural interactions and the participation of individuals from such backgrounds in the evolution of Québec society in order to contribute to the cultural enrichment of society and the development of a common culture in harmony with the democratic and Québec values expressed in the Charter of human rights and freedoms."[96] Finally, there is nothing in the language of the secularism bills discussed above that suggests that they were developed with a view to promote other intercultural objectives such as maintaining openness to "indeterminancy" and to the "uncertainty" required by the principle of hospitality,[97] promoting a re-examination and re-imagination of the majority "Self," enshrining "continual dialogue," or engendering the concomitant entrenchment of multinational federalism, or both. Can a formal constitution bring Quebec closer to achieving these and other intercultural objectives?

## IV. THE FORMAL CONSTITUTION'S LIMITATIONS AND THE INFORMAL CONSTITUTION'S POTENTIAL

In this book, Daniel Turp[98] points to interculturalism and its inconsistency with Canadian multiculturalism as a reason for Quebec to affirm its "constitutional identity." Reversing the causal arrows of this contention, there are three reasons for which we do not believe that adopting a formal constitution in Quebec will actually aid in fulfilling interculturalism's potential.

For one, it is unclear how a formal constitution at this temporal juncture will help to engender "continual dialogue" between majorities and minorities. As some new institutionalists[99] have pointed out the timing and sequencing of institutional design is critical in setting society and politics down a path that is difficult if not impossible to deviate from. Consequently, it is worth considering what the long term impact on majority-minority relations in Quebec might be if Quebec's founding constitutional moment occurred at a time when successive governments of all political stripes have introduced legislation designed specifically to bring a conversation to an end.

Secondly, and in opposition to the principle of "indeterminancy," adopting a formal constitution at this moment also risks freezing the identities of the majority and minorities in a particular time and place. This could also be understood as a "relational" challenge presented by the prospect of a formal constitution in Quebec. Elke Winter[100] argues that real pluralism can only be achieved if "civic" majorities acknowledge that identity formation is "relational" (meaning oppositional), that majorities often claim that their identities are "civic," that by consequence the minority "Other" is often unfairly construed (or self-construed) as an illiberal "ethnic," and that any claim of a clear distinction between ethnic and civic identities is dubious. Therefore, formalizing a Quebec constitution at this particular time – and particularly in the wake of the adoption of Bill 21 – may risk crystalizing an artificial dichotomy between a secular-civic majority and a religious-ethnic-minority, legitimizing the assimilation of "ethnic" minorities into a "civic" culture. This would also prevent any real or profound re-examination of the majority "Self."

Third, it seems unlikely that the adoption of a formal constitution may solve the constitutional impasse and help to kickstart a new round of constitutional negotiation with Canada that could result in a substantive move towards multinational federalism. As we have discussed elsewhere[101] there are significant "roadblocks" to the institutionalization of multinational federalism despite an emerging normative consensus that federal states marked by deep national and ethnic cleavages should adopt asymmetrical institutional arrangements. The "roadblocks" to multinational federalism include inter alia the centralizing imperatives of central governments, a bias in favour of the institutional status quo, as well as a pan-Canadian identity that has been historically deployed to counteract subnational mobilization.[102] Furthermore, a transition to institutional multinational federalism does not necessarily entail the development of substantive multinational federalism. The substantive deepening of multinational federalism requires the robust enshrinement of individual, group, and community rights across the polity and within minority nations.[103] Given that Bill 21 was adopted notwithstanding rights protected under the *Canadian Charter of Rights and Freedoms*, picking the current political conjuncture as the foundational moment for a Quebec constitution is unwise if the desired objective is the development of a truly substantive multinational federation respectful of all its components.

In light of these objections, it might be tempting to argue that if Quebec were to institutionalize interculturalism, as Member of the National Assembly Catherine Fournier proposed when she tabled Bill 493 on 30 October 2019, and thus reverses course on state laicity then this might present a more propitious environment for the development of a formal constitution.[104] However, this also might prove to be problematic given that the formal enshrinement of diversity can be used, ironically, to commodify diversity and, in so doing, to demobilize minorities.[105] This would go against interculturalism's ideal of promoting active citizenship as well as the principle of "hospitality" which requires "not only recognizing intra-national minorities but also empowering them to mobilize on collective lines."[106] Paradoxically, the institutionalization of diversity might engender passive citizenry.

No matter how one slices it, we argue that now is not the time for more institutionalization. In light of the on-going mobilizations for racial justice and decolonization in the United States and around the world, a push for more rule-making in this context may justifiably be seen as a rearguard action by a majority afraid of losing its privilege and as an avoidance of another important intercultural objective: the erosion of hierarchies.

This contribution therefore makes the case for a return to the notion of the informal constitution. Quebec's informal constitution is an aggregate of laws including the *Charter of the French Language*, the Quebec *Charter of Human Rights and Freedoms*, Quebec's laws for popular referendum, the financing of political parties, and closer to us, the *Act respecting the Exercise of the Fundamental Rights and Prerogatives of the Québec People and of the State of Québec* (which achieved assent on 13 December, 2000). Together, these laws form an informal constitution, so to speak, whose political impacts deserve to be highlighted, as they have already created a sense of general agreement, even amongst populations of nonfrancophone origin. This informal constitution gives Quebec's government and society a set of positive guidelines that have been internalized and that have been (and continue to be) gradually adopted in policies, by judges, social actors, and the general population in their day-to-day relations. It is these elements that have long provided Quebeckers with the norms of coexistence and it is upon these elements that an ethic of dialogue, engagement, and reciprocity can be built.

Based on our analysis, a reinvigoration of these norms may be the way forward. Bill 96 –*An Act respecting French, the official and common language of Québec*, introduced by Simon Jolin-Barrette on 13 May 2021, could provide the basis for this reinvigoration by reaffirming French as Quebec's common public language and as the "language of intercultural communication."[107] Given that Bill 96 received unanimous cross-party support when it was introduced,[108] it is clear that there is, at least initially, general agreement amongst both proponents of laicity and between supporters of interculturalism over one of the linchpins of Quebec's informal constitution – the *Charter of the French Language*. At the time of writing, however, it is unclear what final form the legislation will take and it is therefore too early to tell whether Bill 96's affirmation of French as the sole official language of Quebec is, as some are arguing,[109] a threat to the survival of Quebec's English-speaking minority communities or whether it will embody a legitimate form of ad hoc precedence of the majority culture. Overall, it is clear that the necessary conditions for a genuine foundational moment to enact a formal Quebec constitution have not yet been attained and it is important that current and future legislative action does not wind up concretizing a legislative trajectory that began with the adoption of a law on State laicity by a divided National Assembly.[110]

## NOTES

1 Stephen Castles, Hein de Haas, and Mark J. Miller, *The Age of Migration: International Population Movements in the Modern World* (Basingstoke: Palgrave Macmillan, 2014), 5.

2 Irene Bloemraad, Anna Korteweg, and Gökçe Yurdakul, "Citizenship and Immigration: Multiculturalism, Assimilation, and Challenges to the Nation-State," *Annual Review of Sociology* 34 (2008): 153–6.

3 Francis Garon, "Policy-Making for Immigration and Integration in Québec: Degenerative Politics or Business as Usual?," *Policy Studies* 36, no. 5 (2015): 487–503.

4 See Jean-François Dupré, "Intercultural Citizenship, Civic Nationalism, and Nation Building in Québec: From Common Public Language to

Laïcité," *Studies in Ethnicity and Nationalism* 12, no. 2 (2012): 227; and Raffaele Iacovino, "Contextualizing the Quebec Charter of Values: Belonging Without Citizenship in Quebec," *Canadian Ethnic Studies* 47, no. 1 (2015): 41.

5 Alain-G. Gagnon and François Boucher, "L'État québécois devant les défis de la diversité ethnoculturelle," in *Les conditions du dialogue au Québec*, eds. Alain-G. Gagnon and Jean-Charles St-Louis (Montréal: Québec Amérique, Débats series, 2016), 173.

6 See Alain-G. Gagnon and Raffaele Iacovino, "Interculturalism and Multiculturalism: Similarities and Differences," in *Multiculturalism and Interculturalism. Debating the Dividing Lines*, eds. Nasar Meer, Tariq Modood, and Ricard Zapata-Barrero (Edinburgh: Edinburgh University Press, 2016), 104.

7 Charles Taylor, "Interculturalism or Multiculturalism?," *Philosophy & Social Criticism* 38, no. 4–5 (2012): 413.

8 Taylor, "Interculturalism or Multiculturalism?," 416.

9 Ibid., 416–7.

10 It could be argued that the differentiation between Canadian multiculturalism and Quebec interculturalism is based on a set of assumptions. To be clear, there is no scholarly consensus on whether multiculturalism and interculturalism are fundamentally different. Some scholars concur that interculturalism and multiculturalism set out to achieve integration in different ways, see for example Eva Segura, "L'interculturalisme québécois, alternative au multiculturalisme canadien? Voie québécoise ou voix québécoise," *Humanisme et Entreprise* 305, no. 5 (2011): 81; Marie-Michèle Sauvageau, "Du «comment» participer à «pourquoi» participer? Analyse de la notion de participation dans le multiculturalisme canadien et l'interculturalisme québécois," *Canadian Ethnic Studies* 43 (2012): 200. Other scholars point to the underlying similarities between multiculturalism and interculturalism, see for example François Rocher and Bob W. White, "L'interculturalisme québécois dans le contexte du multiculturalisme canadien," *Étude IRPP* (2014): 49; Micheline Labelle, "Multiculturalisme, interculturalisme, antiracisme: le traitement de l'altérité," *Revue européenne des migrations internationales* 31, no. 2 (2015): 31; Avigail Eisenberg, "The Rights of National Majorities: Toxic Discourse or Democratic Catharsis?," *Ethnicities* 20, no. 2 (2020): 312.

11 Taylor, "Interculturalism or Multiculturalism?," 418.

12 Ibid., italics added.

13 Gérard Bouchard, "What is Interculturalism?," *McGill Law Journal* 56, no. 2 (2011): 435–51.

14 Ibid., 454.
15 Ibid., 453.
16 Ibid., 467.
17 Ibid.
18 Alain-G. Gagnon, *Minority Nations in the Age of Uncertainty. New Paths to National Emancipation and Empowerment* (Toronto: University of Toronto Press, 2014), 52.
19 See Alain-G. Gagnon, "Plaidoyer pour l'interculturalisme," *Possibles* 24, no. 4 (2000): 11.
20 See Alain-G. Gagnon, "The New Vivre-Ensemble and Interculturalism," *Social Alternatives* 30, no. 3 (2011): 43.
21 See Gagnon, *Minority Nations in the Age of Uncertainty* and Alain-G. Gagnon, "Appraising Interculturalism and Refusing Canada's Constitutional Stalemate," paper presented at the Institute of Intergovernmental Relations School of Policy Studies, Queen's University, October 2017.
22 Jean-François Caron and Guy Laforest, "Canada and Multinational Federalism: From the Spirit of 1982 to Stephen Harper's Open Federalism," *Nationalism and Ethnic Politics* 15, no. 1 (2009): 46.
23 See Dimitrios Karmis, "Pluralism and National Identity(ies) in Contemporary Québec: Conceptual Clarifications, Typology, and Discourse Analysis," in *Québec: State and Society*, 3rd edition, ed. Alain-G. Gagnon (Peterborough, Ont: Broadview Press, 2004), 69.
24 Ibid., 73.
25 Ibid., 80.
26 Ibid.
27 See Marie McAndrew, "Competing Visions and Current Debates in Interculturalism in Québec," CLC*web: Comparative Literature and Culture* 18, no. 4 (2016): 1.
28 Ibid., 5.
29 Ibid.
30 See Daniel Salée, "Penser l'aménagement de la diversité ethnoculturelle au Québec. Mythes, limites et possibles de l'interculturalisme," *Politique et Sociétés* 29, no. 1 (2010): 145.
31 Ibid., 152.
32 Ibid., 155–6.
33 Ibid., 157 (authors' translation).
34 Ibid., 168–72.
35 Charles Herrera and Guy Lachapelle, "Politicians, Public Opinion, and Reasonable Accommodation in Québec," *Quebec Studies* 49 (2010): 87–97.

36 The duty to provide reasonable accommodation on religious grounds stems, in Canadian jurisprudence, from the Supreme Court of Canada's decision in *Ontario (Human Rights Commission) v. Simpsons-Sears Ltd*, [1985] 2 SCR 536. The decision imposed "the duty of accommodation [that] compels in certain cases the state, individuals and private business to modify, legitimate and justify norms, practices and policies which apply to all without distinction, in order to take into account the particular needs of certain minorities"; see Jean-Guy Vaillancourt and Élisabeth Campos, "The Regulation of Religious Diversity in Québec," *Quebec Studies* 52 (2011): 111–4 (quoting José Woehrling). In Quebec, reasonable accommodation is deemed to have a legal basis (ibid.) in article 10 of the Quebec *Charter of Human Rights and Freedoms, 1975* and it is also viewed as "norm" or societal convention; see Jocelyn Maclure, "Between Cultural and Civic: The Rocky Road of Reasonable Accommodation," *Cités* 23, no. 3 (2005): 57–65. Article 10, the legal basis of reasonable accommodation, is a nondiscrimination measure that prohibits "exclusion or preference" on the basis of thirteen characteristics: race, colour, sex, pregnancy, sexual orientation, civil status, age, religion, political convictions, language, ethnic or national origin, social condition, or handicap.

37 Thierry Giasson, Colette Brin, and Marie-Michèle Sauvageau, "Le bon, la brute et le raciste; analyse de la couverture médiatique de l'opinion publique pendant la 'crise' des accommodements raisonnables au Québec," *Canadian Journal of Political Science* 43, no. 2 (2010): 379–81.

38 Liz Ferguson, "A One-Year Chronology of the Province's 'Reasonable Accommodation' Controversy," *Gazette*, 3 February 2007, https://login.libproxy.uregina.ca:8443/login?url=https://search-proquest-com.libproxy.uregina.ca/docview/434434704?accountid=13480.

39 Alexandre Shields, "Tempête «identitaire» au Québec. Charest affirme que «les Québécois ne sont pas racistes», Dumont rejette le «vieux réflexe minoritaire," *Le Devoir*, 16 January 2007, http://www.ledevoir.com/societe/actualites-en-societe/127579/tempete-identitaire-au-quebec.

40 For some commentators, it was this appeal that helped the ADQ garner enough political support to win thirty-seven additional seats in the Quebec National Assembly and, in so doing, to present the first significant threat to the longstanding PQ-PLQ two-party hegemony in Quebec politics; see Tim Nieguth and Aurélie Lacassagne, "Contesting the Nation: Reasonable Accommodation in Rural Quebec," *Canadian Political Science Review* 3, no. 1 (2009): 1; and Herrera and Lachapelle, "Politicians, Public Opinion, and Reasonable," 87.

41 Beverley Baines, “Must Feminists Support Entrenchment of Sex Equality? Lessons from Quebec,” in *Constituting Equality: Gender Equality and Comparative Constitutional Law*, ed. Susan Hoffman Williams (Cambridge: Cambridge University Press, 2011), 136–46.

42 Darryl Leroux, “The Bouchard-Taylor Commission, the Hérouxville Code of Conduct, and Québec’s Immigrant Integration Policy,” *Quebec Studies* 49 (2010): 107–13.

43 Gérard Bouchard and Charles Taylor, *Building the Future: A Time for Reconciliation* (Québec: Gouvernement du Québec, 2008), 33.

44 Ibid., 35.

45 Ibid., 18.

46 Ibid.

47 Ibid.

48 Ibid., 22.

49 Ibid., 113.

50 Ibid., 118.

51 Ibid., 119.

52 Ibid., 118.

53 Ibid.

54 Ibid., 154.

55 Ibid., 137.

56 Ibid., 138.

57 Ibid., 149.

58 Ibid., 150.

59 Ibid., 151.

60 Ibid.

61 Ibid., 150–4.

62 Which was passed on 26 May 2008.

63 Kevin Dougherty, “We’ll Keep Crucifix Up, Charest Says; Unanimous Vote Motion Also Reaffirms Promotion of French,” *Gazette*, 23 May 2008, https://login.libproxy.uregina.ca:8443/login?url=https://search-proquest-com.libproxy.uregina.ca/docview/434645466?accountid=13480.

64 Bouchard and Taylor, *Building the Future*, 20.

65 This measure came into effect on 1 January 2009. It applies solely to economic and family reunification immigrants.

66 Daiva Stasiulis, “Worrier Nation: Quebec’s Value Codes for Immigrants,” *Politikon* 40, no. 1 (2013): 183–5.

67 Bouchard and Taylor, *Building the Future*, 53.

68 Bill 94, *An Act to establish guidelines governing accommodation requests*

*within the Administration and certain institutions*, 1st Sess., 39th Leg., Quebec, 2010, c. 6, cl. 6.

69 See Kyle Conway, "Quebec's Bill 94: What's 'Reasonable'?: What's 'Accommodation'?: and What's the Meaning of the Muslim Veil?," *American Review of Canadian Studies* 42 (2012): 195.

70 For a detalied analysis of Bill 94 and its implications see Chantal Maillé, Greg M. Nielsen, and Daniel Salée, eds. *Revealing Democracy: Securalism and Religion in Liberal Democratic States* (Brussels: Peter Lang, Diversitas series, 2013).

71 See Martin Patriquin and Charlie Gillis, "About Face: A Bill Banning the Niqab – Supported by a Majority of Canadians: How Did our Multicultural, Tolerant Nation Get Here?," *Maclean's*, 7 April 2010, http://www.macleans.ca/news/canada/about-face/.

72 Bill 60, *Charter affirming the values of State secularism and religious neutrality and the equality between women and men, and providing a framework for accommodation requests*, 1st Sess., 40th Leg., Quebec, 2013, div. II, cl. 5.

73 See Robert Dutrisac, "Pauline Marois au Devoir – L'étapisme pour la Charte des valeurs," *Le Devoir*, 6 September 2013, https://www.ledevoir.com/politique/quebec/386822/pauline-marois-au-devoir-l-etapisme-pour-la-charte-des-valeurs (authors' translation).

74 See Andrew Coyne, "Far from Certain Quebecers Will Side with PQ on Values Charter," *National Post*, 11 September 2013, https://nationalpost.com/opinion/andrew-coyne-far-from-certain-quebecers-will-side-with-pq-on-values-charter.

75 See Benjamin Shingler, "'Problematic' and a 'Dog's Breakfast': Quebec Face-Covering Ban Panned by Authors of Landmark Report," CBC News, 20 October 2017, https://www.cbc.ca/news/canada/montreal/quebec-bill-62-bouchard-taylor-1.4362278.

76 This is Bill 62's final title. It was previously titled: "An Act to foster adherence to State religious neutrality and, in particular, to provide a framework for religious accommodation requests in certain bodies."

77 Bill 62, *An Act to foster adherence to State religious neutrality and, in particular, to provide a framework for requests for accommodations on religious grounds in certain bodies*, 1st Sess., 41st Leg., Quebec, 2015, (assented to 18 October 2017), c. I, cl. 1.

78 Ibid., div. II, cl. 10.

79 Ibid., div. III.

80 Emmet Macfarlane, "Quebec Law Banning Face Coverings Is Neither

Neutral Nor Constitutional," CBC News, 19 October 2017, https://www.cbc.ca/news/opinion/quebec-neutrality-law-1.4360942.

81 Paul Wells, "Why Quebec's Bill 62 Is an Indefensible Mess," *Maclean's*, 23 October 2017, https://www.macleans.ca/politics/ottawa/why-quebecs-bill-62-is-an-indefensible-mess/?google_editors_picks=true.

82 Aangelyn, Francis, "Opinion: Bill 62 Is What Islamophobia Looks Like," *Maclean's*, 26 October 2017, https://www.macleans.ca/politics/opinion-bill-62-is-what-islamophobia-looks-like/.

83 See Joseph Facal, "Comprendre Gérard Bouchard?," *Journal de Montréal*, 13 April 2019, https://www.journaldemontreal.com/2019/04/13/comprendre-gerard-bouchard> (authors' translation).

84 Shingler, "'Problematic' and a 'Dog's Breakfast'."

85 Bill 21, *An Act respecting the laicity of the State*, 1st Sess., 42nd Leg., Quebec, 2019, (assented to 16 June 2019) c. I, cl. 1.

86 Ibid., c. III.

87 Ibid., c. II.

88 Ibid., Schedule II.

89 Quebec, National Assembly, Committee on Institutions, *Journal des débats* (*Hansard*) de la Commission permanente des institutions, 1st Sess., 42nd Leg., vol. 45, no. 34 (9 May 2019) (M. Gérard Bouchard), at 17.

90 Quebec, National Assembly, Committee on Institutions, *Journal des débats (Hansard) de la Commission permanente des institutions*, 1st Sess., 42nd Leg., vol. 45, no. 33 (7 May 2019) (M. Charles Taylor) at 38.

91 See Audrey Ruel-Manseau, "Legault présente un projet de loi sur la laïcité «modéré» dans une allocution," *La Presse*, 31 March 2019, https://www.lapresse.ca/actualites/politique/201903/31/01-5220294-legault-presente-un-projet-de-loi-sur-la-laicite-modere-dans-une-allocution.php (authors' translation).

92 See Andrea Chandler, "The Politics of Face Coverings and Masks in Russia, France, and Quebec," *Review of European and Russian Affairs* 9, no. 2 (2015): 1; and Jean-Marc Fournier and Stéphanie Vallée, "Opinion: Quebec's Bill 62 Promotes Living in Harmony," *Edmonton Journal*, 4 November 2017, https://edmontonjournal.com/opinion/columnists/opinion-quebecs-bill-62-promotes-living-in-harmony.

93 Quebec, National Assembly, Committee on Institutions, *Journal des débats (Hansard) of the Committee on Institutions,* 1st Sess., 42nd Leg., vol. 45, no. 34 (9 May 2019) (M. Jolin-Barrette), at 18–19.

94 See Jean-François Dupré, "Intercultural Citizenship, Civic Nationalism, and Nation Building in Québec: From Common Public Language to Laïcité," *Studies in Ethnicity and Nationalism* 12, no. 2 (2012): 227; and Raffaele

Iacovino, "Contextualizing the Quebec Charter of Values: Belonging Without Citizenship in Quebec," *Canadian Ethnic Studies* 47, no. 1 (2015): 41.

95 Eisenberg, "The Rights of National Majorities," 325.

96 See Bill 493, *Interculturalism Act*, 1st Sess., 42nd Leg., Quebec, 2019, Explanatory Notes.

97 See Gagnon, *Minority Nations in the Age of Uncertainty.*

98 Daniel Turp, "Oui, Quebec Needs a Written Constitution," in *Does Quebec Need a Written Constitution?*, eds. Richard Albert and Leonid Sirota (Montreal and Kingston: McGill-Queen's University Press, forthcoming), 31.

99 See Paul Pierson, *Politics in Time: History, Institutions, and Social Analysis* (Princeton, NJ: Princeton University Press, 2004).

100 See Elke Winter, "How Does the Nation Become Pluralist?," *Ethnicities* 7, no. 4 (2007): 483.

101 See Alain-G. Gagnon and Arjun Tremblay, "Federalism and Diversity: A New Research Agenda," in *A Research Agenda for Federalism Studies,* ed. John Kincaid (Northampton: Edward Elgar Publishing, 2019), 129; and Alain-G. Gagnon and Arjun Tremblay, eds., *Federalism and National Diversity in the 21st Century* (Cham, Switzerland: Palgrave Macmillan, 2020).

102 Gagnon and Tremblay, "Federalism and Diversity: A New Research Agenda," 133–4.

103 Gagnon and Tremblay, *Federalism and National Diversity in the 21st Century*, 320–1.

104 Turp, "Oui, Quebec Needs a Written Constitution," 34.

105 See Yasmeen Abu-Laban and Christina Gabriel, *Selling Diversity: Immigration, Multiculturalism, Employment Equity, and Globalization* (Peterborough, Ont: Broadview Press, 2002).

106 Gagnon and Tremblay, *Federalism and National Diversity in the 21st Century*, 327.

107 Bill 96, *An Act respecting French, the official and common language of Québec*, 1st Sess., 42nd Leg., Quebec, 2021, c. VIII.2, cl. 88.9(1).

108 There were 121 votes in favour of Bill 21 at its first reading, with no votes against and no abstentions.

109 See Andrew Caddell and Colin Standish, "Opinion: Task Force on Linguistic Policy Fights for Quebecers' Rights. Quebec's New Language Legislation and Ottawa's Bill C-32 to Revamp the *Official Languages Act* Are a Double-Whammy for Quebec Anglos," *Gazette* (Montreal), 2 August 2021, https://montrealgazette.com/opinion/opinion-task-force-on-linguistic-policy-fights-for-quebecers-rights.

110 There were seventy-three votes in favour of Bill 21's passage and thirty-five against, with no abstentions.

# 6

# Constitutive Power and the Nation(s) of Quebec

*Mark Walters*

## I. DOES QUEBEC NEED A WRITTEN CONSTITUTION?

In seeking to address this question, I begin with something of a confession: the standard idea of constitution-making leaves me with a vague but real sense of unease. I know, the making of a constitution by a people is supposed to be, according to the standard view, the highest form of self-determination. The exercise by the "nation" of its "constituent power," proclaimed Emmanuel Joseph Sieyès, is an exercise of a pure sovereign will that sets forth the law that will bind the institutions it constitutes; but it is also, he insisted, an exercise of power that cannot itself be constrained by law.[1] Now power unconstrained by law may not be so troubling if the people themselves wield this power. But invariably some people end up speaking for other people, one nation for other nations, and the ascendance of one voice will mean the silencing of other voices. If the making of ordinary law involves violence that kills alternative legal possibilities, as Robert Cover provocatively stated, then the making of supreme laws may be seen to kill alternative visions about basic normative assumptions and aspirations.[2] The birth of one constitution will be the death of others.

In response to these concerns, it may be said that not only have I struck a needlessly depressing note for the beginning of an analysis of whether Quebec should adopt a written constitution, but also that I am deeply confused. Surely, it will be said, it is the very existence of moral, political, cultural, and national pluralism within and between people who find themselves (usually for reasons beyond their control) living with each other that creates the need for a single, stable normative order. A regime of legality in these circumstances requires *a* constitution. I agree. But once we accept that constitutions are made in order to secure a regime of legality, or the rule of law, then I think the standard view of constitution-making advanced by Sieyès must be questioned. There may be good reason to resist the idea that the "constituent power" of the "nation" can be exercised in a legal or juridical void. It may, in the end, be found that writing a constitution is not so very different from reading a constitution – that both tasks involve an exercise of constructive interpretation that seeks to identify what the demands of legality mean for the people(s) who find themselves living together within the same normative space. The task of writing the constitution is, on this view, inseparable from the task of justifying the constitution – and both tasks may be seen as informed by ordinary forms of legal discourse.

In this essay, I will suggest that the exploration of the question of whether Quebec needs a written constitution helps to shed light on the general concept of constituent power for two reasons. First, because Quebec is already a component part of a constitutional system, it is unclear whether the constitution that it could make for itself today would be an exercise of constituent power in the standard sense of that term. Considering this point may shed light upon what constituent power really means. Second, given the constitutional and national pluralism that defines Quebec's legal character today, it is unclear whether there is a nation that could be the holder of a constituent power. In particular, I am interested in exploring how the nation-to-nation relationship that Quebec has developed with Indigenous nations bears on this point. This too may assist our inquiry into whether the standard view about constituent power is valid.

## II.

It is important to begin by observing that today Quebec already has a constitution, and much of it is written. As a province within the Canadian federation, certain key parts of its constitution are found in Part V (entitled "Provincial Constitutions") of the *Constitution Act, 1867*.[3] The courts have recognized that provincial constitutions also include a variety of other statutory, common law, and conventional sources.[4] One reason for adopting a written constitution for

Quebec, then, would simply be to consolidate or codify these diverse constitutional sources, or both, or at least the important ones, in a single written document in order to make the provincial constitution accessible and transparent. In the course of this exercise, however, it may be found that modifications to the provincial constitution are warranted, in which case Quebec could exercise its authority under section 45 of the *Constitution Act, 1982* to amend its provincial constitution, something that could be achieved unilaterally through an ordinary statute.[5]

From one perspective, then, this effort at constitution-writing in Quebec looks like a kind of housekeeping exercise. However, it could be much more. Certainly proponents of a written constitution for Quebec from both federalist and sovereigntist camps have something grander in mind. Benoît Pelletier argues that through the process of consolidating and modifying the provincial constitution, it is possible that the foundations of the Quebec polity could be affirmed in a solemn fashion, and that the resulting document might thereby gain moral authority and reflect a real social contract.[6] "Il me semble impérieux,' he writes, 'que nous déterminions tous ensemble ce que nous sommes et où nous voulons aller collectivement."[7] Sovereigntists go a step further. The real point of writing a Quebec constitution, writes Michel Seymour, is to present a fundamentally new vision of Canada to the rest of the country, one in which Quebec's distinct national identity is properly acknowledged and accommodated, and if the other parties to Confederation fail to respond within a prescribed period of time, Quebec can then initiate a process of secession from Canada.[8] What appears at first as mere housekeeping within Quebec's present constitutional home could emerge quickly into something closer to the exercise (or attempted exercise) of constituent power, in the sense Sieyès invokes, to build a new constitutional home.

The distinction that Daniel Turp makes in a recent essay between original constituent power and derivative constitutent power therefore appears, at first glance, very helpful for understanding these different dimensions of constitution-writing in Quebec.[9] Relying upon the work of Kemal Gözler, Turp says that original constituent power is the standard kind, the legally-unlimited power of the nation to constitute legally-limited institutions, whereas derivative constituent power is the exercise by constituted institutions of powers of constitutional amendment conferred by existing constitutional law.[10] So, it would follow that a sovereign Quebec would exercise original constituent power in making its first constitution, but the province of Quebec would exercise derivative constituent power in writing up a new provincial constitution.

This distinction seems logical enough. However, it seems to me that Professor Pelletier's comments quoted above suggest that the distinction is unstable: he seems to say (though he does not use the expression) that derivative constituent power could be used to establish a new social contract, and therefore to redefine in an original way the "nous" in Quebec. The same instability is apparent in Professor Turp's analysis of the idea of constitution-making in Quebec. The two senses of constitutent power seem to elide in his argument: a written constitution for Quebec adopted through an exercise of derivative constitutive power might, he seems to say, fit within the Constitution of Canada and yet also represent the kind of original constitutive power necessary for the eventual emergence of Quebec as an independent state. This "démarche constituante," as he puts it, might not quite fit the existing Canadian Constitution; rather, it would prompt amendments agreed upon by other political actors to make it fit so that Quebec would find itself within a constitutional system to which it had fully consented, or, if not, it would prompt Quebec's independence.

Turp gives as a model for this sort of constitutional strategy a 2013 draft entitled *Constitution de la Nation et de l'État du Québec* which proclaims in its Preamble that "la Nation du Québec est libre d'assumer son proper destin," but which then also acknowledges the recognition of Indigenous peoples, which "forment des nations distinctes," as well as the anglophone community and the contribution of ethnic minorities to Quebec's development; and, then, this hypothetical constitution, after stating, "*NOUS, DU QUÉBEC* par la voix de Parlement" (a voice that presumably speaks for everyone in Quebec, including the above-mentioned distinct nations and minorities), procedes to outline a constitution for Quebec that would require fundamental changes to the Canadian Constitution to be legal, together with a statement that if these amendments are not forthcoming within three years Quebec independence would be declared.[11] This kind of constitution-making blurs the distinction between original and derivative constituent power – it seems to be both at once.

In fact, examples of the collapsing of derivative and original constituent power are probably more common than one might think, and perhaps theoretically inevitable. As Hans Lindahl has argued, the exercise of constitutive and constituted power, or the actions of the nation and its institutions, are "reflexive," meaning that both are impossible without the other already in play.[12] One example, in my view, can be found today in the Quebec statutebook: the *Loi sur les droits fondamentaux du Québec*, enacted by the Quebec National Assembly in 2000, a statute that Turp describes as the sketch of a Constitution for Quebec.[13] This statute proclaims (inter alia): "The Québec people has the inalienable right to freely decide the political regime and legal status of Québec" (s. 2). This is certainly the assertion of a democratic principle, though, it should be clear, one that is arguably opposed to the principle of democracy articulated by the Supreme Court of Canada in the *Quebec Secession Reference*.[14] It is also, arguably, both the assertion and denial of the idea of derivative constituent power. Gözler, it should be noted, separates theories of constituent power into positivist and materialist camps, the former permitting derivative constitutional change of any kind through legal forms so long as constituted authorities are duly authorized by the constitution to make the change, the latter denying the very idea of derivative constituent power because of the view that the (original) constituent or sovereign power of the people or nation can never be limited by law. The materialist view was, Gözler notes, most famously advanced by Carl Schmitt and his followers.[15] While Schmitt thought that the people had to act through political institutions when exercising its constituent power, he also insisted (following Sieyès) that the sovereignty of the people could never be derived from or limited by law. Schmitt also thought, controversially, that the essential task of sovereign or constituent power is to define the nation or the people – to determine who was in and who was out, who was friend and who was enemy. Constituent power from this view is paradoxically constitutive of the very nation or people wielding it.

Is this kind of constituent power implicit within the hypothetical and embryonic written Quebec constitutions mentioned above? What does it mean to say that writing a Quebec constitution responds to the need "exprimé par les Québécois et les Québécoises de consolider leur identité nationale"?[16] What are the implications for the commitment to legality and respect for moral, political, cultural, and, also, national pluralism? What are the implications of an understanding of constitutent power and constituted power as "reflexive"?

## III.

Before examining these questions, it will be helpful first to sketch, at least in a rough sense, the ways in which Quebec may be said to be a multinational jurisdiction. The following account of the legal position of Indigenous nations in Quebec is admittedly brief and incomplete – but I hope it provides some context for considering the idea of constituent power in Quebec.

By resolution passed in 1985, the Quebec National Assembly acknowledged the existence in Quebec of ten Indigenous or Aboriginal nations (an eleventh being acknowledged several years later), namely, the Abenaki, Algonquin, Attikamek, Cree, Huron, Micmac, Mohawk, Innu, Naskapi, Inuit, and Malecite nations.[17] The geographical, cultural, political, and legal situation of these nations, most of which consist of two or more communities, varies considerably. But for our purposes, they may be grouped into three categories based upon their proximity in time and place to non-Indigenous settlement and resource development. As this discussion unfolds, it will be important to recall that by virtue of section 35 of the *Constitution Act, 1982* the "existing Aboriginal and treaty rights" of the Aboriginal peoples in Canada are constitutionally protected, including rights secured or that may be secured through modern land claim settlement agreements.

As British forces converged on Montreal in the late summer of 1760, the British superintendent general for Indian affairs in the northern parts of North America, Sir William Johnson, engaged in a series of diplomatic meetings with representatives of the various *nations domiciliées* that were strategically located near French-Canadian settlements. The villages of these nations were centred around Jesuit or Sulpician missions established in the seventeenth and early eighteenth centuries, and they included the Huron village at Jeune-Lorette near Quebec (now recognized under the federal *Indian Act* as the "Indian" or First Nation reserve of Wendake); the Abenaki villages of Saint Francis and Bécancour (now the First Nation reserves of Odanak and Wôlinak); the Iroquois-Mohawks of Sault St Louis or Caughnawaga across the St Lawrence River from Montreal (now the First Nation reserve of Kahnawake); the Iroquois-Mohawk (and initially Algonquin and Nippissing) village at Lake of Two Mountains or Canasadaga just west of Montreal (now the First Nation reserve of Kanesatake); and the Mohawk village on the upper St Lawrence River at St Regis or Akwesasne (now the First Nation reserve of Akwesasne).[18]

Though in close physical proximity to European settlements, these nations had retained a cultural and legal distance from Canadian settlers and French authorities and they remained a significant military factor in 1760.[19] In a series of treaty councils, Johnson persuaded most of them to come over to the British side prior to the final assault on Montreal. On 15–16 September at the Mohawk village of Caughnawaga, about one week after the French capitulated at Montreal, Johnson met in council with representatives from all of these nations to affirm a "Covenant Chain" treaty relationship with them according to Indigenous customs and ceremonies.[20] When tensions arose in subsequent years, political actors would turn to this treaty council as the source of normative structure for the evolving relationship between the Crown and these nations. It was at "the Treaty held at Caghnawagey," Johnson wrote after the Caughnawaga Mohawks complained of mistreatment by British soldiers, that the Crown gave the nations of Canada the "greatest assurances" of his protection.[21] The "Indians in Canada" were "received ... into our alliance," said Johnson in 1763, and, as they themselves insisted in the same year, that meant that they were to regard the King as their "Common Father."[22] The covenant chain had by this time a very distinctive meaning. It was an alliance and friendship in the Indigenous sense, meaning that it was a close relationship of care and trust between peoples who were equally free.[23] Today these communities are (from the Canadian legal perspective) "bands" with "reserved lands" and local powers of governance under the federal *Indian Act*.[24] However, they continue to see their relationship with non-Indigenous peoples in Canada in light of their initial treaty relationship with the Crown. In upholding one of the treaties made in September of 1760 as constitutionally protected by section 35 of the *Constitution Act, 1982*, the chief justice of Canada, Antonio Lamer, observed that "Indian nations had sufficient independence and played a large enough role in North America for it to be good policy to maintain relations with them very close to those maintained between sovereign nations."[25] What does that mean for relations between these nations and Canada and Quebec today? Is a degree of sovereignty left with these nations today, as they insist? For now, it is sufficient to say that this question is the source of ongoing tension and dialogue. In recent years, the Government of Quebec has acknowledged their autonomy over various issues falling within provincial legislative jurisdiction through a variety of sectoral devolution agreements.

In contrast to this first group of nations, the Algonquin, Attikamek, and Innu peoples whose traditional territories stretched north and west from the St Lawrence River valley maintained a degree of measured distance from European influence for a longer period of time. At least part of their territories fell within the protections for Indian lands established by the *Royal Proclamation of 1763*. Initially, the colonial government in Quebec assumed that their land rights were thus protected.[26] However, in time the theory was developed that because no treaties had been made for Indigenous lands during the French regime, no Aboriginal title or other rights survived within the original boundaries of the province of Quebec as established after the defeat of New France by the British.[27] The theory, which was advanced by Quebec lawyers before the Supreme Court of Canada (which rejected it) as late as 1996, explains why there were historically no land surrender treaties in Quebec.[28]

In fact, as we shall see below, Quebec began negotiating Indigenous land claims in the 1970s before it accepted that it had a legal obligation to do so. Negotiations with the Attikamets, Innu, and other nations have proceeded, on and off, for many years. I will mention just one recent development as an example relevant to the question of nations within Quebec. In 2004, the governments of Canada and Quebec signed an agreement in principle with four Innu First Nations that established a framework for a general land claim and self-government agreement that will, when completed, be a constitutionally-protected treaty.[29] The treaty will not involve the surrender of any Aboriginal rights to the Innu traditional territory, Nitassinan, but rather it will provide for the suspension of certain Innu rights and the articulation of certain other Innu rights, particularly regarding ownership rights over areas known as Innu Assi. The treaty will protect the Innu in the exercise of "Innu Aitun," the pursuit of activies relating to "the national culture, fundamental values and traditional lifestyle of the Innus associated with the occupation and use of Nitassinan" (art. 1.2). The treaty will also recognize rights of self-government. Each First Nation will "adopt its own Constitution" which will have "the status of a fundamental law" binding on the "legislative, executive and judicial" institutions to be established by the Innu (art. 8.1). Broad legislative powers will be acknowledged.

Innu laws will to apply "on Innu Assi and persons thereon," and in certain cases to Innus of the signatory nations on the Nitassinan of these nations, for example, Innu laws relating to the practice of Innu Aitun (8.3.3.). The *Canadian Charter of Rights and Freedoms* will apply to the Innu governments, but each First Nation will also adopt "an Innu Charter of Rights and Freedoms which shall bring out its distinctive philosophy, traditions and cultural practices" (art. 8.4.1.2.). Although federal and provincial laws will continue to apply to the Innu, in certain areas and on certain issues (relating to culture, language, family law, resource use and development) Innu laws will prevail in the event of conflict. It might be tempting to say that here we will have constitutions (Innu) within a constitution (Quebec) within a constitution (Canada); but in fact the Innu constitutions will have a constitutional status derived from a tripartite treaty and so they will really cut across federal-provincial lines.

Land and self-government claims by the Attitakmeks, Algonquins, other Innu communities, and other Indigenous nations in Quebec remain unresolved. Indeed, an Innu agreement would be only the fourth modern land claim treaty in Quebec, and the first in almost forty years. We turn lastly, then, to a brief discussion of the first modern treaties in Quebec – the "James Bay and Northern Quebec Agreement" (1975) and the "Northeastern Quebec Agreement" (1978). These agreements were made with Cree, Inuit, and Naskapi peoples whose traditional territories fell within the massive area of land that was added to the province of Quebec in 1898 and 1912. After doubts were raised by the Crees about the legality of massive hydro-electric developments initiated by the Quebec government in Eeyou Istchee, the Cree traditional territory, the "James Bay and Northern Quebec Agreement" was made between the Crees and Inuit and the governments of Quebec and Canada in 1975 (a similar agreement was made with the Naskapi in 1978).[30] The James Bay Agreement involved the surrender by the Cree and Inuit of their Aboriginal rights to about 410,000 square miles.

For the purposes of this discussion, it is perhaps sufficient to address the impact of the Agreement on the James Bay Crees. The Agreement defines three categories of land. Category I lands (2,158 square miles) are set aside for the exclusive use of eight (now nine) Cree bands, with Category IA lands (1,274 square miles) being under federal legislative authority and Category IB lands (884 square miles) being under provincial legislative authority. Category II lands

(25,130 square miles) are provincial lands under provincial legislative authority in which the Crees have exclusive hunting, fishing, and trapping rights together with certain replacement or compensation rights when resource development interferes with these activities. The remainder of the territory constitutes Category III lands that are provincial lands under provincial legislative authority with more limited Cree rights of hunting, fishing, and trapping. Category IA lands are divided among the nine Cree communities and, like "reserves" under the *Indian Act*, they fall within federal legislative authority; however, unlike reserves, the federal *Indian Act* no longer applies and instead enhanced powers of self-government are conferred upon each Cree band by a federal statute, the *Cree-Naskapi (of Quebec) Act*.[31] Category IB lands are also divided among the nine Cree communities, though in relation to these lands the bands are incorporated by provincial statute as municipal authorities with some powers of local government.[32] Finally, a central Cree body is constituted by provincial law; it was initially called the Cree Regional Authority and given few powers, but, as we shall see below, it has since been renamed and has been given increased powers under both federal and provincial legislation.

Implementation of the Agreement proved controversial, and provincial resource development in Category II and III lands provoked Cree opposition and litigation. In 2002, the "Agreement Concerning a New Relationship" (or "Paix des Braves") was concluded between the Crees and the Quebec government in order to address these concerns.[33] The substance of the Agreement is remarkable (a multi-billion dollar deal stretching over fifty years with increased power to the Crees over resource development), but the language used is significant too. The parties state that the Agreement "marks an important stage in a new nation-to-nation relationship" (art. 2.3), and that "[b] oth the Cree Nation and the Québec Nation agree to place emphasis in their relations on those aspects that unite them as well as on their common desire to continue the development of Northern Québec and the self-fulfilment of the Cree Nation" (art. 2.1).[34]

In 2008, the Crees entered into a "New Relationship Agreement" with the federal government as well.[35] One principal objective of this Agreement is to provide a process for negotiating a governance agreement that would establish "a Cree Nation Government" with powers and authorities beyond those provided by the *Cree-Naskapi (of Quebec) Act* for Category IA lands (art. 2.1(d)). The Agreement provides: "The Cree Nation will develop a Constitution which shall reflect its values and beliefs, be effective as the fundamental law of the Cree Nation, and be consistent with the Governance Agreement" (art. 3.10). The Agreement has already led to increased powers for the Cree Regional Authority over Category IA lands.[36]

Parallel negotiations for enhanced governance powers have taken place on the provincial level. In 2012, the Crees entered an "Agreement on Governance" with the Quebec government. As "another important stage in the new Nation-to-Nation relationship" (Preamble), and "[i]n order to promote the autonomy and development of the Cree Nation" (art. 2), the parties agreed to reconstitute the Cree Regional Authority as the "Cree Nation Government" ("Eeyou Tapayatachesoo" in Cree and "Gouvernement de la nation crie" in French) (art. 12).[37] The Agreement provides for innovative and complex multilevel governance structures for Category II and III lands.[38] In Category III lands, the old municipal governance structure is dismantled and a new regional authority, the Eeyou Istchee James Bay Regional Government, is constituted consisting of equal representation from Cree and "Jamésian" (non-Indigenous) communities. In Category II lands, the Cree Nation Government will have control over land and natural resource planning, development, and municipal government.[39]

This brief discussion should be enough to illustrate the complexity of governance in modern Quebec. Some Indigenous nations assert rights to autonomy under an ancient covenant chain treaty, others are developing their own constitutions under modern land claims settlements, and still others have Aboriginal rights that have yet to be acknowledged through treaty or judicial pronouncement. Even where, as in the case of the James Bay Crees, governance structures are established through federal and provincial statute, there remains within Indigenous nations an unshakeable view that they exercise powers as sovereign nations. Before examining this point, however, we must first return to the question of nationalism in Quebec.

## IV.

If Quebec wants to adopt a written constitution, how could that constitution accurately acknowledge the complex and unfolding constitutional relationship that it has with Indigenous nations, a relationship that is partly tied to tripartite agreements that include the Government of Canada and that embraces both multilevel or co-management governance structures and also internal constitutions for self-governing Indigenous nations? Indeed, because the Constitution of Canada allocates principal responsibility for Indigenous peoples to the federal legislature, and because the constitutional protection of Aboriginal and treaty rights falls within a part of the Constitution that is outside of the meaning of "provincial constitution" as that expression is used in Part V of the *Constitution Act, 1867* and section 45 of the *Constitution Act, 1982*, it is doubtful that a new written provincial constitution for Quebec could include substantive provisions relating to all aspects of the complex relationships that have emerged between Canada, Quebec, and Indigenous nations. Of course, if the constitution-writing exercise in Quebec involves a more ambitious objective than just writing a "provincial constitution," then presumably the new constitution would have to address the reality of Indigenous identities in Quebec. For those advocates of this more ambitious project – for those who see the constitution-writing process as part of a nation-building exercise of (original) constituent power – the place of Indigenous nations within the process raises complex questions.

That there is a deep, rich, and sincere sense of national identity felt within Quebec – that there is *une nation québécoise* – is undoubted. It is, needless to say, far beyond my capacities and the scope of this essay to explain when and how it emerged, how it relates to the idea of an *identité canadienne-française*, or even how it came to include a territorial or spatial dimension that embraces lands that until just over a century ago lay beyond the boundaries of Quebec. To address the idea of constituent power in Quebec, however, I do need at least to touch upon the controversial question of whether Indigenous nations form part of the *nous* that is supposed to express the constitution-making will of *la nation québécoise*.

The theoretical literature on nationalism within Quebec is vast.[40] Even if there is a general sense that Quebec nationalism is now largely a civic nationalism coupled with strong cultural and linguistic elements – that is, that it is a socio-political nationalism – there is no agreement, even among theorists sympathetic to the sovereigntist cause, on what this means for Indigenous nations whose national identities also have civic as well as cultural dimensions. While Gérard Bouchard writes hopefully of a new national memory or narrative that envisages a Quebec nationalism open to diversity, one in which it is possible to say that Indigenous nations are not First Nations but "premiers Québécois," Michel Seymour argues that on socio-political terms Indigenous nations and *la nation québécoise* must be regarded as wholly separate.[41] For Seymour, the idea of forging one nation through the forcible inclusion of other nations is morally corrupt. "En effet," he writes, "il n'existe pas de contrat social véritable qui lie les nations autochtones à la nation québécoise ... [les autochtones] ne semblent pas se percevoir comme des membres de la société québécoise."[42]

Of course, the constitution-making process could be one that consciously seeks to change this state of affairs, that is, to establish a new social compact bringing Indigenous nations within *la nation québécoise*; indeed, perhaps this is what Pelletier has in mind when he argues that it is necessary "que nous déterminions tous ensemble ce que nous sommes" and that the writing of a constitution would encourage this process to unfold. Perhaps. However, as we have seen, the trajectory of the compacts that Quebec has entered into with Indigenous nations all go the other way: agreements with the Cree speak of "the Cree Nation and the Québec Nation" and a "Nation-to-Nation" relationship. These agreements suggest that Indigenous nations are more interested in pursuing inter-national (using that term in a broad rather than technical sense) relations than forging a single national identity.[43]

The position of the Quebec government is less clear. The nation-to-nation expressions to which it has agreed stand beside the statement in the *Loi sur les droits fondamentaux du Québec* (which, as we have seen, Professor Turp describes an an embryonic constitution for Quebec), that "[t]he Québec people has the inalienable right to freely decide the political regime and legal status of Québec." Joseph Facal, who introduced the bill into the National Assembly, explained that the notion "peuple québécois" was intended to be taken "au sens civique du terme" and thus it embraces all persons without distinction living within the territory of Quebec, including Indigenous nations.[44] So does the Quebec people contain a Quebec nation and Indigenous nations? Or does the Quebec nation itself contain Indigenous nations?

On this point, consider one of the bills that has been introduced into the Quebec National Assembly (but not enacted) to establish a written constitution for Quebec:

> NOUS, PEUPLE DU QUÉBEC,
> CONSIDÉRANT que les Québécois et les Québécoises forment une nation et que le Québec est une nation francophone;
> CONSIDÉRANT la presence au Québec des Premières Nations et de la nations inuite;
> CONSIDÉRANT l'existence de la communauté angophone du Québec;
> CONSIDÉRANT l'apport des Québécois et les Québécoises de toute origine au développement du Québec.[45]

Here, it is unclear whether Indigenous or First Nations are part of the Quebec nation or not, but it is clear that the "nous, peuple du Québec" who, through their parliament, were to have made this constitution, purported to do so for or on behalf of Indigenous nations and everyone else within Quebec's borders. Consider also, in this respect, a 2011 Quebec government document that explains that the eleven Indigenous nations of Quebec "cohabitent avec la nation québécoise," and then proceeds to explain "l'évolution de leurs relations avec la nation québécoise"; that relationships with them have led to "la création d'une société nouvelle, faite de multiples influences"; and, finally: "Aujourd'hui plus que jamais, l'identité québécoise se construit et s'affirme dans le respect des différences. Ainsi, l'avenir d'un Québec prospère, juste et équitable réside dans la convergence des efforts des nations autochtones et de la nation québécoise ainsi que dans la coexistence pacifique de leurs droits respectifs."[46] In these various documents, subtle but important distinctions are thus being drawn between the concepts of "people," "nation," "society," and "identity" – but there is little doubt, from the non-Indigenous governmental perspective, where ultimate sovereignty lies.[47]

## V.

Indigenous peoples also make claims of peoplehood, nationhood, and sovereignty. The Crees issued the following statement in October of 1995:

> We are Eeyou.
> We are a sovereign Peoples.
> We are the original inhabitants of Eeyou Estchee and are one

> with Eeyou Estchee. Our power derives from the Creator, from the Eeyou and from the living spirit of the land and waters.
> [...]
> We have the inherent right to self-determination and the right to govern ourselves. We have a distinct identity reflected in a distinct system of laws and government, philosophy, language, culture, heritage, values, customs, traditions, beliefs and territory.
> [...]
> We do not accept the status quo regarding our present relationships with Quebec and Canada. Cree consent is required and mandatory for any changes to our status as Eeyou or to the status of Eeyou Estchee.
> As Peoples with a right to self-determination, we shall freely decide our political status and associations and freely pursue our future as a people.
> We will assert and defend our inherent right of self-determination and the protection of Eeyou and Eeyou Estchee.[48]

Other Indigenous nations have issued similar statements, as has the Quebec Assembly of First Nations.[49]

Although the various governance rights exercised by the Crees described above may be seen, from one perspective, to be powers delegated to them by federal and provincial statute, from another perspective these powers emanate from the treaty pursuant to which these statutes are made, and so arguably they emanate from the inherent capacities of the Crees as a nation or people. There is some support for this view legally.

In the judicial and academic writing on Aboriginal rights in Canada, the case of *Eastmain Band v. Gilpin* is not often referenced. It is a lower court decision, a judgment of (what was then called) the Quebec Court of Sessions of the Peace. But it deserves more attention than it has received. Justice Denis Lavergne, in reviewing the legality of a curfew by-law passed by the Eastmain Cree Band Council, considered the general legal character of the governmental powers exercised by Cree communities under the *Cree-Naskapi (of Quebec) Act*. Counsel for the Cree had submitted in this case, first, that the statute was merely a "legislative expression" of Cree rights recognized in the James Bay Treaty, and that these rights had become constitutionally-protected "treaty rights" by virtue of section 35 of the *Constitution Act, 1982*; second, that the law-making powers exercised by Cree bands pursuant to the act "are not delegated to them by the Parliament of Canada but stem from their own internal, residual sovereignty and are recognized, not created, by Parliament in the Act"; and, third, that therefore general principles of administrative law regarding the delegation of powers are inapplicable because a Cree band exercises its law-making authority "pursuant to its own internal sovereignty, not as a result of delegation by another sovereign body."[50] Justice Lavergne hesitated about this argument. It seemed to him at first that the idea that there might be "Native sovereignty" over the land occupied by the Crees was somehow inconsistent "with our country's history." However, once he analysed the Treaty and the implementing legislation, it became clear to him that the Cree "power of self-government" was wholly unlike subordinate legislative power delegated by statute to a municipal or administrative body. Here was a self-government power arising from treaty that was made with a "distinct social and cultural group," a power that was now, at least in certain areas, beyond the reach of ordinary federal or provincial legislative authority. "In this perspective," Justice Lavergne said, "the Court agrees with the proposition that the Crees hold some sort of residual sovereignty as regards their local governments."

The conclusion in *Eastmain Band v. Gilpin*, that the Crees retain some kind of residual sovereignty, has never been explicitly rejected by the higher courts. Indeed, the *Eastmain* case has been cited with apparent approval by other judges, albeit without direct reference to the point about "residual sovereignty."[51] It is worth noting as well that the Crees have pressed the sovereignty argument in other cases. In litigation concerning the proposed Great Whale hydroelectric project, the Crees again argued that they exercised "internal sovereignty on their traditional lands," sovereignty which they said excluded the jurisdiction of either federal or provincial authorities to intervene without their consent. Although they did not need to resolve this point in the case before them, and they did not cite *Eastmain*, three judges of the Quebec Court of Appeal, including two future Supreme Court of Canada justices, did observe that the constitutionalization of Aboriginal rights in Canada in 1982 appeared to "introduce a third component in the operation of Canadian federalism which should be taken into account in the distribution of powers between the provincial legislatures and the Parliament of Canada."[52] It is also worth observing that the *Eastmain* case is broadly consistent with the conclusion reached in the case of *Campbell v. British Columbia*, that Indigenous peoples are "independent nations and political communities whose sovereign rights were diminished rather than extinguished by the assertion of [Crown] sovereignty"; that "a right to self-government akin to a legislative power to make laws, survived as one of the unwritten 'underlying values' of the [Candadian] Constitution outside of the powers distributed to Parliament and the [provincial] legislatures [by the *British North America Act*] in 1867"; and that modern treaties (in this case the Nisga'a Treaty in British Columbia) could give these values concrete legal effect.[53]

These lower court opinions have received some support at the highest levels. After citing the American cases on tribal sovereignty as well as the decision of *Campbell v. British Columbia*, Justice Binnie (with Justice Major), in a 2001 case involving the Mohawks of Akwesasne, left open the possibility that there might be in Canada, as in the United States, a residual sphere of Indigenous sovereignty forming the basis of meaningful Indigenous governmental and legislative powers today.[54] Then, in 2004, the Supreme Court of Canada rendered its historic decisions in the cases of *Haida Nation* and *Taku River*. Writing for a unanimous Court, Chief Justice Beverley McLachlin stated that modern treaties serve "to reconcile pre-existing Aboriginal sovereignty with assumed Crown sovereignty," or "*de facto* Crown sovereignty," the respective "sovereignty claims" being "reconciled through the process of honourable negotiation."[55] So, when in 2004 Justice Lavergne, now sitting as a judge of the Court of Quebec, Civil Division, cited with approval his own conclusion from the case of *Eastmain Band v. Gilpin* twenty years before, that the James Bay Crees exercised "some sort of residual sovereignty as regards their local governments," he remained on solid legal ground.[56]

Once the terms of treaties are examined in light of the evolving jurisprudence of the courts, I think it is possible to say that the concept of "nation" when used in relation to the Indigenous peoples of Canada and Quebec is much more than a socio-political concept. It is a legal-constitutional concept that implies certain inherent rights of self-determination or a "residual sovereignty." It is difficult to see how this conclusion could not affect in profound ways the task of writing a constitution for Quebec.

## VI.

I began this essay by stating that I was uneasy about the general idea of constitution-making. Constitutionally-formative moments can be healthy for peoples and nations. However, when deep divisions exist about who the people are who are making the constitution, committing a particular constitutional vision to writing may prove damaging. It may close down prematurely or unjustly avenues of constitutional development that might otherwise have emerged through unwritten or less formal ways. There remains a palpable sense of constitutional loss – the loss, though perhaps not forever, of a particular vision of Canadian federalism – resulting from the last major round of constitution-writing in Canada.[57] I have no doubt that a written constitution could accommodate the complex ideas that underlie the simultaneous assertions by peoples in Quebec of "We are Eeyou" and "Nous, du Québec." Accommodation of unity and diversity, of the multiple allegiances we all have to different communities, is what the principle of federalism, in its biggest sense, can allow.[58] However, I do wonder whether the conditions in Quebec exist just now for accommodation like this on the grand scale of constitution-writing.

There is a deeper theoretical concern that I have about the idea of constituent power that informs my conclusions in this respect. I should be clear: my concern is not with the incommensurability of visions about identity or sovereignty. Jeremy Webber has recently argued, with considerable care and force, that Canada has sustained a polity without needing to define a single constitutional vision for its members; that fundamental questions of identity and even sovereignty can be, and have been, held in abeyance and unanswered; and that instead of judges or legislators dictating substantive outcomes or attempting to produce a comprehensive and unified theory of constitutionalism, judges and legislators have tended, where possible, to articulate strategies or frameworks for an on-going dialogue between political actors directed toward pragmatic forms of accommodation.[59] "This might be called," Webber writes, "*agonistic constitutionalism*: a constitutionalism in which contending positions are seen to be essential to the society, animating it, and where these positions are not neatly contained within a comprehensive, overarching theory."[60]

Strategically, at least, I agree. It is often best to decline to make monolithic and authorative pronoucements of constitutional absolutes in favour of a discursive, delibertative approach. But at the level of theory there is a problem. The concept of agonism in democratic theory is ultimately based upon a sense that pluralistic views of the good are always incommensurable and no rational basis can exist for their coordination or accommodation.[61] Within this view, endless dialogue is the best we can do with only contingent and transient power-based accommodations possible. The agonistic view of democracy is often traced back to the constitutional theory of Schmitt – that is, that, in the end, constituent or sovereign power is purely a matter of power, wholly uncontrained by law, and it is exercised to determine who is in and who is out of the "people" or "nation," who is friend and who is enemy.[62] Despite attempts by leading agonists to soften this view of constituent power by suggesting that the very exercise of sovereignty is constrained by internal juridical limits concerning the public good, the theory still denies the aspirational ideal of legality or the rule of law.[63]

The difficulty with the idea of constituent power, I think, is that it is premised upon an anemic conception of law that is thoroughly linear in essence: legal rules must be traced back in linear fashion to an originating source external to law; law must have someone or something to hold up the string of legal rules for the system. However, to posit the existence of a source of law that is not law is, in the end, to deny the normative value of legality or the rule of law. Once law is conceived in a circular fashion, or, in other words, as an interpretive enterprise that seeks to understand legal rules in light of the underlying principles that they presuppose in a way that brings a sense of integrity or equilibrium to the body of legal rules and priniciples considered, a discursive enterprise that constantly reassesses what we accept as law with what we expect of law, then the idea of an extralegal source for law, or a constituent power, including the constitution of a people or nation, ceases to have any real meaning.[64] Constitutions may still have to be written, of course, but the task of writing a constitution, which may indeed include an attempt to identify the people whose constitution it is, will be seen as an effort to interpret what constitutionalism, or legality, means for the people or peoples affected – a distinctively rational, normative, and legal enterprise, though, we may add, a legally ordinary enterprise, in that it engages ordinary legal interpretive methods.

There is an answer about how to accommodate Indigenous and Quebecois nationalism, but we can only find it by engaging in an interpretive enterprise that seeks to show how our conclusions in this respect cohere with the general values of equality and integrity that these conclusions presuppose. To write a constitution for Quebec that fully accommodates the complex and dynamic normative realities of Indigenous governance in a morally justifiable way would, I think, be possible in theory, if one were (as the legal philosopher Ronald Dworkin would say) a juridical Hercules.[65] However, for mere mortals, I think it might be best for that constitution to evolve, in the incremental fashion that legal interpretation enables, as our sense of integrity and justice and our appreciation for the diversity and the unity of views about equality and respect for others deepen and converge over time and with experience.

## NOTES

1 Emmanuel Joseph Sieyès, *Qu'est-ce que le Tiers état?* 1789 (Paris: Éditions du Boucher, 2002); Emmanuel Joseph Sieyès, *What is the Third Estate?*, ed. S.E. Finer and trans. M. Blondel (London: Phaidon Press Ltd., 1964).

2 Robert M. Cover, "The Supreme Court 1982 Term Forward: *Nomos* and Narrative," *Harvard Law Review* 97, no. 1 (1983): 4–68.

3 *Constitution Act, 1867*, 30 & 31 Vict. c. 3 (UK).

4 *Att. Gen. of Quebec v. Blaikie et al*, [1979] 2 SCR 1016; *Ontario (Attorney General) v. OPSEU*, [1987] 2 SCR 2.

5 *Constitution Act, 1982*, being Schedule B to the *Canada Act, 1982* (UK), 1982, c. 11 s. 45: "Subject to section 41, the legislature of each province may exclusively make laws amending the constitution of the province."

6 Benoît Pelletier, *Une certaine idée du Québec: Parcours d'un federaliste. De la réflexion à l'action* (Québec: Presses de l'Université Laval, 2010), 169 (adoption of the constitution would represent "l'affirmation solennelle des assises de l'État québécois et conférer au texte à venir une autorité morale certaine, bref, établir un réel contrat social").

7 Ibid., 172.

8 Michel Seymour, "La nation québécoise peut-elle se donner la constitution de son choix?" *Revue Québecoise de Droit International* 28, no. June Special Issue (2015): 341–58.

9 Daniel Turp, "Le pouvoir constituant et la constitution du Québec" in Eugénie Brouillet and Patrick Taillon, eds. *Un regard québécois sur le droit constitutionnel. Mélanges en l'honneur d'Henri Brun et de Guy Tremblay* (Montréal: Éditions Yvon Blais, 2016).

10 Kemal Gözler, *Pouvoir constituant* (Bursa, Turquie: Éditions Ekin Kitabevi, 1999).

11 Daniel Turp, *La Constitution québécoise: Essais sur le droit du Québec de se doter de sa proper loi fondamentale* (Montréal: Éditions JFD, 2013), 591–603.

12 Hans Lindahl, "Constituent Power and Reflexive Identity: Towards an Ontology of Collective Selfhood," in *The Paradox of Constitutionalism: Constituent Power and Constitutional Form*, eds. Martin Loughlin and Neil Walker (Oxford: Oxford University Press, 2007), 9–24.

13 Turp, *La Constitution québécoise*, 222 (referring to *Loi sur l'exercise des droits fondamentaux et des prerogatives du people québécois et de l'État du Québec*, RSQ E-20.2, as "l'esquissse du texte d'une Constitution du Québec").

14 *Reference re Secession of Quebec*, [1998] 2 SCR 217.

15 Carl Schmitt, *Constitutional Theory* [1928], trans. J. Seitzer (Durham: Duke University Press, 2008); Carl Schmitt, *The Concept of the Political* [1932], trans. G. Schwab (Chicago: University of Chicago Press, 2007).

16 Daniel Turp, *La Constitution québécoise*, 364.

17 Québec, Assemblée nationale, *Journal des débats* (19 March 1985), 2,533.

18 Denys Delâge, "Les Iroquois chrétiens des 'réductions', 1667–1770," *Recherches Amérindiennes au Québec* 21, no. 1–2 (1991): 59–70; Jean-Pierre Sawaya, *La fédération des sept feux de la vallée du Saint-Laurent: XVIIe-XIXe Siècle* (Sillery: Les Éditions du Septentrion, 1998), 21–3; Denys Delâge and Jean-Pierre Sawaya, *Les Traités des Sept-Feux Avec Les Britanniques: Droits et Pièges d'un Héritage Colonial au Québec* (Sillery: Les Éditions du Septentrion, 2001), 13, 18; Lucie Gill, "La nation abénaquise et la question territorial," *Recherches Amérindiennes au Québec* 33, no. 2 (2003): 71–4; M. Jean Black, "A Tale of Two Ethnicities: Identity and Ethnicity at Lake of Two Mountains, 1721–1850," in *Papers of the Twenty-Fourth Algonquian Conference*, ed. William Cowan (Ottawa: Carleton University, 1993), 1–7; Jan Grabowski, "The Common Ground: Settled Natives and French in Montréal, 1667–1760" (PhD thesis, Université de Montréal, 1993), 81–4.

19 Michel Morin, *L'Usurpation de la souveraineté autochtone: Le cas des peuples de la Nouvell-France et des colonies anglaises de l'Amérique du Nord* (Québec: Éditions du Boréal, 1997); W.J. Eccles, "Sovereignty-Association, 1500–1783," *Canadian Historical Review* 65, no. 4 (1984): 475–510, at 487–8; Jan Grabowski, "French Criminal Justice and Indians in Montreal, 1670–1760," *Ethnohistory* 43, no. 3 (1996): 405–29; Denys Delâge and Étienne Gilbert, "Les Amérindiens face à la justice coloniale française dans le gouvernement de Québec, 1663–1759," *Recherches Amérindiennes au Québec* 33, no. 3 (2003): 79–90.

20 See "Council, Montreal [Caughnawaga] 16 September 1760," in James Sullivan, ed., *The Papers of Sir William Johnson* (Albany: State University of New York, 1921–65), vol. XIII, 163–6. See also Jean-Pierre Sawaya, *Alliance et dépendance: comment la couronne britannique a obtenu la collaboration des Indiens de la vallée du Saint-Laurent entre 1760–1774* (Sillery, Québec: Septentrion, 2002), 20–4.

21 Sir W. Johnson to D. Claus, 20 May 1761, National Archives of Canada, MG19 (Claus Papers), vol. 1, 48–9.

22 "Sir W. Johnson to the Lords of Trade, 25 September 1763," in E.B. O'Callaghan, ed., *Documents Relative to the Colonial History of the State of New York* (Albany, NY: Weed, Parsons, & Co, 1856–1861), vol. VII, 559–62, and "Message of the Canada [Indians] to the Western Indians, August 1763," vol. VII, 544–5.

23 Mark D. Walters, "Brightening the Covenant Chain: Aboriginal Treaty Meanings in Law and History after Marshall," *Dalhousie Law Journal* 24, no. 2 (2001): 75–138; Mark D. Walters, "'Your Sovereign and Our Father': The Imperial Crown and the Idea of Legal-Ethnohistory," in *Law and Politics in British Colonial Thought: Transpositions of Empire*, eds. Shaunnagh Dorsett and Ian Hunter (Houndmills: Palgrave Macmillan, 2010), 91–108.

24 *Indian Act*, RSC 1985, c. I-5.

25 *R. v. Sioui*, [1990] 1 SCR 1025 at 1,052–3.

26 Mark D. Walters, "The Aboriginal Charter of Rights: The Royal Proclamation of 1763 and the Constitution of Canada," in *Creating Canada: From the Royal Proclamation of 1763 to Modern Treaties*, eds. Terry Fenge and Jim Aldridge (Montreal and Kingston: McGill-Queen's University Press, 2015).

27 E.g., *St Catharines Milling and Lumber Co. v. The Queen* (1886) 13 SCR 577, esp. the reasons of Justice, Sir Henri-Elzear Taschereau.

28 *R. v.* Côté, [1996] 3 SCR 139, Lamer CJC at para. 53: "[T]he [Québec government's] proposed interpretation risks undermining the very purpose of s. 35(1) [of the *Constitution Act, 1982*] by perpetuating the historical injustice suffered by Aboriginal peoples at the hands of colonizers who failed to respect the distinctive cultures of pre-existing Aboriginal societies."

29 *Agreement-in-Principle of General Nature between the First Nations of Mamuitun and Nutashukuan and the Governments of Canada and Quebec* (2004), accessed 23 February 2016, http://www.aadnc-aandc.gc.ca/eng/1100100031951/1100100032043 .

30 Government of Quebec, *James Bay and Northern Québec Agreement and Complementary Agreements* (Québec: Les Publications du Québec, 1998).

The agreement which was implemented by federal and provincial legislation: *James Bay and Northern Quebec Native Claims Settlement Act*, SC 1976–77, c. 32; *Act approving the Agreement concerning James Bay and Northern Québec*, SQ 1976, c. 46.

31 SC 1983–1984, c. 18.

32 *The Cree Villages and the Naskapi Village Act*, SQ 1978, c. 88, RSQ c. V-5.1.

33 *Agreement Concerning a New Relationship Between le Gouvernement du Québec and the Crees of Québec* (2002), accessed 23 February 2016, http://www.autochtones.gouv.qc.ca/relations_autochtones/ententes/cris/entente- 020207_en.pdf .

34 See in general Caroline Desbiens, "Nation to Nation: Defining New Structures of Development in Northern Quebec," *Economic Geography* 80, no. 4 (2004): 351–66.

35 *Agreement Concerning a New Relationship Between the Government of Canada and the Cree of Eeyou Istchee* (2008), accessed 23 February 2016 http://www.ainc-inac.gc.ca/ al/ldc/ccl/agr/croei/agrnr-eng.pdf.

36 *An Act to amend the Cree-Naskapi (of Quebec) Act*, SC 2009, c. 12.

37 *Agreement on Governance in the Eeyou Istchee James Bay Territory between the Crees of Eeyou Istchee and the Government of Québec* (2012).

38 *An Act Respecting the Cree Nation Government*, RSQ G-1.031; *An Act Establishing the Eeyou Istchee James Bay Regional Government*, RSQ G-1.04.

39 On these developments, see Brain Craik, "Multilevel Regional Governance in the Eeyou Istchee James Bay Territory," in *Aboriginal Multilevel Governance*, eds. Martin Papillon and André Juneau (Montreal & Kingston: McGill-Queen's University Press, 2015), 99–108.

40 For an overview, see Simon Langlois, "Refondation de la nation au Québec," in *L'annuaire du Québec* 2003, dirs Roch Côté and Michel Venne (Montréal: Fides, 2002), 5–26.

41 Gérard Bouchard, *La Nation québécoise au futur et au passé* (Montréal: VLB éditeur, 1999), 117; Michel Seymour, *La Nation en question* (Montréal: Hexagone, 1999), 16.

42 Ibid., 178. See also, Fernand Dumont, *Raisons communes* (Montréal: Boréal, 1995), 63–4.

43 See, for example, Ghislain Picard, Chief of the Assembly of First Nations of Quebec and Labrador: "it is time to set things straight … First Nations members are not Quebecers and are able to decide their own future"; Assembly of First Nations Quebec-Labrador, "Quebec Sovereignty: First

Nations Will Decide Their Future," press release, 14 March 2014, accessed 24 February 2016, http://www.apnql-afnql.com/en/actualites/pdf/comm-2014-03-14.pdf.

44 Journal des débats (*Hansard*) of the Committee on Institutions, 1st Sess., 36th Leg., vol. 36, no. 80, 30 May 2000. The sovereigntist view has been to define *la nation québécoise* in a manner that integrates civic with ethnic or cultural nationalism, and to insist that all citizens within Quebec are part of the nation; on this view, Indigenous peoples are, along with the anglophone community, one of the so-called historic minorities within the Quebec nation: Daniel Salée, "L'État québécois et la question autochtone," in *Québec: État et société*, vol. II, ed. Alain-G. Gagnon (Montréal: Les Éditions Québec/Amérique, 2003), 117–47, 129, 144–5. See also Claude Bariteau, "Pour une conception civique du Québec," *L'Action nationale* 76, no 7 (1996): 105–168 at 156 – argues that the Quebec nation is a civic nation, and Indigenous peoples belong to it.

45 *Constitution québécoise*, "Projet de loi no 196," [Bill 196] 18 October 2007.

46 *Améindiens* et Inuits: Portrait des nations autochtones du Québec, 2nd ed. (Gouvernement du Québec, 2011), 5, 6, 47.

47 We may note, on this point, that in the debates on the resolution passed by the Canadian House of Commons recognizing "that the Québécois form a nation within a united Canada" ("que les Québécoises et les Québécois forment une nation au sein d'un Canada uni") the question of who "the Québécois" are was avoided by most members of Parliament: Canada, House of Commons Debates, *Hansard*, 39th Parliament, 1st Sess., no. 087, 27 November 2006.

48 "Eeyou Estchee Declaration of Principles," 19 October 1995, accessed 23 February 2016, http://www.gcc.ca/gcc/other.php.

49 "Déclaration de souveraineté d'Atikamekw Nehirowisiw," 8 September 2014, 18, accessed February 2016, http://www.atikamekwsipi.com/fichiers/File/declaration_souverainete_signe.pdf. See also Assembly of the First Nations of Quebec and Labrador Chiefs' Assembly, "Declaration on a First Nations of Quebec and Larador Sovereignty Affirmation Process," 27 November 2008, accessed 24 February 2016, http://www.apnql-afnql.com/en/actualites/pdf/comm-2008-11-27.pdf.

50 *Eastmain Band v. Gilpin*, [1987] RJQ 1637, 3 CNLR 54 (Que. Prov. Ct).

51 *Cree Regional Authority v. Robinson*, [1991] 4 CNLR 84 (Fed. Ct Tr. Div.), per Justice Rouleau (citing the case for the proposition that the James Bay Treaty is now constitutionally protected); *Tawich Development Corporation v. Deputy Minister of Revenue of Quebec*, [1997] 2 CNLR 187 (Que. Ct C

Div.), per Vermette JQC at para. 20 (acknowledging the support for the Cree position on residual sovereignty found in *Eastmain Band v. Gilpin*); *Cree School Board v. Canada (Attorney General)*, [1998] 3 CNLR 24 (Que. Sup. Ct), per Croteau SCJ at para. 160 ("*Eastmain Band v. Gilpin* ... discuss[es] the nature and scope of the JBNQ Agreement"); this decision was affirmed on appeal, though no mention was made of *Eastmain*: *Cree School Board v. Canada (Attorney General)*, [2002] 1 CNLR 112 (Que. CA); leave to appeal denied [2001] CSCR no 563.

52 *Hydro-Quebec v. Canada (AG) and Coon Come*, [1991] RJQ 922, [1991] 3 CNLR 40 (Que. CA), per LeBel JA at CNLR 59–60 (Vallerand and Fish JJA concurring).

53 *Campbell v. British Columbia (Attorney General)*, [2000] BCJ No 1524, 2000 BCSC 1123, 189 DLR (4th) 333 (BCSC), per Justice Williamson at paras 93, 81.

54 *Mitchell v. MNR*, 2001 SCC 331, [2001] SCR 911, per Justice Binnie (Justice Major concurring) at paras 134–5, quoting the Royal Commission on Aboriginal Peoples, *Final Report*, vol. 2 at 214.

55 *Haida Nation v. British Columbia (Minister of Forests)*, 2004 SCC 73, [2004] 3 SCR 511 at para. 20; *Taku River Tlingit First Nation v. British Columbia (Project Assessment Director)*, 2004 SCC 74, [2004] 3 SCR 550 at para. 42.

56 *Danyluk v. Wemindji Band (Wemindji Eeyou)*, [2004] 1 CNLR 87 (Que. Ct C Div.) at para. 75.

57 Jean-François Gaudreault-DesBiens, "The 'Principle of Federalism' and the Legacy of the Patriation and Quebec Veto References," *Supreme Court Law Review* (2d) 54 (2011): 77–115.

58 Mark D. Walters, "Federalism in Its Biggest Sense: Justice Louis LeBel and the Federal Idea in Canadian Constitutional Law," *Supreme Court Law Review* (2d) 70 (2015): 307–36.

59 Jeremy Webber, *The Constitution of Canada: A Contextual Analysis* (Oxford and Portland: Hart Publishing, 2015), 8.

60 Ibid. (emphasis added).

61 Chantal Mouffe, *The Democratic Paradox* (New York: Verso, 2000); Chantal Mouffe, *Agonistics: Thinking the World Politically* (London and New York: Verso, 2013).

62 Chantal Mouffe, *On the Political* (Abingdon and New York: Routledge, 2005); Chantal Mouffe, "Democracy and Pluralism: A Critique of the Rationalist Approach," *Cardozo Law Review* 16, no. 5 (1995): 1533–46; Chantal Mouffe, "Carl Schmitt and the Paradox of Liberal Democracy," *Canadian Journal of Law & Jurisprudence* 10, no. 1 (1997): 21–33.

63 Martin Loughlin, *Foundations of Public Law* (Oxford: Oxford University Press, 2010); Martin Loughlin, "The Concept of Constituent Power," *European Journal of Political Theory* 13, no. 2 (2014): 218–37. For a critique of Loughlin's views, see Mark D. Walters, "Is Public Law Ordinary?" *Modern Law Review* 75, no. 5 (2012): 899–918; David Dyzenhaus, "Constitutionalism in an Old Key: Legality and Constituent Power," *Global Constitutionalism* 1, no. 2 (2012): 229–60; David Dyzenhaus, "The Question of Constituent Power," in *The Paradox of Constitutionalism: Constituent Power and Constitutional Form*, eds. Martin Loughlin and Neil Walker (Oxford: Oxford University Press, 2007), 129.

64 See for greater elaboration of these ideas, Mark D. Walters, "The Unwritten Constitution as a Legal Concept" in *The Philosophical Foundations of Constitutional Law*, eds. David Dyzenhaus and Malcolm Thorburn (Oxford: Oxford University Press, 2016), 33–52.

65 Ronald Dworkin, *Law's Empire* (Cambridge, MA: Belknap Press of Harvard University Press, 1986).

# 7

# Why Alberta Needs a Constitution

*F.L. Morton*

## INTRODUCTION

Both Quebec and more recently Alberta have shown interest in developing modern, democratic provincial constitutions. Quebec nationalists and sovereigntists have discussed the idea of a Quebec constitution for several decades.[1] In Alberta, citizens unhappy with their province's treatment by the federal government have advocated a provincial constitution as part of a package of "home rule" reforms to strengthen the political autonomy of the province.[2]

In Alberta, a constitution is also seen as a means of reigning in spiraling government spending and debt. Alberta enters the third decade of the twenty-first century with an accumulated public debt of over $59 billion dollars and the highest per capita deficit of any Canadian province.[3] This is a far cry from 2005, when then Premier Ralph Klein announced that Alberta was "debt free"; made the first deposit of energy revenues in the Heritage Fund in twenty years; and enacted a balanced budget law (BBL) that was intended to prevent future governments from ever running deficits again. This statutory BBL lasted only as long as oil prices remained above $100 per barrel. It was amended in Budget 2009 to allow temporary deficits. Since then, five different premiers from three different parties chose to run large budget deficits to fund large spending increases with the hope of winning their next elections.

Alberta's experience proves that statutory rules are not sufficient to protect a positive fiscal legacy. Alberta's balanced budget law, flat tax rates, and protections of the Heritage Fund were all removed by simple majority votes in the Alberta legislature. Any meaningful re-instatement of these policies will require that they be put beyond the reach of future governments of whatever party – that is, that they be constitutionally entrenched.

Such reforms should have a special urgency for the recently elected United Conservative Party (UCP) government of Premier Jason Kenney. When the UCP defeated the New Democratic Party (NDP) government of Premier Rachel Notley in 2019, the Kenney government inherited a $40 billion dollar debt and annual structural deficit of $8 billion dollars. Ironically, the four year NDP spending spree was made possible by the fiscal achievements of the Klein era (1993–2006) – elimination of the provincial debt and the highest savings, the lowest corporate and personal taxes, and the highest credit rating of any Canadian province. The NDP government was able to use Alberta's top credit rating to borrow billions of dollars to build new schools, roads and hospitals, and increase the size of the public sector workforce – all with the aim of winning re-election in the 2019 election.

Kenney defeated the NDP by campaigning on the promise of a return to fiscal responsibility and a balanced budget by 2023. This would have been no easy task – even before the Covid crisis and the collapse of the Alberta energy sector in 2020. But budget cuts and tax increases by themselves will not be enough. The Kenney government will also have to put some meaningful constitutional fences around future tax increases or deficit spending, or both. They will also have to politician-proof the Heritage Fund from future vote-hungry governments. Failure to enact such reforms risks simply setting the fiscal table – again – for the NDP to win the next election with big spending promises made possible by the UCP's fiscal discipline.

This is not just an Alberta problem, but a problem faced by all democratically elected governments. Very few governments choose to pursue a policy of long-term public good – for example, balanced budgets – if the short-term effect is to increase the risk of electoral defeat in the next election. In democratic politics, short-term electoral self-interest almost always trumps longer-term public interest.

This chapter explains how the failure to entrench such rules led to Alberta's current $70 billion deficit-debt spiral; how balanced budget laws (BBLs) and tax and expenditure limitations (TELs) could be used to ensure greater fiscal responsibility in the future; why these rules must be constitutionally entrenched, not statutory; some of the problems associated with a provincial constitution; and how those problems might be resolved.

Specifically, these last two sections reach the same conclusion as Daniel Turp's contribution to this book: that the power to appoint provincial judges must be returned to provincial governments. If the goal is increased political autonomy, what sense does it make to have a provincial constitution whose final interpretation – and thus meaning – is made by nine justices on the Supreme Court in Ottawa?

## BUILDING THE ALBERTA ADVANTAGE: THE KLEIN ACHIEVEMENT, 1993–2006

By the early 1990s, the Alberta government's fiscal ineptitude had reached its apogee. Through runaway program and capital spending, the government had amassed $22.7 billion in debt. With its financial profligacy threating its grip on power, the Progressive Conservative Party of Alberta (PCA) opportunistically used a leadership change to try to get government finances – and its own electoral prospects – back on track.

In 1992, political outsider Ralph Klein won the PC leadership race, and launched what would come to be known as the "Klein Revolution" in Alberta politics. Choosing market forces over political micromanagement to grow the economy, Klein cut spending; eliminated the deficit (*Deficit Elimination Act, 1993*); made it illegal for a government to have a deficit (*Balanced Budget and Debt Elimination Act, 1995*); increased transparency in the government's accounting practices (*Government Accountability Act, 1995*); required a referendum before any future government could introduce a sales tax (*Tax Payer Protection Act, 1995*); and privatized a number of services (liquor sales, motor vehicle licensing).

In 1996, the Klein government enacted the *Business Financial Assistance Limitations Act* to stop loans, loan guarantees, and outright subsidies to business (the exception being small businesses),[4] and lived up to its new mantra – "Government is not in the business of business" – by turning off the taps on a number of diversification initiatives and divested the government of its interest in a number of others. In 1999, the Klein government enacted the *Fiscal Responsibility Act*, which prohibited budget deficits (operating and capital) and forbade borrowing.

In 2002, Klein appointed a private commission to advise the government on how to avoid Alberta's petro-state, boom-bust, surplus-deficit syndrome. The subsequent report recommended the creation of a new savings account, in addition to the Heritage Savings Fund, "to provide for a gradual but sustained reduction in our reliance on natural resource revenues and a focused attempt to build financial and other strategic assets to maintain and improve the Alberta Advantage."[5]

The Klein government responded by amending Alberta's *Fiscal Responsibility Act* to create a new "Sustainability Fund" that would alleviate the stop-and-go capital spending patterns of preceding years.[6] Under the amendment, only the first $3.5 billion of resource revenues would be allowed to go into general revenues. The rest, if any, would be allocated to the new Sustainability Fund, which would be available to cover any budget deficits if energy revenues did not reach $3.5 billion in a future year. For example, the "balanced budgets" reported by the Stelmach government in 2008 and 2009, were actually cash expenditure deficits, and were only "balanced" through the use of transfers from the Sustainability Fund. The maximum balance of the Sustainability Fund was initially capped at $2.5 billion.[7]

In 2005, the $23-billion-dollar net debt inherited in 1993 was officially paid off, and Klein celebrated Alberta's new "debt free" status and budget surplus by sending out $400 "Prosperity Bonus cheques" – or "Ralph Bucks" – to every Alberta resident. With respect to the future, Klein proudly declared: "Never again will this government or the people of this province have to set aside another tax dollar on debt ... Those days are over and they're over for good, as far as my government is concerned, and if need be we will put in place legislation to make sure that we never have a debt again."[8] But within only four years, Budget 2009, the law prohibiting deficits was repealed, and Alberta has not had a balanced budget since.[9]

Ed Stelmach succeeded Klein as premier in 2006, and by 2007 and 2008 virtually every resource dollar was being spent. When energy prices crashed in the wake of the 2008 financial crisis, so did government revenues. In a scenario eerily similar to the Lougheed-Getty era, the PC governments of Ed Stelmach and Allison Redford and Jim Prentice began to run "temporary" budget deficits. By the time they were defeated in 2015, the Stelmach-Redford-Prentice PC governments ran seven consecutive deficits and burned through over $16 billion dollars in savings in the now defunct Sustainability Fund, which Redford abolished in her 2013 budget. Indeed, measured by the overall decline in net financial assets, the loss was even greater – from $35 billion dollars in 2008 to $3.9 billion in 2015.[10]

## NDP BUDGETS 2015–19: $40 BILLION DOLLARS OF BORROWING

Rachel Notley's new NDP government did not invent spending money it does not have. The PC governments of Stelmach and Redford had already paved the way to deficit spending well before the NDP's surprise victory in May, 2015. During the last decade of PC governments (2004–15), program spending doubled, increasing almost two times faster than population growth plus inflation.[11] What was novel about Premier Notley's NDP budgets is how they were financed: over $70 billion dollars of borrowing – all on the back of the Triple AAA credit rating she inherited from her PC predecessors.

Since its election in 2015, the NDP government posted budget deficits of $10.8 billion, $8 billion, $6.7 billion, and $12.2 billion. When measured as a percentage of provincial gross domestic product, the 2017 deficit was 4.2 per cent, which made it the largest deficit in Canada. The Dominion Bond Rating Agency downgraded Alberta's long-term debt from "stable" to "negative," noting that "[t]he Negative trend reflects the fact that Alberta continues to erode its low debt advantage through sustained deficit spending. Moreover, the Province has yet to provide a credible plan to restore balance. ... [T]he fiscal plan demonstrates a lack of willingness to contain debt growth."[12]

By 2019, the NDP government had run Alberta's net debt to $40.1 billion dollars. The comparable figure for 1993 at the end of the Getty government's deficit-streak was $23 billion. In 1993, this meant that 44 cents of every tax dollar (corporate and personal) collected went to pay for interest on the debt.[13] On the expenditure side, debt servicing costs were equivalent to 33 per cent of the health budget or 75 per cent of all social service spending.[14] Today's historically low interest rates have rescued Alberta from this calamity so far. Currently debt servicing now consuming 3 per cent of total government revenues. But interest rates are rising, and this figure is projected to double by 2023.[15]

A significant part of the NDP's spending problem was their predictable failure to rein in public sector salaries – especially in the SHE domain – social services, health, and education. Public sector unions constitute the political base of the Alberta NDP, and the Notley government was not going to ignore them. SHE spending has tripled in the past seventeen years and now consumes $4 out of every $5 dollars of program spending.[16] While former PC Premiers Stelmach and Redford share the blame for this, during the NDP's four years public sector compensation constituted about half of the entire budget.

The other budget buster was the NDP's well publicized plan to spend $30 billion dollars over their four-year mandate on infrastructure – new schools, health facilities, roads – all to be paid for with borrowed money. Their bet was that most of the voting public would not understand or care where this money came from or how it would ever be paid back. They hoped voters would see the new schools, hospitals, and roads in their communities and reward the NDP with another majority.

The PC governments' failure to constitutionally protect the fiscal policies that created the much celebrated "Alberta Advantage" effectively handed Rachel Notley's NDP government the political equivalent of a platinum credit card to spend and borrow with the hope of winning the next election.

That hope was defeated in 2019 by Jason Kenney and the newly formed United Conservative Party (UCP). Kenney campaigned on the promise of a return to fiscal responsibility and a balanced budget by 2023.This would have been no easy task – even before the Covid crisis and the Alberta energy sector's economic collapse in 2020. He inherited a structural deficit of about $8 billion dollars a year. In its first full budget year, 2020, the UCP tabled a budget with a deficit of $7.5 billion, but with a projected balanced budget by 2023.[17] This lasted less than a month. The double whammy of Covid 19 and the collapse of oil and gas revenues blew the lid off the UCP budget. By August, the projected deficit was revised to $24.2 billion.[18]

But budget cuts and tax increases by themselves will not be enough. The Kenney government will also have to put some meaningful constitutional fences around future tax increases or deficit spending, or both. They will also have to politician-proof the Heritage Fund from future vote-hungry governments. Failure to do this will simply be setting the fiscal table again for some future government – UCP or NDP – to use the spend-now-pay-later strategy to try to buy the next election.

## CONSTITUTIONALIZING FISCAL RESPONSIBILITY: BALANCED BUDGET LAWS AND TAX AND EXPENDITURE LIMITATIONS

If the Kenney UCP government wants to make fiscal responsibility a permanent feature of Alberta government budgets, then they will need to constitutionally entrench a set of fiscal and budgetary rules that cannot be easily changed by simple majority votes in the Alberta legislature. The good news is that there are practical models from other jurisdictions on how this can be done successfully – the balanced-budget laws (BBLs) and tax-and-expenditure limitations (TELs) used in many US state governments. The not so good news is that for these fiscal restraints to be successful, they must be constitutionally entrenched – something that is legally problematic, but not impossible, for Canadian provinces. This section of the chapter summarizes successful examples of BBLs and TELs from US and Canadian experience.[19] Below (Provincial Constitutions in Canada: Opportunities and Obstacles ), I explain the potential legal obstacles to implementing similar fiscal policies in Canadian provinces, and how these obstacles could be resolved.

A BBL basically requires a government or legislature to balance expenditures with revenues. Some BBLs require this on annual basis, by prohibiting any annual deficits. Others allow a deficit or two in recession years, but then require a net balance over the business cycle – typically three or four years. Most US state BBLs apply only to operating budgets and not to capital budgets. They allow state governments to borrow and use debt to pay for longer-term infrastructure. There are sound reasons for this distinction. Unlike operating expenses such as salaries or supplies, a new school or hospital provides benefits for citizen-taxpayers for years into the future. But they must be paid for when they are built.

For this reason, Alberta (like most Canadian provinces and US state governments) uses what are know as accrual accounting rules. In a given budget year, while the full costs of new school or road must be paid in full, accrual accounting rules allow only the project's annual depreciation to be counted as an in-year "expense," even though actual "expenditures" are much higher.

While there are sound accounting principles to support accrual accounting, in public sector accounting this can lead to misleading communication about whether or not a government's annual budget is balanced. While every first-year accounting student learns that "CAPEX is greater than DEPRECIATION," the general public (and, in my experience, most members of Caucus) don't.

In Alberta during the years that surging oil and gas royalties were creating huge, multi-billion-dollar budget surpluses (2005–08), this distinction did not make any practical difference. When this abruptly ended in 2008, the Stelmach government was able to cover the CAPEX-DEPRECIATION shortfalls with transfers from the $18 billion dollar rainy-day savings in the Sustainability Fund. This allowed the government to tell Albertans that it had "balanced the budget" in 2009 and 2010. This was technically correct, but also misleading and self-serving. What the government did not tell Albertans was that its own internal projections showed that the Sustainability Fund would be drawn down to zero by 2014. In reality, it was empty by 2013. This explains – but does not excuse – why in 2013 the Redford government abolished the Sustainability Fund, changed Alberta's budget definitions that had been in place since 1993, and then told Albertans that the budget was still balanced.

A tax-and-expenditure limitation [TEL] is related to but distinct from a BBL. TELs constrain the growth of government spending and taxation year over year. The most common type of TEL limits the rate of annual budget growth to population growth plus inflation. Under this rule, governments or legislatures can increase annual spending to pay for more services for more people, but real per capita spending cannot increase year over year.

US experience confirms that a BBL by itself does little to slow the increase in the size of government or increases in taxes. So long as tax revenues rise at the same rate as government spending, the budget may be balanced, but there is no cap on the growth rate of government. Accordingly, advocates of lower taxes and smaller governments advocate the simultaneous use of both BBLs and TELs.

US experience demonstrates that the most effective forms of both BBLs and TELs are those that are constitutionally entrenched rather than simple statutes.[20] Studies found that for the latter, legislatures were able and willing to circumvent the spending and taxing limitations by simply amending the statute.

Canadian experience has followed a similar pattern. By the end of the 1990s, eight out of ten provinces had enacted some form of BBL, including all four Western provinces.[21] While their specifics varied, all eight took the form of statutes. Their sponsors understood that this made them vulnerable to reversal by future governments through simple majority votes but hoped that "the high costs associated with altering the regime ... an immense supply of time, political capital, and other resources, none of which a government is likely to possess during an economic downturn ... would deter future politicians from doing so."[22] This hope turned out to be unduly optimistic.

A 2003 study found that these BBLs were initially successful. Five of the eight – including Alberta – achieved balanced budgets or budget surpluses following adoption of their BBLs. But six of the eight – including Alberta – also experienced increases in the growth rate of government spending.[23]

The early success of provincial BBLs evaporated in the wake of the 2008 recession. Faced with plummeting revenues, all of the Western provinces save Saskatchewan amended their BBLs to allow deficits.[24] Alberta was the first to cave. The Stelmach government amended Klein's *Fiscal Sustainability Act* to help pay for operational expenses by withdrawing funds from the Sustainability Fund and to borrow to pay for new infrastructure spending. "Temporary deficits" of $2.4 billion and $1.8 billion were forecast for 2010 and 2011, couched in promises to be "back in the black" by 2012. The deficits were not temporary and the promises were never kept.

In retrospect, this is hardly a surprise. Without some form of constitutional entrenchment or super-majority amending formula, a statutory "balanced budget law is only as effective as the political will and public support surrounding it."[25] But precisely when BBLs are most needed – during economic downturns – is when the "political will" is most lacking. Always with an eye to the next election, "political leaders believed that there was greater political risk associated with spending cuts than running a deficit."[26]

What if Alberta had entrenched a BBL and a TEL in 2004 – the year of the last election when the PCs were led by Ralph Klein? A recent study found that if the departing Klein regime had imposed a "population plus inflation" TEL on its successors, Alberta would have sustained a balanced budget though 2017.[27] During the Stelmach-Redford decade (2004–15), program spending increased an average of 7.1 per cent per year. This was nearly double the combined rate of population growth plus inflation – 4.4 per cent. Total program spending in 2004 was $24 billion. By 2015, it had doubled to $48.2 billion. Had there been an entrenched TEL to constrain spending growth to 4.4 per cent, program spending in Budget 2015 would have been $38.9 billion, and Alberta "would have run surpluses in every year ... rather than 8 deficits in 9 years."[28] It would also still have had at least $35 billion in net assets, the highest of any Canadian province. Instead, in 2017, for the first time since 2000, Alberta fell into a net debt position – where its debts now exceed its total financial assets.[29]

Canadian experience confirms what has happened in the US. The key to successful BBLs or TELs is to make them difficult for future governments or legislatures to repeal, amend or otherwise circumvent. This requires that they be constitutionally entrenched or require some other form of super-majority process to be repealed or amended in the future. How this could be done in Canadian provinces is explained below (Provincial Constitutions in Canada: Opportunities and Obstacles).

## POLITICIAN-PROOFING THE HERITAGE FUND

A unique and important aspect of Alberta's fiscal system is the Alberta Heritage Savings Trust Fund. Established by Premier Peter Lougheed in 1976, the fund served several purposes.

The Heritage Fund held out the opportunity for Alberta to avoid the pitfalls that await wealthy petro-state regimes. The Heritage Fund would not only save current energy revenues for that inevitable future day that its non-renewable resources begin to decline. It would also reduce revenue volatility in annual budgeting cycles. The requirement that 30 per cent of the province's annual non-renewable resource revenues (NRRR) must be transferred to the Heritage Fund would curb the political temptation to overspend in high revenue years. There would be 30 per cent less revenue available. Conversely in low NRRR years, the interest and earnings from the Heritage Fund would provide a stable, alternative source of government revenues and reduce the probability of the three alternatives: raise taxes, cut services, or run deficits. This is not just theory. As the Kneebone-Wilkins study confirms, for the past fifty years seven consecutive Alberta governments from three different political parties have ramped up spending during years of high NRRR, and then ran deficits when oil and gas prices inevitably declined.[30]

Initially the Heritage Fund was managed according to these rules. Between 1976 and 1982, it accumulated assets with a net value of $8.3 billion dollars.[31] It did not hurt that the price of oil had tripled not once but twice during the decade of the seventies – first after the 1973 Yom Kippur Arab-Israeli War and then again in 1979–80 following the Iranian revolution. Early estimates were that the Heritage Fund could top $50 billion dollars by 2000.

This was short-lived. As the price of oil dropped, NRRR declined. Faced with an election in 1982, the Lougheed government reduced deposits into the Heritage Fund to 15 per cent and used the remaining revenues to maintain spending and help win the election. Four years later, his PC successor, Premier Don Getty, had to deal with another election and even lower oil prices. In 1986 the Getty government "temporarily" reduced NRRR transfers to 0 per cent. Other than the three one-off deposits in the boom-year budgets of 2005–07, that is where they have stayed ever since.

The one variation from this depressing pattern was Premier Ralph Klein's decision in 2005 to give each Alberta resident a "Prosperity Bonus" cheque, more commonly remembered as "Ralph Bucks." All Alberta residents and their children each received a $400 cheque that was not taxed by either level of government. The total cost of the program was $1.4 billion dollars, which represented 20 per cent of that year's $6.8 billion dollars budget surplus. While Klein said that there might be more such cheques in the future, there never were. NRRR peaked that year at over $12.5 billion dollars, never to reach that level again.

The result is that in real dollars – accounting for inflation – the Heritage Fund's current value of $17 billion dollars is actually less than it was thirty years ago.[32] Other than the inflation proofing that began in 2005, under current government policy, virtually all of the fund's realized annual earnings are transferred to General Revenue for in-year spending. This means that the fund's value cannot grow as the market goes up. Indeed, when there are down years – such as 2009 – investment losses permanently reduce the size of the fund. Combine this with the fact that the Alberta government has made only three new deposits in the fund since 1987, and the fund begins to resemble the old slinky toy – holding steady in good years but dropping down in bad years – slowly but steadily working its way to the bottom.

The deteriorating value of the Heritage Fund is even worse when population growth and inflation are taken into account. Prices have increased four-fold since the fund started in 1976. Alberta's population has grown by more than 130 per cent. As presented in the

Figure 7.1 | The inflation adjusted per capita market value of the Alberta Heritage Savings Trust Fund (2018, Canadian dollars)

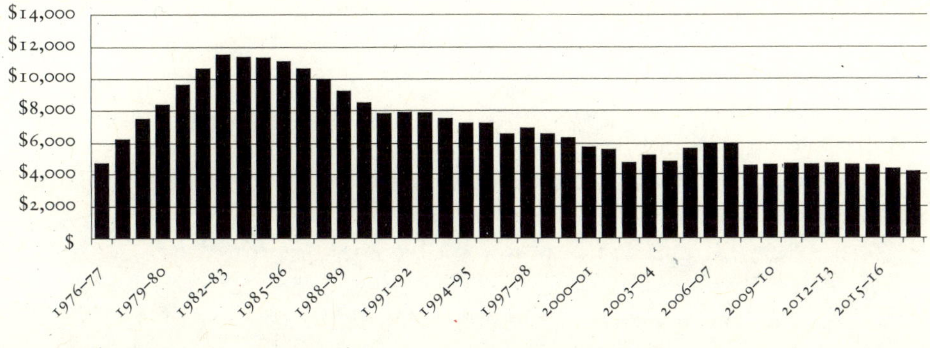


Source: *Alberta Heritage Savings Trust Fund: 2017–2018 Annual Report* (Edmonton: Alberta Treasury Board and Finance, 2018), 12.

figure above, in per capita real dollars, the fund's value peaked in 1983 at $11,507 per Albertan. The most recently available figure is $4,034.[33]

The sad fact is that of the $216 billion dollars in NRRR collected by the Alberta government between 1977 and 2013, less than 6 per cent was saved. The fund's current value is approximately $17 billion dollars. If the $9.7 billion that sat in the Heritage Fund in 1982 had remained untouched (and no further contributions made) and allowed to grow simply at the rate of inflation, the value would have stood at $24.2 billion in 2010.[34] Instead, Heritage Fund earnings were diverted to finance a plethora of spending initiatives. Since 1976, approximately $39.2 billion has been transferred from the fund to the province's general revenues.[35] If this continues, the Heritage Fund will be slowly drained.

Compare this to Alaska's Permanent Fund. Created in 1977 – the same year as the Heritage Fund – the Permanent Fund now has a current balance of $68 billion dollars.[36] And that is after paying out $20 billion dollars in "dividends" to Alaska residents. Norway's NRRR savings fund was started later – 1990 – and now has a balance of over $1 trillion dollars.[37]

How have Alaska and Norway succeeded where Alberta has failed? The Alaska Fund was created by a constitutional amendment that mandates that 25 per cent of annual energy royalties and rents must be deposited in the Permanent Fund. Unlike the Alberta Fund, which was created by a statute, this means that deposits cannot be reduced or stopped when oil prices drop, and the government wants more revenue to fund program spending. In Alaska, this would require a constitutional amendment and a referendum. For reasons explained below, no government has ever proposed this, knowing that it would be political suicide.

Norway's fund is not constitutionally entrenched in a legal sense, but it is universally understood to be off-limits to the governments of the day. In Canadian terminology, we could say the fund's status as politically untouchable is a "constitutional convention" – widely recognized and followed. Originally named the Petroleum Fund of Norway, its name was changed in 2006 to the Government Pension Global Fund. While it is clearly not a pension fund in the normal sense (i.e., member-funded), this name change emphasizes that the fund belongs to the people of Norway – not the government of the day. In short, the Alaska and Norway funds were made politician proof by protecting them from the inevitable short-term priorities – that is, winning the next election – of the governments of the day.

The three funds also differ in how they allocate their respective annual earnings. In the case of Norway, the government is allowed to spend the fund's annual earnings – estimated at approximately 4 per cent – to pay for what it calls its "net oil deficit." However, there was never a net withdrawal from the fund until 2016.[38]

The annual earnings of the Alaska fund are automatically transferred to general revenues, but they can only be used for three specified purposes: returned to the fund for inflation proofing; paying for the operating costs of the fund; and paying an annual "dividend" to all Alaska residents. These annual dividends have varied from a low of $331 per person in 1984 to a high of $2,072 in 2015. Historically these dividends consume 50 per cent of the fund's earnings. When oil prices dropped in 1999, the Alaska legislature tried to reduce the size of the dividends and use the "savings" to help balance their budget. Before making this change, a referendum was held. The "NO" option – blocking the transfer – won 84 per cent of the vote.

Thirdly, the three funds differ in how their principal is managed and invested. The Alaska and Norway funds cannot be used for domestic "economic development," the kinds of politically useful but economically risky projects that Alberta governments indulged in during the 1980s.[39] In that decade, the Lougheed-Getty governments lost over $2.2 billion dollars using the Heritage Fund to make "investments" in new Alberta start-up companies.[40] In 1996, the Klein government put an end to using the Heritage Fund for high-risk "diversification" projects, and instead directed it to be used to maximize long-term returns. The creation of the Alberta Investment Management Company (AIMCO) a decade later further insulated the fund from cabinet micro-management. AIMCO's directive emphasizes that these moneys are to be professionally managed for the long-term interests of Albertans, not the short-term interests of the government of the day. Recent developments, however, suggest that these past mistakes are being ignored.

Premier Redford's 2014 budget proposed to resurrect the practice of using money in the Heritage Fund for "strategic investments." Bill 1, misleadingly named the *Savings Management Act*, would have diverted $2 billion dollars from the Heritage Fund into a new spending program to "provide government with the financial resources to take advantage of new opportunities, yet to be determined, that may require a large, one-time investment from the province."[41] Such politically driven "investments" are all but guaranteed to achieve the same dismal results as they did during the 1980s. Following Redford's resignation in March, 2014, Bill 1 was never implemented. But it is another reminder of the vulnerability of the Heritage Fund to short-term political objectives.

The NDP's first budget directed the Alberta Investment Management Company (AIMCO) to invest $540 million from the Heritage Fund into Alberta-based "growth companies" to promote diversification of Alberta's economy. This "directive" not only eroded the independence and autonomy of AIMCO, but risked further financial losses for the Heritage Fund.

To put the Heritage Fund back on a sound financial footing and to begin to achieve results similar to Alaska and Norway, Alberta will have to resurrect the original Lougheed policy of legally mandating that a set percentage of NRRR be deposited in the Heritage Fund each year. Given Alberta's current structural deficit, initially it could not be 30 per cent. But it could start small – say 5 per cent – and be gradually increased in legally required increments over the next decade or two. More importantly, this time the contribution rule must be constitutionally entrenched; that is, put beyond the reach of simple legislative majorities. The same rule should apply to the fund's principal. Without this reform-- a constitutional ring-fence around the annual contribution rule and the principal – it will continue to be raided by the governments of the day for short-term political gains. The models of success are out there – Norway and Alaska – to be adopted by and adapted to Alberta.

## PROVINCIAL CONSTITUTIONS IN CANADA: OPPORTUNITIES AND OBSTACLES

Constitutionally entrenched fiscal rules – such as a BBL, a TEL, or the mandatory transfer of a defined per cent of annual NRRR to the Heritage Fund – would increase fiscal stability and decrease volatility in Government of Alberta finances. It would enhance economic security for future generations of Albertans. But implementing such rules is not a simple process.

For students of comparative federalism, Canada is an anomaly. Canadian provinces are arguably stronger (both politically and jurisdictionally) than their counterparts in other federal democracies. Yet, unlike the latter, no Canadian province, save one, has a written constitution. Even the one – British Columbia's – is only a statute, and so can be easily amended by the normal legislative process. For our present purposes, this means there is currently no clear or simple legal process for a province to entrench a new constitutional rule, such as a BBL or TEL.

The source of this anomaly can be traced to Canada's heritage as a former British colony and the complementary British traditions of "parliamentary supremacy" and an "unwritten constitution." In 1867 at the time of Confederation, each of the original four colonies had their own "unwritten constitutions" – a combination of British and colonial statutes, Royal Proclamations and charters, custom and convention – and these were duly noted and respected in the *British North America Act (BNA Act)* of 1867. Sections 58–90 of the BNA *Act* address the subject of "Provincial Constitutions," but with the exception of the executive office of the Lieutenant Governor (the Queen's representative), the provinces were given complete authority to amend their constitutions as they see fit. Under this authority, for example, several provinces unilaterally abolished the upper chambers of their legislatures. The provinces' "exclusive" authority over their respective constitutions (save the office of the Lieutenant Governor) was re-affirmed more recently in section 45 of the *Constitution Act, 1982*.[42]

Notwithstanding such authority, all provinces, save British Columbia, have chosen to adhere to the British practice of an "unwritten constitution," or, to use more contemporary terminology, a "flexible" rather than a "rigid" constitution. In so doing, all provincial constitutions still adhere to the principle of "parliamentary supremacy," within the confines of their section 92 powers and the limitations imposed by the 1982 *Canadian Charter of Rights and Freedoms*. This means that any attempt to define a province's constitution produces a lengthy list of statutes, orders-in-council, the rules of order and procedure of the legislatures, and constitutional conventions.

For example, the Alberta attorney general's office, when asked to identify the written documents that are included in the "constitution of Alberta," replied that there was "no listing or definitive statement," but identified 23 Acts that might be included.[43] The author cautioned that this list did not preclude other acts and added that the departmental acts and the Rules of the Legislature might well be included as well. And this is only for the written portion of Alberta's constitutionThe predictable result has been that provincial constitutions are barely acknowledged in either the practice or the theory of Canadian politics. As Wiseman has recently observed, "Provincial constitutions barely dwell in the world of the [Canadian] subconscious. They are too opaque, oblique, and inchoate to rouse much interest, let alone passion."[44]

The absence of provincial constitutions in Canada (like the absence of a democratically elected and effective Senate) distinguishes Canada from other mature federal democracies. In the majority of mature federal countries,[45] the sub-units (US states, Swiss cantons, German länder) have their own written constitutions. The six Australian states also have their own written constitutions, but they are not entrenched. Even most of the newer federal states[46] have more developed provincial constitutions than Canada.

Canada shares with India the dubious honour of being one of only two mature federal democracies with no subnational constitutional systems. This omission reflects mid-nineteenth-century British parliamentary and imperial practice, and the centralist and anti-democratic biases of the two nations' original constitution writers. It is not by coincidence that India and Canada are also the only two English-speaking federations in which state or provincial judges are appointed by the federal government.[47] Both practices are outdated relics of nineteenth century British imperial rule that have no place in modern democratic federations.

Both Quebec and more recently Alberta have shown interest in developing modern, democratic provincial constitutions. Quebec nationalists and sovereigntists have discussed the idea of a Quebec constitution for several decades.[48] In the run up to the 2003 Quebec election, all three major political parties endorsed the idea of a provincial constitution. The Action Démocratique du Québéc (ADQ) proposed "La Charte du Québéc" that would serve as "une document de base... la loi des lois de notre communauté politique" and would affirm "la liberté politique de Québéc," including the right to self-determination.[49] In 2003, when an "Estates General" was convened by the Parti Québécois government to discuss constitutional changes for Quebec, 82 per cent of the delegates voted in support of "une réforme qui mène à une constitution québécoise."

In Alberta, citizens unhappy with their province's treatment by the federal government have advocated a provincial constitution as part of a package of "home rule" reforms to strengthen the political autonomy of the province.[50] In response, the Government of Alberta struck a legislative committee to consult with Albertans on "How to strengthen Alberta's role in Confederation."[51] My own submission to this commission was to adopt a new provincial constitution to coincide with the province's centennial celebration in 2005.[52] However, the commission's final report did not accept this recommendation.

In 2019, the newly elected UCP government struck a "Fair Deal Committee" to consult with Albertans on options to strengthen and improve Alberta's position in Confederation. One of the options studied was a provincial constitution. The Committee's final report stated that it was "unable to unanimously agree if we should recommend a formal constitution for Alberta." However it went on to say that, "we do agree that an urgent need exists to explore ways to affirm, in law and government policy, Alberta's cultural, economic and political uniqueness, and its value, not only to Albertans, but also to Canada as a whole."[53] This message was amplified in a chapter in a new book advocating reforms to create more autonomy for Alberta from Ottawa: "codifying an Albertan Constitution could go a long way to giving the province some real measure of agency and independence without ever leaving country."[54]

This constitutional status quo need not be permanent. Alberta, and every other province, have the constitutional authority to create and entrench a provincial constitution. There are two options – one unilateral, Alberta acting alone; the other bilateral, Alberta engaging with and obtaining the consent of the federal government.[55]

The bilateral option may be the most straight-forward. A provincial government may negotiate an amendment to the Constitution of Canada that affects only that province – subject to the approval of the House of Commons and the Senate. Such an amendment could be used to "patriate" the *Alberta Act* from Ottawa to Alberta, just as Canada "patriated" the BNA *Act* from London in 1982. (The *Alberta Act* is currently part of the federal constitution.) This type of bilateral constitutional amendment (i.e., Ottawa and one province) is authorized by section 43 of the *Constitution Act, 1982*, and has already been used successfully by Quebec and Newfoundland to change provisions respecting separate school boards. Alberta could include in its "patriation package" a new supermajority amending formula – such as a two-thirds approval vote in the legislature or approval by way of referendum, or both. Then, once the power to amend the *Alberta Act* is formally given to the province, Alberta could then make further changes per its new amending formula – such as adding a BBL or a TEL.[56]

Assuming cooperation from the federal government, this bilateral amendment would appear to be the simplest way to entrench a provincial constitution. There is, however, a potential downside to provincial constitution making in Canada. If the purpose is to strengthen provincial self-government and democratic accountability within the province, adopting an entrenched constitution could end up having the opposite effect. Under Canada's current legal system, the final authority for interpreting a provincial constitution would be the Supreme Court of Canada. These judges are appointed unilaterally by the prime minister of Canada, usually along partisan party or ideological lines, or both, and with little to no consultation with provincial governments.

This would hardly make sense for a province like Alberta. The meaning and enforcement of constitutional rules for Alberta would be made by a court on which there might not be a single Alberta judge! If the goal is to increase self-government for Albertans, entrenching a provincial constitution could end up having the opposite effect. The final word on their constitution's meaning would rest with nine, non-Alberta judges in Ottawa. Even allowing the Alberta Court of Appeals to serve as the final interpreter – analogous to the practice in the fifty US states – would be problematic, since its members also are all appointed by Ottawa.

This made-in-Ottawa risk would be amplified if a provincial constitution contained broad guarantees such as "principles of fundamental justice" and "equal protection of and equal benefit of the law." Experience since adopting the 1982 *Canadian Charter of Rights and Freedoms* has shown that broad concepts such as these are subject to unanticipated, unintended, and controversial interpretations, depending on the personal experiences, subjective values, and policy preferences of any given judge.

By contrast, this concern or risk could be minimized if (at least in the beginning) the provisions of a new provincial constitution were limited to clear, explicit rules with broadly agreed-upon, objective meanings. Presumably a BBL or a TEL could be framed in this manner.

For these reasons, a provincial constitution adopted via the bilateral amending process could actually weaken provincial autonomy, unless it were accompanied by constitutional amendments that transferred the power to appoint provincial superior court judges to provincial governments; and made provincial courts of appeal, not the Supreme Court of Canada, the final and exclusive interpreters of provincial constitutions.

Fundamental constitutional changes such as these would have to be extended to all provinces, not just to Alberta. Accordingly, they would engage a broader set of political interests and actors, and make approval under the "7/50" general amending formula more difficult. But without such amendments, adding a provincial constitution might have the opposite of its intended effect.

For this reason, the unilateral option may be the more appropriate way to proceed.[57] Under section 45 of the 1982 *Constitution Act*, "Subject to section 41, the legislature of each province may exclusively make laws amending the constitution of the province."[58]

As Wiseman observes, "Provincial constitutions – with the exception of the federal principle and parts of the Charter – are what provincial legislatures say they are."[59] So per section 45, a province could unilaterally enact an amending formula – say a two-thirds vote in its legislature, combined with majority approval (50 per cent +1) in a referendum. Following this logic, a BBL or TEL could then be added to the constitution, thereby putting such fiscal rules beyond the reach of simple legislative majorities. Indeed, Alberta has enacted legislation that places procedural limits on future Alberta governments twice since 1982.[60] But it is not this simple.

An ordinary statute, enacted by a simple majority vote, that explicitly restricts the substantive policy choices of future legislative majorities violates the principle of "parliamentary supremacy." Under the British-Canadian system of parliamentary supremacy, it is impermissible for a present government to bind the policy discretion of a future government.

Fortunately, there is an important exception. Reasonable procedural or "manner and form" limitations have always been permitted. The Supreme Court of Canada has upheld several such procedural restrictions such as the requirement that all bills must be enacted in both English and French; or that tax increases must first be approved by a referendum.[61]

But, as constitutional expert Peter Hogg notes, these kinds of procedural restrictions are temporary not permanent checks on future legislatures, because they can be repealed by simple majority votes. They do not have the permanence of a true constitutional rule. Hogg argues that this weakness of normal "manner and form" rules can be remedied by what he calls "double entrenchment.": "[I]n order to be fully effective in law, a manner and form provision must apply to itself (be self-referencing or doubly-entrenched). The manner and form provision must not only apply to the protected category of laws … it must also apply to laws amending or repealing the manner and form provision itself."[62]

While this "double entrenchment" would solve the "easy-to-repeal-problem," it runs into a second problem. Hogg is clear that a current legislature may not bind a future legislature with respect to the "substance" of policy. This includes "an ostensibly procedural requirement that is virtually impossible of fulfillment, such as approval by 80 per cent of the voters in a referendum."[63] What is not clear is at what point does "entrenching the entrenching procedure" become "an ostensibly procedural requirement that is virtually impossible of fulfillment"?

There are good reasons why any substantive policy restrictions on future governments must meet a higher standard of support than just a simple majority vote in a current legislature. Today's democratically elected majority should not be allowed to protect its own policy preferences from future revision or repeal by a future democratically elected majority. If this were allowed, a government facing an imminent election and negative polling numbers might be tempted to entrench its own key policies against repeal by its soon to be victorious political opponents – a clear violation of democratic accountability.[64] To take a recent example, Alberta's NDP government was not able to "entrench" its newly enacted carbon tax – a policy that UCP leader Jason Kenney promised to repeal if elected – which he did. The American scholarship describes this as "legislative entrenchment," and rejects it for the same reasons.[65]

A middle ground and a path forward is found in what is called "symmetrical entrenchment."[66] There is a robust scholarship on this subject in the United States: whether, or how, a current legislature can enact rules that limit or restrict what future legislatures may do. Symmetrical entrenchment basically means that a policy restriction on a future government must be enacted under the same super-majority procedures that would be needed to repeal it.[67] More formally stated, "Symmetrical entrenchments are those that employ the same voting rule to govern the enactment of the entrenched measure as would be required to repeal it."[68]

Under this procedure, a government is legally required to achieve the same super-majority or double-majority support that it seeks to impose on future governments. By meeting the same higher, super-majority bar, this achieves a level playing field between current and future governments and passes the test of democratic accountability.

Symmetrical entrenchment could be used to implement the practical task of Alberta (or any other province) unilaterally entrenching constitutional rules. The parliamentary supremacy principle argument could be met by ensuring that any new entrenched provincial constitutional limitation is first approved by the same higher threshold that it seeks to impose on future legislatures. This adoption procedure would satisfy the "manner and form" requirements that are part of Canada's parliamentary tradition and, in fact, would replicate the "manner and form" in which the *Charter* was adopted in 1982 – with the support of nine of ten provinces and both houses of Parliament.

Suffice it to recognize here that at a certain point "manner and form" requirements that are themselves "entrenched" become indistinguishable from a formally entrenched constitutional amending formula, such as, since 1982, is now found in the Constitution of

Canada. The new amending formula, combined with the adoption of the *Charter* in 1982, marks Canada's departure from and modification of Dicey's classical model of parliamentary supremacy. If entrenched constitutional limitations are now permitted in Canada's national constitution, there is no longer a principled reason why they cannot be included in a new provincial constitution, provided it is created using symmetrical entrenchment.

For this same reason, unilateral entrenchment, done as proposed above, would not trigger the only other limitation that constrains the provincial amending power. According to Wiseman, section 45 does not permit "a profound constitutional upheaval by the introduction of political institutions foreign to and incompatible with the Canadian system."[69] Since 1982, neither entrenched rights nor a super-majoritarian amending formula are foreign to Canada.

The same holds true for the use of popular referenda to approve or disapprove proposals to amend the constitution. Whatever its prior legal status might have been,[70] the use of the referendum to approve or disapprove proposals for constitutional change has become well entrenched in Canadian practice since 1982. Both the federal government and several provinces used the referendum procedure to decide the fate of the 1992 *Charlottetown Accord*, a collection of constitutional amendments that was decisively rejected by the voters. Quebec, Alberta, and British Columbia all have statutory requirements that proposed amendments to the federal constitution must first be approved by the people in a referendum. Quebec has twice used the referendum process to vote on proposals to secede from Canada, in 1980 and again in 1995. In its 1998 ruling in the *Quebec Secession Reference*, the Supreme Court of Canada conferred constitutional legitimacy on the use of referenda by declaring that they embodied the unwritten constitutional principle of democracy. The subsequent enactment of the *Clarity Act* by the federal government (1999) and Bill 99 by the National Assembly of Quebec (1999), while diametrically opposed, both presuppose the use of and legitimacy of popular referendums for purposes of deciding constitutional amendments.[71]

In sum, under section 45, Alberta (and by extension, any other province) could unilaterally entrench a BBL, TEL, or Heritage Fund contribution rule, if it used the same super-majority process to approve the new rules that it imposes on any future government to amend or repeal the rules.

Notwithstanding this capacity, unilaterally created provincial constitutional rules face the same paradox and risk as the bilateral option: that under the constitutional status quo, the meaning of such rules would ultimately be interpreted by the Supreme Court of Canada, a body on which Alberta has no guarantee of representation and no role in nominating or approving its nine judges.

This made-in-Ottawa risk could be mitigated if Alberta's initial constitution is limited to just a set of fiscal rules such as BBLs, TELs, or mandatory minimum deposits of energy revenues into the Heritage Savings Fund. These rules would all be relatively straightforward and objective, leaving little room for judicial (mis-) interpretation. Presumably such objective rules would be interpreted and enforced the same ways by judges in either Edmonton and Ottawa, regardless of which party appointed them.

US state constitutions and Canadian provincial statutes provide many different models of both BBLs and TELs. Every state except Vermont has some form of BBL. They vary in stringency. Some are statutory, but most are constitutional. Of the forty-nine states with BBLs, one study ranked thirty-six as "rigorous," four as "weak," and the others in between. There is also the choice whether to make a BBL an annual requirement or allow a more flexible term of "business cycle" or before the next election – typically two to four years. Some models require that the budget as enacted be balanced. Others require balancing of expenditures and revenues by the end of the fiscal year. Almost all BBLs have explicit exceptions that allow for temporary operating deficits. These typically include wars, natural disasters, or a dramatic collapse in revenues – usually defined as greater than 5 per cent.

Almost all state BBLs exclude capital spending from the calculation. This means that their BBL requirement typically applies to only 50 to 60 per cent of total state spending. As noted earlier, there are solid policy reasons not to apply a strict BBL to capital expenditures. But the failure to have any restrictions runs the risks of politically-motivated overspending and fiscally unsustainable debt accumulation. In most states, this risk is minimized by making it difficult to impossible for either governors or legislatures to unilaterally issue debt. Most states require special legislation to issue general obligation "revenue bonds," and many require voter approval of such bonds via referendum. Some then require the creation of stand-alone revenue stream to repay the bonds. The result in these states is that "debt is fully in the public view," and that it is almost unheard of for state governments to borrow to pay for annual operating expenses.[72] These are practices that a future fiscally responsible Alberta government should consider.

One interesting variation in some of the Canadian BBLs is the imposition of financial penalties on members of executive council (e.g., cabinet ministers) in a government that fails to meet the BBL requirement. The prospect of losing 20 to 40 per cent of one's annual salary would presumably serve as great incentive for cabinets to balance expenditures with revenues! These are all some of the practical choices that would have to be made should Alberta choose to adopt a constitutionally entrenched BBL or TEL.[73]

## CONCLUSION

In 2003, in preparation for Alberta's 2005 centennial celebration, I wrote: "A made-in-Alberta constitution could provide many benefits to Albertans, and any other provinces that chose to do the same. It would allow Albertans – if they chose – to 'cement in' some of the most important Klein achievements by way of constitutional (as opposed to statutory) requirements for balanced budgets and referendums to approve tax increases. An entrenched Alberta Constitution could also be used to protect the Alberta Heritage Fund from future raids by vote-hungry politicians."[74]

Would have … could have … should have. That fork in the road is now $70 billion dollars ago and long past. But it is not too late. The Kenney UCP government should undertake the constitutional entrenchment of the fiscal restraint rules described in this chapter.

Given the relative risks of the two entrenchment options, it would be prudent for Alberta to proceed in a staged approach: begin with the unilateral option, and then pursue the bilateral option, with the other necessary amendments, over the medium term. Ideally the first could pave the way to the second.

Even the unilateral approach would require some rules to mitigate the risks of leaving final power of interpretation with the Supreme Court of Canada, a court on which Alberta has virtually no representation.

There are several options. Judicial decisions based on a new provincial constitution could be defined as "advisory only," with final decisions left to the elected government. This is the approach

Great Britain has chosen to use with respect to its recently adopted Declaration of Human Rights.

There is also the existing "Canadian solution" adopted in the 1982 *Charter* – the notwithstanding power – which allows a government to overrule an adverse judicial decision by re-enacting the impugned statute with the declaration that it shall take effect "notwithstanding" the specified section of the *Charter*.[75] The political stigma attached to the "notwithstanding" clause and the resulting reluctance of governments to use it makes this a less preferable choice.

A third possibility would be a modified version of the British rule: judicial decisions that were unanimous would be final and binding, but decisions with one (or more?) dissenting opinion would be advisory only. This rule would capture "clear violations" of the constitution but would leave constitutional issues over which there is "reasonable disagreement" to be resolved by the provincial legislature. This approach would capture the benefit of an entrenched provincial constitution – placing enforceable limits on the government of the day – but minimize the downside of final decisions being made by a far-away court in Ottawa with no Alberta judges.

The made-in-Ottawa risk could also be reduced or eliminated by two additional reforms. One would be a pair of constitutional amendments: one that transfers the power to appoint superior court judges to the provinces; and a second that confers exclusive final jurisdiction over provincial constitutions on provincial courts of appeal. Under this scenario, provincial constitutions would receive their final and authoritative interpretations by provincially appointed judges.

Alternatively, provinces could be given the power to nominate their own justices to the Supreme Court. This type of reform was discussed and agreed to in principle during the Meech-Charlottetown constitutional negotiations of the 1990s. More recently, Ottawa gave the Quebec government a direct role in nominating justices for the three seats on the Court that are legally reserved for Quebec. Ottawa's press release emphasized that this new process "ensures greater participation by its government in the selection process of judges from the province."[76]

Alberta (and the other provinces) could demand the same consideration given to Quebec, or better yet, constitutionalize this process for all provinces. A provincial role in the appointment of Supreme Court justices would make for a more regionally representative Court, and also increase the political diversity of the justices appointed. For the past century, the national Liberal and Conservative parties have enjoyed a monopoly on these appointments. Given the much greater diversity of political parties at the provincial level, sharing the appointment power with provincial governments would open the door to a wider spectrum of political views.[77]

To garner support from provinces other than Quebec and Ontario, the size of the Supreme Court would also have to be expanded. Currently, Quebec has a legal guarantee of three seats, while Ontario by convention also has three. An expanded Court would ensure that the other provinces or regions would be legally guaranteed at least one justice. A more representative model could expand the Court to eleven members: leave Quebec with three; give Ontario four; and then three for the West and one for Atlantic Canada.[78]

Presumably Alberta would have Quebec as an ally in such amendments. In his contribution to this book, Daniel Turp explicitly calls for returning the power to appoint Quebec's judges to the government of Quebec.[79] In addition to its longstanding and multi-partisan interest in a constitution of its own, in 2017 the then Quebec premier, Phillipe Couillard, released a two-hundred page policy document – "Quebecers: Our Way of Being Canadians" – that seeks to expand Quebec's capacity for democratic self-government and policy autonomy within Canada.[80] Clearly this objective would be strengthened by either or both of the two sets of amendments proposed here. Presumably other provinces would also be supportive of gaining the authority to appoint their own superior court judges, or their justices to the Supreme Court, or both.

While these amendments might appear radical, in fact they would implement in Canada what is already the norm in almost all other mature federal states. As noted earlier, returning the authority to appoint provincial superior court judges to provincial governments would remove an outdated relic of nineteenth-century British imperial rule that has no place in modern democratic federations. With respect to provincial governments' nominating justices to the Supreme Court of Canada, this would basically replicate the practice of the European Union. The European Court of Justice, the final court of appeals for the European Union, each member state is guaranteed a seat and appoints the judge that fills that seat.

For these same reasons, Alberta should concurrently propose the abolition of the federal powers of disallowance and reservation.

There is little purpose in going through the time and trouble to draft and ratify provincial constitutions, if the government in Ottawa retains the power to change unilaterally the division of powers – powers completely at odds with the very concept of federalism. Yes, there is already a strong unwritten convention of non-use for disallowance and reservation. But why not use this opportunity to entrench these conventions into Canada's written constitution? Again, support from Quebec would be all but certain. Quebec has already enacted legislation declaring that any use of either the disallowance or reservation powers to reverse policies enacted by its National Assembly would be "illegal."[81] It is hard to imagine opposition from any other province.

At the federal level, there is a precedent. In 1970 then Prime Minister Pierre Trudeau indicated a willingness to abolish these powers in return for provincial support for a new bill of rights that would apply to both levels of government. Perhaps Canada's current prime minister could be persuaded to complete a journey his father began but never finished – "renewed federalism."

## NOTES

1 See Daniel Turp, "Oui, Quebec Needs a Written Constitution," chapter 1 of this book.

2 See Ted Morton, "A Provincial Constitution: A Centennial Project for Alberta," Fraser Forum, November 2003, 15–16.

3 Steve Lafleur, Ben Eisen, and Milagros Palacios, "Race to the Bottom: Comparing the Recent Deficits of Alberta and Ontario," Fraser Institute, May 2017, https://www.fraserinstitute.org/sites/default/files/race-to-the-bottom-comparing-the-recent-deficits-of-alberta-and-ontario.pdf

4 Bill 31, *Business Financial Assistance Limitations Statutes Amendment Act*, 4th Sess., 23rd Leg., 1996.

5 Financial Management Committee, *Moving from Good to Great: Enhancing Alberta's Fiscal Framework* (Edmonton: Government of Alberta, 2002), 4.

6 *Budget 2003 Speech*, (Edmonton: Government of Alberta, 2003), 4–5.

7 Unfortunately, no sooner was this new savings rule created than it was broken. As energy resource revenues soared, the Klein government amended the act to allow for more than the original $3.5 billion to be allocated to general revenues. In 2004, the limit was raised to $4 billion; in 2005, to $4.75 billion; and in 2006, to $5.3 billion.

At the same time, the "rules" governing what to do with resource revenues in excess of the $2.5 billion mandated for the Sustainability Fund were soft and vague. "Surplus funds" could be directed into additional savings, but they could also be directed into the Capital Account or into "balance sheet improvements," which turned out to mean just more program spending.

8 See Jared J. Wesley and Wayne Simpson, "Promise Meets Reality: Balanced Budget Legislation in Western Canada, 1991–2010," paper delivered at the Annual Meeting of the Canadian Political Science Association, Wilfrid Laurier University, 16 May 2011.

9 In 2014–15 Alberta's operating budget was balanced, but there was still a net deficit when borrowing for capital spending is included.

10 Steve LaFleur et al., "Alberta's Budget Deficit: Why Spending Is to Blame," Fraser Research Bulletin, January 2017, 3.

11 Lafleur et al., "Alberta's Budget Deficit," 4.

12 Province of Alberta, Alberta Capital Finance Authority, "DBRS Confirms Province of Alberta at AA (high) and R-1 (high), Changes Trend on Long-Term Ratings to Negative," DBRS Morningstar, 7 July 2017, https://www.dbrsmorningstar.com/research/312862/dbrs-confirms-province-of-alberta-at-aa-high-and-r-1-high-changes-trend-on-long-term-ratings-to-negative.

13 In the budget of 1993 debt servicing was $1.654 billion dollars, while combined personal ($2.877 billion) and corporate ($854 million) income taxes totaled $3.731 billion. See Ron Kneebone, "Alberta Budget Data, 1965–2017," in Ron Kneebone and Margarita Wilkins, "50 Years of Government of Alberta Budgeting," University of Calgary: The School of Public Policy Publications 11, no.26 (October 2018).

14 M. Milke, "Alberta's Prosperity Is Ralph Klein's Legacy," *National Post*, 5 April 2013, https://nationalpost.com/opinion/mark-milke-albertas-prosperity-is-ralph-kleins-legacy.

15 Steve Laflleur and Joel Ames, "Alternative Paths for Alberta's Budget: Balance by 2023/24 is Not Enough," Fraser Institute, February 2018, https://www.fraserinstitute.org/sites/default/files/alternative-paths-for-albertas-budget-balance-by-2023-24-is-not-enough.pdf.

16 Lafleur and Ames, "Alternative Paths for Alberta's Budget."

17 President of Treasury Board and Minister of Finance, *Fiscal Plan: A Plan for Jobs and the Economy 2020–23* (Edmonton: Alberta Treasury Board and Finance, 2020), https://open.alberta.ca/dataset/05bd4008-c8e3-4c84-949e-cc18170bc7f7/resource/79caa22e-e417-44bd-8cac-64d7bb045509/download/budget-2020-fiscal-plan-2020-23.pdf.

18 Sammy Hudes, "Alberta's Deficit Could Balloon to $24.2 Billion; Finance

Minister Warns of Future Cuts to Services," *Calgary Herald*, 27 August 2020, https://calgaryherald.com/news/politics/albertas-deficit-could-balloon-to-24-2-billion-finance-minister-warns-of-future-cuts-to-services.

19 Most of the information used in this section is drawn from the excellent study done by the Fraser Institute: Jason Clemens et al., "Tax and Expenditure Limitations: The Next Step in Fiscal Discipline," Fraser Institute, October 2003, https://www.fraserinstitute.org/studies/tax-and-expenditure-limitations-next-step-in-fiscal-discipline.

20 Clemens et al., "Tax and Expenditure Limitations," 17–19. Two other differences that increased the efficacy of TELs in US states were initiation by citizen initiative or referendum, or both, and inclusion of municipal government spending as well as state spending.

21 Wesley and Simpson, "Promise Meets Reality."

22 Ibid., 4.

23 Clemens et al., "Tax and Expenditure Limitations," 11.

24 Wesley and Simpson, "Promise Meets Reality," 21–2.

25 Ibid., 40.

26 Ibid.

27 LaFleur et al., "Alberta's Budget Deficit."

28 Ibid., 1, 5.

29 Ibid., 7.

30 Kneebone and Wilkins, "50 Years Government of Alberta Budgeting."

31 Robert L. Mansell, "Fiscal Restructuring in Alberta," in Christopher Bruce et al., *A Government Reinvented: A Study of Alberta's Deficit Elimination Program* (Oxford: Oxford University Press, 1997), 24.

32 Wallis Snowdon, "Province to Review Investment Strategy for Alberta's Battered Heritage Fund," CBC News, 30 October 2020, https://www.cbc.ca/news/canada/edmonton/alberta-heritage-trust-fund-review-1.5783754.

33 Alberta Heritage Savings Trust Fund, *Alberta Heritage Savings Trust Fund: 2017–2018 Annual Report* (Edmonton: Alberta Treasury Board and Finance, 2018), https://open.alberta.ca/dataset/3675e470-646e-4f8a-86a7-c36c6f45471a/resource/1f86ad5d-923c-47d0-816a-063fd6cacbf4/download/2017-18-heritage-fund-annual-report.pdf.

34 Herb Emery and Ron Kneebone, "Alberta's Problems of Plenty," *Policy Options*, May 2011, 11.

35 Alberta Treasury Board and Finance, "Heritage Fund – Frequently Asked Questions," Government of Alberta, accessed 14 January 2015, http://www.finance.alberta.ca/business/ahstf/faqs.html.

36 Elwood Brehmer, "Alaska Permanent Fund up 4% for 2Q, 5% for FY20," *Alaska Journal of Commerce*, 19 February 2020, https://www.alaskajournal.com/2020-02-19/alaska-permanent-fund-4-2q-5-fy20.

37 Norges Bank Investment Management, "Market Value," accessed 20 September 2021, https://www.nbim.no/en/the-fund/market-value.

38 International Monetary Fund, "Norway: 2017 Article IV Consultation – Press Release and Staff Report," 15 June 2017, IMF Country Report, no. 17/182 (July 2017): 12.

39 See Ted Morton and Meredith McDonald, "The Siren Song of Economic Diversification: Alberta's Legacy of Loss," The School of Public Policy Publications, March 2018, https://www.policyschool.ca/wp-content/uploads/2016/03/siren-song-economic-diversification-morton-mcdonald.pdf.

40 See Morton and McDonald, "The Siren Song of Economic Diversification."

41 Government of Alberta, "Putting Alberta's Growing Savings to Work for Our Future," press release, 4 March 2014, accessed 19 January 2015, http://www.alberta.ca/release.cfm?xID=359728D5EF19F-D565-C959-7EFD9867C9BC38F7.

42 See *Constitution Act, 1982*, Part V, being Schedule B to the Canada Act, 1982 (UK), 1982, c. 11, s. 45 ("Subject to section 41, the legislature of each province may exclusively make laws amending the constitution of the province."). Section 41 exempts the Office of the Lieutenant-Governor from this power.

43 These included the *Alberta Bill of Rights*, the *Auditor General Act*, the *Regulations Act*, the *Languages Act*, the *Ombudsman Act*, the *Electoral Finances and Contribution Act*, and the *Justices of the Peace Act*. See Nelson Wiseman, "Clarifying Provincial Constitutions," *National Journal of Constitutional Law* 6, no. 2 (1996): 269–94, at 289.

44 Wiseman, "Clarifying Provincial Constitutions," 270.

45 United States, Switzerland, Austria, Germany, the four South American federations – Argentina, Brazil, Venezuela, and Mexico, and most recently Ethiopia. In the past decade Italy and Spain, while not technically federal states, have devolved significant powers to regional governments, which have in turn adopted constitution-like documents for governance.

46 Spain, Russia, South Africa, Bosnia and Herzegovina.

47 Austria and Venezuela are two other federations in which this anti-federal practice occurs. In Venezuela, it reflects the centralist bias of South American political development.

48 Turp, "Oui, Quebec Needs a Written Constitution," chapter 1 of this book.

49 "L'ADQ propose d'adopter une Charte du Québéc," *Le Devoir*, 1 June 2001, A-7.

50 These ideas were advanced by the Alberta Residents League and the Citizens Centre, for instance.

51 Dawn Walton, "Seeking to Address Alberta's Anger," *The Globe and Mail*, 8 March 2004, http://www.theglobeandmail.com/news/national/seeking-to-address-albertas-anger/article994970/

52 F.L. Morton, "Constituting Democracy in Alberta," 15–16.

53 Fair Deal Panel, *Report to Government* (Government of Alberta, May 2020), 49, https://open.alberta.ca/dataset/d8933f27-5f81-4cbb-97c1-f56b45b09a74/resource/d5836820-d81f-4042-b24e-b04e012f4cde/download/fair-deal-panel-report-to-government-may-2020.pdf.

54 Richard Albert, "Secession and Constitution in Alberta," in Jack Mintz, Ted Morton, and Tom Flanagan, eds., *Moment of Truth: How to Think About Alberta's Future* (Toronto: Sutherland House, 2020).

55 The same two options are recognized in the Clemens et al. study. See Clemens et al., "Tax and Expenditure Limitations."

56 Rather than immediately entrench the entire *Alberta Act*, it would be more prudent simply to provide a procedure by which selected sections of the act could be entrenched in the future. There may be sections of the act that are no longer relevant or archaic that Albertans may want to delete or amend without having to go through the burdensome procedure (double-majority or referendum, or both) required for formal constitutional amendment.

57 Wiseman seems to imply that the only way a province can place an "entrenched" constitutional limitation on itself is through amending the Constitution of Canada by using the s.43 bilateral amending procedure. See Wiseman, "Clarifying Provincial Constitutions," 279. For the reasons that follow, it is equally plausible that a province could use section 45 amending formula and would not need to get Ottawa's permission to entrench a constitution of its own.

58 Section 41 exempts the Office of the Lieutenant-Governor from this power. *Constitution Act, 1982*, s. 45.

59 Wiseman, "Clarifying Provincial Constitutions," 282.

60 Alberta has in fact bound future legislatures in its *Constitution of Alberta Amendment Act, 1990*, which deals with Métis settlements and stipulates that its amendment or repeal "may be passed be the Legislative Assembly only after a plebiscite of settlement members." Similarly, Alberta's

*Constitutional Referendum Act, 1992*, requires a referendum before ratification "of a possible change to the Constitution of Canada" and further declares the result "is binding on the Government of Alberta." Based on the argument that follows, I believe that the *Metis Settlements Act, 1990* is in fact unconstitutional, since it purports to bind a future parliament with an amending or repeal procedure, or both, that was not used for its original enactment.

61 See Peter W. Hogg, *Constitutional Law of Canada* (Toronto: Carswell, 5th edition, 2007, annually supplemented), 12.3(b), 12–11.

62 Hogg, *Constitutional Law*, 12.3(b), 12–13.

63 Ibid., 12.3(b), 12–18, fn. 71.

64 Ibid., 12.3(b), 12–8.

65 See John O'McGinnis and Michael B. Rappoport, "Symmetrical Entrenchment: A Constitutional and Normative Theory," *Virginia Law Review* 89, no.2 (2003): 385–445. This article is a reply to and rebuttal of an earlier article. See Eric A. Posner and Adrian Vermeule, "Legislative Entrenchment: A Reappraisal," *Yale Law Journal* 111, no. 7 (2002): 1,665–1,705.

66 See O'McGinnis and Rappoport, "Symmetrical Entrenchment" and Posner and Vermeule, "Legislative Entrenchment."

67 O'McGinnis and Rappoport, "Symmetrical Entrenchment," 426.

68 Ibid., 417.

69 Wiseman, "Clarifying Provincial Constitutions," 285.

70 See *Reference re Manitoba Initiative and Referendum Act*, [1919] AC 3 WWR 1, 48 DLR 18.

71 Following the adoption of the *Clarity Act* by the federal government, the Quebec provincial government adopted Bill 99, *Act respecting the exercise of the fundamental rights and prerogatives of the Québec people and the Québec State*, CQLR c. E-20.2. This Quebec act emphasizes the right to self-determination according to public international law. Article 13 responds to the Canadian federal *Clarity Act* by stating: "No other parliament or government may reduce the powers, authority, sovereignty or legitimacy of the National Assembly, or impose constraint on the democratic will of the Québec people to determine its own future."

72 The US National Conference of State Legislatures has several useful publications that review the many different forms of state BBLs and TELs. See National Conference of State Legislatures, "State Balanced Budget Requirements," accessed on 19 September 2021, http://www.ncsl.org/research/fiscal-policy/state-balanced-budget-requirements.aspx.

73 For examples of these choices, see Clemens et al., "Tax and Expenditure Limitations."

74 Morton, "A Provincial Constitution," 15–16.

75 Section 33 of the *Constitution Act, 1982* reads: "Parliament or the legislature of a province may expressly declare in an Act of Parliament or of the legislature, as the case may be, that the Act of a provision thereof shall operate notwithstanding a provision included in section 2 or sections 7–15 of this Charter." The federal government has not yet used the "notwithstanding" clause, but it has been used several times by provincial governments. See Centre for Constitutional Studies, "Notwithstanding Clause," accessed on 19 September 2021, https://www.constitutionalstudies.ca/2019/07/notwithstanding-clause.

76 Just months before the 2019 federal election, the Trudeau government announced the creation of a new advisory board for Supreme Court appointments from Quebec. All eight members of the board must be functionally bilingual and two are chosen by the Quebec minister of justice. The government's press release emphasized that this new process "ensures greater participation by its government in the selection process of judges from the province." Government of Canada, "Prime Minister Announces Advisory Board to Select the Next Supreme Court Justice," 14 May 2019, https://pm.gc.ca/en/news/news-releases/2019/05/14/prime-minister-announces-advisory-board-select-next-supreme-court.

77 See Ted Morton, "The Status Quo Must Go," in Mintz, Morton, and Flanagan," *Moment of Truth*.

78 Tom Flanagan, Jack Mintz, and Ted Morton, "Alberta's Future: Concluding Thoughts," in Mintz, Morton, and Flanagan," *Moment of Truth*.

79 See Chapter IV ("The Judiciary of Quebec") in Turp, "Oui, Quebec Needs a Written Constitution," chapter 1 of this book.

80 Canadian Press, "Couillard Wants National Unity Dialogue Despite Little Interest to Reopen Constitution," *The Globe and Mail*, 1 June 2017.

81 Bill 99, *Act respecting the exercise of the fundamental rights and prerogatives of the Québec people and the Québec State*, CQLR c. E-20.2.

PART THREE

# Insights from Abroad

# 8

# Political Functions and Limitations of Contemporary State Constitutions in the United States

*Jonathan L. Marshfield*

## INTRODUCTION

The United States has a long history with "layered" constitutionalism. Since the adoption of the Articles of Confederation in 1781, the United States has had a written "national" constitution as well as written constitutions for each of the constituent states.[1] Throughout this long history, state constitutions have evolved in their substance and function.[2] During the revolutionary period, some of the then-colonies used state constitutions to signal independence from Great Britain.[3] In the period before the Civil War and the incorporation of the *United States Bill of Rights*, state constitutions were the primary source of law restricting (or failing to restrict) state government intrusion on individual rights.[4] And, during the conservative years of the Burger Court, state constitutions became the focus of efforts to expand individual rights that the United States Supreme Court had restricted under the federal Constitution.[5]

In this essay, I draw attention to two particularly striking features of contemporary state constitutionalism that may be relevant to the broad question of whether subnational[6] units within a federal system should adopt their own written constitutions, and, more specifically, whether Quebec needs a written constitution. Of course, state constitutionalism does not provide an archetype for how subnational constitutionalism should be implemented in any particular federal system, and lessons from state constitutionalism may not translate to other situations. The comparative value of the American experience is surely limited by many factors. Nevertheless, the United States' long history with state constitutionalism may provide some helpful information for constitutional designers in other systems. With these qualifications and limitations in mind, I focus on two themes in state constitutionalism that may be particularly relevant to the Quebec question.

First, state constitutions have a mixed track record as devices for fostering or preserving subnational political identities.[7] One of the most intuitive reasons for a subnational jurisdiction to adopt a constitution is to express and preserve the political priorities of an identifiable subnational community.[8] As A.E. Dick Howard has argued: "no function of a constitution, especially in the American states, is more important than its use in defining a people's aspirations and fundamental values."[9] Yet, state constitutions have done this only sporadically and with limited success. Instead, the dominant trend in state constitutions is for convergence around various national political identities and issues. Although there is evidence that this is the result of unique environmental factors in the United States, there are also good theoretical reasons to believe that subnational constitutions are not especially effective at preserving subnational political communities.[10]

Second, contemporary state constitutionalism is characterized by frequent formal amendment of constitutional texts through popular political processes.[11] This has resulted in a form of constitutionalism that often bypasses representative decision-making and prioritizes swift responsiveness to majoritarian preferences rather than fidelity to entrenched prior commitments.[12] This version of constitutionalism stands in stark contrast to the rigidity of the federal constitutional text and the informal methods of amendment that characterize federal constitutional change.[13] Moreover, recent comparative scholarship suggests that the United States' experience is not idiosyncratic.[14] In fact, most layered constitutional systems around the world experience more formal amendment and popular constitutionalism at the subnational level. Constitutional designers should be aware, therefore, that energized popular constitutionalism seems to follow written subnational constitutions.[15]

These two observations may raise important considerations for the Quebec question. First, to the extent the movement for a written Quebec constitution is motivated by Quebecois nationalism, proponents should take seriously the limitations on using a written constitution to preserve substate political communities. Currently, provincial constitutional change in Quebec seems highly institutionalized and opaque,[16] which might contribute to its entrenchment and the preservation of a Quebecois national identity as the status quo. Codifying Quebec's constitutional law in a written constitution could have the counter-intuitive result of making it less entrenched, and, consequently, less effective in preserving Quebec's national identity. This may be an unlikely outcome based on the longstanding cultural and political circumstances in Quebec, but it should inform expectations regarding the efficacy of a written Quebec constitution.

Second, if written subnational constitutions tend to catalyze pressure for more direct popular involvement in constitutional change, then a written constitution for Quebec would likely raise interesting legal questions regarding a province's authority to craft amendment rules that incorporate referendum or public initiative options. Although a written Quebec constitution may enhance pressure for these devices, such changes may run afoul of Canada's parliamentary tradition and even the Canadian Constitution.[17] Even if the Canadian Constitution permits Quebec to adopt alternative amendment procedures, Quebec reformers should nevertheless be mindful of how democratic amendment processes might further energize popular constitutional politics.

This essay has two major parts. In part one, I explore how state constitutions have performed in fostering subnational political identities and provide a few thoughts on what this might mean for a written Quebec constitution. In the second part, I explore the stark contrast between the processes of constitutional change under the United States Constitution and methods of change under state constitutions. I also explore likely causes of this contrast and provide a few preliminary thoughts on the relevance of the United States experience for Quebec.

## STATE CONSTITUTIONS DO NOT NECESSARILY ENSURE THE PRESERVATION OF SUBNATIONAL POLITICAL COMMUNITY

Perhaps the most intuitive reason for a subnational unit to adopt a constitution is to preserve an identifiable subnational political community within a larger constitutional system.[18] This approach to subnational constitutionalism is common in divided societies that are comprised of geographically clustered political communities.[19]

Subnational constitutions provide a mechanism for these communities to exercise some degree of political self-determination while remaining under a national constitutional structure. On this view, subnational constitutions help express and preserve the values and identity of a self-aware political community.

In this section, I consider the extent to which state constitutions have been successful in expressing or preserving state political identities. I conclude that the evidence is conflicting. A few states have been successful, at times and in limited ways, in using state constitutions to preserve a unique political identity. Most states, however, seem to be characterized by increased convergence with national political identities. In all, the United States experience with written state constitutions suggests that subnational constitutions can facilitate the preservation of political community, but they do not guarantee it.

### *Examples of the Preservation of Unique State Political Identities*

State constitutions provide examples of the effective expression and preservation of unique state identity. The Texas and New Mexico constitutions are particularly illustrative, but Alaska, California, Colorado, Hawaii, and New York, provide further examples, among others. I briefly discuss examples from each.

The Texas Constitution contains evidence of a distinct constitutional narrative for the state. As the Supreme Court of Texas has proudly noted, the Texas Constitution "bears the distinction of being the only state constitution that was derived form its own independent, national constitution."[20] Indeed, as one Texas judge explained: "Texas was never a territory. We were an independent nation from 1836 to 1846 and we joined the Union then by treaty – one sovereign to another. After joining the Union we carried over the written principle upon which our Country (Texas) was founded into the principles of government of our State. As such we have and we pride ourselves in having our own concepts of what our Constitution means to us."[21] Texas's current constitution reflects the state's proud independent tradition and prioritization of self-governance. The constitution's opening declares: "Texas is a free and independent State, subject only to the Constitution of the United States, and the maintenance of our free institutions and perpetuity of the Union depend upon the preservation of the right of local self-government, unimpaired to all the States."[22]

The Texas Constitution has been at least somewhat effective in preserving this identity. The Supreme Court of Texas and the Texas Court of Criminal Appeals have, on various occasions, relied on the Texas Constitution as a basis for resisting convergence with federal constitutional precedent.[23] In *Heitman v. State*, for example, the Texas Court of Criminal Appeals overturned a lower court decision interpreting the Texas Constitution in lockstep with the Fourth Amendment of the United States Constitution.[24] The court held that "clearly our own state constitution was not intended by our own founding fathers to mirror that of the federal government."[25] To be sure, the Texas high courts have not always been consistent in their approach,[26] but to the extent the Texas constitution embodies the fundamental values and unique political character of Texas, state courts have acknowledged and implemented those priorities from time to time.

New Mexico provides another example. The New Mexico Constitution contains a series of unique provisions designed to protect Spanish-speaking residents.[27] Article XII, section 8, for example, provides: "The legislature shall provide for the training of teachers in the normal schools or otherwise so that they may become proficient in both the English and Spanish languages, to qualify them to teach Spanish-speaking pupils and students in the public schools and educational institutions of the state."[28] Article VII, section 3, similarly provides that all New Mexicans have a right to "vote, hold office or sit upon juries" that "shall never be restricted, abridged or impaired on account of … inability to speak, read, or write the English or Spanish languages."[29]

These provisions reflect a deep and lasting commitment to a bilingual and multicultural polity.[30] The provisions were included in the state's initial constitution drafted in 1910, and were "deemed of sufficient importance to be worthy of special protection" through "extraordinary requirements for amendment."[31] Ordinarily, amendments to the New Mexico Constitution must be approved by a majority of both legislative chambers and a majority of voters.[32] The provisions related to Spanish-speaking residents, however, must be approved by three-quarters of the legislature and the electorate.[33]

New Mexico courts have been especially sensitive to the values expressed in these provisions. In *State v. Samora*, the New Mexico Supreme Court considered whether a trial judge violated the state constitution when he dismissed a Spanish-speaking juror "who had difficulty understanding the English language."[34] In finding that the dismissal was unconstitutional, the court explained that the constitution "unambiguously protects the rights of non-English speakers to serve on our state juries."[35] The court further explained that "this unique right has been part of our judicial history since our territorial days" and that "New Mexico courts are required to make every reasonable effort to accommodate a potential juror for whom language difficulties present a barrier to participation in court proceedings."[36]

Hawaii provides another important example. In 1978, Hawaiians convened a constitutional convention. The convention considered several important reforms related to preservation of traditional Hawaiian identities and customary rights.[37] These included a provision recognizing Hawaiian as an official language, guaranteeing traditional subsistence gathering rights at certain fisheries and land, and establishing public education programs regarding Hawaiian culture and heritage.[38] A key purpose of these provisions, which were ratified by voters and added to the constitution,[39] was to protect and promote Hawaiian heritage in the face of opposition from existing state government which had "resulted in making Hawaiians strangers in their own homeland."[40] These reforms appear to have significantly advanced and entrenched Hawaiian identities; at least as compared to the prior state constitutional structure. Hawaiian courts have, for example, relied on these provisions to require county planning commissions to "preserve and protect" the exercise of customary Hawaiian rights.[41] Courts have also relied on these provisions to require state agencies to consider customary access rights when granting special use permits.[42]

Other examples of political identity in state constitutions can be found in Alaska, California, Colorado, and New York, among others. In *Ravin v State*, the Alaska Supreme Court famously held that the Alaskan Constitution embodies a unique commitment to "individuality" that allows citizens "to achieve a measure of control over their lifestyles which is now virtually unattainable in many of our sister states."[43] Similarly, the California Supreme Court, has found that the California Constitution contains a unique commitment to robust and independent protection of individual liberties.[44] The Colorado Supreme Court has held that its constitution prioritizes direct democracy by establishing a fundamental collective right to referenda, initiatives, and recall procedures.[45] Finally, the New York Court of Appeals has reiterated New York's unique commitment to freedom of expression and robust free speech protections.[46]

These rulings and constitutional provisions provide some evidence that state constitutions can effectively express and preserve subnational political identities in the states. They are not the whole picture, however.

*State Constitutions and Constitutional Convergence*

Despite the examples discussed above, there is evidence that the dominant trend in state constitutional law is towards convergence.[47] State constitutional designers, for example, have shown an increasing propensity to model new state constitutions after federal provisions or archetype state constitutions (such as the National Municipal League's Model State Constitution).[48] State constitutions have also increasingly borrowed provisions from each other.[49] This modeling and borrowing has resulted in a greater "degree of uniformity"[50] on both structural and rights issues[51] that reflects a common understanding regarding the nature of American constitutionalism.

As an historical matter, state constitutional convergence seems to have begun in the decades following World War II as the result of pressure to "modernize" state constitutions.[52] New Jersey, Hawaii, and Alaska all adopted constitutions during this period that were modeled heavily after the Municipal League's Model State Constitution.[53] A study of twentieth-century conventions in Rhode Island, New York, New Mexico, Maryland, Arkansas, and Illinois found that proposals in all those states moved closer to the Model State Constitution.[54] Indeed, as James Gardner has observed, "[b]y the late nineteenth century, American state constitutions largely converged on a common model for structuring the institutions of governance."[55]

This is not so say that state constitutions no longer contain idiosyncrasies or unique provisions. The increasing use of the initiative and referendum to amend state constitutions has resulted in many unique state constitutional provisions. In general, however, these changes often reflect popular national trends and sentiments rather than unique state values. Alan Tarr has observed, for example, that following the postwar convergence of state constitutions, many states adopted amendments that reflected broad-based popular skepticism regarding the efficiency and responsiveness of government officials.[56] Although many states adopted unique language to address these issues, the amendments are more a reflection of a broad populist movement throughout the country than the values of any particular state community.[57] More recently, the wave of marriage amendments adopted across many states seems to reflect broad-based national political and cultural cleavages rather than any particular state's identity.[58]

Studies have also shown that despite persistent pressure on state courts to interpret state constitutions by reference to state-specific values and history, state courts tend to interpret state constitutions by reference to national norms.[59] As Joseph Blocher has observed, most state courts "bow to the nationalization of constitutional discourse" and "adopt federal constitutional law as their own."[60] Thus, in both constitutional drafting and constitutional interpretation there has been a trend towards significant convergence in state constitutionalism, and a reluctance to use state constitutions to express or preserve unique constitutional values within states.

There are various possible explanations for this trend. One explanation is that contemporary state populations do not contain consolidated political communities that share fundamental values or even a common political identity. James Gardner is the most notable proponent of this view. He explains: "The claim that the populations of the various American states today constitute meaningfully distinct peoples with meaningfully distinct characters and values is dealt a serious and probably fatal blow simply by consideration of some of the most glaringly obvious features of modern American society: the ease and frequency of mobility; the dominance of mass media and mass marketing of national scope; and the increasing globalization of economic activity. These factors have made state boundaries extremely porous – indeed, for many purposes, such boundaries have become irrelevant."[61] Gardner acknowledges that American society contains many meaningful sub-communities.[62] He maintains, however, that state boundaries do not track those communities, and, therefore, it "simply makes no sense" to talk about state constitutions as expressing the fundamental values of nonexistent groups.[63] The operative communities, according to Gardner, are national in dimension and not confined to particular state boundaries.[64]

Gardner's explanation is explicitly empirical. State constitutions, he maintains, do not express or preserve state values because there is no state community in the first instance.[65] Although Gardner's theory may provide a compelling explanation for why contemporary state constitutions have converged, it is largely unhelpful in assessing whether subnational constitutionalism (as an institution) can be effective in fostering or preserving subnational identities when in fact they exist.

Gardner has, however, articulated a broader theory of subnational constitutionalism that might shed light on that issue. In an important but often overlooked paper titled *In Search of Sub-National Constitutionalism*, Gardner explores the conditions under which subnational constitutions are likely to become "meaningful players in intergovernmental negotiations concerning rights," and, in consequence become "meaningful bulwarks of protection against government tyranny."[66] He identifies three requirements for subnational constitutions to operate effectively in protecting subnational communities: (1) a subnational "populous must come to self-consciousness as a populous, it must understand itself to be a politically distinct group entitled to exercise some significant degree of self-rule"; (2) "this populous must possess sufficient actual autonomy to undertake the enterprise of meaningful self-governance"; and (3) the polity "must commit itself to self-restraint under the rule of law through the adoption of a constitution."[67]

Under these conditions, Gardner argues, subnational constitutions may be effective in protecting subnational communities, so long as other external factors do not undermine their utility.[68] Specifically, he notes that if national laws and institutions provide easy and accessible remedies for subnational communities, subnational constitutions are likely to fall by the wayside. Similarly, if supranational and international organizations provide redress for subnational communities, then subnational constitutions are likely to be insignificant.[69]

This broader theory of subnational constitutionalism likely provides a more complete explanation of state constitutional convergence. Not only have many state populations lost any sense of self-consciousness regarding a unique political identity, but federal law has significantly restricted the degree of autonomy available to states. This is in part because of the expansion of federal constitutional rights applied to the states through the Fourteenth Amendment. As federal constitutional protections have grown, state autonomy has shrunk. Additionally, to the extent American society is comprised of culturally distinct subcommunities, those communities have often found more effective protection through the enforcement of federal constitutional rights. All of these forces, combined with the practical reality that citizens do not primarily sort themselves by state boundaries – might explain why state constitutions have failed to assume a meaningful role in protecting subnational communities.

There is, however, a more theoretical hypothesis to explain state constitutional convergence that is based on Tom Ginsburg and Eric Posner's work. Posner and Ginsburg postulate that subnational constitutions are not particularly effective at resisting pressure for popular constitutional change.[70] Consequently, when majorities shift, subnational constitutions tend to change. To the extent subnational constitutions reflect communal values and identity, therefore, this is often in response to a contemporary majority that has shaped the constitution and not a rigid constitution that has shaped the contemporary majority.[71] In other words, because of their democratic responsiveness, subnational constitutions often change to reflect contemporary political associations rather than preserve preexisting identities by slowing contemporary changes.

Obviously, shifts in political community and constitutional expression are complex and affected by many variables. The account above is overly simplistic in many respects. There is significant evidence, however, that subnational constitutions provide no guarantees regarding the longevity of political community, and this evidence should inform constitutional designers' expectations.

### *What this Might Mean for a Written Quebec Constitution*

The narrative from state constitutionalism in the United States can be helpful in assessing the likely impact of a written constitution for Quebec. A written constitution is surely not a panacea for a subnational community striving for greater recognition and protection. As Gardner has theorized, the efficacy of a subnational constitution implicates a variety of complex variables. It likely depends on the degree of autonomy provided to Quebec under the Canadian Constitution, and the extent to which the people of Quebec form a self-aware political community with a distinct identity. Yet, a written constitution can surely help in perpetuating and formalizing salient political identities. Hawaii's experience is perhaps illustrative of this.

Moreover, to the extent a written constitution is motivated by Quebecois nationalism, reformers should carefully consider whether Quebec's current constitutional system is necessarily inferior to a written constitution for their objectives. As Nelson Wiseman has observed, "provincial constitutions barely dwell in the world of the

[Canadian] subconscious" and "[t]hey are too opaque, oblique, and inchoate to rouse much interest let alone passion."[72] To the extent this observation remains true, it might contribute to the current entrenchment and preservation of Quebecois nationalism in Quebec's political culture. Provincial constitutional change in Quebec seems dominated by representative decision-making and mediated processes of informal constitutional change.[73] These processes can have a slowing effect on constitutional change that might benefit existing political communities. If constitutional law in Quebec is codified in a written constitution, it creates the possibility that constitutional change will be more popularized and more volatile. Although this might benefit Quebecois nationalism, it also creates the possibility that the status quo might be more easily disturbed. From this perspective, a written constitution for Quebec might create more risk for Quebecois nationalism than reward.

Again, this is an oversimplification of the many variables that could impact the effectiveness of a subnational constitution for Quebec. However, state constitutionalism and theoretical research regarding subnational constitutionalism suggests that subnational constitutions may only preserve subnational identities under particular circumstances. This should at least be a consideration for those interested in a written Quebec constitution.

## STATE CONSTITUTIONS HAVE FACILITATED CONTEMPORARY POPULAR INVOLVEMENT IN CONSTITUTIONAL CHANGE

Although some early written constitutions did not contain procedures for amendment,[74] all national written constitutions now contain explicit rules for how the constitutional text can be changed.[75] There are good theoretical and practical reasons for this approach to constitutional change. From a practical perspective, empirical research has shown that a constitution is more likely to last if it is subject to regular formal amendment.[76] From a theoretical perceptive, amendment rules are useful because they establish an ordered process for resolving conflicts regarding fundamental issues of governance.[77] If we take as our starting point, therefore, that a written constitution is likely to contain rules allowing for its amendment, then important design questions include how those rules will be structured, and, in turn, how the chosen amendment rules will affect constitutional politics.

In this section, I explore whether the United States experience with state constitutions sheds light on this issue. I conclude that when state constitutions are viewed from a comparative perspective, there is good evidence to suggest that written constitutions adopted by subnational units often facilitate popular involvement in constitutional change through frequent formal amendment. Frequent amendment, in turn, often promotes a more populist form of constitutionalism that "privileges democratic responsiveness over fidelity to commitments made in the past."[78] I conclude with a few brief thoughts on what this might means for a written Quebec constitution.

### *Characteristics of State Constitutional Change*

Constitutional politics in the United States is a story of stark contrasts. At the federal level, constitutional change occurs primarily through informal amendment of a relatively static constitutional text. Although article V of the Constitution establishes procedures for formal amendment, those procedures are notoriously arduous. Indeed, those who have tried to measure the relative difficulty of amendment rules consistently identify the United States Constitution as having one of the most difficult amendment procedures in the world.[79]

The actual amendment rate (twenty-seven since 1789) is also extremely low relative to other constitutional democracies around the world.[80] In the seminal study regarding relative amendability, Donald Lutz found that the average annual amendment rate for constitutional democracies is 2.54 amendments per year.[81] At the time of his study, the amendment rate for the United States Constitution was only 0.13.[82] In addition, both Richard Albert and Darren Latham have observed that the United States amendment rate has been decreasing over time.[83] In other words, formal amendment of the United States Constitution is relatively uncommon, and it is becoming more uncommon with time.

As a result, constitutional change at the federal level occurs mostly through informal amendment.[84] Informal amendment occurs when political actors and institutions effectively modify constitutional rules without altering the constitutional text, and it can happen in a variety of ways.[85] Bruce Ackerman has famously argued that the Constitution is changed informally through "constitutional moments" that are triggered by significant institutional conflict, followed by dialogue and indirect popular endorsement.[86] Informal constitutional change may also occur through "super-statutes" that are elevated over time to "quasi-constitutional" status.[87] Perhaps the most salient process of informal constitutional change is the Supreme Court's exercise of judicial review. As the final arbiter of constitutional meaning, the Supreme Court can issue binding constitutional decisions that change constitutional rules without any formal change to the Constitution.

One of the main criticisms of informal constitutional change in the United States – especially through judicial review by the Supreme Court – is that the processes lacks democratic legitimacy and undermines popular sovereignty.[88] On this account, article V is a preferable device for at least some constitutional changes because it establishes processes that are more directly tied to democracy, political accountability, and popular sovereignty.

These critics often point to constitutional changes through judicial review as the strongest example of the democratic deficiencies associated with informal constitutional change. Over time, the Supreme Court has rendered various high-profile decisions that changed binding constitutional rules without any changes to the constitutional text. These changes were decided by nine unelected Justices with minimal political accountability because of their protected life tenure.[89] From this perspective, judicial review is a rather undemocratic method of constitutional change that limits opportunities for direct popular involvement in constitutional politics.

Of course, Supreme Court rulings are not self-enforcing. They require the eventual backing of other political institutions to effectuate the Court's ruling. And most of these institutions – such as the President and Congress – are comprised of democratically elected officials. In this sense, even constitutional changes announced by the Court are at least somewhat connected to democratic processes and popular preferences.

Indeed, defenders of informal constitutional change argue that its legitimacy is ultimately grounded in popular sovereignty.[90] Bruce Ackerman's theory of "constitutional moments," for example, involves a multi-step process outside of article V that nevertheless requires indirect popular ratification.[91] The process begins with a constitutional impasse between institutions followed by an electoral mandate to address the impasse. It culminates with a "national election to serve as a referendum" on the resolution of the constitutional impasse.[92] According to Ackerman, this process is tied to popular sovereignty because "popular sovereignty is not a matter of a single moment; it is a sustained process that passes through a series of stages – from the signaling phase through the culminating acts of popular decision to consolidation."[93] Similarly, according to David Strauss, "the people rule not through discrete, climatic, political acts like formal constitutional amendments, but in a different way – often simply through the way they run their nonpolitical lives, sometimes combined with sustained political activity spread over a generation or more."[94]

Even if we accept these accounts of informal amendment, they present only an indirect and protracted connection to democratic processes and popular politics. Indeed, Heather Gerken has defended informal amendment processes precisely because they promote gradual change through deliberative processes.[95] One virtue of informal amendment, according to Gerken, is that it is not "encapsulated in a thin textual reference" adopted by a particular group of people locked in a particular moment.[96] Informal amendment, according to Gerken, involves "repeat encounters with a similar problem over time."[97]

Regardless of whether one agrees with the normative bases for informal constitutional change, most scholars recognize that, as an empirical matter, federal constitutional change occurs primarily through informal processes.[98] For better or worse, the infrequently of formal amendment has forced constitutional change into informal processes. The result is very few opportunities for immediate popular input regarding constitutional reform.

State constitutions present a stark contrast to this picture.[99] If federal constitutional change is dominated by protracted processes of informal change, state constitutional change is characterized by frequent and immediate formal amendment.[100] Indeed, states have amended their current constitutions more than 7,495 times and the states have collectively adopted 144 different constitutions.[101] On average, states formally amendment their constitutions at least once every three years.[102] Although there is some variety in amendment rates between states, even the most static state constitution (Vermont) is amended at least once every two years on average.[103]

Moreover, state constitutional amendment rules generally emphasize popular participation in constitutional change.[104] All states except Delaware require a new constitution to be approved by citizens at a referendum.[105] Similarly, all states except Delaware require all constitutional amendments to be ratified by public referenda.[106] Eighteen states permit citizens to bypass government officials altogether and amend their constitutions directly through the public initiative.[107] Additionally, fourteen state constitutions mandate that there be a regular public referendum on whether the state should hold a constitutional convention to revise or replace the constitution.[108] Two states even allow voters to call a constitutional convention by initiative.[109] All of these amendment processes prioritize direct popular involvement in constitutional change in a way that contrasts with constitutional change under the federal Constitution.

Thus, as John Dinan has observed, state constitutional amendment activity reflects a fundamentally different form of constitutionalism than experienced at the federal level.[110] Under the federal Constitution, popular involvement in constitutional change is protracted, mediated, and severely limited. Indeed, even formal amendment through article V does not require a public referendum of any kind to ratify amendments. At the state level, however, popular involvement is often direct and immediate. In fact, state constitutions are frequently criticized because they appear to change on a whim in response to every hot-button issue in American society.[111]

Consequently, state constitutions often reflect contemporary political preferences rather than a set of deep, enduring commitments passed on from prior generations.[112] They also tend to be very specific in substance and address myriad policy issues that one might consider to be more properly addressed through legislation.[113] Additionally, it is not uncommon for state amendments to directly invalidate unpopular judicial rulings.[114]

This populist form of constitutional is not necessarily invalid. Indeed, I have suggested elsewhere that the populist nature of state constitutions balances the formal rigidity of the federal approach and contributes to the overall health of United States constitutionalism.[115] But the populist nature of state constitutionalism should raise questions for constitutional designers about the likely consequences of having written constitutions for subnational jurisdictions. If the United States experience is mostly the result of idiosyncratic environmental factors, then it may not provide much guidance for constitutional decision makers in other systems. On the other hand, if state constitutionalism is the result (at least in part) of more universal principles of constitutional design, then it may warrant more careful attention.[116]

*Explanations for "Popular" State Constitutionalism*

The causes of state constitutionalism's popular influence have been explored and debated by various scholars. Stephen Griffin, has argued that the states' "permissive attitude toward constitutional amendment" is a "descendant of Anti-federalist beliefs."[117] On this account, state constitutionalism grew from the historical conflict during the framing of the United States Constitution between the federalists and anti-federalists.[118] Because the federal Constitution ultimately adopted the federalists' preference for a rigid, framework-type document, state constitutionalism became the locale for alternative constitutional theories.[119] Christian Fritz, for example, has observed that although the federal Constitution rejected Thomas Jefferson's vision of periodic constitutional revision, Jefferson's "vision assumed considerable importance in the intellectual life of state constitution-making."[120]

John Dinan has offered another historical account. Based on an extraordinary review of the records from most state constitutional convention proceedings, Dinan concludes that states initially maintained very rigid amendment procedures.[121] According to Dinan, it was not until the nineteenth and early twentieth centuries that states began to adopt more flexible amendment rules in response to various concerns.[122] Specifically, Dinan notes that amendment rules were first liberalized during the nineteenth century in order to address entrenched geographic interests that skewed the balance of power in the states.[123] Then, in the twentieth century, states further liberalized amendment procedures to ensure that citizens could "overcome special interests and intransient judges" who "blocked popular social and economic reform measures."[124] Although Dinan's account is more nuanced, it nevertheless suggests that state constitutionalism is mostly the result of unique historical factors and does not identify any transferrable principles of constitutional design that might help inform constitution-makers in other places.

There is, however, a comparative account of state constitutionalism that might shed light on its causes in a way that is more useful for constitutional design. In an important article titled "Subconstitutionalism," Tom Ginsburg and Eric Posner conduct a comparative study of subnational constitutions in the United States and other two-tiered constitutional systems (i.e., systems where there is a "superconstitution" that operates above a set of constituent units with separate "subconstitutions").[125] Ginsburg and Posner explore whether subconstitutions are likely to be designed differently because they are subordinate to superconstitutions.[126] They conclude that subconstitutions are likely to be easier to amend and "weaker" in their ability to constrain majorities than superconstitutions because agency costs are lower at the substate level.[127]

Because agency costs are lower for substates, Ginsburg and Posner observe that there is likely a disparity in constitutional stability between "states" and "substates."[128] High agency costs mean that national constitutional constraints must be relatively strong, static, and difficult to change.[129] Substate constitutions, however, can be relatively more fluid and responsive to public input because agency costs are lower.[130]

As I have explained elsewhere, Ginsburg and Posner's basic intuition is that there are strong incentives for a national constitution to be stable in its creation of core government institutions and protection of essential individual liberties. A stable national constitution, in turn, creates incentives for subnational constitutions to be more responsive to contemporary popular preferences.[131]

Although Ginsburg and Posner note that their empirical analysis is "exploratory," they see evidence of their theory in the United States, the European Union, and Mexico.[132] They also note that they did not find any "subconstitutional system that is more difficult to amend than that of its superstate."[133] Other comparative case studies have found evidence in Austria and Switzerland of a correlation between subconstitutionalism and popular involvement in constitutional change.[134]

Another factor that might explain the correlation between popular constitutionalism and subnationalism is democratic scale.[135] Subnational constitutionalism necessarily involves smaller jurisdictions with fewer participants than the entire national population. Smaller jurisdictions can provide stronger incentives for grassroots political activity if citizens sense that their participation is more likely to impact the outcome in a smaller jurisdiction. As a corollary, smaller jurisdictions might increase the influence of special interests because they are often more cohesive and therefore easier to capture than larger, more diverse jurisdictions. In either case, decentralizing constitution-making to smaller jurisdictions might create stronger incentives for citizens or organized groups to actively pursue formal amendments at the subnational level. This is especially true when constitutional rules are codified in a written constitution with a clear process for amendment.

Thus, there seems to be good evidence that the populist nature of state constitutionalism in the United States is not simply a result of idiosyncratic historical forces. When subnational units adopt written constitutions that operate under enforceable national constitutional law, it is likely that the subnational constitutions will be weaker in their ability to constrain majorities and more majoritarian in nature.[136]

### *What this Might Mean for a Written Quebec Constitution*

Predicting constitutional outcomes can be a particularly dubious exercise. There are many variables and it is very hard to account for all of them in any single analysis. Political culture, for example, can be hard to identify and articulate, but it can be a powerful influence on how constitutional rules are deployed. Nevertheless, the field of comparative constitutional design aspires to identify reliable and transferable relationships between constitutional rules and outcomes. Thus, it is worth commenting here on what popular state constitutionalism might mean for a written Quebec constitution.

First, as noted above, a written constitution for Quebec would likely require the design of formal amendment rules for that constitution. This would raise the legal question of what discretion Quebec has under the Canadian Constitution to craft its own amendment rules.[137] Section 45 of the *Constitution Act, 1982* provides that "[s]ubject to section 41, the legislature of each province may exclusively make laws amending the constitution of the province."[138] As Alan Tarr has observed, "by lodging the power of amendment 'exclusively' in provincial legislatures, [s]ection 45 may preclude provinces from devising alternative mechanisms" for amendment.[139] However, under the parliamentary tradition, provinces can impose upon themselves "manner and form" requirements that could, at least in theory, include a requirement for ratification by popular referendum.[140] Additionally, F.L. Morton has suggested that provincial amendment rules incorporating a referenda requirement would likely be constitutional based on contemporary practice and precedent under the Canadian Constitution.[141] In any event, a written Quebec constitution would very likely raise this issue under Canadian constitutional law.

Second, the above evidence suggests that codifying higher law for the province of Quebec could create incentives for relatively flexible and democratically accountable amendment procedures. This, in turn, could incentivize popular participation in constitutional issues and result in constitutional law that "privilege[s] democratic responsiveness" over entrenched counter-majoritarian commitments.[142] The result is likely a constitution that changes often (or at least more often than the national constitution) to reflect the contemporary preferences of the prevailing majority.[143]

As noted above, this version of constitutionalism is not necessarily problematic. It does, however, come with a particular set of costs and benefits that constitutional designers should consider and explore. It is not my purpose (nor within my field of expertise) to conduct that analysis here regarding Quebec and Canadian constitutionalism. My more modest goal is to flag for those who might pursue a written constitution for Quebec the possibility that it will likely gravitate towards a particular version of constitutionalism; one that is characterized by more frequent popular amendment than experienced under the Canadian Constitution. This might signify a change in the type of constitutionalism currently experienced in Quebec, which I understand to be dominated by representative decision-making and other mediated forms of constitutional change.[144] Of course, to the extent that Quebecois nationalists imagine a written constitution for Quebec to be a first step towards full independence under that constitution, this concern may be inapposite.

Of course, this is by no means a foregone conclusion. Constitutional change in any system is complex and hard to predict. I understand, for example, that much of Canada's constitutional law is found in uncodified constitutional conventions that are not subject to formal amendment in any direct way.[145] This culture of uncodified constitutional law might affect how Canadians approach constitutional change, even under a written provincial constitution. It could, for example, mitigate the usual incentives towards frequent popular amendment.[146] On the other hand, the hydraulics associated with introducing a written constitution into a system dominated by informal methods of constitutional change might catalyze popular energy for formal amendment. In any event, decision makers considering a written constitution for Quebec should give serious thought to how it might affect the nature of constitutionalism in the province.

## CONCLUSION

Drawing comparisons between constitutional systems has many limitations. My goal here is not to suggest that the Quebec question can be answered by any particular comparisons to state constitutionalism in the United States. There is value, however, in studying the experiences of other constitutional systems before making design choices. My hope is that the two aspects of state constitutionalism I have discussed here will at least suggest lines of inquiry relevant to whether Quebec needs a written constitution.

## NOTES

I am grateful to Richard Albert for inviting me to contribute to this important volume. I am thankful for helpful research assistance from Gene Franco.

1 See Akhil Reed Amar, "Of Sovereignty and Federalism," *Yale Law Journal* 96, no. 7 (June 1987): 1,437–1,520.

2 See generally G. Alan Tarr, *Understanding State Constitutions* (Princeton: Princeton University Press, 2000) (describing the many developments in state constitutionalism over time).

3 Mark A. Graber, "State Constitutions as National Constitutions," *Arkansas Law Review* 69, no. 2 (2016): 385–97.

4 Prior to ratification of the Fourteenth Amendment, the states' constitutional space had been demarcated primarily by US Const. art. I, s. 10, which expressly prohibited the states from doing various things. Regarding individual rights, the only meaningful prohibitions contained in that section relate to bills of attainder, impairment of contract, and titles of nobility (ibid.). The Fourteenth Amendment fundamentally changed this by explicitly prohibiting the states from making or enforcing "any law which shall abridge the privileges or immunities of citizens of the United States; ... deprive any person of life, liberty, or property, without due process of law; [or] deny to any person within its jurisdiction the equal protection of the laws" (*US Const. amd. XIV*). But see James A. Gardner, *Interpreting State Constitutions* (Chicago: University of Chicago Press, 2005), 29–36 (recounting confusion in courts' applications of these doctrines before incorporation).

5 See A.E. Dick Howard, "State Courts and Constitutional Rights in the Day of the Burger Court," *Virginia Law Review* 62, no. 5 (June 1976): 874–9. These are only some of the many mutations of state

constitutionalism in the United States over the last two centuries. Indeed, each state constitution has its own unique history that is lost in these broad-brush characterizations.

6 Throughout this essay, I use the phrase subnational to refer to sub-state jurisdictions within a federal system. I understand that this terminology is awkward in the Canadian case because Quebec represents a nation in its own right, albeit within the larger Canadian constitutional structure. Although "sub-state" might be a better phrase to capture the relationship between Quebec and Canada, this phrase introduces confusion when discussing state constitutions in the United States. Thus, as others have done, I use the phrase "subnational" throughout this paper to refer to any sub-state jurisdiction within a federal system, but I do not mean to suggest that Quebec does not retain its own national identity. See G Alan Tarr, "Subnational Constitutions and Minority Rights: A Perspective on Canadian Provincial Constitutionalism," *Rutgers Law Journal* 40, no. 4 (Summer 2009): 769 (using "subnational" to refer to Quebec with a similar qualification).

7 See generally James A. Gardner, "The Failed Discourse of State Constitutionalism," *Michigan Law Review* 90, no. 4 (February 1992): 761–837.

8 See Tarr, "Subnational Constitutions," 783.

9 A.E. Dick Howard, "The Renaissance of State Constitutional Law," *Emerging Issues in State Constitutional Law* 1, no. 1 (1988): 14.

10 See Gardner, *Interpreting State Constitutions*, 61–72 (explaining that state populations do not correspond to meaningful political communities); Tom Ginsburg and Eric Posner, "Subconstitutionalism," *Stanford Law Review* 62, no. 6 (June 2010):1,620–2 (theorizing that under certain usual conditions subnational constitutions are likely to experience pressure to converge on common themes).

11 See Mila Versteeg and Emily Zackin, "American Constitutional Exceptionalism Revisited," *University of Chicago Law Review* 81, no. 4 (2014): 1,679–80.

12 Ibid., 1,679.

13 See Richard Albert, "American Exceptionalism in Constitutional Amendment," *Arkansas Law Review* 69, no. 2 (2016): 224.

14 See Ginsburg and Posner, "Subconstitutionalism," 1,600 ("We know of no subconstitutional system that is *more* difficult to amend that that of its superstate"); John Dinan, "Patterns of Subnational Constitutionalism in Federal Countries," *Rutgers Law Journal* 39, no. 4 (Summer 2008): 842 ("It turns out that subnational amendment procedures are often quite

different from the corresponding national procedures, and, in particular, are invariably more flexible and wide-ranging"); Jonathan L. Marshfield, "Dimensions of Constitutional Change," *Rutgers Law Journal* 43, no. 4 (Spring/Summer 2013): 595–6 ("the growth of subnational constitutionalism has coincided with an expansion of mechanisms for direct democracy and popular participation in constitutional reform").

15 From a normative perspective, frequent formal amendment and popular involvement in constitutional change are not necessarily problematic. See Versteeg and Zackin, "American Constitutional Exceptionalism Revisited," 1,699–1,705 (arguing for recognition of a constitutional theory that prioritizes flexibility and detailed instructions over long-term stability). It could be a desirable consequence of adopting a subnational constitution.

16 See Nelson Wiseman, "Clarifying Provincial Constitutions," *National Journal of Constitutional Law* 6, no. 2 (1996): 270 (explaining stagnant nature of provincial constitutionalism in Canada).

17 See *Constitution Act, 1982*, s. 45, being Schedule B to the *Canada Act, 1982* (UK), 1982, c. 11 [*Constitution Act, 1982*] ("the legislature of each province may exclusively make laws amending the constitution of the province."); Tarr, "Subnational Constitutions and Minority Rights," 789–91 (discussing potential limitations under section 45).

18 See Jonathan L Marshfield, "Models of Subnational Constitutionalism," *Penn State Law Review* 115, no. 4 (Spring 2011): 1,169.

19 Ibid., 1,171–22 (describing this model of subnational constitutionalism in Nigeria, South Africa, Iraq, India, Switzerland, and Ethiopia).

20 *Davenport v. Garcia*, 834 SW (2d) 4 at 15 (Tex 1992) [*Davenport*].

21 *Osban v. State*, 726 SW (2d) 107 at 119–20 (Tex Crim App 1986) (Judge Miller, dissenting).

22 Tex. Const. art. I, s. 1.

23 See e.g., *Heitman v. State*, 815 SW (2d) 681 at 690 (Tex Crim App 1991) [*Heitman*]; *Davenport*, 17.

24 *Heitman*, 690.

25 Ibid.

26 See Gardner, "The Failed Discourse," 789–90 (tracking inconsistencies in Texas high courts' approaches).

27 See generally Jonathan L. Marshfield, "Amendment Creep," *Michigan Law Review* 115, no. 2 (November 2016): 145–7 (describing New Mexico's protection of Spanish-speaking residents).

28 NM Const. art. XII, s. 8; see NM Const. art. XII, s. 10 ("Children of Spanish descent in the state of New Mexico shall never be denied the right and privilege of admission and attendance in the public schools or other

public educational institutions of the state, and they shall never be classed in separate schools, but shall forever enjoy perfect equality with other children in all public schools and educational institutions of the state").

29 NM Const. art. VII, s. 3.

30 See generally Richard H. Folmar, *Piecemeal Amendment of New Mexico Constitution* (Santa Fe: New Mexico Legislative Council Service, 2005), 8.

31 Ibid.

32 See NM Const. art. XIX, s. 1.

33 Ibid.

34 *State v. Samora*, 307 P (3d) 328 at 330 (NM 2013).

35 Ibid., 332.

36 Ibid.

37 *Proceedings of the Constitutional Convention of Hawaii of 1978* (Honolulu: State of Hawaii, 1980), 426–55.

38 Ibid., 426–8.

39 See Haw. Const. art. X, s. 4 (education); art. XV, s. 4 (language); art. XII, s. 8 (customary rights).

40 *Proceedings of the Constitutional Convention Hawaii*, 426.

41 *Pub. Access Shoreline Haw. v. Hawai'i Cty. Planning Comm'n*, 903 P (2d) 1246 at n. 43 (Haw 1995).

42 *In re Contested Case Hearing re Conservation Dist. Use Application (CDUA) Ha-3568 for the Thirty Meter Telescope at the Mauna Kea Sci. Res.*, 431 P (3d) 752 (Haw 2018).

43 *Ravin v. State*, 537 P (2d) 494 at 503–4 (AK 1975) (interpreting Alaskan constitutional provision protecting individual privacy to allow home use of marijuana).

44 See *Raven v. Deukmejian*, 801 P (2d) 1077 at 1088 (Cal 1990) (finding that Cal. Const. art. I, s. 24, which states "Rights guaranteed by this Constitution are not dependent on those guaranteed by the United States Constitution," demonstrates California's commitment to the independent adjudication of individual rights issues).

45 See *Bernzen v. City of Boulder*, 525 P (2d) 416 at 419 (Col 1974).

46 See *Immuno AG. v. Moor-Jankowski*, 567 NE (2d) 1270 at 1277 (NY 1991).

47 See generally Scott Dodson, "The Gravitational Force of Federal Law," *University of Pennsylvania Law Review* 164, no. 3 (February 2016): 703–54.

48 See Tarr, *Understanding State Constitutions*, 153–7; Michael Schwaiger, "Understanding the Unoriginal: Indeterminate Originalism and Independent Interpretation of the Alaska Constitution," *Alaska Law*

*Review* 22, no. 2 (December 2005): 302–3 (providing explanation of how Hawaii and Alaska constitutions were developed based on the "Model State Constitution").

49 See G. Alan Tarr, "Models and Fashions in State Constitutionalism," *Wisconsin Law Review* 1998, no. 3 (1998): 733–6.

50 Ibid., 734.

51 See Tarr, *Understanding State Constitutions*, 12 ("over time state bill of rights have come to more closely resemble federal bill of rights"); Dodson, "The Gravitational Force of Federal Law," 753 ("Yet state constitutional autonomy has not materialized. Instead, all states have declarations of rights that track the federal Bill of Rights, sometimes with a startling degree of mimicry").

52 See Tarr, *Understanding State Constitutions*, 152–4.

53 Ibid., 153.

54 See Elmer E. Cornwell, Jr et al., *State Constitutional Conventions: The Politics of the Revisions Process in Seven States* (New York: Praeger Publications, 1975), 156–9.

55 James A. Gardner, "Practice-Driven Changes to Constitutional Structures of Governance," *Arkansas Law Review* 69, no. 2 (2016): 354; see generally James A. Gardner, "Autonomy and Isomorphism: The Unfilled Promise of Structural Autonomy in American States," *Wayne Law Review* 60, no. 1 (Spring 2014): 31–68; James A. Gardner, "State Constitutional Rights as Resistance to National Power: Toward a Functional Theory of State Constitutions," *Georgetown Law Journal* 91, no. 5 (June 2003): 1,029 ("The texts of the state constitutions are, at many critical points, similar or even identical to one another and to parallel provisions of the US Constitution").

56 See Tarr, *Understanding State Constitutions*, 157. Citizens amended their constitutions to include recall procedures, term limits, and resolve contentious policy issues (such as gambling, gay rights, and tort reform) that state legislatures had avoided. (Ibid.).

57 See ibid.

58 See generally Justin R. Long, "Guns, Gays, and Ganja," *Arkansas Law Review* 69, no. 2 (2016): 453–76.

59 See Dodson, "The Gravitational Force of Federal Law," 725 ("state court interpretations of state constitutions have tended to follow federal court interpretations of the US Constitution"); Lawrence Friedman, "Path Dependence and External Constraints on Independent State Constitutionalism," *Penn State Law Review* 115, no. 4 (Spring 2011):

783–6; Justin R. Long, "Intermittent State Constitutionalism," *Pepperdine Law Review* 34, no. 1 (2006): 41–5.

60 Joseph Blotcher, "Reverse Incorporation of State Constitutional Law," *Southern California Law Review* 84, no. 2 (January 2011): 339.

61 Gardner, *Interpreting State Constitutions*, 69.

62 Ibid., 68.

63 Gardner, "The Failed Discourse," 812.

64 Gardner, *Interpreting State Constitutions*, 69–72.

65 See ibid., 68.

66 James A. Gardner, "In Search of Subnational Constitutionalism," *European Constitutional Law Review* 4, no. 2 (September 2008): 326.

67 Ibid., 327–8.

68 Ibid., 330.

69 Ibid.

70 Posner and Ginsburg, "Subconstitutionalism," 1,584–6. I discuss this idea in more detail in the next section of this essay.

71 This seems to be the conclusion reached by Versteeg and Zackin regarding state constitutions. See Versteeg and Zackin, "American Constitutional Exceptionalism Revisited," 1,679–80.

72 Wiseman, "Clarifying Provincial Constitutions," 275.

73 See Tarr, "Subnational Constitutions and Minority Rights," 787–90.

74 See Tarr, *Understanding State Constitutions*, 62.

75 Jonathan L Marshfield, "Decentralizing the Amendment Power," *Lewis & Clark Law Review* 19, no. 4 (2015): 972.

76 See Zachary Elkins et al., *The Endurance of National Constitutions* (New York: Cambridge University Press, 2009), 7–11, 94–103 (noting that all else being equal constitutions tend to fail if they are too difficult to amend or extremely easy to amend).

77 Sanford Levinson, "Introduction: Imperfection and Amendability," in *Responding to Imperfection: The Theory and Practice of Constitutional Amendment*, ed. Sanford Levinson (Princeton: Princeton University Press, 1995), 4.

78 Versteeg and Zackin, "American Constitutional Exceptionalism Revisited," 26.

79 See e.g., Donald S. Lutz, *Principles of Constitutional Design* (New York: Cambridge University Press, 2006), 154; Richard Albert, "The Difficulty of Constitutional Amendment in Canada," *Alberta Law Review* 53, no. 1 (2015): 86 (discussing empirical research into relative amendment difficulty).

80 See Albert, "American Exceptionalism," 224–8.
81 Lutz, *Principles of Constitutional Design*, 169–71.
82 Ibid. The current rate is slightly less at 0.12; or one amendment every 8.4 years. See Albert, "American Exceptionalism," 227.
83 See ibid., 224–5; Darren R. Latham, "The Historical Amendability of the American Constitution: Speculations on an Empirical Problematic," *American University Law Review* 55, no. 1 (October 2005): 255.
84 See Albert, "American Exceptionalism," 224 ("This decelerating pace of formal amendment is paired with a modern fact of constitutional law in the United States: constitutional change today occurs 'off the books.'").
85 See Richard Albert, "Constitutional Disuse or Desuetude: The Case of Article V," *Boston University Law Review* 94, no. 3 (May 2014): 1,031 (describing informal amendment and listing ways it can occur).
86 See Bruce Ackerman, "The Living Constitution," *Harvard Law Review* 120, no. 7 (May 2007): 1,762. Professor Ackerman initially articulated his theory in slightly different terms. See Bruce Ackerman, *We The People: Transformations* (Cambridge: Harvard University Press, 1998), 20.
87 See William N. Eskridge, Jr and John Ferejohn, "Super-Statutes," *Duke Law Journal* 50, no. 5 (March 2001): 1,230–1.
88 See generally Sanford Levinson, *Our Undemocratic Constitution* (New York: Oxford University Press, 2006).
89 See ibid., 123–39.
90 See generally Heather K. Gerken, "The Hydraulics of Constitutional Reform: A Skeptical Response to *Our Undemocratic Constitution*," *Drake Law Review* 55, no. 4 (2007): 935–6.
91 See Ackerman, "The Living Constitution," 1,762.
92 Ibid.; see Gerken, "The Hydraulics," 934 (describing Ackerman's theory).
93 Ackerman, "The Living Constitution," 1,807.
94 David Strauss, "The Irrelevance of Constitutional Amendments," *Harvard Law Review* 114, no. 5 (March 2001): 1,505; see Gerken, "The Hydraulics," 936 (describing Strauss's theory).
95 Gerken, "The Hydraulics," 935–6 ("change is recorded over time and across factual scenarios").
96 Ibid., 934–5.
97 Ibid., 936.
98 See e.g., Albert, "American Exceptionalism," 224 (describing this as a "modern fact").
99 See generally Versteeg and Zackin, "American Constitutional Exceptionalism Revisited."

100 See Cornwell et al., *State Constitutional Conventions*, 5 ("Whereas the Federal Constitution has been adapted to a changing society by a liberal interpretation of the delegated powers contained in that document, states have more often than not resorted to the formal amending procedure and wholesale revision as methods to keep pace with an increasingly complex society").

101 John Dinan, "State Constitutional Developments in 2015," in *Book of the States* (Lexington: Council of State Governments, 2016), 9, table 1.1.

102 See Jonathan L Marshfield, "Improving Amendment," 488.

103 See Dinan, "State Constitutional Developments," 9.

104 See generally Versteeg and Zackin, "American Constitutional Exceptionalism Revisited," 1,677–8.

105 G. Alan Tarr and Robert F. Williams, "Getting from Here to There: Twenty-First Century Mechanisms and Opportunities in State Constitutional Reform," *Rutgers Law Journal* 36, no. 4 (Summer 2005): 1,081.

106 Ibid.

107 See Marshfield, "Improving Amendment," *Arkansas Law Review* 69, no. 2 (2016): 488–9. The commitment to popular involvement in constitutional change is also evident in the many procedures that state constitutions include for recalling government officials and electing judges. These procedures are ostensibly designed to reduce agency costs and ensure fidelity between the people's preferences and the actions of government officials.

108 Tarr and Williams, "Getting from Here to There," 1,079.

109 Ibid., 1,081.

110 See John Dinan, "'The Earth Belongs to the Living': The Development of State Constitutional Amendment and Revision Procedures," *The Review of Politics* 62, no. 4 (Autumn 2000): 645.

111 See James Gray Pope, "An Approach to State Constitutional Interpretation," *Rutgers Law Journal* 24, no. 4 (Summer 1993): 985 (describing state constitutions as "a textual foundation that changes with every legislative or popular whim"). State constitutions have been amended to address pressing but unsettled social issues like marriage equality and affirmative action. They have also been amended to tackle large but controversial policy issues like government healthcare and gun control.

112 See Versteeg and Zackin, "American Constitutional Exceptionalism Revisited," 1,677 (observing that state constitutions tend to "privilege democratic responsiveness over fidelity to past commitments").

113 See Pope, "An Approach," 985.

114 See John Dinan, "State Constitutional Amendments and Individual Rights in the Twenty-First Century," *Albany Law Review* 76, no. 4 (2012–13): 2,113–18 (collecting and describing amendments that overruled state high court decisions regarding criminal procedures, tort law, and abortion rights).

115 See Marshfield, "Models of Subnational Constitutionalism," 1,196–8.

116 This dichotomy is, of course, an oversimplification of the comparative exercise.

117 Stephen Griffin, *American Constitutionalism: From Theory to Politics* (Princeton: Princeton University Press, 1996), 35.

118 Ibid., 973.

119 Ibid.

120 Christian G. Fritz, "The American Constitutional Tradition Revisited," *Rutgers Law Journal* 25, no. 4 (1994): 973.

121 Dinan, "State Constitutional Amendments," 651; see John Dinan, *The American State Constitutional Tradition* (Lawrence: University Press of Kansas, 2009), 29–32.

122 Dinan, "State Constitutional Amendments," 650.

123 Ibid., 650–1.

124 Ibid., 650.

125 See Ginsburg and Posner, "Subconstitutionalism," 1,584.

126 Ibid., 1,584–5.

127 In this context, agency costs refer to the inefficiencies in government resulting from actions taken by government officials that benefit officials at the expense of the public. (Ibid., 1,585). Ginsburg and Posner conclude that agency costs are lower at the sub-state level because superconstitutions must place limits on theoretically unlimited government power, but subconstitutions are legally subordinate to their respective superconstitutions. (Ibid., 1,596). Moreover, there is no effective enforcement mechanism operating above a superconstitution, but national government provides an effective monitoring and enforcement mechanism regarding sub-state abuses of power. (Ibid., 1,596–7). Finally, if sub-states abuse power, they are more likely to lose citizens to neighboring sub-states because mobility within a country is easier than international immigration. (Ibid.).

128 Ibid., 1,593–4.

129 Ibid.

130 Ibid.

131 See Harry L. Witte, "Rights, Revolution, and the Paradox of Constitutionalism: The Processes of Constitutional Change in Pennsylvania," *Widener Journal of Public Law* 3, no. 1 (1993): 475 (reaching a similar conclusion regarding the United States federal system: "[O]ur federalism permits vigorous popular democracy to operate in the states because the Federal Constitution places checks on majoritarian excesses.").

132 Ginsburg and Posner, "Subconstitutionalism," 1,627.

133 Ibid., 1,600.

134 See Marshfield, "Dimensions," 599–602 (summarizing these studies).

135 See ibid., 607 (exploring this possibility).

136 See Dinan, "Patterns," 842 (conducting comparative study of amendment procedures and finding that subnational amendment procedures are usually easier to amend and amended more frequently). But see Versteeg and Zackin, "American Constitutional Exceptionalism Revisited," 1697–9 (resisting this view).

137 See Tarr, "Subnational Constitutions and Minority Rights," 790–1 (raising this issue).

138 *Constitution Act, 1982*.

139 See Tarr, "Subnational Constitutions and Minority Rights," 790.

140 Ibid.

141 See F.L. Morton, "Provincial Constitutions in Canada" (unpublished manuscript, 4 April 2004), https://statecon.camden.rutgers.edu/sites/statecon/files/subpapers/morton.pdf.

142 Versteeg and Zackin, "American Constitutional Exceptionalism Revisited," 1,677.

143 See ibid., 1,679–80 (describing state constitutions in this way).

144 See Tarr, "Subnational Constitutions and Minority Rights," 771.

145 See ibid.

146 See ibid., 791 (noting that the "absence of supermajority requirements or popular ratification could, alternatively, simply reflect Canadian political culture, which has shown a distrust of referenda unlimited popular sovereignty").

# 9

# The Brazilian Experience with Subnational Constitutions: What Went Wrong?

*Débora Costa Ferreira and Juliano Zaiden Benvindo*

## 1. INTRODUCTION

Would the enactment of a constitution for Quebec help structure and clarify the constitutional identity of its citizens, enhancing thereby democratic participation?[1] Would it provide the maintenance and enhancement of Quebec's multicultural heritage?[2] In other words, the discussion is whether the existence of subnational constitutions strengthen provincial autonomy in a federal state. This paper aims to address, from the Brazilian experience with subnational constitutions, some important insights about the role subnational constitutions may play in a federal state. Evidently, Brazil's federalism is very distinct from Canada's in many respects, and the way subnational constitutions have been drafted over history in Brazil is not easily comparable to the debate that is now gaining momentum in Canada. Yet, comparative law is also aimed at bringing these very differences as well as some interesting connections into the spotlight. As a country with twenty-six states and a federal district – each one with its own constitution – there are naturally important facts, data, and analyses that can be drawn from such a reality. From this brief discussion of the Brazilian subnational constitutional system, we hope to bring some contribution to the debate over whether Quebec should have its own constitution.

Although the existence of state constitutions is a prerequisite of Brazil's federalism,[3] most citizens do not have any knowledge of their existence and do not see them as something that really matters for their lives. One reasonable explanation for such a behaviour is that most state constitutions basically repeat norms from federal constitutions in a mimicry process,[4] a movement that has intensified in the most recent constitutions.[5] The reasons for this lie mostly in five features of Brazilian constitutionalism: (i) the short drafting period that state constitutions had after the enactment of federal constitutions; (ii) the centralized federal model, which was intensified in dictatorial regimes, leaving thereby a narrow space for constitutional innovation; (iii) the uncertainty about the current margin of state constitutional autonomy as such defined by the judiciary and its centralizing tendency; (iv) the overlapping structure of judicial review in constitutional states; and (v) the reinforcing tendency of mimicking, which has been catalyzed by subnational amendment procedures. Therefore, under some specific institutional and legal conditions – like the ones that led to the irrelevance of state constitutions in Brazil – our conclusions clearly point out that it might not be worth enacting subnational constitutions.

If those conditions apply for Quebec, even though Brazil is quite a diverse paradigm, our conclusions may serve as a cautionary case of how subnational constitutions may not be that powerful tool to reach the expected sociocultural goals normally connected to this debate.

In the following sections, we will describe the mimicry process observed in constitutions in Brazil and explain each of its causes.

## 2. THE MYTH OF STATE AUTONOMY AND THE MIMICRY PROCESS

The Brazilian constitutional literature generally upholds the importance of subnational constitutions, pointing out that it is part of the very essence of Brazil's federal model and a vital feature of each state's autonomy. For example, Anna Cândida Ferraz argues that "the first element of state autonomy is the capacity assigned to the federated unit to grant itself a particular constitution."[6] Cláudio Pacheco sustains that "autonomy is the faculty of granting their own constitutions, and to be *a fortiori* governed by them, but according to pre-existing norms."[7] The underlying argument lies in establishing and strengthening, through such constitutions, both federalism and regional identities. Naturally, for these features to prove true, it is at least expected that subnational constitutions provide some originality, which means that they cannot be "a copy of the Federal Constitution" and comprise the fundamental rules and principles of the organization and main activities of the member states.[8]

Historically, these premises were part of the mainstream understanding of federalism in the first years of Brazil as a republic. In 1890, just some months before the Constitution of 1891, which established a republican government after years of monarchy, the idea that states had to exert their autonomy also through their own constitutions gained momentum. The chief of the provisory government, General Manoel Deodoro da Fonseca, somehow influenced by American federalism, enacted the Decree 802,[9] which determined that the states had to enact their own constitutions by their legislative assemblies before the enactment of the Constitution of 1891. The need to draft the subnational constitutions before the federal one was well explained in the following words from that decree:

> Whereas the constitutional organization of the states is the necessary complement of the regime laid out in the federal Constitution of 22 June;
>
> Whereas, even after the future Congress adopts this constitutional pact, we will not have established the legality prescribed therein while the various states do not have their respective constitutions;
>
> Whereas, before such a fact, it will be impossible for the next National Congress to draft the organic laws of the country and even the normal budget of the Republic, since the estimate of federal resources and obligations requires a precise differentiation between the administration, the judiciary, the state income, [on the one hand], and the income, the judiciary, the general administration [on the other].
>
> Whereas Congress cannot naturally fulfil its ordinary duties after having exercised its constituent mandate, while the constituent assemblies in the states have not gathered and enacted their constitutions.
>
> Whereas, therefore, once the Constitution has been approved and the Supreme Justices of the Republic have been elected, the next Congress will determine the adjournment of its sessions until the states enact their constitutions.

> Whereas, consequently, the urgent need to speed up this work of local organization, so that the National Congress, still in mid-1891, begins to ordinarily work in the regular exercise of the legislative power, as the Chamber and the Senate.

It is clear from such words that, in the origins of Brazilian federalism, there was a strong subnational constitutional project. Yet, as time went by, that project was set aside in favour of a model of federalism that was paradoxically centralist by gradually bestowing greater powers on presidents.[10] The following constitutional frameworks already pointed to an increasing process of subnational constitutions that simply mimicked the federal one, and, even with the transition to democracy in 1985, this trend was kept strong in the years following the Constitution of 1988. Indeed, current state constitutions have as a common ground the high similarity with that Constitution.

In a very interesting empirical research, Cláudio Couto, Gabriel Bellon, and Victória Gandolfi[11] concluded that there is a narrow variation in length between subnational constitutions and the federal Constitution (22.5 per cent using the word count criterion or 20.5 per cent using the number of articles criterion), with a negligible linguistic variability and practically the same order of chapters (nine out of ten chapters are identical).[12] Table 9.1 shows the relative[13] and the general[14] equivalence index between state constitutions (SC) and the federal Constitution (FC). It proves that subnational constitutions are more similar to the federal Constitution than among themselves, thus revealing that mimicking the federal Constitution has been the rule in state constitutions.

The state whose constitution presents a higher similarity to the federal Constitution is Rio Grande do Norte (RN), with an index of 58.74 per cent of its constitutional text, and the lowest is the Constitution of Rio Grande do Sul (RS), whose index is 20.43 per cent. A comparison among state constitutions also shows that Rio Grande do Sul (RS) is the most original one (figure 9.2). Rio Grande do Sul (RS) and Pernambuco (PE) are states normally deemed as carrying a high autonomist tradition and their citizens have a strong sense of identity,[15] which may help explain their lower similarity to other constitutions. This thesis becomes even more consistent because that research was not able to identify any significant influence of a regional factor on the equivalence index.

Table 9.1 | Equivalence indexes

| Statistics | Relative equivalence index | | | General equivalence index | | |
|---|---|---|---|---|---|---|
| | SC x SC | FC x SC | SC x FC | SC x SC | FC x SC | SC x FC |
| Mean | 26.24% | 24.66% | 34.81% | 8,003.23 | 10,650.92 | 10,653.58 |
| Standard deviation | 7.33% | 5.54% | 8.72% | 2,060.33 | 2,394.14 | 2,388.67 |
| Coefficient of variation | 27.91% | 22.48% | 25.05% | 25.74% | 22.48% | 22.42% |
| Minimum | 8.73% | 11.08% | 20.48% | 2,865 | 4,786 | 4,866 |
| Maximum | 48.54% | 33.74% | 58.74% | 14,264 | 14,576 | 14,554 |

Source: Couto et al., *Constituições Estaduais e Centralização Federativa*, 14.

This conclusion may be an interesting point for Quebec's debate over the need of its own constitution as it may provide some insights about the relevance of supporting an identity for a constitutional project. Turp's argument that "Today, Quebec does not have a clear constitutional identity,"[16] if true, can be interpreted as a red flag since it may point towards a potentially higher risk of a mimicry process in any future Quebec constitution. However, there are some methodological caveats: the comparable contextual variables between Brazil's and Canada's experiences differ significantly, the sample is very limited, and cultural identity does not necessarily mean constitutional identity – one could argue, for instance, that both Rio Grande do Sul and Pernambuco have a strong cultural identity, but not a constitutional one.

The difference between what was expected of Brazilian federalism in the first years of republic, based on Decree 802, and what it turned out in the following years, is astonishing. More striking is to observe that the first years of the republic were also characterized by a creative moment of subnational constitution-making.

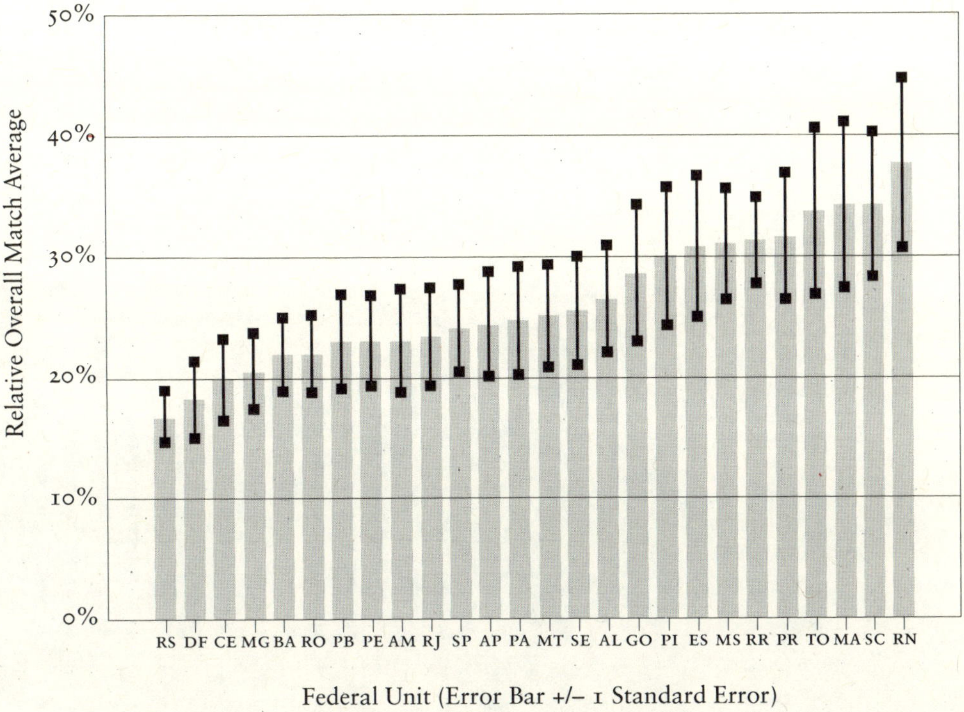


Figure 9.1 | Equivalence between federal and state levels

Couto, Bellon, and Gandolfi's research[17] also empirically proves that the first subnational constitutions were much less similar to the first federal constitutions than what came out as a pattern in the most recent constitutional frameworks in Brazil. Their study compared the Constitution of 1891 with five subnational constitutions: São Paulo and Minas Gerais, by reason of their notorious political relevance at the federal level; Rio Grande do Sul, Pernambuco, and Pará, since they are recognized as endowed with a considerable autonomous vocation and also as regionally economic and cultural powers at least since the First Republic.

The greater degree of similarity was observed in Minas Gerais' Constitution, with 17.08 per cent, followed by the Constitutions of Pará (16.80 per cent), São Paulo (7.99 per cent), Pernambuco (4.41 per cent), and Rio Grande do Sul (2.75 per cent). The higher sense of identity and autonomy may explain their extremely low degree of

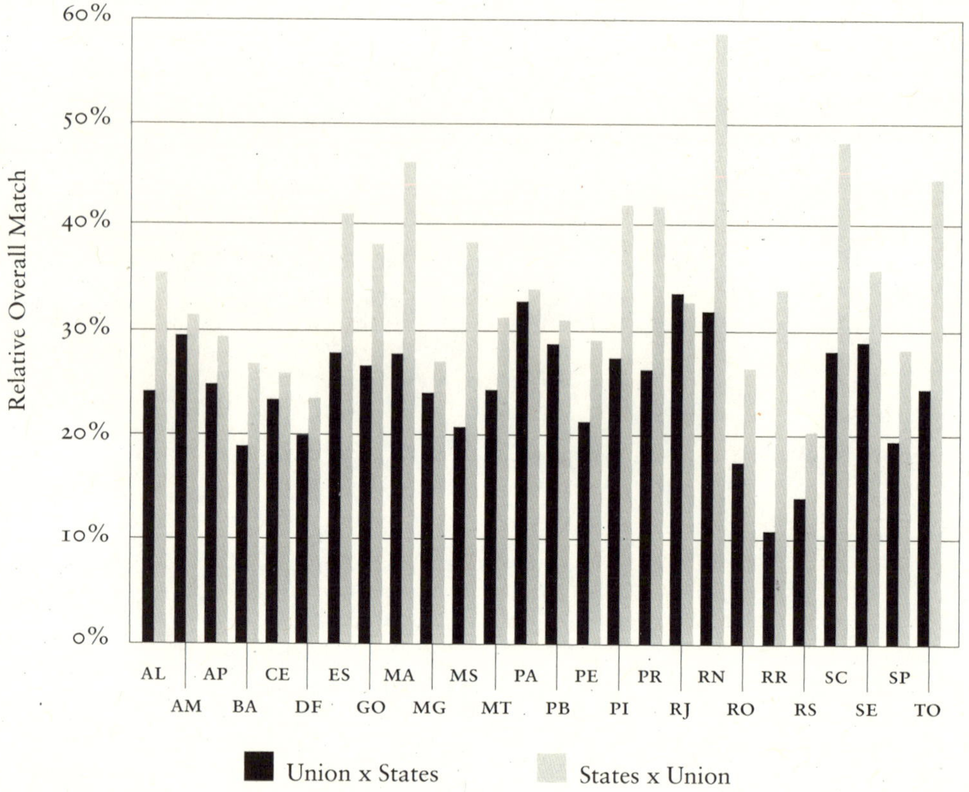


Figure 9.2 | Average interstate equivalence

similarity. As shown before, however, these levels of similarity have increased over time (Rio Grande do Sul: 20.43 per cent; Pernambuco: 29 per cent), though the degrees of similarity of Minas Gerais and Pará have remained relatively identical as of today. Although a higher sense of identity may play a role for greater originalism in some subnational constitutions, there are naturally other more structural causes for such a behaviour. History clearly points out that constitutional creativity slowed down over the years and even in such states deemed as owning a stronger sense of identity and autonomy. What went wrong? What might explain the increasing mimicry process?

## 3. WHAT WENT WRONG? REASONS FOR THE MIMICRY PROCESS

In our investigation of this phenomenon, we found five main factors that can better explain the failure of the Brazilian subnational constitutional project by reason of an increasing mimicry process. These factors are presented below.

### *3.1 Temporal Constraints to Enact State Constitutions in New Constitutional Frameworks*

It has been a common pattern of Brazilian constitutionalism since the proclamation of the republic in Brazil in 1889 to determine that each state must have its own constitution, which has been normally followed by temporal constraints imposed at the federal level. Unlike what seemed to be the spirit of the Decree 802 of 1890, the Constitution of 1891 already laid down explicit constraints aimed at pushing state constituent powers to draft their constitutions until 1892 or their respective states would have their constitutions as simple copies of another state's constitution, even if amendable according to its rules. This is what article 2 of the transitory provisions prescribes: "The State which, by the end of the year 1892, has not enacted its own constitution shall be submitted, by act of Congress, to that of one of the others which seems more convenient for this adaptation, until the state subject to that regime amends it by the process determined therein."[18] Although, in the end, every state, naturally eager to be autonomously constituted, proclaimed their own constitution, that pattern was set.[19] The following Constitution of 1934 would not be that different in determining a temporal constraint, but now for only four months, according to article 3 of the transitory provisions:

> Art. 3. Ninety days after the promulgation of this Constitution, elections will be held for the members of the Chamber of Deputies and the Constituent Assemblies of the States. Once inaugurated, the latter will elect the Governors and the representatives of the States in the Federal Senate, swear them into office and, within a maximum period of four months, draft their respective constitutions, which will then be transformed into

> ordinary Assemblies, taking care to ensure that the representation of the professions is met.
>
> Paragraph 6 – The State that, at the end of the term of this article, has not enacted its Constitution shall be submitted, by deliberation of the Federal Senate, to that of one of the others that seems more convenient, until it amends it by the process determined therein.[20]

The Constitution of 1937, which inaugurated the Estado Novo dictatorial regime of President Getúlio Vargas, suspended this practice, because, as it is expected from an authoritarian government, it centralized even further the federal government and expanded presidential powers. Article 187 of the Constitution provided that it would be "submitted to a national plebiscite," which never took place. National Congress, the state legislative assemblies, and the Municipal Chambers were all dissolved (article 178). All states were instead regulated by the Decree-Law n. 1.202 of 8 April 1939,[21] which directly submitted state governors to the authority of the president. Only at the end of the regime were elections for state governors and members of the state legislative assemblies set according to the Decree-Law n. 8.063, of 10 October 1945.[22] Yet, before those elections and in a similar pattern to previous constitutional frameworks, article 2 of that Decree-Law established a temporal constraint of only twenty days for state governors or intervenors to enact their respective constitutions.

After the end of Estado Novo and already under the liberal Constitution of 1946, that pattern of setting out temporal constraints on state constitution-making remained practically untouched. Article 11, paragraph 9, of the transitory provisions stated: "Any state which, up to four months after the installation of its assembly, may not have decreed its constitution, shall, by deliberation of the National Congress, be submitted to the constitution of whichever other state may be deemed most suitable, until it has been amended by the process determined therein."[23] The authoritarian Constitution of 1967 also determined a temporal constraint, now of only sixty days, but, unlike the previous constitutions, the focus was on amending the already existent state constitutions by adapting them to the new federal – and authoritarian – constitutional order. Article 188 says: "The states shall amend their constitution within sixty days to adapt them, where necessary, to the standards of this Constitution, which, at the end of that period, shall be considered automatically incorporated into the state constitutions."[24] The transition to a democracy in 1985 would not change this scenario.

The current Constitution of 1988 would follow the same pattern of defining a temporal limit for each state to promulgate their own constitutions. Article 11 of the *Act of the Temporary Constitutional Provisions* sets down: "Each Legislative Assembly endowed with constituent powers shall draft the State Constitution within one year as from the promulgation of the Federal Constitution, with due regard for the principles of the latter."[25] A temporal constraint was also set out for the so-called Organic Laws of the municipalities in the sole paragraph of the same article: "After the promulgation of the State Constitution, it shall be incumbent upon the City Council, within six months, to vote the respective Organic Law, in two discussion and voting turns, with due regard for the provisions of the Federal and State Constitutions."[26] Unlike the previous constitutions, the Constitution of 1988 did not define the penalty of temporarily adopting other state constitutions, were a state not able to draft its own constitution during that period of one year. Yet, it clearly maintained the mindset that a short amount of time is enough to grapple with the complexities of constitutional design.[27] There was no perspective whatsoever of the need of each state to work with the particularities that might play a role based on its constitutional identity and what the people of that state might deem as representative of their will. Rather, the quickest response was to basically mimic the federal Constitution, with some originalism being found in those state constitutions that have historically shown a more autonomous behaviour.

In such constitutions with a stronger sense of identity, the costs of writing down their social values in the constitutional text may prevail over the inertial costs of simply mimicking the federal or another state constitution, even more so if their citizens are more consensual about their values. It would also be more socially costly to accept other state values or even the federal ones in detriment of their own. In any case, the mimicry process prevailed in most of the constitutions – and, though less pronounced, also in those traditionally more autonomous states. The inertial effect would also impact the very capacity of constitutional change after those state constitutions had been enacted: changes aimed at translating such identities into the constitutional text, once the primary constituent power was already over, would likely require a stronger endeavour of political actors.

The lesson from Brazil for Quebec is that time matters a great deal: it allows for a more appropriate balance between strengthening the provincial's own identity and the natural costs of inertia. It also helps engender the necessary debates and reflections on how to draft constitutional clauses that better serve the needs of Quebec, avoiding the less demanding behaviour of simply mimicking the federal constitution's clauses.

Other factors, however, would also play a significant role in hampering originality and autonomy at the subnational level.

### 3.2 *Identity Destruction by Dictatorial Regimes and the Centralizing Heritage*

In addition to temporal constraints, the very centralizing heritage of Brazilian federalism matters significantly for the low degree of originality of state constitutions, more even so if this heritage becomes more pronounced as a consequence of the dictatorial regimes that plagued the country in the twentieth century. Dictatorial regimes imposed a broadly centralized model, with a narrow space of autonomy to state-members, disrespecting thereby constitutional identities already established in the previous constitutional orders. It practically decimated any sort of creativity in state constitutional-making. The Constitution of 1937, during the Estado Novo, as Pacheco argues, "heavily compressed the margin of state autonomy, expanding the federal intervenient power, and, most drastically, degraded the federal state to the point of not collecting enough revenue to maintain its services for three consecutive years."[28] Likewise, the Constitution of 1967 determined the automatic incorporation of its provisions to subnational constitutions.[29] The amendment n. 1 of 1969 to the Constitution of 1967 followed suit and went even more radically in determining that "the provisions contained in this Constitution are incorporated, where necessary, into the constitutional law drafted by the states."[30] Authoritarianism has thereby strongly affected the people's capacity to adopt state constitutions as a means to impose limits on the federal government.

This centralizing heritage has then played a great part in the Brazilian federative model, even though the country transitioned to a democracy more than thirty years ago. In some respects, we could argue that it has, either unconsciously or consciously, internalized this centralized framework. Therefore, there is little space for subnational entities to create their own constitutionalisms in a way that both complements and specifies the federal one according to their own particularities. The mimicry process is thereby a predictable consequence and is "an element that reinforces the interpretation of the Brazilian federalism as being of a considerably centralized type."[31]

It is no wonder that the Constitution of 1988 explicitly restricts constitutional authority of member-states while keeping many of them in the hands of the Union,[32] and, in some cases, of the municipalities.[33] More serious, the Union has all the tools to force federal entities to comply with certain rules, either directly – for example, through federal intervention, though needing authorization by the Supreme Court[34] – or, indirectly, due to its tight grip on taxes and revenues, which shows the imbalance of economic power in favour of the Union. There is a top-down institutional mechanism of coercion that significantly constrains the states to follow the standards as defined by the Union.[35] This feature increases the cost of innovation due to the risks of being penalized for challenging such standards. It is small wonder that it has jeopardized even the innovative energy of most autonomist states.

Even though Canada features a more robust democratic framework and tradition, the Brazilian experience shows that also democratic constitutions, such as Brazil's current one, can adopt distinct mechanisms to constrain autonomy and curb constitutional innovations. The questions that should be raised in this regard are whether the central government have such instruments and whether Canadian federalism is structured in a way that enables, even indirectly, the Union to suffocate Quebec's constitutional identity. If so, perhaps the effects foreseen by Turp may not happen in the extent he envisions.

### *3.3 Uncertainty about the Current Margin of State Constitutional Autonomy as Such Defined by the Courts and Their Centralizing Tendency*

Uncertainty about the limits of constitutional autonomy at the subnational level naturally increases the cost of innovation, which has intensified because of the centralizing heritage of the dictatorial years. The uncertain margin of innovation can foster constitutional review and a stronger intervenient role by the judiciary. Such an outcome is obviously not ideal as it entails political costs of not taking advantage of a greater electoral legitimacy to define, through constitution-making, the autonomy and the identity a state aims to preserve. Yet, for a country whose states have not really fought for autonomy, the alternative of simply copying another state's constitution or the federal one might sound reasonable and, as a practical matter, engender minimal costs, even though suffocating their autonomy – which may not have been a serious issue at first place. After all, if a state is uncertain about how far it can go in defending its autonomy, perhaps it will be better off by not even experimenting any avenue that might challenge federal standards. In other words, the Union takes advantage of the benefit of the doubt.

Thus, only states with a broad sense of identity and which have strongly defended their autonomy might be willing to channel their energies into innovation and operate in the grey zone of constitutional battles and legal uncertainties. The inertial movement favours, after all, the simplest avenue – in this case, basically copying another state constitution or the federal one – if the preservation of autonomy and identity has not been deemed such a serious matter to the point of needing to be institutionalized through constitutional means. The very restrictive and centralizing interpretation of federalism can turn the imitation of the federal Constitution or another state constitution into a better strategy, even for states with a stronger identity. Perhaps this premise may help explain why the similarity rate of the constitutions of well-known states for defending their identity, such as Rio Grande do Sul and Pernambuco, is higher today than during the First Republic.[36] The centralizing heritage combined with unclear limits has raised institutional incentives that are contrary to innovation and experimentalism.

History may help explain how such institutional incentives have played out as a growing barrier to innovation and experimentalism. It also shows that the original idea of providing greater autonomy to the states have proven irreconcilable with the centralizing tradition that would react more explicitly in the following constitutional frameworks. For example, when the Constitution of 1891 was enacted, it set a very general and vague material limit for constitution-making at the subnational level: "Each State shall be governed by the Constitution and laws adopted by it, provided that the constitutional principles of the Union be respected."[37] Therefore, at that moment, states needed only to observe the "constitutional principles of the Union." Naturally, such vague clause engendered some important legal battles and both courts and doctrine attempted to settle the high level of uncertainty it created. "The absence of express enumeration of constitutional principles became a source of innumerable constitutional and political problems," said Ana Cândido Ferraz.[38] In 1926, therefore, a constitutional reform was introduced to set out the so-called sensitive constitutional principles that states had to comply in their constitutional systems with, which were later reinforced and expanded in the Constitution of 1934. They were:

> Article 7. It appertains exclusively to the States:
> I. To decree the Constitution and the laws by which they may govern themselves, observing the following principles:
> (a) Representative republic form;
> (b) Independence and coordination of powers;
> (c) Temporary duration of elective functions, limited to the same periods of time as the corresponding Federal positions, and prohibiting the re-election of governors and prefects for the period immediately following;
> (d) Economy of Municipal Districts;
> (e) Guarantees of the local Judicial Power and of the Attorney General;
> (f) Presentation of accounts of the administration;
> (g) Possibility of constitutional reform and competence of the legislative power to decree it;
> (h) Representation of the professions.[39]

Along with the democratization process, the Constitution of 1946 adopted an analog clause to that of the Constitution of 1891: "Each State shall govern itself by the Constitution and the laws it may adopt, the principles established in this Constitution being duly observed."[40] The interpretation at that time was that these principles were not only those that could justify federal intervention, but also those explicitly or implicitly directed at states. At least formally, therefore, it seemed that this new constitutional order would grant states greater autonomy. Yet, the following authoritarian Constitution of 1967, while keeping a similar structure, enumerated some restrictions,[41] thereby increasing uncertainty: "It is not surprising that the state constituent power practically 'copies' the Federal

Constitution, driven, perhaps, by the fear of 'forgetting the principles' or – who knows? – by the difficulty in distinguishing which principles must be copied from those that must be assimilated and adapted, and which principles of the Federal Constitution have no need to be adopted by the states."[42]

The Constitution of 1988 practically repeated the model of the Constitution of 1891. Article 25 provides that "The states are organized and governed by the Constitutions and laws they may adopt, in accordance with the principles of this Constitution."[43] It went even further in declaring that "all powers that this Constitution does not prohibit the states from exercising shall be conferred upon them."[44] This vague clause, more than in the previous federal constitutions, received a great attention from constitutional scholars and the courts. Yet, the uncertainty has remained strong, first, because of the very theoretical difficulty in defining the "principles of this Constitution," and thus determining which norms states must comply with, and, second, because such a definition would reach the Supreme Court, a player that has proven unable to settle controversies in this matter – in fact, the opposite is true.

Uncertainty about the federal corresponding principles the subnational constitutional should embrace has potentially significant effects on constitutional design. In this matter, like the previous ones, it impacts how constitutional drafters should appropriately balance the level of desired autonomy with the shared values of the federation as well as foresee potential court's behaviours thereafter. This is an important aspect that Turp did not mention directly but which should not be forgotten.

These difficulties in defining the "principles of this Constitution" – norms that states have to comply with – are also visible in the Brazilian constitutional literature. Since the promulgation of the Constitution of 1988, there has been a fruitful debate over the principles of the Constitution that the states' constituent powers must comply with. Basically, the main argument has focused on interpreting the Constitution as the guidance and the source of validity, whose effects irradiate on the entire legal system and provide it with homogeneity and coherence. In this regard, for example, Raul Machado Horta argues that "it is in the federal Constitution that lays the legal source of the member state's constituent power."[45] This premise of the Constitution representing the core of a "minimum of identity" is also Leo Leoncy's main argument: "it is common for the legal order of a federal State to attribute to the [federal] entities a set of competences, faculties, rights, and duties arranged in a differentiated and asymmetric manner. On the other hand, it is also appropriate that the same legal order imposes certain normative standards in a uniform way as necessary for the maintenance of a minimum of identity among the various political bodies which are members of the pact."[46]

Therefore, based on the scope of each norm in the federal framework as a core providing a "minimum identity," they can be interpreted as being binding, permitted, or prohibited at the subnational level.[47] Such a classification is what normally leads to the distinction between constitutional principles of binding compliance and those of nonbinding compliance. Yet, disagreement prevails when it comes to defining the extension of such a vague clause of "principles of this Constitution." As a provider of "minimum identity," the Constitution also acts as conditioning state constitutions to "be inserted in the context of the federal Constitution in a harmonic way,"[48] which is not always an easy content for interpretation. In this context, Tércio Sampaio Jr acknowledges that copying provisions of the Constitution in state constitutions was the way subnational political actors found to enhance the legitimacy of their state orders: "We must acknowledge that, in order to observe principles, the constituent power need not repeat them in the state constitution, although nothing prevents him or her from doing so … A principle is not fulfilled by repeating its content, but by issuing rules that create a hierarchically harmonic framework. Since principles do not require a specific behaviour and are not applicable in an 'all or nothing' fashion, observing them means following their guidance in setting out state constitutional rules. This provides the constituent power with a certain degree of legitimacy that makes its authority a conditioned but not a limited power. On the other hand, the non-compliance with such principles raises the illegitimacy of the constituted rules, whose consequence is the disregard of the constituent power."[49]

It is inevitable that such difficulty in defining the extension of mandatory compliance of state constitutions to the federal norms would reach the Supreme Court. If the Constitution is the core of this "minimum identity" and, therefore, the source of the basic principles to be coherently followed at the subnational level, state constitutions would represent a partial constitutional framework supplementing federal principles with local norms. Constitutional design, with such a mindset, clearly interprets state constitutions as playing an ancillary role.

It is thus consequential of this movement towards centralization that the Supreme Court would behave as favouring the Union over the states. Based on that vague clause of "principles of this Constitution," the Supreme Court would apply the so-called principle of symmetry, which requires that state constitutions reproduce the federal constitutional framework as much as possible, while any innovation should be the outcome of a prudent analysis and self-restraint.[50] Such an interpretation would represent a powerful barrier against any attempt to more deeply deviate from the Constitution. Couto, Bellon, and Gandolfi, in this regard, argued that "there is some room for variation and innovation, but this is a frequent target of judicial inquiries, which tend to reinforce the centralizing trend."[51] Souza, by the same token, concluded that "the few attempts to create rules not explicitly specified in the Federal Constitution, though not forbidden, were declared unconstitutional by the Supreme Court."[52]

The Supreme Court's precedent on this matter firmly sustains the "principle of symmetry," whose origins, by the way, date from 1967, exactly during the dictatorial regime and the 1967 authoritarian Constitution.[53] The unanimous precedent refers to a direct action of unconstitutionality (ADI) – ADI 486 – an action of the abstract system of judicial review judged in 1997, which questioned the constitutionality of a constitutional amendment that set out a higher threshold for amendment to the Constitution of the State of Espírito Santo in comparison to the federal Constitution. That amendment would change article 62, paragraph 5, of that state Constitution by raising the quorum for amendment from three-fifths, as defined in the federal Constitution, to four-fifths of the members of the Legislative Assembly. Justice Celso de Mello, the rapporteur, after a long defence of the importance of the autonomy of the member states and the decentralized model the federal Constitution enshrined, argued that "the autonomy of the member-states is one of the essential cores in the conceptual configuration of the federative organization."[54] He simply applied the general centralizing mindset that has prevailed in Brazilian constitutionalism:

> It should be noticed as necessary that this view of the subject, related to the essentially limited character and the secondary legal nature of the constituent power of the member states, has

> been stressed by the precedents of the Supreme Court, whose lessons identify, in the very text of the Constitution of the Republic, the irradiation – and also restriction – of the core of this special legal-political prerogative granted to the regional units that are part of the federal pact.
> [...]
> This means that all formal and material procedures and requirements pertaining to the reform of the Political Charter, as such defined in the federal Constitution, cannot be suppressed nor modified by the member states based on their reformist authority, whose exercise suffers, for such matters, unquestionable constraints of legal nature imposed by the primary constituent legislator.
> [...]
> This is the reason why the acts of constitutional change, especially those originated from member states, whose reformist power suffers even deeper constraints than those affecting and concerning the National Congress' derived constituent power, can also be unconstitutional, which results from the breach, by the competent legislative body (the Legislative Assembly, in the case of member states), of the legal constraints as such superiorly defined in the text of the Constitution of the Republic by the institution exerting the role of primary or original constituent power. [55]

Justice Celso de Mello's words could not be more direct in justifying the secondary role of subnational constitutions and their need to symmetrically comply with the general principles set out in the Constitution. This precedent has been regularly deployed in various other cases. For example, the Supreme Court settled that the principles and contents protected by the unamendable clauses of the Constitution (article 60, section 4) cannot be modified or extended to other hypotheses at the subnational level.[56] It has also decided that state constitutions "cannot create new avenues for a power to affect another power, unless the provision directly or indirectly stems from a rule or a principle of the Constitution."[57] In these and other cases, what has prevailed is an increasing intervention of the Supreme Court judging unconstitutional any innovation that deviates from the standards of the Constitution,[58] as data from the Supreme Court cases proves (table 9.2).

Table 9.2 | Percentage of questioned state norms that are declared unconstitutional

| *Year* | *Declared unconstitutional* | *Questioned* | % |
|---|---|---|---|
| 2014 | 44 | 56 | 78.57% |
| 2015 | 49 | 69 | 71.01% |
| 2016 | 41 | 62 | 66.13% |
| 2017 | 54 | 68 | 79.41% |
| 2014–17 | 188 | 255 | 73.78% |

Source: own elaboration. Data: 2014–17 Annual Report of the Judiciary. Conjur, "De cada 10 leis julgadas em ADIs pelo STF, 6 são inconstitucionais," *Consultor Jurídico*, 13 April 2015, https://www.conjur.com.br/2015-abr-13/cada-10-leis-julgadas-adis-stf-sao-inconstitucionais; Robson Pereira, "Sete em cada dez leis analisadas pelo STF são inconstitucionais," *Consultor Jurídico*, 24 April 2016, https://www.conjur.com.br/2016-abr-24/sete-cada-dez-leis-analisadas-stf-sao-inconstitucionais; Robson Pereira, "De cada três leis, duas foram julgadas inconstitucionais pelo STF em 2016," *Consultor Jurídico*, 29 May 2017, https://www.conjur.com.br/2017-mai-29/cada-tres-leis-duas-foram-julgadas-inconstitucionais-2016; Lilian Matsuura, "Oito em cada dez leis foram julgadas inconstitucionais pelo STF em 2017," *Consultor Jurídico*, 2 May 2018, https://www.conjur.com.br/2018-mai-02/oito-cada-dez-leis-foram-julgadas-inconstitucionais-stf.

The same reasoning could perhaps be extended to the Supreme Court of Canada. A clear understanding of existent precedents on federalism and their extension to distinct types of relationship between the Union and the provinces should be subject of concern for Quebec's constitutional design. Evidently, the same difficulties in comparing such distinct realities apply here, but it should always be noticed that Supreme Courts have increasingly played a more intervenient role in matters as such, and Canada, like Brazil, does not seem to deviate from this trend.

### 3.4 *The Overlapping Structure of Judicial Review of State Constitutions*

In Brazil, the system of judicial review takes place, at the federal level, at the Brazilian Supreme Court (Supremo Tribunal Federal), and, at the state level, at the State Court of Appeals (Tribunal de Justiça). This overlapping structure of judicial review often creates an interesting cascade effect: whenever the Supreme Court decides that a state constitutional provision is unconstitutional, the likelihood that other state constitutions might need to be amended to comply with that precedent is high. As Souza says: "Therefore, any innovation created by the state constitutional framers which would strengthen the autonomy of the states tend to be subject of a stricter scrutiny by the Supreme Court through the federal judicial review of local constitutional provisions.

As a consequence, it is expected that part of the constitutional amendments at the state level will come as a response to the declaration of unconstitutionality of state constitutional provisions by the Supreme Court. In addition, it is expected that decisions of state courts on the constitutionality of state laws and amendments to the state Constitution vis-à-vis the Federal Constitution provide a response from the state legislatures through corrective constitutional amendments and legislative changes."[59] This overlapping structure, however, increases uncertainty. After all, there is no efficient mechanism that guarantees that the Supreme Court's decision, which is based on the Constitution, will necessarily serve as a natural precedent for state courts, which exert the judicial review based on state constitutions. This situation becomes more worrisome as long as some state courts frequently interpret that the only limits for constitutional amendment are the unamendable provisions set out in the state constitutional text, which may vary among the states.

A very interesting example of such behaviour is found in the following precedent of the Court of Appeals of the State of Paraná, whose Constitution, unlike the federal one, does not contain explicit unamendable clauses:

> In order to challenge, in the centralized system of judicial review, state statutes in light of the federal Constitution, the only existing avenue is the direct action of unconstitutionality before the Supreme Court (CF, art. 102, I, 'a'). If the claim is

> to exert judicial review based on both the federal and the state Constitutions, it rests with state courts only the exam of the cause of action with reference to the state Constitution [...]. Judicial review by local courts on constitutional amendments to the state Constitution is confined exclusively to the potentiality of a breach of some of the limitations on the power of amendment as set out in the state Constitution. Article 64 of the Constitution of the State of Paraná, which sets formal ... and circumstantial limits, does not provide any material limits, thereby not reproducing article 60, § 4, of the federal Constitution. Therefore, bearing in mind the state parameter for judicial review of constitutional amendments (article 64), all actions based on material breach are inadmissible, since there are no unamendable clauses in the state Constitution.[60]

Such uncertainty over the limits of constitutional amendment at the subnational level, the state courts' deference to the Supreme Court, and the Supreme Court's centralizing behaviour foster an environment that is safer for political players to target the federal Constitution as the sole parameter for legislation. Since any state statute or constitutional amendment can be questioned both in state courts and in the Supreme Court, a design that is more in line with the federal standards tends to prevail, increasing then the likelihood of homogeneity and the lack of innovation and creativity at the state level. In other words, the overlapping structure of judicial review, while aimed at favouring a division of labour among federal and state courts, has not really strengthened the protection of state constitutions, but, rather, increased the likelihood of those constitutions to assimilate even further the federal standards.

Such a model may indicate that subnational judicial systems may, in the end, be subjugated by the federal system, and, like Brazil, decisions made at the provincial courts can be overruled by precedents of the Supreme Court of Canada. Especially in a context where "conservatism of subnational constitutions culture" and imperfect provincial constitutions prevail,[61] there is the risk of some overlap as the Brazilian experience demonstrates.

### *3.5 The High Rate of Constitutional Amendment at the Subnational Level*

Jonathan L. Marshfield argues that constitutional amendments, at the state level, are more frequent at the state level than at federal one in the United States, because of a higher democratic participation. According to him, such democratic engagement is able to adapt the subnational constitutions according to the local customs and identities as well as the political and civil precommitments reached over the years.[62]

This high rate of constitutional amendment is also a reality in Brazil, though it varies greatly among the states. The reasons for such a phenomenon, nonetheless, are diverse. They are caused especially by: (i) the need to update the state constitutions according to changes in the federal Constitution; (ii) the use of such amendments as a political-electoral strategy. There is no immediate connection with the need to constitutionalize social identities and values in those constitutions.

The first reason stems from the fact that state constitutions repeat verbatim most of the provisions of mandatory compliance of the federal Constitution, which demands update as soon as the federal Constitution has been amended (by 2022, the federal Constitution was already amended 125 times). Though such updates are not homogeneously carried out among the states, "there is evidence that state constitutional amendments are somehow directly influenced by the federal amendment of the previous year."[63] This phenomenon proves that amendments, at the state levels, are clearly based on mimicking the federal ones. In this way, these state constitution amendments reinforce the mimicry process already observed during the constituent moment. Evidence of this findings is seen in the similarity of the substance of federal and state amendments distributed within the chapters (see figure 9.3).[64]

The second reason that fosters amendments derives from: (i) the constitutionalization of public policies;[65] and (ii) the fact that procedural rules for constitutional amendments do not require the governor's approval. The first situation increases the likelihood that any change in public policies become a matter of constitutional change. The second case, in turn, is intimately related to how political players can use different strategies to tighten their grip on power. As constitutional amendments do not require the governor's approval, the local Parliament can strike down his or her proposal, especially when there is a greater political fragmentation or

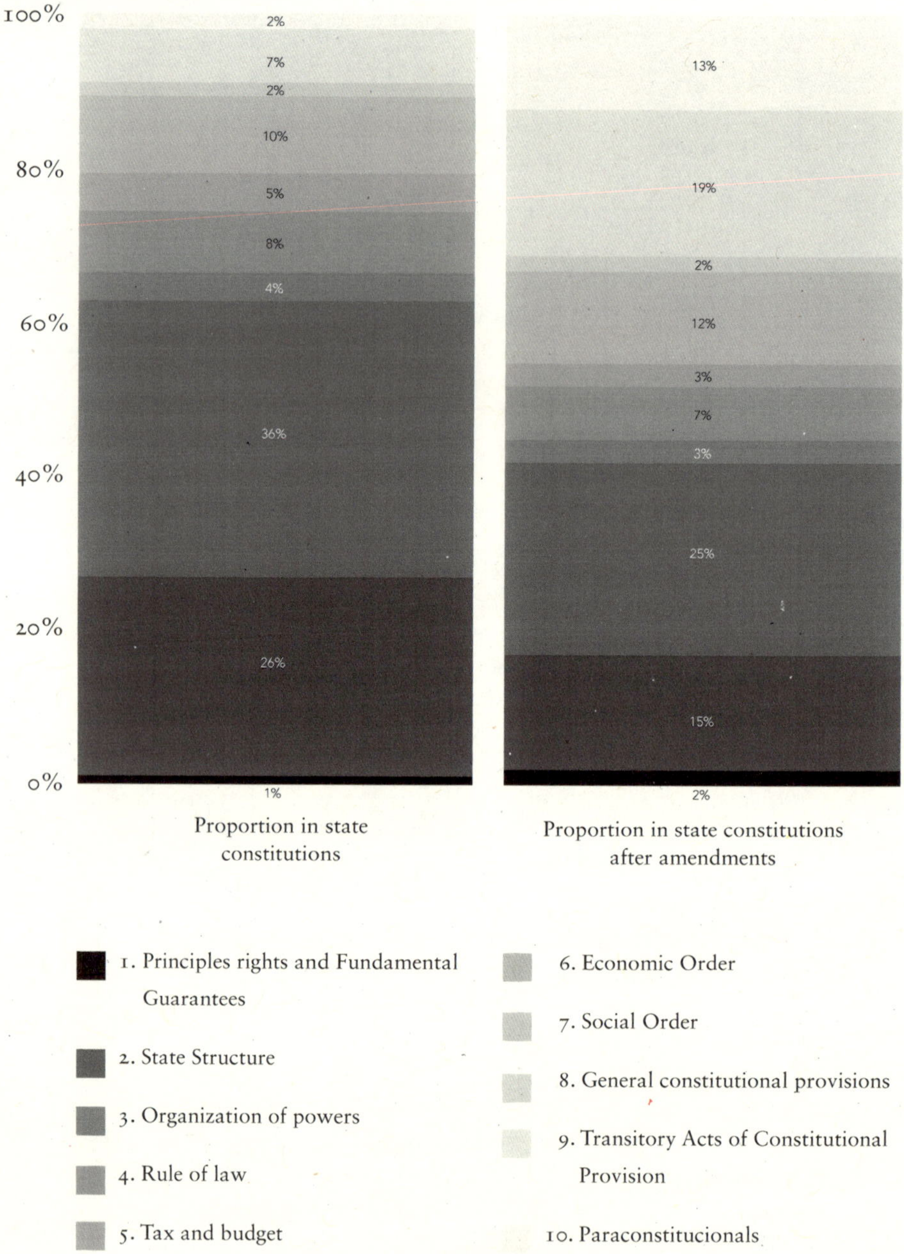


Figure 9.3 | Relative proportion of the titles in the means of the state constitutions and in the federal Constitution

when they are willing to implement their interests through amendments (80 per cent of such amendments are originally from local Parliaments).[66] The combination of these two factors fosters a permanent constituent agenda driven by political competition among state actors, which has nothing to do with their original duties.[67] Nelson Wiseman[68] foresees this process even before the enactment of Quebec's constitution, as he recognizes the project of enacting a constitution "a rhetorical device in election campaigns," with "pure cosmetic value."[69] Ferreira, Meneguin, and Bugarin show that this tendency is higher in states with weak judicial review systems.[70]

The outcome of this behaviour is a high rate of judicialization of constitutional amendments as a way for governors to reverse the political strategies of the local Parliament. According to the 2016 annual report of the judiciary,[71] 42 per cent of all direct actions of unconstitutionality were filed in the Supreme Court by state governors, and 76 per cent among them were held to be well-founded.

Therefore, state constitutions and constitutional change at the subnational level have been used more as a political strategy than as an avenue to channel local identities and values. They have become increasingly a mere verbatim copy of the federal Constitution and any change is normally due to either a mere update based on changes at that federal Constitution or the consequence of electoral-political strategies, not to legitimately express the will of their own people. Such a reality may not be different in Canada, as Daniel Turp has also argued.

## 4. CONCLUSION

Comparative constitutional law has naturally in such comparisons of very distinct federal frameworks difficulties of various sorts. For this reason, those five factors discussed above have to be interpreted as ontologically related to how Brazilian legal, political, and social institutions have behaved over history, not as a generalized symptom that could easily migrate to the Canadian or other constitutional systems. As seen, some of the causes that have strongly disrupted the subnational constitutional system in Brazil are intimately connected to a history that, while subtly embracing legal pluralism – as it should be expected from a federal country – does not provide the tools to make such pluralism a reality. It is also a history that, though democracy has strengthened over the years, has still many wounds of authoritarianism, and it is no wonder that, instead of facing the real challenges of a subnational constitutional framework, it has strategically resorted to rhetorical narratives of federalism while, in practice, centralization is the norm.[72]

This strategy has, in fact, proven quite effective. Sociologists and political scientists have argued that Latin American, in general, and Brazilian citizenry, in particular, tend to believe in the drafting or reform of constitutions as a mechanism to promote a fairer society. Yet, such a belief is normally not followed by the trust in the capacity and legitimacy of constitutions – and the law, more generally – to coordinate their own behaviours.[73] This conclusion may help explain why legal narratives usually have a high symbolic effect and are often built up against a self-learning process where individuals, through trial and error, could themselves learn from past experiences. In practice, a paternalistic mindset prevails in the end, curbing thereby the autonomy of individuals, while the narrative still empowers them at the theoretical level. In this context, the Brazilian constitutional literature and legal precedents celebrate the subnational autonomy, while mistrusting the ability of subnational actors to draft a coherent and viable constitutional order. It would not be difficult to conclude that the emphasis on subnational constitutions, at least in Brazil, is a powerful and persuasive strategic solution which, in the end, paradoxically serves as a tool to maintain the control of the central government over the states in a safe level.

The Brazilian experience is a clear example of subnational constitutionalism going wrong. It has not historically proven a feasible avenue to strengthen the autonomy of a federal state nor has it provided sociocultural gains that are normally deemed a significant reason for such a movement. It is also a cautionary tale that may provide important insights about the risks and challenges a subnational constitutional framework may endure as well as the strategies that should be adopted to face them. In this regard, some useful conclusions can be drawn from the Brazilian case that may contribute to the debate over the need of a constitution for Quebec.

First, any constitution-making process should be provided enough time to better grapple with the complexities of constitutional design at the state level, especially in view of the centralizing behaviour that has proven a typical tendency of federal systems. Second, there should be some guarantees that the central power will not disrespect constitutional identities already set out in the previous subnational constitutional orders, which could be done by defining sufficient competences to the federated unit. Third, constitutional drafters ought to set clear boundaries of provincial competences in the Constitution as a guidance for constitutional interpretation. Fourth, the Canadian Supreme Court ought to support innovation rather than presumably construe it as an attack on the federal system. Fifth, constitutional drafters should avoid designing a system of judicial review that may lead to continuous overlaps of legal power, increasing thereby uncertainty. Sixth, constitutional amendment at the state level should legitimately express the will of the people and not become a mechanism to strengthen electoral-political strategies. Finally, and above all, subnational constitutionalism should not be the scenario where, in the end, paternalism and mistrust prevails.

## NOTES

We are grateful for the opportunity to participate in this fascinating debate and hope that our contribution may help Quebec make the best decision. Translations from Portuguese to English are our own.

1 Daniel Turp, "Oui, Quebec Needs a Constitution," in this volume. See also Daniel Turp, *Nous, Peuple du Québec: Un Projet de Constitution du Québec* (Québéc, QC: Éditions du Québécois, 2005); Daniel Turp, *L'Avant-Projet de Loi sur Souveraineté du Québec* (Cowansville, QC.: Éditions Yvon Blais, 1995); and Daniel Turp *La Mise en œuvre du Pacte International Relatif aux Droits Civils et Politiques à la Lumière de l'Expérience du Canada et du Québec*, (Thèse de Doctorat d'État, Université de Droit, d'Économie et de Sciences Sociales de Paris (Paris II), 1990).

2 Alain-G. Gagnon, "Diversity and Québec's Place Alongside the Canadian Federation," in *A Constitution for Quebec: Challenges and Prospects* (forthcoming 2023).

3 "The first element of state autonomy is the capacity assigned to the federated unit to grant itself a particular constitution." Anna Cândida da Cunha Ferraz, *Poder Constituinte dos Estados-Membros* (São Paulo: Ed. Revista dos Tribunais, 1979), 54, para. 2 (showing how the legal doctrine considers subnational constitutions a requirement of federalism).

4 See Cláudio Gonçalves Couto, Gabriel Luan Absher Bellon, and Victória Ermantraut Gandolfi, "Constituições Estaduais e Centralização Federativa: Considerações sobre o Caso Brasileiro (2017)," 10th Meeting – Brazilian Association of Political Science (ABCP), https://cienciapolitica.org.br/system/files/documentos/eventos/2017/04/constituicoes-estaduais-e-centralizacao-federativa.pdf.

5 Ibid.
6 Ferraz, *Poder Constituinte dos Estados-Membros*, 54. See also José Luiz de Anhaia Mello, O *Estado federal e as suas Novas Perspectivas* (São Paulo: Max Limonad, 1968), 87; A. de Sampaio Dória, *Direito Constitucional* (São Paulo: Max Limonad, 1976), 56.
7 Cláudio Pacheco, *Tratado das Constituições Brasileiras* (Rio de Janeiro: Freitas Bastos, 1965), 318.
8 "This [stablishing basic guidelines and fundamental principles] must be done in each state's own constitution, which may be a "copy" of the federal Constitution, it must be a set of rules and fundamental principles which inform the organization of the member states and their fields of action." Ferraz, *Poder Constituinte dos Estados-Membros,* 56.
9 Decree 802, 4 October 1890.
10 *See* Roberto Gargarella, *Latin American Constitutionalism, 1810–2010: The Engine Room of the Constitution* (Oxford: Oxford University Press, 2012) (arguing that one of the features of Latin American constitutionalism is hyperpresidentialism).
11 Couto et al., *Constituições Estaduais e Centralização Federativa: Considerações sobre o Caso Brasileiro,* 1–26.
12 Chapters: 1. The Fundamental Principles, Rights and Guarantees; 2. The State; 3. The Organization of Powers; 4. Public Security. 5. Taxation and Budget. 6. The Economic Order; 7. The Social Order; 8. General Constitutional Provisions; 9. Transitory Constitutional Provisions Act.
13 The number of words in sentences considered similar according to the established parameters.
14 Ratio between the quantity and the length of the constitutional text in question.
15 Couto et al., *Constituições Estaduais e Centralização Federativa,* 17.
16 Turp, "Oui, Quebec Needs a Constitution," in this volume.
17 Couto et al., *Constituições Estaduais e Centralização Federativa,* 21–3.
18 *Constitutional Act, 1891*, article 2, section of the transitory provisions.
19 João Barbalho, *Constituição Federal Brasileira. Comentários* (Rio de Janeiro: Typ. da Cia, 1902), 26.
20 *Constitutional Act, 1934*, article 3, section of the transitory provisions.
21 Ferraz, *Poder Constituinte dos Estados-Membros* ,77.
22 Ibid., 77–8.
23 *Constitutional Act, 1946*, article 11, paragraph 9, of the transitory provisions.
24 Constitutional Act, 1967, article 188.

25 Constitutional Act, 1988, article 11 of the *Act of the Temporary Constitutional Provisions*.

26 Constitutional Act, 1988, article 11, sole paragraph, of the *Act of the Temporary Constitutional Provisions*.

27 As Mark Walters argues, because "deep divisions exist about who the 'people' are who are making the constitution," it is necessary to "accommodate the complex ideas that underlie the simultaneous assertions by peoples" and "the complex and dynamic normative realities of aboriginal governance in a morally justifiable" in a sufficient period. Mark D. Walters. "Constitutive Power and the Nation(s) of Quebec," in in this volume.

28 Pacheco, *Tratado das Constituições Brasileiras*, 347.

29 See previous section.

30 Amendment n. 1 of 1969 to the 1967 Federal Constitution, article 200.

31 Maria Hermínia Tavares de Almeida "Recentralizando a Federação?," *Revista de Sociologia e Política* 24, (2005): 29–40; Marta Arretche, *Democracia, Federalismo e Centralização no Brasil* (Rio de Janeiro: FGV Editora, 2012). See also Couto et al., *Constituições Estaduais e Centralização Federativa,* 1.

32 Federal Constitution of 1988, article 22.

33 Federal Constitution of 1988, article 30.

34 Federal Constitution of 1988, article 34.

35 See Claudio Gonçalves Couto and Gabriel Luan Absher Bellon, "Imitação ou Coerção? Constituições Estaduais e Centralização Federativa no Brasil," *Revista de Administração Pública* 52, no. 2 (2018): 323–4 (showing how such top-down coercion is a strong mechanism against state autonomy).

36 See Couto et al., *Constituições Estaduais e Centralização Federativa,* 21–3.

37 *Constitutional Act, 1891*, article 63.

38 Ferraz, *Poder Constituinte dos Estados-Membros,* 150.

39 *Constitutional Act, 1891*, article 7.

40 *Constitutional Act, 1946*, article 18.

41 *Constitutional Act, 1967*, article 13.

42 See Ferraz, *Poder Constituinte dos Estados-Membros*, 158.

43 1988 Federal Constitution, article 25.

44 1988 Federal Constitution, article 25, s.1.

45 Raul Machado Horta, "Poder Constituinte do Estado-Membro," *Revista de Direito Público* 88, no. 5 (1989): 23

46 Léo Leoncy Ferreira, *Controle de Constitucionalidade Estadual: As Normas de Observância Obrigatórias e a Defesa Abstrata da Constituição do Estado-Membro* (São Paulo: Saraiva, 2007), 6.

47 See Raul Machado Horta, *Direito Constitucional*, 5th ed. (Belo Horizonte: Del Rey, 2010).

48 Tércio Sampaio Sampaio Jr, "Princípios Condicionantes do Poder Constituinte Estadual em face da Constituição Federal," in *Revista de Direito Público* 92 (1989): 37.

49 Ibid., 45.

50 See Marcus Vinícius Furtado Coêlho, "O Controle de Constitucionalidade das Constituições Estaduais," in *Conjur*, 21 August 2016, https://www.conjur.com.br/2016-ago-21/constituicao-controle-constitucionalidade-constituicoes-estaduais.

51 Couto et al., *Constituições Estaduais e Centralização Federativa,* 1.

52 Celina Souza, "Federalismo, Desenho Constitucional e Instituições Federativas no Brasil Pós-1988" in *Revista de Sociologia e Politica* 24 (2005): 105–11.

53 Marcus Vinícius Furtado Coêlho,"O Controle de Constitucionalidade das Constituições Estaduais," 52.

54 See ADI 486, *Attorney General v. Legislative Assembly of Espírito Santo*, reporting justice: Min.[What is Min.? It doesn't appear in the folloing note] Celso de Mello, 1997, 8–10.

55 ADI 186, *Attorney General v. Legislative Assembly of Paraná*, reporting justice: Celso de Mello, 1995, 11–32.

56 "The procedure and all formal and material requirements concerning the reform of the Constitution, as devised in the federal Constitution, cannot be suppressed by member states or be modified by them based on their reformist authority, whose exercise suffers, on such matters, unquestionable legal limitation imposed by the primary constituent legislator" (ADPF 33/PA, Governor of Pará (PA) v. Instituto de Desenvolvimento Econômico-Social do Pará (IDESP-PA), reporting justice: Gilmar Mendes, 2005, http://redir.stf.jus.br/paginadorpub/paginador.jsp?docTP=AC&docID=363288).

57 ADI 3.046-9 SP, *Governor of the State of São Paulo (SP) v. Legislative Assembly of the State of São Paulo*, 2004, reporting justice: Sepúlveda Pertence, http://redir.stf.jus.br/paginadorpub/paginador.jsp?docTP=AC&docID=363288.

58 See Alexandre Costa and Juliano Benvindo, *A Quem Interessa o Controle Concentrado De Constitucionalidade? – O Descompasso entre Teoria e Prática na Defesa dos Direitos Fundamentais*, 1 April 2014, https://ssrn.com/abstract=2509541 or http://dx.doi.org/10.2139/ssrn.2509541.

59 Souza, "Federalismo, Desenho Constitucional e Instituições Federativas no Brasil Pós-1988," 111.

60 AI 516425-4, TJPR, Reporting justice: Carlos A. Hoffmann, 2009.

61 Gerald Baier, "Canada: Federal and Sub-national Constitutional Practices," in *Constitutional Dynamics in Federal Systems: Sub-national Perspectives* (Montreal; Kingston, ON: McGill-Queen's University Press, 2012), 190.

62 Jonathan L. Marshfield, "Political Functions and Limitations of Contemporary State Constitutions in the United States," in in this volume.

63 See Gabriel Luan Absher Bellon, *Constituições Estaduais Pós-1989: O Processo de Emendamento e seus Determinantes* (São Paulo, 2015), http://www.teses.usp.br/teses/disponiveis/8/8131/tde-14032016-101816/pt-br.php.

64 Chapters: 1. The Fundamental Principles, Rights and Guarantees; 2. The State; 3. The Organization of Powers; 4. Public Security. 5. Taxation and Budget. 6. The Economic Order; 7. The Social Order; 8. General Constitutional Provisions; 9. Transitory Constitutional Provisions Act.

65 See Rogério B. Arantes and Cláudio G Couto, "Uma Constituição Incomum," in *A Constituição de 1988. Passado e Futuro* (São Paulo: Aderaldo & Rothschild: Anpocs, 2009), 28; Rogério B. Arantes and Cláudio G. Couto, "Constitutionalizing Policy: The Brazilian Constitution of 1988 and its Impact on Governance," in *New Constitutionalism in Latin America from a Comparative Perspective: A Step Towards Good Governance?* (United Kingdom: Ashgate Publishing Limited, 2012).

66 Gabriel Luan Absher Bellon, "Constituições Estaduais pós-1989: O Processo de Emendamento e seus Determinantes," *Orientador Rogério Bastos Arantes* (São Paulo, 2015), 126, http://www.teses.usp.br/teses/disponiveis/8/8131/tde-14032016-101816/pt-br.php.

67 Rogério B.Arantes and Cláudio G Couto, "Uma Constituição Incomum," in *A Constituição de 1988. Passado e Futuro* (Aderaldo & Rothschild: Anpocs, 2009), 45.

68 "Nevertheless, however decorative and superficial a codified Quebec constitution may appear at present, it might turn out to give rise to momentous political implications and unpredictable legal consequences." Nelson Wiseman, "A Codified Quebec Constitution: A Vain Pursuit or the Making of a Sovereign People?" in this volume.

69 Josée Legault, "Editorial: If Change Is to Come, Let It Be for the Better," *Gazette* (Montreal), 30 August 2012.

70 See Débora Costa Ferreira, Fernando B. Meneguin, and Maurício Soares Bugarin, "Atuação do Poder Legislativo Estadual: Análise dos Incentivos dos Deputados Estaduais na Atividade Legislativa," EPRG Working Paper Series 84 (2018), https://econpolrg.files.wordpress.com/2018/07/eprg-wp-2018-84.pdf.

71 Conjur, "O Anuário da Justiça Brasil 2016," *Consultor Jurídico*, April 2016, https://www.conjur.com.br/loja/item/anuario-justica-brasil-2016.

72 See Luis Eduardo Abreu, "Tradição, Direito e Política," 59, in DADOS – *Revista de Ciências Sociais* (2016): 139–70.

73 Ibid. See also Mauricio García V and César A. Rodríguez, "Derecho y Sociedad en América Latina: Un Debate sobre los Estudios Jurídicos Críticos," *Instituto Latinoamericano de Servicios Legales Alternativos*, Bogotá (2003).

10

# Constitutionalization *à l'Écosse*: Subnational Constitutionalism as Constitutional Reconciliation

*Erin F. Delaney*

## 1. INTRODUCTION

It is the scholarly convention to evaluate subnational constitutionalism on its success in providing diversity across a federal system, in ensuring robust democratic accountability and meaningful subsidiarity, or in creating vibrant subnational political communities or identities. This chapter takes a decidedly different tack. It explores whether and how subnational constitutionalism might affect national constitutionalism more broadly.[1] In short, it goes beyond the volume's implied question, "does Quebec need a written constitution?" and asks "does Canada need a written Quebecois constitution?"

In raising this possibility, the experience of Quebec and the debate over provincial constitutionalism take on new import. Due to fundamental disagreements within the Canadian federation, even "the management of what should be day-to-day political issues has a tendency to mutate into quasi-constitutional negotiations, with the ironical result that Canada, for wanting to avoid its constitution, finds itself locked in a state of permanent constitutional debate."[2] And this constitutional uncertainty has been heightened by Quebec's holdout position on the 1982 constitutional changes and the repeated failures at grand-bargain constitutional negotiation. Can subnational constitutionalization serve as a mechanism of subnational influence to extract concessions or achieve change at the federal or national level? Could robust Quebecois constitutionalism lead to constitutional reconciliation?

The current approach to Quebecois constitutionalism foregrounds the Quebecois frustration with the federal constitution and its failure to recognize Quebec as a distinct society. Quebec provincial constitutionalization thus has a substantive focus on identity formation and value articulation, with an aim of wresting recognition from the rest of Canada.[3] Section 2 of this chapter addresses how and why provincial constitutionalism has taken on these aspects and reviews the challenges to achieving success on these terms.

To provide a concrete example of subnational constitutionalization as subnational influence, section 3 turns to the Scottish Constitutional Convention of 1989–95. The Convention was able to wrest self-government and autonomy from a hitherto recalcitrant central government, and in developing Scottish constitutionalism through a focus on democracy, accountability, and good governance, it had an important effect on British constitutionalism more broadly. The experience of the Scottish Constitutional Convention is unusual; certainly later constitutionalization efforts on the part of the Scottish independence movement share more elements in common with the Quebecois approach, prioritizing statements of values and solidifying a shared identity in opposition to or to contrast with the Westminster model.[4] Nevertheless, the undeniable success of the Scottish Constitutional Convention demonstrates the virtue of thinking more creatively about subnational constitutionalism and constitutionalization.

By situating subnational constitutionalization into a broader schema of subnational influence, section 4 highlights the ways in which Scotland achieved its goals of increased autonomy by extracting concessions from Westminster while simultaneously challenging hoary British constitutional precepts. The devolution of legislative power to Scotland has contributed to a weakening of parliamentary sovereignty,[5] perhaps even opening the door to British constitutional renewal. This story of influence may not be easily transferable, and the section goes on to catalogue both the opportunities and pitfalls for Quebec. But the comparative endeavour is one of exploration and creativity, to identify new possibilities for solving old problems. The Scottish experience suggests, at minimum, that there is potential for provincial constitutionalism to promote constitutional reconciliation.

## 2. CONSTITUTION AS IDENTITY: CALLS FOR A CONSTITUTION OF QUEBEC

The relationship between Quebec and Canada has long been fraught; it is well documented and does not need expansive treatment here. Nevertheless, a brief review of some of the more recent tensions contributing to the current constitutional crisis at the federal level sheds light on the concurrent demands for a Quebecois constitution at the provincial level. This section first outlines some aspects of the ongoing constitutional impasse related to Quebec's unwillingness to join the rest of Canada in recognizing the *Constitution Act, 1982*. It then proposes that one way to understand contemporary enthusiasm for provincial constitutionalism in Quebec is as a substitute for the demands unmet through grand-bargain constitutional change at the federal level. But it argues the likelihood of achieving broader goals through provincial constitutionalism is undermined by an approach to constitutionalization that focuses on identity creation and proceeds through legislative enactment.

### *Ongoing Constitutional Crisis*

Structured by the 1867 *British North American Act*, the federal system in Canada displays many of the tensions common in federations – chief among them, differing understandings about the nature of the federative contract leading to (and caused by) the omnipresent interplay between centripetal and centrifugal forces. The difficulty is heightened in Canada due to the cultural and linguistic overlay that separates Quebec from English Canada. And an overlap – real and perceived – between English Canada and federal Canada gives added momentum to Quebecois calls for more autonomy.

The passage of the *Constitution Act* in 1982 contributed to the most recent set of constitutional controversies. In response to pressure to patriate or decolonize the federal constitution, the United Kingdom acted to relinquish its formal power to amend the Canadian Constitution.[6] In turn, the *Constitution Act, 1982* confirmed Canada's complete sovereignty and introduced a number of changes and clarifications to the Canadian Constitution, including a new amending formula and the *Canadian Charter of Rights and Freedoms*. The entire project raised the specter of centralization and was considered by some in Quebec to be in contravention of the intentions of the original founders and the spirit of the *BNA Act*.[7] Quebec was the only province that refused to agree to the constitutional changes of 1982. That decision spurred litigation,[8] resulted in extensive political negotiation, and as I will argue below, has contributed to the drive for a written provincial constitution.

Efforts to reconcile Quebec to Canada led to two major rounds of constitutional negotiations. The first attempt at a grand constitutional bargain resulted in the Meech Lake Accord – a set of compromise positions that gave a number of assurances to Quebec in exchange for the province's embrace of the *Constitution Act, 1982*. In discussions leading to the Accord, Quebec sought recognition as a distinct society and the affirmation that the Government of Quebec could and would "preserve and promote the distinct identity of Quebec." Other demands included expanded bilingualism, increased provincial control over judicial nominees, and enhanced provincial participation in immigration.[9] The Meech Lake Accord required approval by all provinces within three years; by June 1990, the proposal had failed.[10] The second attempt at reconciliation was at Charlottetown, but that plan for constitutional reform was defeated in a national referendum in 1992. Since the rejection of the Charlottetown Accord there have been no attempts at wholesale constitutional reform.[11]

## *Provincial Constitutionalism*

In the mid 1980s, Jacques-Yvan Morin, an academic, politician, and Quebec sovereigntist, wrote a seminal article arguing for a new, written, Quebecois constitution. He posited that a provincial constitution would reflect "les préoccupations particulières qui correspondent aux besoins et aux aspirations de sociétés distinctes, exprimant de la sorte leur autonomie plus fermement que les lois ordinaires."[12] Furthermore, Morin saw provincial constitutionalism as part of the broader strategy of negotiating with "le Canada anglais."[13] The language he used – distinct societies, autonomy – foreshadowed the Meech Lake and Charlottetown proposals. When those efforts failed, calls for a written provincial constitution became an alternative method for seeking some of the same ends.[14]

A mantle taken up by others and retaining vibrancy today, "Quebecois constitutionalism" is not driven by core constitutional or governance needs; a written constitution is not required to structure the government, ensure democracy, or delineate and protect new rights. Those elements of constitutionalism are rooted in the existing and uncodified provincial constitution – found in statutory laws with constitutional import and present in conventions and practices.[15] Rather, the creation of a written constitution would provide "un texte fondamental auquel les citoyens peuvent d'identifier."[16] It would distinguish Quebec from the rest of Canada by reinforcing Quebec's position that the 1982 repatriation of the federal constitution was against Quebec's will,[17] and by highlighting the contrasts between broader Canadian values and those of Quebec.[18] It would serve to create an ideal portrait of a distinct society and force the rest of Canada to take note, possibly achieving at some level the goal frustrated by the failures of national grand-bargain constitutionalism.

To the extent there is an external-facing purpose in broadcasting Quebecois identity through a provincial constitution, it is not clear that such a clarification is needed; there is no real sense that Canadians are confused about Quebec's claims to be a distinct society. Rather, it is those very claims that create anxiety about provincial equality and reluctance to allow for more constitutional asymmetry. Assuming, however, that the focus on provincial constitutionalism is, at least in part, a move to generate increased bargaining power for Quebec in the context of constitutional renegotiation, it is likely to be stymied by the broader context of provincial constitutionalism in Canada. Provincial constitutionalism must contend with limitations imposed by a history of unwritten constitutionalism and the legacy of the British parliamentary system, as well as with constraints created by the federal constitutional framework.

Notwithstanding its French lineage, Quebec has "l'héritage du droit constitutionnel non écrit de la Grande-Bretagne, que le Québec partage avec les provinces Anglophones du Canada."[19] And, given this context, the problems of collation and codification are serious.[20] The political focus on identity formation has meant that less attention has been paid to the challenges of codification, apart from an assumption that key documents, such as the *Charter of Human Rights and Liberties* and the *Charter of the French Language*, would be included.[21] And there are additional factors weighing against detailed explication. The *BNA Act* provided each provincial legislature the right to amend "the Constitution of the Province," subject to exceptions expanded and clarified under the *Constitution Act, 1982*.

Neither act, however, defined "the Constitution of the Province."[22] As a result, questions surrounding what may be changed by provincial legislatures have made their way to the courts, and the Supreme Court has weighed in on a variety of cases.[23] This posture means that the Government of Quebec, at least, has been reluctant even to identify a list of what might be in the provincial constitution, "pour ne pas préjuger de positions que pourraient ultériurement prendre le procureuer général du Québec devant les tribunaux dans certain litiges constitutionnels."[24]

The British tradition of parliamentary sovereignty adds another layer of complexity. In 2007, Daniel Turp introduced Bill 191, *Constitution of Québec*, to the National Assembly. By focusing primarily on Quebec's values and its "territory, heritage, national capital, language, symbols and national holiday,"[25] Bill 191 largely avoided the codification and collation issues. It could not, however, resolve another challenge of provincial constitutionalism: the idea that one parliament cannot bind another.[26] Scholars of parliamentary sovereignty debate whether a parliament has the ability to impose procedural restrictions through "form and manner" exceptions.[27] The Bill was not enacted, but to make it enforceable would require accepting that the National Assembly itself could entrench a "Constitution of Quebec" with a supermajority requirement for amendment.[28]

Finally, the federal constitutional framework creates obstacles: it has been described as a "carcan politique" for the evolution of Quebecois constitutionalism.[29] The very structure of the federal constitution – the two lists of divided competences – places a heightened responsibility (and concomitant control) at the federal level for maintaining (or ensuring) provincial powers. Furthermore, even if a provincial constitution were to claim supremacy in its sphere, its attempt at autonomy would be stymied by the broader Canadian judicial system. The Canadian judiciary is an integrated judicial system under federal control.[30] Although provincial legislatures have (federal) constitutional authority to create courts,[31] section 96 of the *Constitution Act, 1982* gives the federal government power to "appoint the Judges of the Superior, District, and County Courts in each Province."[32] Only specialized courts of limited jurisdiction at the bottom of the judicial hierarchy have judges appointed by provincial governments. In other words, the final word on a provincial constitution's meaning would rest at the Supreme Court in Ottawa, and "even allowing the provincial Court of Appeals to serve as the final interpreter ... would be problematic, since its members too are all appointed by Ottawa."[33]

These complications for provincial constitutionalism are part of the reason that provincial constitutions do not get a lot of attention,[34] and why most provinces dispense with any pretense of creating or drafting one.[35] But using subnational constitutionalism as a mechanism for federal bargaining has been tried in other contexts. The Quebec approach may not have been effective thus far, but looking to the experiences of subnational communities in other systems may provide useful insights.

## 3. CONSTITUTION AS GOVERNANCE: THE SCOTTISH CONSTITUTIONAL CONVENTION

Much like Quebec, Scotland has fostered a distinct society and a singular Scottish identity for centuries, notwithstanding its political absorption into Great Britain. Even after the *Acts of Union* in 1707 that abolished the Scottish Parliament and created the unitary state, Scotland maintained a separate legal system and its own Scottish Church. It is not surprising that political pressure in Scotland for home rule has a rich heritage.[36] And indeed, the Scottish Constitutional Convention of 1989–95 was not the first effort at constructing a Scottish constitution.[37] It was, however, the most effective. Its early results were increased autonomy and regional power, and in 2018, the Westminster Parliament recognized the right of Scots to self-determination. Although identity was always part of Scottish nationalism, the focus of the Scottish Constitutional Convention was on governance.

* * *

The genesis for the Scottish Constitutional Convention occurred a decade before its first meeting, when the Campaign for a Scottish Assembly (CSA) formed following the failure of the devolution referendum in 1979. In the late 1960s and 1970s, the British government created a Royal Commission on the Constitution, known as the Kilbrandon Commission, to look into devolving power to the regions.[38] The Commission recommended legislative devolution, and in light of that recommendation, a referendum question on the issue was put to voters in Scotland. The Scots voted 51.6 per cent in favour of devolution to 48.4 per cent against on a turnout of 63.6 per cent, but the referendum failed. The act enabling the vote had included a threshold requirement: 40 per cent of the total electorate had to vote yes for success. The Scots only managed 32.8 per cent.[39] There is reason to believe this threshold requirement was added to protect the unitary state, and many Scots were frustrated by the defeat.

The Campaign for a Scottish Assembly gained strength in the late 1980s, as the distance grew between political preferences in Scotland and the policies of the Conservative government under Margaret Thatcher, and in 1987, after another landslide conservative victory, the CSA formed the Constitutional Steering Committee (CSC).[40] The CSC was comprised of "prominent Scots, representing all sections of Scottish society (but not including prominent politicians)."[41] It issued a report in 1988, *A Claim of Right for Scotland*, which did not shy away from nationalism and identity. The report contended that "The United Kingdom is a political artifact put together at English insistence."[42] It further articulated a demand for self-determination, asserting "the sovereign right of the Scottish people to determine the form of government best suited to their needs."[43] And, critically, it argued that the British constitution itself was flawed in its "failure to provide good government for Scotland."[44]

*A Claim of Right for Scotland* called for a constitutional convention to "be established to draw up a scheme for a Scottish Assembly or Parliament."[45] And the Convention that was formed brought together elected officials and leaders of community and ecclesiastical organizations; it was "part political coalition, part a more broadly based movement in civil society."[46] It did not secure representation from all national or regional political parties – the Conservatives did not participate, and the Scottish National Party (SNP) withdrew because they did not feel "the option of independence would be seriously considered."[47] But the Labour Party and the Liberal Democrats were intimately involved, a fact that would help to bring "the convention proposals to fruition" in the fullness of time.[48]

The Convention's first work product, *Towards Scotland's Parliament*, was produced in November 1990; barely twenty pages, it presented sweeping plans without much detail, permitting a focus on the generalities that gained consensus.[49] It did, however, highlight the interconnection between the rethinking of Scottish governance and constitutional reform in the United Kingdom more broadly:

"The aim is to strengthen the United Kingdom by establishing that our constitutional structure is sufficiently flexible to accommodate Scotland's needs."[50] Not only was the linkage made between the strength of the region and the strength of the central system, but further, the document recognized that other regions would be affected: "The North of England, Wales and the South West of England have suffered as certainly as Scotland from the centralization of power. People living there will want to put in place the right solutions for their particular needs."[51] The report concluded that its content was "an honest attempt and we believe a successful attempt to combine the interest of the United Kingdom with Scotland's needs."[52] The express focus on both levels of government and the benefits that would accrue to each was a marked change from earlier attempts at Scottish constitutionalization.[53]

The next stage of the Convention spanned a five-year period focused on finding compromise and creative solutions to the disagreements among members, spearheaded by a new committee: the Scottish Constitutional Commission. This process resulted in a refined and more detailed report that spoke in pragmatic, governance-focused terms. The Convention's final report, *Scotland's Parliament, Scotland's Right*, opened with stark language: "This report is about practical intent. It says: 'Here is what we are going to do,' not 'here is what we would like.' Those who seek inspirational home rule rhetoric are respectfully directed elsewhere ... We have moved on."[54] Not only was the language expressly devoid of dramatic identity-laden rhetoric, but the arguments presented drew from universalist, not exceptionalist, values and norms. As the report continued: "present constitutional circumstance denies Scotland responsive and effective *democracy*."[55] This democratic deficit "is a matter of fairness and justice, [... that] chimes well with the powerful trend internationally towards democracy, accountability and constitutional renewal."[56]

The convention's choice to root the demand for a Scottish quasi-constitution in shared values was a savvy decision with implications both for Scotland and Britain. To understand why, it is first necessary to detail the significant background challenges to a separate Scottish constitutionalism in the British system: the authority of the Westminster Parliament over Scotland (since the 1707 *Acts of Union*) and the concomitant doctrine of parliamentary sovereignty that underpins the British constitution itself. The authority of the Westminster Parliament means that, in the absence of formal rupture or independence, Scotland can have no claim to form a Scottish assembly or parliament without an act of Parliament.[57] Furthermore, given the doctrine of parliamentary sovereignty and the inability of a parliament to bind itself into the future, an act of Parliament could not entrench a law to give it protected status. Thus, as the Convention itself noted, "in theory under Britain's unwritten constitution such an Act [creating a Scottish Parliament] can be repealed or amended without restriction."[58] But universalist themes of democracy, fairness, justice, and good governance are as much part of the self-conception of the British as the Scottish. It is a shared identity. The convention responded to a troubling democratic deficit with an "unprecedented" consensus-based solution of a Scottish parliament, and it posited that "[n]o Westminster government would be willing to pay the political price of neutralizing or destroying a parliament so firmly rooted in, and supported by the people of Scotland."[59] As history has unfolded, the Convention has been correct; the threat of an omnipotent parliament at Westminster rescinding devolved power is vanishingly small.

The Convention's efforts were instantiated in the *Scotland Act, 1998*, which gave "institutional form to nearly all of the Constitutional Convention's desires."[60] Although technically, "[t]he power of the Westminster Parliament to make laws for Scotland is not affected by Scotland's power to make laws" for Scotland,[61] concurrent with the act's passage, it was announced that "Westminster would not normally legislate with regard to devolved matters in Scotland without the consent of the Scottish Parliament."[62] Known as the Sewel Convention (after Lord Sewel who announced the policy),[63] the self-limitation of the Westminster Parliament provided some assurance that the *Scotland Act, 1998* would be treated differently from mere ordinary legislation.[64] And the construction of the £414 million Scottish Parliament Building in Edinburgh provided a physical instantiation of institutional stability.[65] Furthermore, because of the broad consensus created by the Convention for the recommendations in its report and the referendum on devolution that preceded the *Scotland Act, 1998*, the act itself can be seen as "quasi-autochthonous,"[66] in which "the authority of the Scottish Parliament rests less on the sovereign legislative power of Westminster than on the consent of the Scottish people themselves."[67]

The Scottish Constitutional Convention introduced calls for self-determination and popular sovereignty within the British system of parliamentary sovereignty, challenging its precepts.[68] Under traditional views, the doctrine of parliamentary sovereignty is incompatible with the concept of popular sovereignty: if Parliament "embodies the people, so that, when Parliament is assembled, the people are there assembled," then there is "no constitutional role for the real people. The people cannot be both embodied in parliament and yet exist *constitutionally* outside Parliament."[69] Nevertheless, as a functional matter, claims of self-determination and popular sovereignty resonate politically. And the manifestation of this commitment to self-determination in Scotland is the Claim of Right – articulated by the Constitutional Steering Committee in 1988, attested to at the opening of the Scottish Constitutional Convention in 1989, a part of the Convention's final report in 1995, and "ceremonially handed over to the parliament's presiding officer for its future keeping" at the 1999 opening of the Scottish Parliament.[70] By 2018, in an Opposition Day debate in the Westminster Parliament, the SNP asked all parties to endorse Scotland's Claim of Right, proposing the motion "That this House endorses the principles of the Claim of Right for Scotland, agreed by the Scottish Constitutional Convention in 1989 [...] and therefore acknowledges the sovereign right of the Scottish people to determine the form of government best suited to their needs."[71] The motion passed.[72]

The *Scotland Act, 1998* and Scottish expressions of popular sovereignty – both products of the Scottish Constitutional Convention – are contributing to a broader weakening of parliamentary sovereignty and may lead (in conjunction with Brexit and other constitutional changes) to a rethinking of British constitutionalism.[73] In this way, the subnational engagement has not only achieved its aims but has had important ramifications at the central level. In the 1990s, scholars wrote that Scotland offered an "opportunity to break with constitutional conservativism in the United Kingdom,"[74] but Scottish democratic constitutionalism has also presented an opportunity to remake constitutionalism in the United Kingdom. And that was an explicit aim of the Convention itself: "We offer, not just a new parliament, but the possibility of a renewed nation, a cathedral of hope and promise for all the people of Scotland, and indeed of the whole United Kingdom."[75]

## 4. THE FEDERAL CONSTITUTIONAL DIMENSION OF SUBNATIONAL CONSTITUTIONAL CHANGE

As practiced by the Scottish Constitutional Convention, subnational constitutionalization served as a mechanism of influencing the central-level government while achieving regional goals and has effected broader discussion about and even change in British constitutionalism itself. That kind of subnational dynamic forces negotiation; it is here where hope might lie for Quebecois provincial constitutionalization to lead to federal constitutional reconciliation. This section first integrates into broader federal theory the ways in which subnational constitutionalization can be understood to function as subnational influence and assesses how the Quebecois and Scottish approaches have differed in their efficacy. It then analyzes specific lessons and limitations of the Scottish experience and their relevance for Quebec.

### *Subnational Constitutionalism as Federal Influence*

In the Scottish and Quebecois contexts, the central-level governments wield power in their ability to frustrate or limit the realization of subnational interests. As part of Great Britain, Scotland could not form its own parliament; it needed the Westminster Parliament to legislate on the creation of a regional assembly. In Quebec, the driving agenda items are protection of Quebecois autonomy and a recognition of its status as a distinct society within Canada; it is the federal level (and other provinces) that must provide these assurances. Each case thus rests on whether there is sufficient subnational influence at the federal level to achieve subnational goals.

In a recent article, Jim Gardner theorizes subnational influence in Canada, presenting a general schema and highlighting three critical mechanisms of influence used by provinces: negotiation and deal-making, ignoring the federal government, and threats.[76] This section argues that the current approach to Quebecois provincial constitutionalization fails to achieve influence, but that subnational constitutionalization of the kind practiced by the Scottish Constitutional Convention presents a fruitful amalgam of these techniques.

Under Gardner's schema, the primary avenue of subnational influence is political negotiation in the first instance. Provincial leaders have many points of access to engage in multilateral negotiations (e.g., first ministers' conferences and first ministers' meetings), all supported by an "elaborate administrative apparatus."[77] And certainly, intergovernmental negotiations can extend "to the terms of the basic constitutional framework itself," whether through efforts to "circumvent the constitutional allocation of powers through the practice of 'inter-delegation'" or in the metaconstitutional politics of Meech Lake and Charlottetown.[78] As detailed above, this route for achieving Quebec's goals has been closed and is unlikely to be reopened.

The other mechanisms of influence, however, require no engagement with the federal government ab initio. Instead, they serve to prompt eventual bilateral negotiation between the province and the federal government. A provincial decision either to ignore or to threaten the federal government can force the federal government to act to protect its rights or to avert a crisis.[79] For example, when provinces can "pursue provincial goals directly, through the direct and unmediated exercise of provincial power,"[80] they can afford to ignore the federal government. And by seizing their authority in uncompromising fashion, they may expand it. Gardner terms this "power entrepreneurialism."[81] If the federal government is unhappy about the results of provincial power expansion, the federal government must open negotiations to introduce cooperative measures.[82] Similarly, threatening the federal government – for example, with secession – may also bring it to the bargaining table.[83]

Quebec's current mode of provincial constitutionalization – a procedural focus on legislative enactment and a substantive focus on identity formation – neither ignores nor threatens the federal government. Enacting a provincial constitution through provincial lawmaking is certainly a "direct and unmediated exercise" of provincial power, but if the ultimate goal is to increase autonomy from the federal level, provincial legislation on its own cannot achieve the constitutional change necessary in the Canadian Constitution. In addition, by operating within the current federal constitutional framework, Quebec cannot ignore the federal government as federal judicial review will necessarily apply to its actions.[84] Furthermore, articulating a distinct identity may indeed threaten the federal government (or other provinces), but the threat is external and zero-sum – this is part of the reason past constitutional negotiations have broken down. Renewing a threat that has not been effective has little purchase. And subnational constitutionalization of distinct society status (short of independence) provides only weak pressure when viewed against the broader historical context of secession movements.

By contrast, the experience of Scottish Constitutional Convention provides a complex and nuanced account of subnational influence, drawing on unconventional strategies of both ignoring and threatening. In its very formation, the Convention ignored the constraints and limitations presented by parliamentary sovereignty and the historical understanding of the British constitution. It relied on extraconstitutional values of popular sovereignty to construct its set of claims. And by achieving broad political consensus around its aims and daring Westminster to ignore it, the Convention developed functional approaches (that operated outside of British constitutional theory) to ensuring entrenchment of the subnational constitution (*Scotland Act, 1998*). Critically, the Convention also threatened Westminster, not through in terrorem claims, but by arguing that Scotland was being deprived of democracy, accountability, and good governance. This universalist language highlighted values integral to the broader British tradition and widely shared across the various regions; the threat was the accusation that by denying Scotland its parliament, Westminster (and the rest of the country) was failing to live up to the aspirations of the British constitution itself.

### *Lessons and Limitations from the Scottish Experience*

The Scottish Constitutional Convention occupied only a few years in a complicated and ongoing constitutional realignment in the United Kingdom; its lessons are necessarily circumscribed and there are clear limitations in its applicability to a Canadian province with its own complex political history operating against a different constitutional background. Nevertheless, a benefit of comparative work lies in the opportunities it provides to question conventional wisdom and behaviour and to engage in imaginative and creative rethinking. In this aspirational vein, the following analysis highlights the opportunities and challenges presented by *constitutionalization à L'Écosse*, addressing in turn the substantive and procedural elements of constitutionalization.

By the time the Scottish Constitutional Convention convened, it was clear that Scotland presented an unusual situation in global democracy: it had its own system of law and an independent judiciary, but "no legislature of its own to determine that law."[85] In the *Acts of Union, 1707*, Scots law was allowed to remain separate from English law,[86] and to protect the integrity of Scottish criminal law in particular, the Appellate Committee of the House of Lords was not given jurisdiction to hear appeals from the High Court of Justiciary, the highest criminal court in Scotland.[87] Scotland's outlier status gave urgency to its demands for legislative authority and allowed it to draw on universalist language of democracy and governance in support of its claims. Quebec, by contrast, has a constitution, albeit unwritten, as well as a legislature, and "ce n'est certes pas l'absence de règles qui inviterait à l'adoption d'une Constitution formelle."[88] But Canadian federalism has its own particularities that Quebec could harness to raise more universalist substantive claims.

Quebec presents the inverse to Scotland's exceptionalism; it has a legislature and provincial law, but it does not have autonomous judicial control over those laws. Canada's integrated judicial system is unusual in federal systems.[89] Its primary characteristic – federal judicial control over appointments to provincial courts – necessarily limits the effectiveness of provincial constitutions as autonomy-protecting. In many ways, the judicial system is a legacy of British imperialism and the system of parliamentary, rather than constitutional, sovereignty. As British constitutional scholar A.V. Dicey understood, federalism stands in tension with parliamentary sovereignty as it gives priority to the judiciary in navigating the metes and bounds of the constitutional agreement.[90] Quebec, which has consistently advocated for rethinking judicial appointments,[91] could raise universalist concerns by highlighting the problems that the Canadian judiciary presents for accountability and autonomy. Indeed, it could claim that a true patriation of the federal constitution requires an updating of the judicial system.

Reassessing the core arguments for a new provincial constitution – and arguing for the necessity of federal constitutional change – are plausible ways in which to mirror the Scottish experience. Shifting focus from identity formation to the fine-grained aspects of governance and institutional structure that implicate autonomy (in this case, the nature of judicial federalism) may serve to "threaten" the federal government by raising universalist critiques that are rooted in global federal experience and have resonance in other provinces.[92]

Notwithstanding these substantive possibilities for influence, procedural challenges will remain: proposing a provincial constitution by operating outside existing constitutional frameworks is likely to prove difficult. First, and more broadly, there is the challenge of creating a robust convention process itself. The Scottish Constitutional Convention was a "civil society convention [... in which] people are represented not only by those whom they have chosen in public elections, but also by leading figures from organized civil society."[93] Creating an effective civil society convention thus requires broad enthusiasm and buy-in, and as the Constitutional Steering Committee acknowledged at the outset, "the authority of the Convention would depend heavily on the range of other organisations represented."[94] In addition, delegates from civil society must carry with them "the full authority and wholehearted support of these organisations."[95] Putting together this type of community is challenging. (Even in the successful Scottish context, observers critiqued the Convention's composition and complained about whether its internal procedures improperly gave more voice to politician delegates.[96])

Second, the success of the Scottish Constitutional Convention rested in part on the presence (or absence) of certain political parties and the internal structure of political parties in the United Kingdom – distinguishing factors unlikely to be replicated in Quebec. The decision by the SNP not to participate in the deliberations allowed the Convention to operate against a backdrop assumption of continued Scottish membership in the United Kingdom. The SNP's absence encouraged parties to negotiate in good faith within the Convention and reinforced the substantive universalist claims presented by the Convention. The contrary choice by Labour and the Liberal Democrats had salutary effects in turn: by participating, these national parties were able to negotiate with one another with no immediate electoral pressure, to resolve their reservations and concerns about Scottish devolution. And other delegates at the Convention were able to operate with hope leading to expectation that the national parties would carry forward their proposals to Westminster. This engagement was facilitated by the fact that the United Kingdom has integrated political parties, so that the Scottish Labour Party operates in conjunction with the national Labour Party. Indeed, when the national political winds changed and Labour was elected in 1997, its commitments to Scotland were clear.

In Quebec, each of these features presents real problems for implementation of the Scottish model. First, it is unthinkable that the Parti Québécois would not participate in a Quebecois Constitutional

Convention, which would leave secession as a latent background threat that might undermine efforts to frame the provincial constitution as a conversation about improving or perfecting the federal constitution. Second, and raising a different set of issues, Canada does not have integrated political parties; in fact, national and provincial parties "are now largely disconnected."[97] Thus, as Gardner notes, "Canadian parties do not offer paths of political influence that cross constitutional lines of authority."[98] There can be no expectation, therefore, of assistance at the federal level in making threats or supporting negotiations. A Quebecois approach to garnering support would need to rely on engaging and activating other provinces interested in advancing true provincial constitutionalism,[99] perhaps by welcoming convention observers from other provinces as non-voting delegates.

## 5. CONCLUSION

The Scottish experience suggests that there is potential for Quebecois provincial constitutionalism to both extract key federal concessions and promote constitutional reconciliation – if those advocating for a Quebecois constitution wish to make the changes necessary to do so. Shifting to questions of governance and autonomy and away from values, identity formation, or indicia of nationalism may not be what leaders of the movement have in mind.[100] If it is not, then perhaps neither are they interested in engaging the federal government in further negotiation. And the implications of provincial constitutionalism in the latter context (whether in Quebec or in post-Brexit Scotland) lead most naturally to independence.

## NOTES

For their substantive contributions, I am grateful to the editors of this collection and the participants at the conference which inspired it. I would like to thank Michael Gajewsky, Ellie Graham, Sarah Reis, and Jack Steele for excellent research assistance. This chapter contains material in French.

1 As do others in this volume, I use the terminology "subnational" to refer to those jurisdictions beneath the central-level government but above local governments in a federal or quasi-federal system. This choice presents particular complications in the context of a comparison between Quebec and Scotland, as not only does Quebec express a national identity distinct

from Canada, but so too does Scotland within Britain. Where possible, I use "provincial" (Quebec) or "regional" (Scotland) as synonyms for "subnational."

2 Marc-Antoine Adam, "Fiscal Federalism and the Future of Canada," in *Canada: The State of the Federation 2006/7*, eds. John R. Allan et al. (Montreal: McGill-Queen's University Press, 2009), 297–8.

3 See, for example, in chapter 1 of this volume, the proposed Constitution of Quebec, which opens in part I with an explicit focus on values, nationality, heritage, emblems, etc., before turning later to powers (part II). Note that part III addresses international relations, which is itself understood as connected to Quebec's identity formation. See Stéphane Paquin, "Identity Paradiplomacy in Québec," *Québec Studies* 66, no. 1 (2018): 3–26.

4 The Scottish Government, *Scotland's Future: From the Referendum to Independence and a Written Constitution*, 6 (2013). See also W. Elliot Bulmer, "An Analysis of the Scottish National Party's Draft Constitution for Scotland," *Parliamentary Affairs* 64, no. 4 (2011): 674–93.

5 Erin F. Delaney, "Judiciary Rising: Constitutional Change in the United Kingdom," *Northwestern University Law Review* 108, no. 2 (2015): 543.

6 *Canada Act, 1982* (UK) c. 11, s. 2 ("No Act of the Parliament of the United Kingdom passed after the Constitution Act, 1982 comes into force shall extend to Canada as part of its law.").

7 Eugénie Brouillet, *La Négation de la Nation* (Sillery: Septentrion, 2005), 379.

8 *Reference re Amendment to the Canadian Constitution*, [1982] 2 SCR 793 (Quebec Veto Reference). See also *Reference re Resolution to Amend the Constitution*, [1981] 1 SCR 753 (Patriation Reference).

9 Meech Lake Communiqué of 30 April 1987.

10 Jean-François Cardin, *A History of the Canadian Constitution* (Montreal: Global Vision, 1996), 29.

11 Jeremy Webber, *The Constitution of Canada: A Contextual Analysis* (Oxford: Hart Publishing, 2015), 52.

12 Jacques-Yvan Morin, "Pour une nouvelle Constitution du Québec," *McGill Law Journal* 30, no. 2 (1985): 176.

13 Ibid., 177.

14 General discussions of provincial constitutionalism in Quebec long predated the Morin article. In 1963, Jean Lesage created a "Commission de la Constitution, chargée d'examiner diverses questions relatives à l'adoption d'une constitution Québécoise." Benoît Pelletier, "La Nature quasi constitutionnelle de *la Charte des droits et libertés de la personne du Québec* et

l'idée d'une constitution Québécoise," *Bulletin Québécois de droit constitutione* (2007), available at http://aqdc.quebec/archives/infolettres/bqdc_no2_hiver2007.html.

15 Benoît Pelletier, *Une Certaine idée du Québec – Parcours d'un fédéraliste de la réflexion à l'action* (Québec: Presses de L'Université Laval, 2010), 165, 172 ("La Québec possède déjà une constitution au sense materiel du terme. Elle est composée de mesures énoncées dans les lois constittutionnelles, de convention et de principles.").

16 Pelletier, *Une Certaine idée du Québec*, 172.

17 Daniel Turp, "Un nouvel essai sur le droit et l'importance pour le Québec de se donner une Constitution," in *La Constitution Québécoise. Essais sur le droit du Québec de se doter de sa propre loi fondamentale.* (Montréal: Éditions JFD, 2013), 564.

18 Ibid., 563 (arguing that the Canadian *Charter of Human Rights and Freedoms* affirms the supremacy of God in contrast to the increasing focus on a secular society in Quebec; and it affirms multiculturalism within Canada in contrast with Quebec's choice of interculturalism).

19 Morin, "Pour une nouvelle Constitution du Québec," 176. He described the Quebecois constitution as "éparse et malaisé d'en discerner les contours." Ibid.

20 See chapter 4 in this volume.

21 See Québec, Bill 191, *Constitution of Québec*, 1st Sess., 38th Leg., 2007 (introduction 22 May 2007) [Bill 191]. See also Turp, "Nous, peuple du Québec," in *La Constitution Québécoise*, 213; see also Pelletier, "L'idée d'une constitution Québécoise."

22 The *Constitution Act, 1982* does define what constitutes the Constitution of Canada, *Constitution Act, 1982*, being Schedule B to the *Canada Act, 1982* (UK), 1982, c. 11, s. 52(2) ("The Constitution of Canada includes *(a)* the *Canada Act 1982*, including this Act; *(b)* the Acts and orders referred to in the schedule; and *(c)* any amendment to any Act or order referred to in paragraph *(a)* or *(b)*."). But even this definition is not considered to be comprehensive, due to the role of unwritten principles and conventions in the Canadian system. See Peter W. Hogg, *Constitutional Law of Canada* (Scarborough, Ont.: Carswell, 5th ed. Supp. 2009), 1-14–1-17 (citing examples including, inter alia, parliamentary privilege, *New Brunswick Broadcasting Co. v. Nova Scotia* 1 SCR 319 (1993), and judicial independence, *Re Remuneration of Judges*, 3 SCR 3 (1997)).

23 See, e.g., *Forest v. Manitoba (Attorney General)*, 2 SCR 1032 (1979); *OPSEU v. Ontario*, 2 SCR 2, 40 (1987). Other areas include "the abolition of a province's Legislative Council (upper house), the public service of the

province, the powers and privileges of the legislative assembly, and the term of the legislative assembly." Hogg, *Constitutional Law of Canada*, 4–33.

24 Nelson Wiseman, "Clarifying Provincial Constitutions," *National Journal of Constitutional Law* 6, no. 2 (1996): 289 (citing correspondence between the author and Jean-K. Samson).

25 Bill 191 (Explanatory Notes).

26 Pelletier, "L'idée d'une constitution québécoise."

27 For a discussion and critique of the terms of this debate, see R. Elliot, "Rethinking Manner and Form: From Parliamentary Sovereignty to Constitutional Values," *Osgoode Hall Law Journal* 29, no. 2 (1991): 215.

28 Ibid. See also chapter 2 in this volume for a skeptical view.

29 Morin, "Pour une nouvelle Constitution du Québec," 177.

30 See Erin F. Delaney, "Reimagining Judicial Federalism," in *Rewriting the Canadian Constitution*, eds. Richard Albert, Kate Glover, Michael Pal, and Wade Wright (forthcoming).

31 *Constitution Act, 1982*, ss 101 & 92(14), being Schedule B to the *Canada Act, 1982* (UK), 1982, c. 11., respectively.

32 *Constitution Act, 1982*, s. 96, being Schedule B to the *Canada Act, 1982* (UK), 1982, c. 11.

33 F.L. Morton, "Provincial Constitutions in Canada," (paper presented at the Conference on Federalism and Sub-national Constitutions: Design and Reform, Center for the Study of State Constitutions, Rockefeller Center, Bellagio, Italy, 4 April 2004), http://statecon.camden.rutgers.edu/sites/statecon/files/subpapers/morton.pdf. See also chapter 7 in this volume.

34 Wiseman, "Clarifying Provincial Constitutions," 270 ("One study of the Canadian Constitution describes them as an 'often-forgotten subject' and barely refers to them.").

35 Only British Columbia has a provincial constitution, see *Constitution Act (BC)*, RSBC 1996, c. 66, available at http://www.bclaws.ca/civix/document/id/complete/statreg/96066_01, but, in addition to Quebec, a movement for constitutionalization exists in Alberta. See chapter 7 in this volume.

36 The Scottish Home Rule Association was founded in 1886, and the National Party for Scotland in 1928. The latter merged with the Scottish Party to become the Scottish National Party (SNP) in 1934.

37 A draft constitution for Scotland was prepared by the Scottish Provisional Constituent Assembly of 1957–64. This "Muirhead Draft" envisioned a "free, independent, democratic nation." Reprinted in W. Elliot Bulmer,

*Constituting Scotland* (Edinburgh: Edinburgh University Press, 2016), 207–20.

38 W. Elliot Bulmer, "The Scottish Constitutional Tradition: A Very British Radicalism?," *Perspectives on Federalism* 7, no. 1 (2015): 34.

39 House of Lords Select Committee on the Constitution, *Referendums in the United Kingdom*, 12th Report of Session 2009–10, (2010), 9.

40 Alan Renwick, *After the Referendum: Options for a Constitutional Convention* (London: The Constitution Society, 2014), 49.

41 Scottish Constitutional Convention, *Towards Scotland's Parliament: A Report to the Scottish People by the Scottish Constitutional Convention*, 4 (Edinburgh, November 1990).

42 Campaign for a Scottish Assembly, *A Claim of Right for Scotland: Report of the Constitutional Steering Committee* (Edinburgh, 1988), 6.

43 Ibid.

44 Ibid.

45 SCC, *Towards Scotland's Parliament*, 4.

46 Robert Hazell, "Reinventing the Constitution: Can the State Survive?," *Public Law* (Spring 1999): 87.

47 Jean McFadden, "Constitutional Law: Framework of Scottish Devolution," in *The Laws of Scotland: Stair Memorial Encyclopedia* (Edinburgh: Lexis Nexis, 2002), 84.

48 Renwick, *After the Referendum*, 51.

49 See SCC, *Towards Scotland's Parliament*, 4; see also Renwick, *After the Referendum*, 54.

50 See SCC, *Towards Scotland's Parliament*, 7.

51 Ibid.

52 Ibid, 13.

53 See Muirhead Draft, reprinted in Bulmer, *Constituting Scotland.*

54 Scottish Constitutional Convention, *Scotland's Parliament, Scotland's Right* (1995), 5.

55 Ibid, 6.

56 Ibid, 6–7.

57 Scholars have argued that the *Acts of Union* had a confederal nature, see, e.g., J.D.B. Mitchell, *Constitutional Law* (Edinburgh: Scottish Universities Law Institute, 2d ed. 1968), 69–70, but in practice they effectuated "the incorporation of the Scots […] legislature within those of England and Great Britain." Alvin Jackson, *The Two Unions: Ireland, Scotland, and the Survival of the United Kingdom, 1707–2007* (Oxford: Oxford University Press, 2012), 108.

58 SCC, *Scotland's Parliament*, 18.
59 Ibid.
60 Bulmer, "The Scottish Constitutional Tradition," 36; see also Renwick, *After the Referendum*, 55 ("The great majority of the Convention's proposals … were subsequently implemented by the Labour government after its election in 1997.").
61 Paul Craig and Mark Wallets, "The Courts, Devolution and Judicial Review," *Public Law* (Summer 1999), 281.
62 592 Parl. Deb. HL (5th ser.) (1998) 791 (UK).
63 Scotland Act, 1998, c. 46, explanatory notes at 40.
64 The Sewel Convention has come under pressure during the lengthy Brexit process. See generally Gordon Anthony, *Devolution, Brexit, and the Sewel Convention* (London: The Constitution Society, 2018); Nicola McEwen, "Is Brexit Eroding the Sewel Convention?," Centre on Constitutional Change, 22 January 2020, https://www.centreonconstitutionalchange.ac.uk/news-and-opinion/brexit-eroding-sewel-convention/.
65 See "£414m Bill for Holyrood Building," BBC News, 21 February 2007, http://news.bbc.co.uk/2/hi/uk_news/scotland/6382177.stm.
66 Brigid Hadfield, "The United Kingdom as a Territorial State," in *The British Constitution in the Twentieth Century*, ed. Vernon Bogdanor (Oxford: Oxford University Press, 2003), 626.
67 Vernon Bogdanor, *The New British Constitution* (Oxford: Hart Publishing, 2009), 274.
68 Bulmer, "The Scottish Constitutional Tradition," 34; Roger Levy, "The Scottish Constitutional Convention, Nationalism and the Union," *Government and Opposition* 27, no. 2 (1992): 224 ("[T]his notion of sovereignty puts any parliament derived from it at odds with the government and constitution of the United Kingdom as a whole.").
69 D.J. Galligan, "The Constitutional Future of the UK: 'Matters of High Concernment'," in *Constitution in Crisis*, ed. D.J. Galligan (London: I.B. Tauris, 2017), 161.
70 Hadfield, "The United Kingdom as a Territorial State," 623.
71 HC, Order Paper no. 162: Part 1, 4 July 2018.
72 644 Parl. Deb. HC (4 July 2018) 456 (UK).
73 See Stephen Tierney, "Reclaiming Politics: Popular Democracy in Britain after the Scottish Referendum," *Political Quarterly* 86, no. 2 (2015): 226; Silvia Suteu, "The Scottish Independence Referendum and the Participatory Turn in UK Constitution-Making," *Global Constitutionalism* 6, no. 2 (2017): 184.

74 Isobel Lindsay, "Democratic Innovation in Scotland" in *Debating the Constitution: New Perspectives on Constitutional Reform*, eds. Anthony Barnett et al. (Cambridge: Polity, 1993), 169.

75 SCC, *Scotland's Parliament*, 31.

76 James A. Gardner, "Canadian Federalism in Design and Practice: The Mechanics of a Permanently Provisional Constitution," *Perspectives on Federalism* 9, no. 3 (2017).

77 Ibid., 16.

78 Ibid., 19–20.

79 Threats may also produce multilateral negotiation, as in the example of secession. Ibid., 22.

80 Ibid., 21.

81 Ibid.

82 Ibid., 22 (using the example of foreign policy).

83 Ibid., 22–3. See also Wade K. Wright, "The Political Safeguards of Canadian Federalism: The Intergovernmental Safeguards," *National Journal of Constitutional Law* 36 (2016): 48–51.

84 And, indeed, federal judicial review may work against Quebec's interest. See Antoni Abat I. Ninet and James A. Gardner, "Distinctive Identity Claims in Federal Systems: Judicial Policing of Subnational Variance," *International Journal of Constitutional Law* 14, no. 2 (2016): 378 (noting the "uniformly hostile reaction" that distinct identity claims receive from constitutional courts).

85 SCC, *Scotland's Parliament*, 15.

86 James E. Pfander and Daniel D. Birk, "Article III and the Scottish Judiciary," *Harvard Law Review* 124, no. 7 (2011): 1,655, n238.

87 See *Bywater v. Crown*, (1781) 2 Paton 563 (HL); Stuart Reid and Janice Edwards, "The Scottish Legal System," *Legal Information Management* 9, no. 1 (2009): 12.

88 Morin, "Pour une nouvelle Constitution du Québec," 190.

89 See Delaney, "Reimagining Judicial Federalism."

90 A.V. Dicey, *Introduction to the Study of the Law of the Constitution*, 7th ed. (London: Macmillan, 1908), 170.

91 See, e.g., Government of Quebec, *Quebecers – Our Way of Being Canadian* (Quebec 2017).

92 See chapter 7 in this volume.

93 Renwick, *After the Referendum*, 48.

94 CSA, *A Claim of Right*, 17.

95 Ibid.

96 Renwick, *After the Referendum*, 56.

97 Kenneth R. Carty and Steven B. Wolinetz, "Political Parties and the Canadian Federation's Coalition Politics," in *Canada: The State of the Federation, 2002*, eds. Peter J. Meekison et al. (Montreal: McGill-Queen's University Press, 2004), 303. See also Wright, "The Political Safeguards of Canadian Federalism," 21–2.

98 Gardner, "Canadian Federalism in Design and Practice," 23.

99 See chapter 7 in this volume. Cf. Wright, "The Political Safeguards of Canadian Federalism," 44–8.

100 Coalition Avenir Quebec's recent efforts to pass Bill 21, banning the wearing of religious symbols by public employees and those working in positions of authority, Quebec, Bill 21, *An Act respecting the laicity of the State*, 1st Sess., 42nd Leg., 2019 (assented to 16 June 2019), demonstrate a continued focus on asserting Quebec's status as a distinct society from the rest of Canada and increasing autonomy through unique provincial identity claims. See, e.g., Marian Burchardt, *Regulating Difference: Religious Diversity and Nationhood in the Secular West* (New Brunswick: Rutgers University Press, 2020), 81; Phil Lord, *What Is the True Purpose of Quebec's Bill 21?* (Montreal: Canadian Race Relations Foundation 2020).

# Should Quebec Adopt a Written Constitution? A (But Not The) Conclusion

*Hoi L. Kong*

In order to answer the question of whether Quebec should adopt a written constitution, we should address two preliminary questions. The first, substantive question is: what is the value of a written constitution to a polity? The second, procedural question is: what is the value of writing a constitution to a polity? Once we have answered those questions, we can turn to articulate the conditions under which the Quebec polity would enjoy the substantive and procedural benefits of adopting a written constitution. These inquiries cannot be separated from issues of positive constitutional law. And our interpretation of that body of law cannot be entirely separated from our best attempts at understanding the underlying purposes and functions of the Canadian Constitution.

The diverse and rich chapters gathered together in this collection revolve around the above set of issues, though not always explicitly and often not on the terms that I have used to frame them. In this conclusion, I will interpret the relevant issues and the contributions of my colleagues in light of a general normative theory of constitutional law. The claim that I shall advance is the following: Quebec should adopt a written constitution if in so doing it gives effect to the values of deliberative constitutionalism.

This conclusion is divided into three parts. In part I, I will define deliberative constitutionalism and argue for its pertinence to Quebec. In the course of this discussion, I will engage with views of Quebec's constitutional identity articulated by some of this collection's authors. In part II, I will argue that, in general, a polity should undertake the process of drafting and entrenching a written constitution if in so doing it achieves deliberative democratic constitutionalism's ends. In this part, I will engage with some authors in this collection who present comparative evidence about the effects of entrenched subnational constitutions, and others who offer arguments about the state of constitutional law in Canada, as it pertains to amending provincial constitutions. In part III, I will examine what it would mean for a process of constitution-making in Quebec to achieve deliberative democratic ends, and I will raise possible normative objections to Quebec's adopting a written constitution, including some raised by contributors to this collection.

## PART I: DELIBERATIVE CONSTITUTIONALISM AND QUEBEC

Ron Levy and I have defined deliberative constitutionalism as a normative theory which claims that the practices of creating, interpreting, and applying a polity's basic norms should occur under conditions of equal inclusion, reflection, adequate information, and flexible, open-minded and reciprocal discussion.[1] In order to appreciate the central insights of the theory, it is perhaps helpful to contrast its conception of legitimacy with that of mainstream constitutional theory. Proponents of the latter typically conceive of constitutional legitimacy as a democratic problem.[2] The central dilemma for this body of theory is how to use law to establish, interpret, and enforce a polity's constitutional commitments – its fundamental institutions, values, and collective mission – without wholly ceding power over those commitments to elites who may be distant from, and unaccountable to, the wider polity. Judges, lawyers, legislators, and administrators have primary responsibility for a constitution's day-to-day functioning. But they are often insulated, sometimes by design, from the influence of the broader public sphere. They are, moreover, accustomed to deploying distinctively legal or technical norms and language. The fundamental question for much of constitutional theory is: are these elite decision-making methods sufficiently alive to the preferences and interests of the citizens who notionally authorize the constitution in the first place?

Deliberative constitutionalism dissipates some of the force of this constitutional legitimacy dilemma by shifting focus. For instance, the theory examines the extent to which judicial review enhances democratic deliberation, as this is what guarantees the legitimacy of constitutional interpretation, and not the bare fact that preferences can be aggregated and interests mobilized to support a given position. In this view, a constitution should construct a set of public processes – including judicial review – for carefully and deliberatively working through social controversies. These processes aim to change social preferences or resolve differences among them and to aid the polity in continually reflecting upon, interpreting and refining its basic laws. Deliberative constitutionalism's general claim about the nature of constitutional legitimacy extends, we shall see, to the process of constitution-making and the substance of a constitution. Moreover, this general, deliberative-democratic understanding of legitimacy requires elaboration in the context of specific constitutional polities.

In order to convey the significance of this view of constitutionalism for Quebec, therefore, I will need to outline some features that define this polity. Confederation would seem to be a good place to focus our analysis but as Mark Walters and others in this collection remind us, there are other moments, including ones in which Indigenous peoples played a central role, that demand our equal attention. Later in this conclusion I will address the significance that that history holds for the question of whether Quebec should adopt a written constitution, but for now let us turn our attention to the Confederation debates.[3]

Some French Canadians at Confederation who sought to create what would become the Province of Quebec believed that it would protect their interests against incursions by an anglophone majority in what was then the colony of the United Province of Canada. By contrast, the policies of a unitary state, in which French Canadians would be a persistent minority would, they feared, be unrelentingly indifferent or hostile to their collective interests. Therefore, some who were present at Confederation, including George-Étienne Cartier, aimed to create a political unit in which this persistent threat would be removed.[4] Under a federalist regime that would give democratically elected and controlled governments in Quebec jurisdictional control over the vast majority of government decisions and policies that would affect citizens' lives, it would no longer be possible for French Canadians (the vast majority of whom would live on the territory of Quebec) to persistently doubt that the institutions of popularly elected government would track their collective interests.[5] The *Constitution Act, 1867* provided such a set of institutions.

Among the defining features of the Quebec polity are its distinctive history and its shared public culture, and these flow in part from its constitutional status. It is important to note that these features and the constitutional identity that they shape do not belong to any single group within Quebec society. They represent, rather, an ongoing narrative to which members of diverse communities, as well as citizens who do not identify with any particular community, contribute. As Gagnon and Tremblay remind us in their chapter, the contours and contents of that narrative are contested, as are the very terms according to which we frame the narrative. It is this ongoing and fluid conversation that constitutes the Quebec polity. The authors of the Bouchard-Taylor report have recently described the sociological fact of ethnocultural diversity in Quebec and offered a way of conceiving of the common culture that incorporates this diversity. The authors of the report write: "[T]he members of the ethnic minorities can become valuable interlocutors in the search for new questions to be asked on Québec's past. They can also substantially enrich Québec's collective memory by contributing to it their own stories. The edification and dissemination of the collective memory can contribute powerfully to making known and promoting common values."[6]

These common values, contested and controversial as they may be, result from a specific history and the manifold contributions of a diverse populace. The values, and the debates that frame and surround them, constitute the basic norms of the Quebec polity and would necessarily be the object of any exercise in constitution-making. Evidence of the breadth of those debates can be found in diverse interpretations of the relevant history, including the interpretations offered by Wiseman and Turp in their respective contributions to this collection.

Recall that deliberative constitutionalism claims that the practices of creating, interpreting, and applying a polity's basic norms should occur under conditions of equal inclusion, reflection, adequate information, and flexible, open-minded, and reciprocal discussion. These conditions render the relevant norms legitimate and they enable a society to respectfully navigate political and social disagreements, including some that go to the very nature of the constitutional polity itself. In the parts that follow, we shall see what it means for constitution-making in diverse societies, such as Quebec, to occur under these conditions and how the contents of a written constitution can satisfy them.

## PART II: DELIBERATIVE DEMOCRATIC CONSTITUTION-MAKING

It is important to be precise about what is meant by a written constitution, in the present context. Elster has argued that there are three senses of the term "constitution": "First, many countries have a set of laws collectively referred to as 'the constitution.' Second, some laws may be deemed 'constitutional' because they regulate matters that are in some sense more fundamental than others. And third, the constitution may be distinguished from ordinary legislation by more stringent amendment procedures."[7] The debate around constitution-making tends to focus on texts that have the defining features of the second and third senses,[8] and I will therefore focus attention on these kinds of documents in this part. For the purposes of this discussion, then, a constitution is a document that regulates matters of fundamental importance to a polity, and is difficult to amend. Some recent scholarship on constitution-making that addresses deliberative constitutionalist concerns has an empirical cast;[9] in what follows, I will focus instead on the normative dimensions of constitution-making, from a deliberative democratic perspective.

Deliberative democratic theorists engage with two aspects of constitution-making. The first is the *means* by which constitutions come into being. For some theorists, the procedures involved in the making of a constitution legitimize the text if they involve wide-spread public debate. Ackerman captures the legitimizing force of this intense public attention with his concept of a "constitutional moment."[10] More recently, Tierney has argued that constitutional referendums can be structured to allow for widespread and meaningful citizen deliberation about what a constitution should contain,[11] and Landemore has examined how a recent experiment in Iceland aimed to maximize public involvement in the very drafting of constitutional text.[12] Running through these deliberative democratic conceptions of constitution-making is a desire to ensure broad public deliberation about a constitution's contents. Yet the idea that widespread democratic deliberation can render a constitutional text legitimate is not universally shared. For instance, Ricoy has argued that because a constitution is hard to amend, those involved in making a constitution have strong incentives to rent seek in order to protect their interests.[13] As a consequence, they will likely not engage in deliberation that satisfies this paper's normative framework. I will return to this point below.

A second aspect of constitution-making that attracts the attention of theorists of deliberative democracy is the *significance* of the very act of enshrining a set of political commitments in a constitutional text. Some theorists with deliberative leanings reject the idea that a constitution (in the sense that I use the term here) can ever be legitimate, because by its very nature, the act of enshrining the will of a polity at a founding moment shuts down public deliberation about matters of ongoing fundamental importance.[14] Drawing on Chambers, I argue that it is possible to understand the making of a constitution, not as a founding moment, but as one moment in an ongoing conversation. In this vein, Chambers has argued against the view that written constitutions are necessarily contracts that comprehensively capture the will of the people. Instead, she claims that they can be instruments through which a polity engages in an ongoing conversation about its deepest commitments.[15] For Chambers, a constitution should entrench a polity's diverse conceptions of justice, acknowledge that these have been accommodated throughout the polity's history, and provide mechanisms for future accommodations.[16] Understood in this light, constitutional entrenchment simultaneously reflects a polity's ongoing debates about its fundamental values, and catalyses further democratic deliberation about them.

When applied to a specific constitutional context, these deliberative democratic views about what renders a constitution and its processes legitimate require careful attention to facts on the ground. Comparative insights can be particularly valuable in helping us to identify potential opportunities and challenges. Consider first the light that comparative law can shed on processes of subnational constitutional change. Instructive in this regard are Delaney's descriptions of broad civil society engagement in the Scottish Constitutional Convention and her analysis of conditions – including the Scottish National Party's decision to not participate – that ensured that parties to the Convention negotiated in good faith. As a consequence, the parties refrained from using the Convention as a pretext or instrument for ending Scotland's membership in the United Kingdom. Bad faith participation in a constitutional convention is manifestly inconsistent with deliberative democratic ideals and Delaney suggests that it may be difficult to replicate in Quebec the conditions for good faith negotiations that were present in the Scottish case.

Comparative constitutional analysis can also point to challenges in relation to the significance that polities ascribe to subnational written constitutions. For example, in his analysis of American state constitutions, Marshfield identifies a form of constitutionalism that emphasizes public initiatives and popular referendums. This form of constitutionalism is not necessarily inconsistent with deliberative democratic ideals. As Levy, O'Flynn and I have argued, constitutional referendums can be designed in ways that render them congruent with those ideals.[17] But the trends that Marshfield identifies suggest that state level constitutionalism is vulnerable to special interest capture and resistant to thoroughgoing deliberation about fundamental values, encouraging instead reflexive responsiveness to hot-button issues. Marshfield thus provides a cautionary note: written constitutions in subnational jurisdictions such as Quebec may fail to catalyse reasoned debate and may unleash instead political forces that deliberative democrats and mainstream constitutional theorists alike would have reason to resist.

The contributions from Marshfield on the one hand, and Costa Ferreira and Zaiden Benvindo on the other, point to another set of concerns that comparative constitutional analysis reveals. According to these authors, courts in the United States and Brazil have not interpreted state constitutions in ways that enable subnational diversity to thrive. These authors therefore recommend that advocates of a written constitution for Quebec be aware of possible unintended consequences of entrenchment. Finally, it is worth noting that Marshfield is writing about the United States, a federation with the kind of dual judicial structure that Morton in his contribution argues should be adopted in Canada. Marshfield's analysis suggests that giving subnational courts exclusive and final jurisdictional authority over some subject matters and populating them with judges appointed by subnational governments may not necessarily turn them into bulwarks against centralization.

## PART III: SHOULD QUEBEC ADOPT A WRITTEN CONSTITUTION? THE VIEW FROM DELIBERATIVE CONSTITUTIONALISM

With these theoretical and comparative stakes in view, we are now in a position to assess the claim that Quebec should adopt a written constitution if in so doing it gives effect to the values of deliberative constitutionalism. In this part, I will briefly discuss the relevant body of positive law and describe how deliberative constitutionalist values may be reflected in a constitution-making process for Quebec. I will close with some objections to the idea that Quebec should adopt a written, entrenched constitution.

### *i. Constitutional Process and Constitutional Substance*

Let me begin this discussion by surveying the different kinds of matters that would qualify as comprising the substance of a written constitution in Quebec. The subject matter of provincial constitutions was considered by a majority of the Supreme Court of Canada in *Ontario (Attorney General) v. OPSEU.*[18] The Court in *OPSEU* noted that the concept of a provincial constitution is nowhere defined in the *Constitution Act, 1867*. Nonetheless, the Court identified the contents of Ontario's constitution: federal constitutional provisions (including sections 58, 70, and 82–7 of the *Constitution Act, 1867*), provincial statutes (including *The Legislative Assembly Act, The Representation Act,* and *The Executive Council Act*), common law rules (including those governing the Royal Prerogative), and conventions (including those relating to responsible government).[19] It is worth quoting in full the Court's definition of a provincial constitution: "the question whether a given enactment forms part of its constitution or amends its constitution could be resolved by only one relatively simple test: is the enactment constitutional in nature? In other words, is the enactment in question, by its object, relative to a branch of the government of Ontario or, to use the language of this Court in *Attorney General v. Blaikie*, [1979] 2 SCR 1016 at p. 1024, does '[i]t bear on the operation of an organ of the government of the Province?' Does it for instance determine the composition, powers, authority, privileges, and duties of the legislative or executive branches or their members? Does it regulate the interrelationship between two or more branches? Or does it set out some principle of government?"[20]

The power of a province to legislate with respect to these constitutional matters, the Court noted, is limited. No province can regulate matters that fall within the scope of a provincial constitution, if in so doing, it would violate the Canadian Constitution. This general statement of law is consistent with the reading of section 45 of the *Constitution Act, 1982* offered by Taillon and Cauchon in their contribution to this collection.

The Court in OPSEU proceeded to identify provincial constitutional matters that lie beyond the power of the provinces to amend unilaterally, including provisions that are entrenched by the federal constitution (for instance, the powers under section 92) and that are, in the words of the Court, "essential to the implementation of the federal principle."[21] Other matters excluded from the power of the provinces to alter unilaterally include those that "constituted a fundamental term or condition of the Union formed in 1867."[22] Section 133 of the *Constitution Act, 1867* was held in *Blaikie* to constitute such a provision and to be a "'part of the Constitution of Canada and of Quebec in an indivisible sense' and not part of the constitution of Quebec within s. 92(1)."[23] Included in this category of fundamental terms are "the office of the Lieutenant-Governor and, presumably and *a fortiori*, the office of the Queen who is represented by the Lieutenant Governor."[24] Finally, the Court in OPSEU reasoned that the power of provinces to alter their constitutions does not authorize a "profound constitutional upheaval by the introduction of political institutions foreign to and incompatible with the Canadian system."[25]

In order to illustrate what incompatibility with the Canadian system entails, the Court in OPSEU invoked a Judicial Committee of the Privy Council case, *In re Initiative and Referendum Act*.[26] The Judicial Committee invalidated Manitoba legislation that purported to enable legislation to be enacted directly by referendum. Such a power, the Judicial Committee held, would bypass the lieutenant governor's essential role in the provincial legislative process. This example represents a hard limit on the aspects of provincial constitutions that provinces can amend unilaterally.

Yet the boundaries of provincial jurisdiction in this area remain unclear. It is, for instance, well-established in Canadian constitutional law that legislatures can impose "manner and form" requirements. Legislatures seem, therefore, to be empowered to attenuate in some respects the ability of subsequent legislatures to regulate matters within their jurisdiction.[27] Two questions arise for present purposes: (1) how specifically is this power to regulate attenuated by manner and form requirements? and (2) does an entrenched provincial constitution fall within the limits of permissible constraint represented by the manner and form requirement, or does it rather represent a constitutional change similar in impact to the plebiscites in the Manitoba case?

It is on this terrain that St-Hilaire and Baud advance their arguments. With respect to the first question, they argue that no clear authority establishes that self-imposed legislative (as opposed to constitutionally mandated) manner and form requirements affect the validity of laws that infringe those requirements. The authors argue that these kinds of manner and form requirements should be understood as modifying common law rules that govern how statutes are to be interpreted, in cases of conflicts between statutory provisions.[28] Therefore, they argue, these rules may affect whether a given statutory provision is operative, but not whether it is valid. This distinction is more than semantic, as an entrenched provincial constitution would purport to render laws inconsistent with it invalid and would thus constrain the principle of legislative supremacy, as it applies to the provinces.

I understand St-Hilaire and Baud to be further arguing that section 52(1) of the *Constitution Act, 1982* is the exclusive locus of constitutional authority for attenuating legislative supremacy within the Canadian constitutional order. Therefore, any attempt by a provincial legislature to grant itself the power to invalidate laws enacted by subsequent legislatures would violate section 52(1). This would be so even if a provincial legislature were to attempt to entrench a written provincial constitution by invoking section 45 of the *Constitution Act,1982*. Such an entrenched constitution would, in the words of the Court in *OPSEU*, create a "profound constitutional upheaval."[29] If St-Hilaire and Baud are correct in their interpretation of the manner and form jurisprudence, an attempt at constitutional entrenchment by a province would be different in kind than a manner and form requirement. In its attempt to arrogate novel powers to a province, a purported unilateral entrenchment of a written provincial constitution would represent an upheaval of the constitutional order.

Since the ambitions of this conclusion are primarily theoretical, I will now bracket this debate, and assume for the purposes of the discussion that follows that it would be possible for a province to enact an entrenched constitution. Yet even if we assume this, we would still need to specify how a process for enacting it would satisfy deliberative democratic norms. It is to this task that I now turn.

### *ii. Constitutional Process, Constitutional Substance, and Deliberative Constitutionalism*

Provinces have routinely altered their constitutions through the ordinary legislative process.[30] In light of this history, there would seem to be no obstacle to enacting a written constitution by means of ordinary legislation. This course of action would likely be acceptable, as a matter of law and prudence, if all that we meant by a written constitution was a statutory compilation of the relevant sources of Quebec's existing constitution. Such an enactment would not be different in kind from the statutes that provinces regularly pass when amending their provincial constitutions. If, however, Quebec were to attempt to enact an *entrenched* constitution, it would be necessary, as a matter of political morality, if not constitutional law, to institute a broader process of public deliberation. In order to understand why this is the case, let us bring deliberative constitutionalism's analytical framework to bear on the analysis.

We have seen that for deliberative constitutionalism, a given political system is rendered legitimate when its constitutional processes are characterized by equal inclusion, reflection, adequate information, and flexible, open-minded, and reciprocal exchange. Underlying this conception of legitimacy is a deep respect for the rational autonomy of citizens. According to the deliberative constitutionalist, citizens should be able to participate, whether directly or through their representatives, in political decisions that affect them, because such participation aims to ensure that state action is supported by reasoned justifications. Defenders of the parliamentary system and of all its defining features claim that it is an effective system for facilitating public deliberation about ordinary legislation.[31] If well-functioning legislatures are part of a system of competitive political parties that present broad policy platforms that are themselves the result of internal party deliberation, and if citizens can vote on platforms with relatively high levels of information, then one can be confident that the ordinary legislative process satisfies the requirements for public justification.[32]

What changes if we are faced with enacting an entrenched written constitution, rather than ordinary legislation? Heightened requirements for public justification are required in the former case, as a matter of political principle, because entrenchment reduces the capacity of ordinary citizens to participate actively in political processes relating to ordinary legislation affected by the entrenchment. Their capacity to exercise their political agency would be reduced as a result. The decision to entrench would require heightened discussion and debate, in order to justify to citizens this lessening of their political power, and the concomitant reduction in the system's respect for their autonomy. That is a procedural reason for heightened public deliberation when any polity decides to entrench a constitution. There is also a substantive reason for greater public deliberation that is related to the diverse nature of modern liberal democracies, such as Quebec.

We saw above that according to Chambers' understanding of constitutional entrenchment, a constitution should set the terms of an ongoing debate about a polity's fundamental commitments. Entrenchment, therefore, should enshrine a polity's diverse conceptions of justice and provide mechanisms for future accommodations of these.[33] To ensure that this would be the case in a polity such as Quebec would require broad and deep public deliberation in the constitution-making process. Recent scholarship on constitution-making suggests that public participation should be pervasive through all phases of the process, including drafting, debate, and ratification.[34] At the drafting stage, this would involve public input, including, for instance, recourse to "a specially elected body" to undertake the drafting.[35] At the debate stage, participation might involve a legislature or constituent assembly, but "civil society and ordinary citizens [would] visibly influence[] debates, undermining experts' abilities to assert monopolies on constitutional wisdom."[36] And at the ratification stage, public involvement would entail a free and fair referendum,[37] that itself was conducted according to deliberative democratic norms.[38] The evidence suggests that these participatory measures contribute to the success of constitutional regimes and their perceived legitimacy. One could add a requirement that ratification in Quebec's National Assembly involve a super-majority vote in order to further heighten political deliberation and increase the likelihood that the entrenched constitution would reflect Quebec's rich diversity.

### *iii. Objections*

The previous sections defended the idea of a constitution for Quebec, on grounds of substance and procedure. Substantively, the idea would be justified if the contents of a written constitution reflected the diversity of conceptions of Quebec's basic norms that are present in Quebec society. Procedurally, the idea would be justified if the relevant processes of constitution-making empowered a broad cross-section of citizens to participate and deliberate. This broad-based participation would aim to ensure that the diversity of voices that contribute to Quebec's political culture would be reflected in the resulting statement of basic norms. This form of participation would further justify the attenuation of political agency in respect of subsequent ordinary law-making that results from any act of constitutional entrenchment. We also saw that the terms of any prospective constitution would need to be consistent with the Canadian Constitution. In what follows, I will target the factual and theoretical underpinnings of these conditional arguments in favour of a Quebec constitution. I will conclude by addressing consequences that likely would result from the inevitable uncertainty around the status, under the Canadian Constitution, of laws made pursuant to a provincial constitution.

Let us examine first, the assumption that an entrenched constitution could in fact capture the diversity of conceptions of the public good that inhere in Quebec society, and could therefore in turn, facilitate future accommodations of this diversity. As we saw above, Ricoy has argued that entrenchment incentivizes powerful special interests involved in constitution-making to rent seek. Entrenchment, therefore, can be an obstacle to engaging in good faith deliberations about shared norms and the public good. Gagnon and Tremblay note in their contribution to this volume that in Quebec, some political contemporary fault lines run very deeply indeed. In conditions such as these, partisans will likely aim to entrench their positions, and not seek accommodations of alternative viewpoints. This is so because once a position is entrenched, subsequent legislative measures that diverge from it will likely be struck down by courts. The temptation to see in an act of constitution-making a founding moment that enshrines a particular and exclusive vision of the polity may be too great to resist. And if it is not resisted, the resulting entrenched text would neither reflect nor facilitate the kinds of ongoing accommodations that we saw above were essential to deliberative constitutionalism's conception of a just constitution.

In his contribution to this volume, Mark Walters identifies a set of theoretical reasons to worry about enacting an entrenched constitution in Quebec. As he notes, the constitutional relationships between Indigenous peoples and the Government of Quebec are complex, variable and contested, and the history of those relationships reaches back to 1760. Walters wonders whether non-Herculean constitutional drafters could capture in a written constitution the on the ground complexity of the longstanding relationships between

Indigenous peoples and the the Government of Quebec. More fundamentally, he worries that constitution-making – understood as a one-time exercise of constituent power – would undermine legal interpretation. According to Walters, those who engage in the distinctively rational, normative, and legal activity of interpretation should endeavour, in an incremental way, to articulate and defend their sense of constitutional justice, as their experience with, and understanding of, differing conceptions of justice deepens over time. This "circular" approach to constitutional interpretation is, Walters argues, undermined by "linear" conceptions of constitution-making that draw on constituent theories of constitution-making. And these linear theories, he notes, are perhaps naturally invoked when a subnational polity attempts to define, in one decisive moment, its constitutional identity.

I close this part by identifying some concerns about whether it is likely that entrenching a constitution in Quebec would facilitate ongoing democratic deliberation within and about the constitutional project of Canadian federalism. Some have noted that it is difficult to draw the line between, on the one hand, matters of fundamental concern only to the provinces and their constitutions, and, on the other hand, those that are also of concern to the Canadian Constitution.[39] Moreover, courts have found ordinary provincial legislation to violate the Canadian Constitution, despite claims by the provinces that they were only altering their own constitutions.[40] These kinds of disagreements can give rise to heated rhetoric. It is likely that the rhetorical stakes would be even higher if federally appointed courts, including the Supreme Court of Canada, were to rule that the Canadian Constitution was to be given priority over the terms of an entrenched provincial constitution. Such interpretive conflicts would not likely result in the kind of ongoing conversation and accommodations envisaged by Chambers in her arguments for a deliberative constitution. Instead, the likely outcome would be entrenched partisanship and hardened preferences that would undercut the conditions necessary for respectful and open democratic deliberation to flourish.

## CONCLUSIONS

In this concluding chapter, I have addressed the question, "should Quebec adopt a written constitution?" and have answered that one should reply "yes," only if the normative conditions set by deliberative constitutionalism are satisfied. I turn now to a fundamental challenge to this paper's theoretical framework. Deliberative democratic constitutionalism has been challenged on "agonistic" grounds.[41] The details of the argument need not detain us here, but the core critique is pertinent and has been forcefully articulated by Chantal Mouffe. She claims that deliberative democratic theory fails to acknowledge that conflict is an ineradicable feature of democracy and that rational consensus on some matters is not possible. One pursuing this agonistic challenge may pointedly ask: is it plausible in multinational federations such as Canada to suppose that there is a reservoir of public reasons upon which a constitution and its reform processes can be founded?

One response to this challenge is simply semantic, and states that a constitution that is not based on such reasons fails to be a constitution in any meaningful sense. Thus, if such public reasons are not possible in multinational federations, then a constitution is not possible for such federations. A second response would address agonism on its own terms. Given that constitutions are a pervasive feature of democracies, the agonist would need to generate criteria for determining whether a given document or set of laws can be understood to be a constitution. In my understanding, agonistic theories require that a particular kind of ethic govern conflicts among individual members and constituent units of a polity. According to this ethic, opponents are to be viewed as adversaries and not enemies. Adversaries share normative commitments, and in a constitutional polity, these include a set of shared beliefs about what membership entails. By contrast, the enemy stands outside of that sphere of shared concepts of belonging, and the benefits of membership that it entails. At a minimum, a constitution draws this boundary of belonging, sets out the relevant concepts and practices of community, and therefore constrains, even if it does not eliminate, conflict. In order to be legitimate, the contents of the relevant concepts and practices, and the criteria for belonging, will need to be acceptable in principle to those who are governed by them, and therefore grounded in something that resembles public reasons. These reasons form, as a result, the contents of even a minimalist and agonistic constitution, and should govern the process and substance of constitution-making and interpretation in all polities, including multinational federations.

In the previous parts of this conclusion, I have identified specific ways in which constitution-making *processes* in Quebec may satisfy or fail to satisfy deliberative constitutionalism's normative requirements. I conclude by noting that the *substance* of an entrenched constitution may fail to meet these requirements, if it imposed burdens on citizens in Quebec that could not be justified to them by appeal to public reasons. The task of identifying such norms would necessarily be interpretive and likely controversial, but a hypothetical norm may illustrate what I have in mind. Recall that Quebec's constitutional narrative comprises the contributions of its diverse communities. Now, imagine an entrenched constitutional norm that expressed hostility towards one of those communities, denied its contributions to Quebec's constitutional narrative, and imposed and enforced limits on that community's interests and activities, without providing any justification for doing so. The relevant affected community, interests and activities may be linguistic, religious, cultural, or other. The objectionable constitutional norm that I have in mind would not treat this community's members as citizens of equal standing, nor would the norm recognize the community (and its advocates) as worthy adversaries in a contest about the shared meaning of Quebec's constitution. Instead, the hypothetical constitutional norm would treat the community's members as enemies and in so doing, would violate the norms of deliberative constitutionalism.

## NOTES

I thank participants in the symposium from which this collection emerged for their very helpful comments. I am grateful to my former colleagues at McGill University's Faculty of Law who participated in a faculty seminar on this paper and provided challenging questions that helped shape the paper's direction. Amy Preston-Samson and Merran Hergert provided outstanding research assistance and Austin Horn did the meticulous, final citation work for this paper. The Social Sciences and Humanities Research Council of Canada supported research on deliberative democracy that informed the arguments presented here.

1 Hoi L. Kong and Ron Levy, "Deliberative Constitutionalism," in *Oxford Handbook on Deliberative Democracy*, ed. Bächtinger et al. (Oxford: Oxford University Press, 2018). The paragraphs that follow draw from that text.

2 See, e.g., Alexander M. Bickel, *The Least Dangerous Branch: The Supreme Court at the Bar of Politics* (Indianapolis: Bobbs-Merill Company, 1962) and Jeremy Waldron, *Law and Disagreement* (Oxford: Oxford University Press, 1999).

3 The following paragraphs draw from Hoi L. Kong, "Republicanism and the Division of Powers in Canada," *University of Toronto Law Journal* 64, no. 3 (2014): 359.

4 See Christopher Moore, *1867: How the Fathers Made a Deal* (Toronto: McClelland & Stewart, 1997): 142–3.

5 See for the relevant history A. I. Silver, *The French-Canadian Idea of Confederation, 1864–1900*, 2nd ed. (Toronto: University of Toronto Press, 1997): chap. 1.

6 Gérard Bouchard and Charles Taylor, *Building the Future: A Time for Reconciliation* (Quebec: Consultation Commission on Accommodation Practices Related to Cultural Differences, 2008): 127.

7 Jon Elster, "Forces and Mechanisms in the Constitution-Making Process," *Duke Law Journal* 45, no. 2 (1995): 364–96, at 366.

8 See, e.g., Elster, "Forces and Mechanisms."

9 See, e.g., Tom Ginsburg, Zachary Elkins, and Justin Blount, "Does the Process of Constitution-Making Matter?" *Annual Review of Law and Social Science* 5, no. 5 (2009); and Todd A. Eisenstadt, A. Carl LeVan, and Tofigh Maboudi, "When Talk Trumps Text: The Democratizing Effects of Deliberation During Constitution-Making, 1974–2011," *American Political Science Review* 109, no. 3 (2015).

10 Bruce Ackerman, *We the People: Foundations* (Cambridge, Massachusetts: Harvard University Press, 1991).

11 Stephen Tierney, *Constitutional Referendums: The Theory and Practice of Republican Deliberation* (Oxford: Oxford University Press, 2012), 24.

12 Hélène Landemore, "Inclusive Constitution-Making: The Icelandic Experiment," *Journal of Political Philosophy* 23, no. 2 (2015): 166.

13 Iñigo González Ricoy, "Participation, Deliberation and Constitutional Rigidity," *Ratio Juris* 27, no. 4 (2014): 525.

14 Marco Goldoni, "Political Constitutionalism and the Question of Constitution-Making," *Ratio Juris* 27, no. 3 (2014): 387.

15 Simone Chambers, "Contract or Conversation? Theoretical Lessons from the Canadian Constitutional Crisis," *Politics and Society* 26, no. 1 (1998).

16 Chambers, "Contract or Conversation," 154.

17 Ron Levy, Ian O'Flynn, and Hoi L. Kong, *Deliberative Peace Referendums* (Oxford: Oxford University Press, 2021).

18 *Ontario (Attorney General) v. OPSEU*, [1987] 2 SCR 2, 41 DLR (4th) 1.

19 *OPSEU* at paras 82–5.

20 Ibid., at para. 86.

21 Ibid., at para. 89.

22 Ibid.

23 Ibid.

24 Ibid., at para. 90.

25 Ibid., at para. 111.

26 *In re Initiative and Referendum Act*, [1919] AC 935, [1998] 2 SCR 217.

27 For an overview of manner and form requirements, and their constitutional limits, see Robin Elliott, "Rethinking Manner and Form: Parliamentary Sovereignty and Constitutional Values," *Osgoode Hall Law Journal* 29, no. 2 (1991).

28 I would add that the on-the-ground effectiveness of manner and form requirements may be attributed to the willingness of actors in the constitutional order to abide by them.

29 *OPSEU* at para. 111.

30 See the examples in Nelson Wiseman, "Clarifying Provincial Constitutions," *National Journal of Constitutional Law* 6 (1,995–6).

31 For a republican version of this argument, see Richard Bellamy, *Political Constitutionalism: A Republican Defence of the Constitutionality of Democracy* (Cambridge: Cambridge University Press, 2007), chap. 6.

32 See also, Adam Tomkins, *Our Republican Constitution* (Portland, OR: Hart, 2005), chap. 4.

33 Chambers, "Contract or Conversation," 154.

34 See, e.g., Eisenstadt, LeVan, and Maboudi, "When Talk Trumps Text."

35 Eisenstadt, LeVan, and Maboudi, 598.

36 Ibid.

37 Ibid.

38 For the criteria governing such referendums, see Tierney, *Constitutional Referendums*.

39 For a summary, see Wiseman, "Clarifying Provincial Constitutions."

40 See, e.g., *Dixon v. British Columbia (Attorney General)* (1986), 7 BCLR (2d) 174, 31 DLR (4th) 546 at 186 [cited to BCLR]; *MacLean v. Nova Scotia* (1987), 35 DLR (4th) 306 (NSTD), 76 NSR (2d) 296. Both cited in Wiseman, "Clarifying Provincial Constitutions."

41 See Chantal Mouffe, "Deliberative Democracy or Agonistic Pluralism," *Prospects for Democracy* 66, no. 3 (1999).

# Contributors

RICHARD ALBERT, born in Quebec, is professor of world constitutions and director of constitutional studies at the University of Texas at Austin. A graduate of Yale, Oxford, and Harvard, he is co-president of the International Society of Public Law and a former law clerk to the chief justice of Canada.

PATRICK F. BAUD is counsel in the Crown-Indigenous Relations, Northern Affairs, and Indigenous Services Legal Services Unit in the Department of Justice. The views expressed in his contribution to this collection are his alone and do not represent the views of the Department of Justice or the Government of Canada.

JULIANO ZAIDEN BENVINDO is professor of constitutional law at the University of Brasília in Brazil, where he is the head of the Center for Comparative Constitutional Studies. A research fellow at the Brazilian National Council for Scientific and Technological Development and a CAPES-Humboldt senior fellow at the Max-Planck Institute for Comparative Public Law and International Law.

HUBERT CAUCHON is a doctoral candidate at Université Laval and a lawyer for the Secrétariat du Québec aux relations canadiennes (Quebec Secretariat for Canadian relations) from the ministère du Conseil exécutif (Executive Council Office).

ERIN F. DELANEY is a professor of law and political science at Northwestern University. Her scholarship explores constitutional design in comparative perspective, with a focus on multi-level governance systems. In 2014, she held the Fulbright Visiting Research Chair in the Theory and Practice of Constitutionalism and Federalism at McGill University.

DÉBORA COSTA FERREIRA is a doctoral student in economic sciences at the University of Brasília, professor of economic analysis of law at Instituto Brasiliense de Direito Público, and a federal auditor for external control at the Federal Court of Accounts.

ALAIN-G. GAGNON is a full professor of political science at the Université du Québec à Montréal (UQAM) and has held the Canada Research Chair in Quebec and Canadian Studies since 2003. From 1982 to 2003, he taught at the universities of Queen's, Carleton, and McGill. He is the founding director of the Centre de recherche interdisciplinaire sur la diversité et la démocratie (CRIDAQ) and the director of the Groupe de recherche sur les sociétés plurinationales (GRSP).

HOI L. KONG is holder of the Rt Hon. Beverley McLachlin PC, Professorship in Constitutional Law at the Univeristy of British Columbia. He researches and publishes in a range of areas of public and constitutional law and theory. Much of his work has focused on how to make the substance and processes of public and constitutional law more legitimate in the eyes of citizens.

JONATHAN MARSHFIELD is associate professor of law at the University of Florida Levin College of Law. His reach focuses on state constitutional law and constitutional change. His most recent work has appeared in the *Northwestern University Law Review*, *Boston University Law Review*, and the *Michigan Law Review*.

F.L. MORTON is a professor emeritus of political science at the University of Calgary. His books include *Charter Politics*, *Morgentaler v. Borowski: Abortion, the Charter and the Courts*; *The Charter Revolution and the Court Party*; and *Law, Politics and the Judicial Process in Canada*, 4th ed. He also served in the Government of Alberta as minister of sustainable development, minister of energy, and minister of finance.

LÉONID SIROTA is associate professor in law at the University of Reading. A graduate of McGill and New York University, he also served as a law clerk at the Federal Court of Canada. His teaching and research focus on public law and legal philosophy. He is also the creator of the Double Aspect Blog.

MAXIME ST-HILAIRE is an associate professor at the Faculty of Law at Université de Sherbrooke (UdeS). His monographs include: *Les Positivismes juridiques au XXe siècle* (UdeS human sciences research award 2021); *La lutte pour la pleine reconnaissance des droits ancestraux* (Minerve award 2014). He served as law clerk to the hon. Marie Deschamps, at the Supreme Court of Canada (2009–10). He holds a doctoral degree in law from Université Laval.

PATRICK TAILLON is professor of law at the Faculty of Law at Université Laval. He is the author of *Le référendum expression directe de la souveraineté du peuple? Essai critique sur la rationalisation de l'expression référendaire en droit comparé* (Dalloz 2012), a member of Centre de recherche interdisciplinaire sur la diversité et la démocratie (CRIDAQ), and the editor-in-chief of the *Bulletin québécois de droit constitutionnel.*

ARJUN TREMBLAY is an associate professor in the department of Politics and International Studies at the University of Regina. He obtained his PhD in political science from the University of Toronto. His research explores the near and longer-term prospects of the politics of diversity from a comparative perspective. He is the author of *Diversity in Decline? The Rise of the Political Right and the Fate of Multiculturalism.*

DANIEL TURP is an emeritus professor of the Faculty of Law of the Université de Montréal. A graduate of the University of Cambridge and of the Université de droit, d'économie et de sciences sociales de Paris (Paris II), he is president of the Association québécoise de droit constitutionnel. His books include *La Constitution québécoise – Essais sur le droit du Québec de se doter de sa propre loi fondamentale.* He also sat as a member of the House of Commons of Canada for the Bloc Québécois as well as in the National Assembly of Quebec for the Parti Québécois.

MARK WALTERS is professor and dean of law at Queen's University. He works in the area of public and constitutional law with an emphasis on the history of legal ideas and the law relating to Indigenous peoples. He is the author of *A.V. Dicey and the Common Law Constitutional Tradition: A Legal Turn of Mind.*

NELSON WISEMAN is a professor emeritus of political science at the University of Toronto. His books include *Partisan Odysseys: Canada's Political Parties*; *The Public Intellectual in Canada;* and *Social Democracy in Manitoba. Choice* magazine designated his book, *In Search of Canadian Political Culture*, as an Outstanding Academic Title.

# Index